Kentucky Baptists
1925-2000

Kentucky Baptists
1925-2000
A Story of Cooperation

James Duane Bolin

Southern Baptist Historical Society
Brentwood, Tennessee
AND
Fields Publishing Incorporated
Nashville, Tennessee

Library of Congress Card Number: 00-102730

ISBN: 1-57843-006-2

Published by

Southern Baptist Historical Society
P.O. Box 728 • Brentwood, Tennessee 37024-0728
800-966-2278
e-mail: cdeweese@tnbaptist.org
and

Fields Publishing Inc.
917 Harpeth Valley Place • Nashville, Tennessee 37221
615-662-1344
e-mail: tfields@fieldspublishing.com

Contents

Foreword

As the twentieth century began to draw to a close, in May 1995, the members of the Kentucky Baptist Historical Commission became aware of a need to update the published histories of Kentucky Baptists. At the urging of Doris Yeiser, for whom the newly established Kentucky Baptist Archives was named, the chairman of the commission, Terry Wilder, appointed a committee to study the feasibility of such a publication. At the December 1995 meeting, the committee, consisting of Barry Allen, Marv Knox, Jim Hawkins, along with Terry Wilder, Ronald F. Deering, and Joe Priest Williams, recommended to the commission that it undertake the publication of such a history to coincide with the turn of the century from the 1900s to 2000.

At the December meeting the commission endorsed the project and a committee was appointed to develop a plan for the history, obtain financing, secure an author, find a publisher, and bring the work to completion.

Kentucky Baptist Executive Secretary Bill Marshall and the Executive Board of the convention generously agreed to provide the financing, and the committee devised the broad outlines of the history of Kentucky Baptists over the period in focus and the general guidelines for the development of the manuscript. A search for a suitable author eventuated shortly in the selection of J. Duane Bolin, Associate Professor of History at Murray State University and an active Baptist layman in the First Baptist Church of Murray.

The committee then engaged in many meetings over the next four years to develop the guidelines of the history, consult with the author during its writing, and to review it with him. At last in December 1999, the work was completed and ready for the publisher, with hopes that it will be a helpful reminder to its readers of the story of Kentucky Baptists in the last three-quarters of the twentieth century, and an inspiration to them on the threshold of the twenty-first century. The work is meant to be a readable story, not a chronicle of all that occurred in this crowded seventy-five years of life and witness for Kentucky Baptists, as many volumes would be required to fully chronicle all the activities and developments of this period. It is at the end a story of cooperation of Baptists in Kentucky working together to extend the saving and redeeming grace of God in the life of his Son Jesus Christ and his followers across the last seventy-five years of the twentieth century.

Much appreciation goes first of all to the author who in his own right has largely determined the content of the book, but also to the committee who guided and supported his work: Barry Allen, Ronald F. Deering (chair), Andrew B. Rawls, Terry Wilder, Joe Priest Williams, Stan Williams, and Kentucky Baptist Archivist Cheryl Doty who served as administrative assistant to the committee and enabled and facilitated its work in many ways. Special thanks is extended to Andrew B. Rawls who provided and prepared the many illustrations and photographs which contribute so much to the volume.

Ronald F. Deering
Louisville, Kentucky
Advent 1999

For

my parents

J. Wesley Bolin

and

Cammie Mann Bolin,

two Baptist saints

Acknowledgments

In 1996, my family and I decided to return to our native state after a four-year sojourn in Arkansas. I had taken a position in the Department of History at Williams Baptist College in 1992. We enjoyed our brief time at Williams, but we yearned to return to the Bluegrass State. So when a position opened up in the Department of History at Murray State University, we eagerly sought the opportunity to come back home. Leaving a Baptist school for a larger, public institution presented new challenges. We wanted to come back to Kentucky badly, but we also cherished our experience at a Baptist college.

Even before our move, my friend and former pastor William E. Shoulta called to ask if I would have any interest in writing a history of the Kentucky Baptist Convention in the twentieth century. He wanted to give my name to the KBC's Historical Commission because they were then in the process of planning the work. Of course, I jumped at the chance. For me, this was a clear indication of the Master's call for us to return to Kentucky. I will always be grateful to Bill Shoulta for thinking of me and to the commission and the convention for placing confidence in me for this task.

The nature of this work required the help of many individuals. A committee of the Kentucky Baptist Historical Commission skillfully guided the project from the outset. Committee members Ronald F. Deering (chair), Barry Allen, Andrew B. Rawls, Terry Wilder, Joe Priest Williams, Stan Williams, and Kentucky Baptist archivist Cheryl Doty faithfully read each chapter of the manuscript and offered helpful suggestions. I owe a special debt to Ron Deering who went beyond the call of duty in making sure that the project would be completed on time, to Cheryl Doty who made available the rich resources housed in the archives, and to Andrew Rawls for his work in locating appropriate photographs.

I appreciate the kind, professional help provided by Charles W. Deweese, my editor, and Tim Fields at Fields Publishing. Also, the project would not have been completed without the careful editing of two friends, Thomas H. Appleton, Jr., editor of the *Register of the Kentucky Historical Society*, and Terry H. Garvin, associate pastor at Murray's First Baptist Church. Tom and Terry read chapter after chapter, lending their time and skill to the manuscript. I am indebted to them.

Along life's pilgrimage, I have been privileged to know and love several special people who nurtured my faith as well as my interest in history. In their Baptist history courses, Albert W. Wardin at Belmont University and Glenn Hilburn at Baylor University taught me the riches of church history. I would also like to thank Roy Z. Chamlee, Jr., my history professor at Belmont. James Leo Garrett and C. Pat Taylor have always been examples to me, representing all that is honorable and good in Christian education. Jerome Browne, my wife Evelyn's friend and former pastor, became my friend as well. He represents the best in the Baptist pastorate. Humbert S. Nelli, my professor and friend at the University of Kentucky, had faith in my work from the start. I will always be grateful for his continued encouragement. My friend and fellow historian, Ken Startup, has provided a model of excellence in his life and work. Although I am the only Baptist among them, my colleagues in the Department of History at Murray State University have been supportive of this project and have provided a friendly, collegial environment in which to work. I am especially grateful to B. Anthony Gannon, James W. Hammack, Jr., and Ken Wolf for their interest and support.

My church family at First Baptist Church, Murray helped sustain me throughout the process of research and writing. My pastors, Terry Ellis, Terry Garvin, and Wendell Ray, and ministers Joetta H. Kelly, Boyd Smith, and Mike Crook, and the members of the Solomon Sunday School class have blessed me beyond measure. I am grateful for Paula Alcott, our skilled church librarian, who gave me access to materials that saved several trips to Middletown. Castle Parker found needed materials for me as well. And I thank Gary and Roberta Jones for their encouragement.

Finally, I must thank my family. My brother Steve, and Sharon and Chris, and my in-laws—Marlin and Jossie Seaton; Rebecca and Lynn; Marilyn, Ken, and Jessica; June, Tim, and Alexis; and Jim and Beth—have been understanding and supportive. My wife, Evelyn, and our children Wesley and Cammie Jo gave of themselves and sacrificed vacation and evening time. Their lives of service and love make them the best Baptists I know. Finally, I must thank my father and mother, J. Wesley Bolin and Cammie Mann Bolin, two Baptist saints. Because of the heritage of faith that they have passed on to me and hundreds of others, this book is dedicated to them.

James Duane Bolin
Murray, Kentucky
Christmas 1999

Prologue

In 1925, messengers to the Southern Baptist Convention adopted the Co-operative Program, a system of giving and budgeting that unified the missions and institutional efforts of convention churches throughout the nation. On November 9, 1926, the 318 messengers of the 89th meeting of the General Association of Baptists in Kentucky gathered in the sanctuary of Lebanon Baptist Church in Lebanon, Kentucky, and unanimously elected George E. Hays as moderator. Hays took the chair and "with a bit of humor" and "after speaking in tender appreciation led the body in prayer to God for guidance."[1] As moderator, Hays, a lay member and deacon of Walnut Street Baptist Church in Louisville, directed the proceedings of the annual meeting the first year after the adoption of the Cooperative Program.

In Kentucky, the denomination included some 1,969 churches and more than 300,000 members in 1926. The fact that members of Southern Baptist churches made up almost 13 percent of the state's population indicated the growing influence of Kentucky Baptists in the life of the commonwealth. Seventy-five years later, as Kentucky Baptists faced a new millennium, the denomination still comprised 13 percent of the population with more than 2,400 congregations and well over half a million members.

The continued growth of the Baptist witness in Kentucky was not certain in 1926. The "Seventy-five Million Campaign," launched in 1919, had resulted in bitter disappointment, the Great Depression loomed, and nagging controversies threatened to weaken the work of Kentucky Baptists. The newly elected moderator of the General Association was not one to shy away from difficulty, however. Just a few months before the annual meeting, Hays underwent surgery at the Baptist Hospital in Louisville. The January 14, 1926, issue of the *Western Recorder* "was glad indeed to report that Brother Hays who is the Chairman of the Board of the Trustees of the Hospital and prominent in other ways in Baptist service, is making a good recovery."[2]

A well-known Louisville businessman, Hays was described by the Kentucky Baptist historian Frank Masters as "a great Baptist layman." Robbie Trent of the *Western Recorder* stated that "everyone in Kentucky knows Brother Hays" and that Hays was "widely loved throughout the South for his services in stewardship and the practice of his Christianity."[3] He not

George E. Hays
Kentucky Baptist lay leader

only served as a deacon and trustee at Walnut Street, teaching the Baraca Sunday School class since 1903; Hays also represented Kentucky Baptists on the commission of the "Seventy-five Million Campaign," on the executive board of the General Association, on the State Board of Missions, and as a member of the Executive Committee of the Southern Baptist Convention. Hays had been elected as a trustee of Georgetown College, an institution that eventually rewarded him for his years of service with an honorary Doctor of Divinity degree. And during World War I, he was the associate camp secretary of the Y.M.C.A. at Camp Zachary Taylor in Louisville. Hays remained active "in Baptist business" until his death in 1965. When he was introduced as moderator of the 1926 annual meeting in Lebanon, there remained many years of service for this Baptist layman.[4]

Only a brief time remained, however, for the earthly service of Edgar Young Mullins, the venerable president of the Southern Baptist Theological Seminary. At the opening of the 1926 annual meeting, Mullins had just returned from a tour of Europe, an excursion that, according to the *Western Recorder*, "meant much for Baptist fellowship and world consciousness." The tour included a series of regional conferences conducted as part of Mullins's responsibilities as president of the Baptist World Alliance.[5] Here was a Kentucky Baptist whose influence was, by 1925, international in scope.

Born in Mississippi in 1860, the son of a Baptist minister, Mullins grew up in various Baptist parsonages in Mississippi and Texas.[6] After undergraduate study at the Agricultural and Mechanical College of Texas (1876-80), young Mullins worked as a telegraph operator to earn money for law school. His plans changed, however, when he was converted during a revival meeting in Dallas led by the noted Baptist evangelist William Evander

Penn. Baptized by his father on November 7, 1880, Mullins within a few months became convinced of a call to the ministry. He entered Southern Baptist Theological Seminary, recently moved to Louisville from Greenville, South Carolina, in time for the fall term in 1881. After his graduation from Southern in 1885, and following pastorates in Harrodsburg, Kentucky, and outside Kentucky in Baltimore and then Newton Center, Massachusetts, Mullins was asked, in 1899, to return to Louisville as president of the seminary.[7]

In the wake of the Whitsitt controversy—centered around the former president, William H. Whitsitt, and his views of Baptist origins—the "tall, thin,

E. Y. Mullins
Baptist statesman and president
of Southern Seminary, 1899-1928

bearded, and somewhat courtly" Mullins assumed the presidency of "one of the world's largest non-Catholic seminaries," a post he would retain for almost twenty-nine years, until his death in 1928.[8] In 1925, Mullins was at the height of his influence and prominence. President of the Baptist World Alliance, he had also served as president of the Southern Baptist Convention from 1921 to 1924. As president at Southern Seminary, Mullins had more than quadrupled the endowment, and he had orchestrated the move, in 1926, of the seminary campus from downtown Louisville to a fifty-eight-acre suburban site on Lexington Road, complete with impressive Georgian structures—costing in excess of $2 million—and magnificent Beech trees.[9]

The seminary's physical campus, dubbed "The Beeches," grew during Mullins's tenure, as did the school's enrollment, from 256 students in 1899 to 501 in 1928. Young men came to study with a faculty growing in numbers (from seven to twelve) and in reputation. The Southern faculty boasted the teacher of Hebrew, John R. Sampey, who would become president after Mullins's death, and Archibald Thomas Robertson, the renowned

Greek scholar, and author of some fifty books, including a massive Greek grammar. Baptist women also benefitted from Mullins's vision to expand the educational program of the seminary. In 1904, at his urging, living quarters for women studying at the seminary were provided; and in 1907, the Woman's Missionary Union of the Southern Baptist Convention, again with the support of Mullins and the seminary, founded a training school for Baptist missionary women. Carrie U. Littlejohn, later named as president of the Training School, wrote that "though he was a very busy man, he gave his interest, his time, and his best thought to the beginning of a project designed to help young women of our denomination receive the specialized missionary training that they needed. With his background, he was not inhibited by the conservatism that made the majority of Southern Baptists of that era slow to embrace new ideas and ways of doing things."[10]

The scholarly Mullins authored ten books, dozens of pamphlets, and over one hundred articles and book reviews. In an 1885 letter to E. M. Poteat, the young and aspiring minister mused, "Why can he not be a man of books and a man of the people both?" That he had achieved this goal was evident. After his death, one admirer concluded that his "brilliance as teacher and writer, his administrative ability, and his firm but conciliatory attitude soon won the confidence of all and gave him a place of leadership in the denomination."[11]

Mullins was not reluctant to use his positions of leadership and influence to steer Kentucky and Southern Baptists away from extreme views and causes that threatened to divide Baptist ranks. In the evolution controversy of the 1920s, he sided with Frank McVey, president of the University of Kentucky, in opposing the passage of anti-evolution laws in Kentucky and other southern states. In denominational affairs, Mullins "eschewed the growing fundamentalism of many of his co-denominationalists while criticizing the liberalism or modernism of many of his northern Baptist colleagues."[12]

Indeed, the seminary's location in Louisville in border-state Kentucky allowed Mullins to function "as the major point of contact between Northern and Southern Baptists."[13] Throughout his seminary presidency, Mullins was a mediator. Yet, his stance against fundamentalism on one hand and liberalism on the other, along with his growing influence in state and national Baptist affairs, failed to satisfy detractors on both sides.

In western Kentucky, Harvey Boyce Taylor, pastor of the First Baptist Church of Murray, was often at odds with the theological and denominational views of the influential seminary president. Mullins sometimes "sustained stinging denunciation" as Taylor's polemics intensified in the denominational controversies of the 1920s.[14] Born in Ohio County in 1870, Taylor became a fourth-generation Baptist minister. A brilliant student at

Harvey Boyce Taylor
Pastor, First Baptist Church, Murray, and
innovator in cooperative giving

Bethel College in Russellville (A.B., 1890, and M.A., 1896) and Southern Seminary (Th.M., 1896), Taylor reluctantly gave up plans to minister on a foreign mission field to stay close to home to help with family financial burdens following the death of his father. He accepted a call in 1896 as pastor—"unseen, unsampled and unheard" as one biographer wrote—of the seventy-two-member congregation of Murray Baptist Church. Within a few years, attendance regularly topped five hundred, the Murray church "became noted as one of the greatest missionary churches in the denomination," and H. Boyce Taylor "became the dominating element in the religious thought of Western Kentucky."[15]

Like many Baptists, Taylor's views were complex. A list of the targets of his criticism is astonishing, defying easy categorization. Through the pages of his paper *News and Truths*, a Baptist weekly personally published in Murray from 1904 to 1932, Editor Taylor lashed out against "unionism," Masonry, questionable social practices, and denominational "bossism."[16] He railed against card-playing, evolution, mixed-bathing, the movies, divorce, bootlegging, gambling, petting parties, and automobiles. In one issue, published in 1930, Taylor listed the subjects "on church truth" to be discussed in future editorials: the "heresies of Methodism, Campbellism, Mormonism, Adventism, Presbyterianism, Holy Rollerism, Mourner's Benchism, Catholicism, Arminianism, Hardshellism, Russellism, Feminism, Unionism, Modernism, Schofieldism, etc."[17]

During World War I—and only shortly after being elected as moderator of the General Association in 1917—Taylor temporarily resigned his church pastorate when his pacifist views discussed from the pulpit and in the pages of *News and Truths* resulted in a storm of protest voiced in secular and church papers throughout the state. In June 1918, Taylor faced "a public inquiry into [his] alleged disloyal utterances" before a committee of the Kentucky Council of Defense. The "inquiry could find no evidence to support the charges," and Taylor was reinstated as pastor of his Murray church; but within five months, the pastor was again embroiled in controversy, this time the result of his refusal to abide by a ban against public gatherings during the 1918 influenza epidemic.[18] When Taylor held worship services in violation of the ban—believing the government was infringing on freedom of religion rights—he was arrested "in the middle of his sermon." Released on bond, and warned, Taylor again ignored the ban and gathered with a few determined members for the church's mid-week prayer service. Arrested again, and refusing to pay the fines, Taylor was jailed for sixty days. He "rejoiced in his martyrdom," and sometimes preached from his cell to gathered church members outside.[19]

Taylor was indeed "a man of controversy," but he was also a person of conviction. As a staunch opponent of the Ku Klux Klan in western Kentucky, as the organizer of the Amazon River Baptist Faith Mission in Brazil, as the originator of the West Kentucky Baptist Assembly and the West Kentucky Bible Institute, as moderator of the General Association and as one invited to preach the annual sermon twice (1902 and 1913), as an early supporter of the "Seventy-Five Million Campaign," Taylor's mark was made beyond the petty controversies in which he was constantly involved. Most significantly, and ironically, Taylor is rightly remembered as a founding leader of the spirit of cooperation among Baptists in Kentucky.

In 1900, Taylor led his church in adopting a unified budget plan of church finances, a system soon followed by other Kentucky churches. And in 1914, before the intense imbroglios of later years, he was asked to serve as chairman of a committee that presented the budget plan to the entire General Association. At the annual meeting at Jellico in 1915, the committee's report was adopted. Kentucky's plan for unification and cooperation served as a model when the Southern Baptist Convention adopted the Cooperative Program in 1925.[20] When moderator George E. Hays called for the "Report of the Executive Board"—a report that encouraged Kentucky churches to support the new Cooperative Program plan for giving—at the annual meeting of the General Association in 1926, the former moderator, an embittered H. Boyce Taylor, following years of debate and controversy, was not in attendance. In the last decade of his life, Taylor had grown disenchanted with denominational life. The irony of the controversial and enigmatic Taylor's role in the founding of the Cooperative Program was indicative of the perseverance of cooperation as a theme of Baptist life in Kentucky in the years from 1925 to 2000.

Just as H. Boyce Taylor was absent from the annual meeting in Lebanon in 1926, so, too, was Eliza Sommerville Broadus. Although women were seated in the meetings of the Southern Baptist Convention as early as 1918, in Kentucky the participation of some one hundred women in the 1908 meeting in Louisville was followed by the 1909 meeting in which "the constitution of the state body was interpreted as allowing for men messengers only."[21] Not until 1956 were women again allowed messenger cards in the state. In October 1926, Broadus met instead with other Baptist women at the twenty-third annual session of the Woman's Missionary Union, eighty miles from Lebanon in Winchester. At the Winchester meeting, another WMU member reported that "Miss Broadus gave us some interesting reminiscences of the past history of the work [of WMU] in Kentucky."[22] Broadus was certainly qualified to present a history of the work. As a participant in a growing women's missionary movement within the Southern Baptist Convention and within the state of Kentucky, she knew of which she spoke.

The eldest daughter of John A. Broadus, a founder and the second president of Southern Seminary, Broadus was born in Charlottesville, Virginia, where her father pastored the First Baptist Church. She grew up in Greenville, South Carolina, but when Southern Seminary moved in 1877, Eliza, now "a mature young woman, well educated under her father's supervision and already his able assistant," moved to Louisville with her family. Never married,

Eliza Broadus
Missions educator, organizer

Broadus devoted herself in Louisville to Baptist work, serving as chair of the Central Committee of Kentucky's women's mission organization from 1887 to 1919, and as vice chair from 1919 to 1929.[23] The "beloved leader of Kentucky Baptist women" also served, in 1904, as a charter member of the Board of Managers of the home for young women studying at Southern Seminary and as a founder of the national Woman's Missionary Union of the Southern Baptist Convention. She served as vice president of the national organization from 1888 to 1920.

In 1925, facing increasing deafness, and following the death of her famous father and stepmother, Broadus lived with her half-sister Ellen and her prominent husband, the seminary professor and Greek scholar A. T. Robertson. It was in their home that Eliza Broadus died in 1931, following years of service for others. A writer in the WMU's *Royal Service* concluded that "few southern Baptist women have equalled Miss Eliza S. Broadus in the service rendered her 'own generation according to the will of God.' Fourscore years and one week were granted her and she not only used them to help lovingly in the home, church, community and state but for more than half of her life she was a most efficient officer of Woman's Missionary Union."[24] Another admirer wrote that Broadus was "one of the women who had faith, perseverance and vision. . . . Eliza 'had faith in God and faith in the future and believed in Missions. She was a woman of vision because she saw the great possibilities in unenlisted women and young people.'"[25] The state missions offering was eventually named the "Eliza Broadus Offering" for this "woman of vision."

As with Eliza Broadus, who devoted her life and work to the Woman's Missionary Union, another individual labored for over fifty years in yet another pioneering area of Kentucky Baptist work. Called "the prophet of Little Cane Creek," Asbel S. Petrey founded twelve churches in Letcher, Perry, Leslie, and Whitley Counties in eastern Kentucky. Born in 1866 in Whitley County, the eldest of eight children, Petrey early accepted the value of cooperation. "We learned," he stated, "in such an aggregation of children, how to share what we had. We learned the lessons of organization and co-operation."[26] Petrey learned his lessons well at home and later as a student at Cora College, a two-year school in Pleasant View, and at Cumberland College in Williamsburg where he was awarded an A.B. degree as a member of the first graduating class of 1893. Following graduation from Cumberland, Petrey attended Southern Seminary "in preparation" for his "life's work."[27]

Petrey's "life's work" was to be varied and productive. He acknowledged that from his ordination in 1891 until his retirement from the active ministry in 1943 he had served as "preacher, pastor, evangelist, missionary, and religious teacher all at the same time."[28] Sporting a mustache, wearing a suit, tie, and white fedora, and with Bible in hand, Petrey proved to be highly effective in his organizational efforts in eastern Kentucky. One writer recalled that his "voice was deep and whispery except in places where he spoke of desperate mountain need" and "low and trembling as it dealt with sacred memories." One touched by his ministry simply remembered that "he just loved his God and he loved the mountain people. The mountain people loved him."[29]

In addition to organizing twelve churches, Petrey also founded Hazard Bible Institute, an institution that at one time provided 75 percent of the public school teachers of Perry County. His biographer asserted that "the story of A. S. Petrey is the story of Hazard Bible Institute."[30] The school was organized in 1903, and Petrey served as the institution's president until 1929. In the depression years when the school was unable to meet the ac-

creditation standards of the Southern Association of Colleges and Secondary Schools, the seventy-year-old Petrey appealed to the Baptist Education Society of Kentucky for continued funding. When his plea failed, the trustees were forced to close the school in 1938.[31] Although he saw "his dreams turn to ashes," the aging Petrey continued with his life's work in mountain missions.

Petrey's life and work—like that of Hays, Mullins, Taylor, and Broadus—included victories and defeats, joys and sorrows. Such is the Kentucky Baptist story. These five individuals—George E. Hays, "prominent in other ways in Baptist Service";

Asbel S. Petrey, "Prophet of Little Cane Creek," (left) with Harold Dye (1949 HMB Photo)

E. Y. Mullins, "a man of books and of the people"; H. Boyce Taylor, "a man of controversy and conviction"; Eliza S. Broadus, "a woman of vision"; and A. S. Petrey, "the prophet of Little Cane Creek"—represented the rich diversity within the life of the Kentucky Baptist Convention in the years after 1925. These individuals do not represent the whole of Kentucky Baptist life, however; neither do they represent the work of the state convention.

Thousands of lesser-known individuals in the churches and communities of the commonwealth have woven their stories of faith and fault, of victory and failure, into the larger fabric of Baptist cooperation. This history of Kentucky Baptists is their story. Variously led by the likes of Mullins and Taylor, by Hays and Petrey, and by Eliza Broadus, thousands of other Baptists, each making his or her own contributions to the Baptist story, have lived and served. This, then, is the story of leaders, and of those willing— and sometimes unwilling—to be led. It is a story that needs to be written, read, and remembered, not because the record indicates a line of continued progress and success—although examples of progress and success abound—but because real men and women, and real boys and girls, contributed much to the story of the commonwealth's largest denomination.

As another writer of Baptist history has written, the real danger in any work of this nature is that history survives "only as a misty, sentimentalized, mythical past which is inhabited by plaster saints whose experiences have little meaning for us because they seem so alien to the real life we experience." "The real past, peopled by real men and women, has much to teach us," the writer concluded, but "the mythical past has little to offer beyond nostalgia."[32] The quest for this "real past" is the challenge for any historian. And it is a daunting challenge, but one well worth the effort. Even a cursory glance at Baptist history in Kentucky invites a realization of how the past is mirrored in the present. Indeed, the issues and challenges and controversies of a new millennium bear a marked resemblance to the issues and challenges and controversies of the 1920s.

In 2000, as in 1925, more Baptists lived in Kentucky than any other religious group. This expression of Christianity, this tradition of faith, has therefore had a significant influence on Kentucky society and on the religious history of the nation and the world. The story of Kentucky Baptists in the years of cooperation from 1925 to 2000, in all of its complexity, deserves a serious recounting. It is a story that begs to be told.

1
chapter

A Foundation
on Which to Build

Before George E. Hays was elected as moderator of the 1926 session of the General Association of Baptists in Kentucky, messengers and visitors joined together in singing a hymn. "How Firm a Foundation" was an appropriate selection, as was the next hymn, "Faith of our Fathers," sung later during that Thursday morning session. For it was the faith of those who had gone before and the firm foundation they laid that allowed for the promise of continued growth and service in the years ahead.[1] At the same time, controversies within Baptist ranks, controversies concerning faith and practice and introduced in the earliest years of the Baptist presence in Kentucky, elicited heated debate into the 1920s, and indeed into the new millennium after 2000.

The history of Kentucky Baptist life before the 1920s has been recorded carefully in a number of studies, beginning with John Henderson Spencer's monumental two-volume *A History of Kentucky Baptists from 1769 to 1885*, published in 1885. In 1922, William Dudley Nowlin attempted to update Spencer's work with his *Kentucky Baptist History, 1770-1922*, and Frank Mariro Masters's encyclopedic study *A History of Baptists in Kentucky*, published by the Kentucky Baptist Historical Society in 1953, brought the story of Kentucky Baptists through the mid-twentieth century. In commemoration of the bicentennial of Baptist preaching in Kentucky, *Baptists in Kentucky, 1776-1976: A Bicentennial Volume* was edited by Leo

T. Crismon and published in 1975. Then, as part of the celebration of the sesquicentennial of the Kentucky Baptist Convention, the convention published Ira (Jack) Birdwhistell's *Kentucky Baptists: 150 Years On Mission Together* in 1987.[2]

Each of these works emphasizes the period before the organization of the Cooperative Program in 1925 and the beginning of the work of the unified budget plan the following year. And rightly so. The first 150

J. H. Spencer, author of A History of Kentucky Baptists from 1769 to 1885

years of Baptist witness in Kentucky provided a strong foundation on which to build the next seventy-five years of cooperation in the twentieth century.

The introduction of Baptist belief and practice in Kentucky coincided with the founding of the Republic. In Kentucky, Baptists "were present . . . from the first days of settlement."[3] In fact, William Hickman preached, in 1776, the first documented sermon by a Baptist preacher in the territory that would become the Commonwealth of Kentucky in 1792. Hickman had been converted under the preaching of David Tinsley, a Baptist preacher in Virginia, and baptized or "dipped . . . all over in water" by Reuben Ford.[4]

Hickman moved from Virginia to Kentucky in February 1776, arriving in Harrodsburg—then known as Harrodstown—on April 1. There, he lodged with Thomas Tinsley, described by Hickman as "a good old preacher," and accompanied Tinsley at Sunday outdoor worship services. In his autobiography, Hickman described his first preaching opportunity:

One Sunday morning, sitting at the head of a spring at this place, he laid the Bible on my thigh and said, "You must preach today." He said if I did not, he would not. It set me in a tremor. I knew he would not draw back. I took the book and turned to the 23rd Chapter of Numbers, 10th verse: "Let me die the death of the righteous and let my last end be like his." I suppose I spoke fifteen or twenty minutes, a good deal scared, thinking if I had left any gaps down, he would put them up. He followed me with a good discourse but never mentioned my blunders.[5]

Hickman's modest attempt at preaching was the beginning of a remarkable ministerial career. Leaving for Virginia soon after that first sermon, he was ordained there in 1778, and returned to Kentucky six years later for his life's work. There, from 1788 until his death in 1834, he pastored the Forks of Elkhorn Baptist Church and "probably baptized more happy converts than any other pioneer preacher."[6] Certainly, individuals responded to his persuasive style. Describing Hickman's preaching, fellow pioneer minister John Taylor stated that his "preaching is a plain and solemn style, and the sound of it like that of thunder at a distance but when in his best gears, his sound is like thunder at home, and operates with prodigious force on the consciences of his hearers."[7] The confident "thunderings" of William Hickman's later years contrasted sharply with the hesitant murmurings of that first sermon in 1776. The preaching development of thousands of Baptist preachers would mirror Hickman's experience in the years ahead.

Of course, Hickman was not the only Baptist voice in the Kentucky wilderness of the later eighteenth century. Squire Boone, "an occasional preacher in the Calvinistic Baptist Church," and the younger brother of Daniel Boone, was "credited with preaching the first sermon in Louisville and also with conducting the first marriage in Kentucky on August 7, 1776."[8] Other pioneer Baptist preachers followed: John Taylor, John Gano, Ambrose Dudley, the Craig brothers—Lewis, Elijah, and Joseph—and James Garrard. Taylor eventually founded ten churches in Kentucky, and Garrard served as the state's second governor (1796-1804). During his second term as governor, Garrard, "the most popular man in Kentucky," according to Kentucky Baptist historian J. H. Spencer, "apparently adopted unitarian views." Although Garrard later served as moderator of the Elkhorn Association (the first association of Baptist churches in Kentucky), was appointed "to examine Josiah Dodge as to his ministerial qualifications," and helped constitute the Mays Lick Church in Mason County in

1789, Spencer concluded that Garrard "had not the gift of ready speech, and was every way better qualified to make laws, than to preach grace."[9]

By the end of the American Revolution, the Baptist presence in Kentucky was evident, although Baptist churches were yet to be established. Frank M. Masters stated that "at the close of the year 1780 there were many Baptists in the scattered settlements in the territory of Kentucky and at least six Baptist ministers, but no church had been constituted."[10] In 1781, however, three churches were founded. Severns Valley, "evidently the first church planted in the great valley between the Allegheny and Rocky Mountains," and certainly the first Baptist church in Kentucky, was organized on June 18, 1781, "under the shade of a large sugar tree" near present-day Elizabethtown. This first congregation experienced the reality of life on the Kentucky frontier when their first pastor, John Gerrard, was captured by Native Americans less than a year after the church's founding. Gerrard was "never again heard of," but the church continued to grow and prosper.[11]

The founding of Severns Valley was followed by the organization of Cedar Creek Baptist Church, located some five miles southwest of Bardstown, on July 4, 1781. The church's founding date was chosen "probably for patriotic reasons" on the fifth anniversary of the Declaration of Independence.[12]

Cedar Creek Baptist (Nelson County)
Organized July 4, 1781, as the second
Baptist church in Kentucky

Then, in December 1781, Gilbert's Creek Baptist Church was established on the south side of the Kentucky River in what would become Garrard County, named after the Baptist minister and Kentucky governor. The Gilbert's Creek church had been organized as the Upper Spotsylvania Church in Virginia where the Baptist believers, and particularly the church's pastor Lewis Craig—and his brothers—had been plagued by the established Anglican church. Like other Baptists in the Old Dominion, these Spotsylvania County Baptists considered issues of church and state to be important, indeed crucial.

Craig persuaded most of the members of the Upper Spotsylvania Church, some five or six hundred strong, to relocate in the Kentucky territory. They gathered, on September 29, 1781, "in their church on the Old Catharpin Road, twenty-two miles below Fredericksburg." There, Craig preached to the anxious Traveling Church members, Captain William Ellis "sounded the tocsin, and the congregation headed its wagons and herds westward."[13] Finally, after a tortuous two-and-a-half-month winter journey through the Cumberland Gap, Craig "placed the church's Bible on a crude stand in the log church at Gilbert's Creek" on the second Sunday of December. The Traveling Church had found a home.[14] But the pilgrims in the Traveling Church found other Kentucky church homes as well. In his *Kentucky Baptists: 150 Years on Mission Together*, Ira (Jack) Birdwhistell asserted that as "the Craig party dispersed, moving closer to the Bluegrass region, other churches were organized from its members: Forks of Dix River (1782), South Elkhorn (1783), Clear Creek (1784), and Great Crossings (1785). Providence Church, Clark County, arrived in Kentucky in early 1784, having been another traveling church from Virginia."[15]

Lewis Craig, the minister who challenged that first Traveling Church congregation, eventually became "a millmaster and distiller in Bourbon County."[16] Craig, and other early church leaders, were themselves, products of the frontier. In *The Baptists*, Frank S. Mead wrote of these early pioneer ministers: "Crude as he was, at times illiterate and unclean, lips stained with tobacco and tongue thick with white liquor, he was nevertheless the saving salt of the whole situation. . . . When he dropped on the wilderness trail, the churches he'd left behind him carried on."[17]

The churches did carry on. And the legacy of pioneer ministers and church members cast a long shadow over the Kentucky Baptist story. Their determination to organize into churches and associations laid the foundation for future cooperation, and issues that those pioneer Baptists wrestled with continued to be debated in the years ahead.

While still in good standing as a Baptist minister, James Garrard served with several other Baptist ministers and laymen as delegates to Kentucky's

Constitutional Convention in April 1792. Although delegates Garrard and David Rice, Kentucky's leading Presbyterian minister, espoused strong antislavery views, "the Pro-Slavery party carried the convention, and Kentucky was admitted into the Union on June 1, 1792, as a slave state."[18] The state's struggle with the slave question would continue to divide Kentuckians and Kentucky Baptists in the years ahead. So, too, would questions of theology. Garrard's divergent unitarian views served as a precursor for continuing debate over Baptist orthodoxy.

In the waning years of the eighteenth century, many Kentucky Baptist churches simply struggled to survive. Still, the development of internal divisions had begun. Birdwhistell summarized the state of Kentucky Baptist affairs at the end of the century:

> In the last two decades of the eighteenth century, the Baptist congregations were scattered and small, most of them meeting only once a month for preaching services. Many of the log, brick, or stone church buildings had balconies or galleries for the slaves of the members of the congregations. The Baptists of Kentucky were categorized as either Regulars, north of the Kentucky River, who were orderly in their worship and practices, or Separates, south of the Kentucky, whose worship was emotional and unstructured. Both groups were divided internally over such issues as slavery, Unitarianism, and the pay of ministers.[19]

By the dawn of the nineteenth century, then, the groundwork for future Kentucky Baptist cooperation and division was laid. Early associational cooperation was established, but, at the same time, divisive issues—temperance, church and state, slavery and race, education for ministers, and theological questions—were introduced.

Only a few years after the first churches were founded on Kentucky soil, those individual, local church bodies associated with other congregations. The Kentucky Baptist historian Wendell Rone concluded that from "their beginnings there had been a kind of practical interrelationship of Kentucky churches."[20] Despite the fact that "distance, wilderness conditions, danger from indians, and some doctrinal variants" discouraged associational development, by 1785 the first Kentucky Baptist associations were formed.[21] Baptist associations often played an ambiguous role in Baptist church life; they "allowed for congregational independence while also providing some guidance by informally resolving disputes between churches on questions of doctrine." Although churches in Baptist associations "were not required to follow the dictates" of the associations, "these regional bodies nevertheless held the power to 'break fellowship' with congregations that violated doctrinal or behavioral standards."[22]

The earliest American Baptists prided themselves in their distinctive belief in "Baptist democracy," the polity of the autonomy of local congregations in the face of "the evils inherent in state-supported religion" in Massachusetts and later in Virginia. In Rhode Island, for example, Roger Williams and John Clarke had been "excluded from Puritan towns for their radical beliefs about the autonomy of individual souls." Indeed, Baptist insistence on complete liberty of conscience and the necessity of the separation of church and state influenced "the framers of the Constitution to enshrine the principle in the founding document of the new nation."[23] Still, the value of voluntary associational organization was not lost on early Baptists in the nation or in Kentucky. The foundation for the "story of cooperation" of Kentucky Baptists from 1925 to 2000 was established in the mid-1780s.

Elkhorn Association minutes
June 12, 1785

Only a month following the organization of the Elkhorn Association—
a "Regular Baptist" association—by representatives of six churches meeting
in the home of John Craig at Clear Creek (Woodford County) on September
30, 1785, "messengers from four churches, in what was then the western
area, met at Cox's Creek and organized Salem Association" on October 29.[24]
The Salem Association also used the moniker "Regular Baptist" to identify
themselves. These Regular Baptists traced their roots back to England and to
the first Baptist presence in the American colonies, and to Roger Williams
and John Clarke, the founders of Rhode Island and the first Baptist churches
in America. To this day Williams's Providence church and Clarke's Newport
church, both founded in 1638, continue friendly rival claims to having been
the first Baptist church founded on American soil.

Characterized "by order and dignity in worship, appreciation for an educated ministry, and a fondness for precise doctrine, such as that enshrined in
the Philadelphia Confession of Faith (1742)," Kentucky's Regular Baptists
gathered initially in congregations north of the Kentucky River in the Bluegrass region and farther to the west in Hardin County and along the Green
River.[25] A decade and a half after the formation of the Elkhorn and Salem Associations in central Kentucky, the Green River Association was constituted
in June 1800, at Mt. Tabor Church in Barren County. Churches in the Green
River Association, all Regular Baptist in origin, eventually emphasized a "hy-
per-Calvinism" and withdrew from cooperation with the majority of Kentucky Baptists after 1840.[26]

South of the Kentucky River in central Kentucky, Baptists "whose tradition originated from the Great Awakening in New England in the 1730s and
1740s" were, at first, opposed to associational organization and concentrated instead on "regenerate conversion, pure membership, and strict local
independence."[27] In Kentucky, these "Separate Baptists," at first opposed to
organization of any sort among local churches, eventually formed associations of their own with the understanding that "no doctrinal agreement"
would be required.[28]

In October 1787, the South Kentucky Association of Separate Baptists,
composed of eleven churches located south of the Kentucky River, was
formed. Because of the lack of any uniformity in doctrinal belief, the South
Kentucky Association was soon racked with divisions and church withdrawals.
Five churches withdrew in 1793 and organized the Tates Creek Association;
the original association split into two divisions in 1801, and in 1803 a rival
Separate Baptist association, calling itself the South Kentucky Association of
Separate Baptists II, was formed.[29] These divisions, growing out of various
doctrinal controversies, indicated a general weakening of Baptist influence in
the years following the admission of Kentucky as the fifteenth state in 1792.

The internal divisions among Separate Baptists in Kentucky were coupled with a growing tension between Separate and Regular Baptists. When Baptists first came to Kentucky, they were primarily of the Separate Baptist persuasion. Masters asserted that "of the first twenty-five preachers, who settled in Kentucky, twenty of them were known to have been Separate Baptists in Virginia and North Carolina."[30] Only one, Joseph Barnett, was identified with the Regular Baptists.[31]

After settling in Kentucky, however, eighteen of the first twenty-five ministers eventually subscribed to the Philadelphia Confession of Faith, and the majority of Kentucky's earliest Baptist churches identified themselves as Regular Baptist. Although at first there was little friction among Separate and Regular Baptist ministers and churches, "as both agreed on the essential doctrines," the formation of the first associations changed the dynamic between the two groups.[32] In fact, when factions in each group worked to magnify "minor points of difference, and at the same time to minimize the points of agreement," the initial fledgling attempts at associational cooperation ironically led to more pronounced division between the two groups.[33]

When the first union between Regular and Separate Baptists was consummated in North Carolina in May 1786, and in Virginia the following year, the United Baptist movement sought to "bury in oblivion" the destructive division. Communication of the union of Baptists in Virginia "was forwarded at once to Kentucky," and Kentucky Baptists were urged to follow suit.[34] The advice of the Virginia Baptists was not heeded in Kentucky until 1801, however, when the union of Kentucky Baptists finally occurred during Kentucky's Great Revival. The union was one of several important results of a movement that "produced far reaching spiritual results in the salvation of thousands of people of all classes and caused a marked change in the social orders of the day."[35]

Masters concluded that "the climax of the fruit of the revival on the Baptists of Kentucky was the healing of the unhappy division between the Regular and Separate Baptists."[36] The healing began with the appointment of a committee at the 1800 session of the Elkhorn Association, a Regular Baptist association, for the purpose of visiting the South Kentucky Association of Separate Baptists "and to join with that body in calling a convention for the purpose of effecting a union."[37]

The convention was called, and two members from each church in each association gathered at Howards Creek, at the "old Providence Meetinghouse" in Clark County "on the second Saturday in October, 1801."[38] The "Terms of General Union" were approved unanimously by the Elkhorn and South Kentucky Associations, and "speedily accepted by all the Baptists in the State."[39] The terms of the union provide a ready reference for the basic beliefs of Kentucky Baptists at the time of the Great Revival:

We, the committees of Elkhorn and South Kentucky Associations, do agree to unite on the following plan:

1st. That the Scriptures of the Old and New Testament are the infallible word of God, and the only rule of faith and practice.

2d. That there is one only true God, and in the Godhead or divine essence, there are Father, Son and Holy Ghost.

3d. That by nature we are fallen and depraved creatures.

4th. That salvation, regeneration, sanctification and justification are by the life, death, resurrection and ascension of Jesus Christ.

5th. That the saints will finally persevere through grace to glory.

6th. That believers' baptism by immersion is necessary to receiving the Lord's supper.

7th. That the salvation of the righteous and punishment of the wicked will be eternal.

8th. That it is our duty to be tender and affectionate to each other, and study the happiness of the children of God in general; to be engaged singly to promote the honor of God.

9th. And that the preaching Christ tasted death for every man, shall be no bar to communion.

10th. And that each may keep up their associational and church government as to them may seem best.

11th. That a free correspondence and communion be kept up between the churches thus united.[40]

J. H. Spencer concluded his listing of the provisions with the optimistic statement: "Now ensued the golden age of the Kentucky Baptists. Their divisions had been healed. Universal harmony prevailed among them, and they were in the midst of the most powerful and extensive revival of religion that had ever been witnessed by them or their fathers."[41]

Spencer wrote that the Great Revival "was one of the most wonderful events of modern times" and "appeared more like the sudden conversion of a nation than the regeneration and reformation of individuals." The Kentucky evangelist and historian illustrated the dramatic results of the revival, results that, he believed, exerted a revolutionary impact on the nation as a whole:

If a traveller had passed through the whole breadth of the settled portions of North America, in 1799, he would have heard the songs of the drunkard, the loud swearing and obscenity of crowds around taverns, and the bold, blasphemous vaunting of infidels, in

Old Stone Meeting House, Providence Baptist Church,
Winchester, site of 1801 union of Separate and Regular Baptists

every village and hamlet. If he had returned in 1801, he would have heard, instead, the proclamation of the gospel to awed multitudes, earnest prayers in the groves and forests, and songs of praise to God, along all the public thoroughfares.[42]

One student of the revival observed that before the revival, Kentucky "had become notorious for the prevailing vice and moral lassitude." The Methodist evangelist Peter Cartwright described pre-revival Logan County as "Rogues' Harbor." Cartwright believed that to Logan County "many refugees, from almost all parts of the Union, fled to escape justice or punishment; for although there was a law, yet it would not be executed, and it was a desperate state of society."[43] The revival's impact was so profound, however, that a later traveler reported that "on my way to Kentucky I was told by settlers on the road that the character of Kentucky travelers was entirely changed, and that they were now as distinguished for their sobriety as they had formerly been for dissoluteness, and, indeed, I found Kentucky the most moral place I have ever been in: a profane expression was hardly heard, a religious awe seemed to pervade the country."[44]

While Spencer concluded that "in no other locality was [the revival] so deep and powerful as in Kentucky," his enthusiasm was tempered with his determination to distance Kentucky Baptists from the excesses of the movement that subsequently swept across the state and the South. Long sections of his history were devoted to "the strange exercises" occurring during revival meetings. "The Falling Exercise," "The Jerking Exercise," "The Rolling Exercise," "The Dancing Exercise," "The Barking Exercise," "The Laughing Exercise," and various "Visions and Trances," all a part of the camp meeting experience, "diverted popular attention from the Bible, which must always be the sole standard of truth among intelligent christians, and fostered a fondness for those mysticisms, superstitions and novelties, so congenial, and yet so degrading to fallen men."[45] New sects, "originating from the Great Revival," such as Marshallites, Stonites or Newlights, and the Shakers or "Millenial Church," were all examples to Spencer of the negative excesses of a generally positive movement.[46] Spencer was consoled, though, that while "the great revival among the Presbyterians and Methodists degenerated into a misguided and corrupting enthusiasm," among the Baptists in Kentucky "the revival began, and continued to its close, in a decorous, orderly manner."[47]

The impact of the Great Revival on the South was indeed significant. John B. Boles, a modern historian of the phenomenon, has asserted that by "the 1830s nearly everyone in the South—the plain folk, wealthy planters, slaves—accepted in broad outline the evangelical tradition that had emerged during the Great Revival. That tradition became one of the essential ingredients of what has been called the mind of the Old South."[48] In Kentucky, and among Kentucky Baptists, the impact of the Great Revival was no less significant.

J. H. Spencer's attempt to separate the revival experience of Kentucky Baptists from other sects in Kentucky and across the South was not far-fetched. Birdwhistell agreed that while Spencer and other writers "were doubtless trying to protect the Baptists from the ridicule and suspicion attendant upon these dramatic manifestations, what they wrote was probably accurate."[49] Baptists, rather than using "the camp meeting approach," relied on the local churches; the impact of the Great Revival on Kentucky Baptists "moved from church to church, from community to community."[50] While critics and secular historians concentrated on the gothic drama of the meeting at Cane Ridge in Bourbon County, historians of Kentucky Baptists have emphasized the impact of the Great Revival on local churches and communities.

At South Elkhorn Baptist Church, for example, where "six only had been received [as new members] in the past six years, three hundred and nine were received during the spring and summer of 1801." At Bryant's Station Baptist Church, 367 baptisms were reported. Indeed, "most of the conversions in Baptist meetings took place before Cane Ridge," and when the Elkhorn Baptist Association met for its annual session on August 8, 1801, the same weekend as the opening of Barton Stone's Cane Ridge meeting, some eight to ten thousand Baptists were in attendance at the session's Sunday worship service.[51]

At the Elkhorn session, a total of 3,001 baptisms in the 36 churches were reported for the previous year, and the total membership of the association's churches had "nearly tripled."[52] Other associations grew as well. By 1803, the 219 Baptist churches in Kentucky's 10 associations boasted a membership of 15,495. Spencer compiled 1803 statistics for each of the state's Baptist associations:

Associations	Number of Churches	Number of Members
Elkhorn	40	4,404
Salem	18	890
Tates Creek	23	1,905
Bracken	16	776
Green River	30	1,763
North District	24	1,745
South District	24	1,468
North Bend	9	429
Long Run	25	1,715
Cumberland	10	400
Totals (10)	219	15,495[53]

The revival's dramatic impact on church membership prompted Masters to conclude that "though they did not join as a denomination with others in promoting it," the revival "proved a great blessing to the Baptists of Kentucky."[54] A great blessing indeed. Between 1800 and 1810, the number of Kentucky Baptists increased from 5,119, or 2.3 percent of the population of the state, to 16,650, or 4.1 percent.[55] The fact that the vast majority of the decade's new Baptist church members came into Kentucky Baptist churches during the revival indicates its impact. The Great Revival, while making a significant impact on other denominations as well, insured that Kentucky Baptists would continue as the leading expression of Christianity in the commonwealth.

Other, more subtle changes came with the revival. Birdwhistell emphasized the "immense socio-economic implications" for Kentucky's Baptist churches. Masters agreed that "the great revival of 1800 produced far reaching spiritual results in the salvation of thousands of people of all classes and caused a marked change in the social orders of the day."[56] The revival increased the democratization of Kentucky Baptists. Most of the converts in Baptist churches during the revival came from the lower rungs of the state's socioeconomic ladder. Many African-American slaves were added to the rolls of Kentucky's Baptist churches.[57] While many of the earliest Baptists in Kentucky were relatively prosperous landowners with aspiring business interests, the Great Revival had its most significant impact on the lower classes. Spencer concluded that:

> The effect of the revival, on Christians, was permanently good. It imbued them more deeply with the spirit of the Master, and gave them clearer views of the spirituality of religion. It turned their minds away from metaphysical abstractions about dogmas, and inspired a greater earnestness for spreading the gospel of salvation. They became more interested in sinners' being "born again," than in determining the comparative orthodoxy of Calvin and Arminius; and were more desirous to promote love and harmony among brethren, than to discover indistinguishable shades of heterodoxy in each other's creeds. The mere forms, of religious morals, ceremonies, and learning catechisms, gave way to a firm belief in the necessity of experimental religion.[58]

And, according to Spencer, the revival "had an especially happy effect on the Baptists." Not only was the rift between Regular and Separate Baptists healed; the revival also instilled a more profound missionary fervor in the various churches and associations. The state's largest and oldest association, for example, responded to a request from the South Elkhorn church "to send missionaries to the Indian nations," and eventually approved John Young for the task. Although Spencer lamented that "we have no knowledge of the length of time he spent among the Red men, or the results of his labors," Young's commission indicated a new concern for missions following the revival.[59]

The revival made a lasting impact on Kentucky and on many Kentuckians. While some "returned quickly to their sinful ways," others "had undergone lifetime changes."[60] After a "season of barrenness" when a seven-year "spiritual dearth" plagued the churches of the commonwealth, another awakening revitalized Kentucky Baptists "with a precious outpouring of his Spirit" in 1810.[61]

The series of revivals beginning in the second decade of the nineteenth century coincided with other phenomena that made a lasting imprint on Kentucky. The New Madrid earthquakes, "the greatest recorded sequence of earthquakes in the history of North America," literally shook the western portion of the state beginning on December 16, 1811. These earthquakes were the first of four major series of earthquakes in a sequence that continued until February 7, 1812, when the largest quake in the sequence rocked the area.[62]

Because of the lack of newspapers at the time, the extent of the damage from the earthquakes is unknown. Certainly, houses and other buildings were destroyed, people were killed in western Kentucky towns, and minor damage was reported in Louisville and as far east as Lexington, Frankfort, and Maysville.[63] The earthquakes' impact went beyond mere damage to the state's physical structures. Some scholars have suggested that the earthquakes influenced the religious life of residents as well. Historian Lowell H. Harrison has written in *A New History of Kentucky* that some "backsliders were reported to have changed direction again in 1811-12, when the great earthquakes repeatedly rocked the eastern half of the nation." When a "bright comet appeared during that period," many "frightened Kentuckians viewed it and the quakes as signs that the world was coming to an end."[64]

Spencer wrote that the quakes "gave much alarm to the people, especially in the western part of the state, where *'the shakes,'* as they were called, were most violent," and concluded that the "phenomenon, doubtless, added much to the seriousness of the people, and probably led many to repentance." When Congress declared war on Great Britain in 1812, the "superstitious" were confirmed in their belief that "'the shakes' betokened some great calamity."[65] The comet, the earthquakes, and the war certainly caused many Kentucky Baptists to think more seriously about their faith and the need to spread that faith to others in need of the gospel in Kentucky and around the world. Spencer asserted that it was following the 1810 renewal, in the years of the calamitous events of the decade, that "the subject of foreign missions first began to be agitated among the Baptists of Kentucky."[66]

A commitment in Kentucky to international missions coincided with a general emphasis among American Christians in missions. Masters concluded that it was "of special interest to observe how God in his providence in a mysterious way thrust American Baptists to the forefront at the very beginning of the great Foreign Mission Movement."[67] As early as 1792, William Carey, a Baptist in England recognized as the "Father of Modern Missions," envisioned a "world-wide missions concept."[68] Carey was appointed, in 1793, as a missionary of England's Baptist Missionary Society, whose organization and funding "stimulated the formation of missionary agencies throughout the Protestant world."[69]

In the United States, the American Board of Commissioners for Foreign Missions, an interdenominational society, was organized in Massachusetts in 1800. On February 18, 1810, this board sent Adoniram Judson as a missionary to India. The day after Judson and his wife Ann set sail from Salem, Massachusetts, Luther Rice and several other appointees sent by the same board for mission work in India sailed for Calcutta from Philadelphia. Within weeks, the Judsons and Rice, all with backgrounds in the Congregational Church, came independently to a decision that would have a profound effect on their future work in Christian missions. Spencer described the decision in his 1885 history:

> During their passage, Mr. Judson thought much of the circum-
> stance, that he was going to Serampore, where all were Baptists,
> and that he should, in all probability, have occasion to defend in-
> fant sprinkling. To be prepared for this exigency, he began to ex-
> amine the foundation of pedobaptism. At an early period of the ex-
> amination, he suggested his difficulties to his wife, and after a
> solemn and prayerful investigation, they both became satisfied
> that the immersion of a believer in the name of Christ is the only
> Christian baptism. They were both baptized, in the Baptist chapel,
> in Calcutta. Mr. Rice, also, entered into an examination of the sub-
> ject, and in a few weeks afterward, he was also baptized.[70]

Because Baptists in America had not yet organized a board or society dedicated to foreign missions, the future work for the Judsons and Rice as new Baptists was uncertain. The Serampore Baptists consulted "the most distinguished Baptists" in America, "recommending to their attention the favorable opening for their enterprise in this great work." The small group was "convinced of the conviction" that the Judsons should go to Burma "as the scene of their future labors," and that Luther Rice should return to the states. There, "sustained by many brethren of enlarged benevolence and influence, and particularly by the special providence that threw this opportunity in their way," Rice would work to organize Baptist missionary societies.[71]

Rice's work resulted in a large number of missionary societies around the country, including six in Kentucky. In fact, Rice spent "the associational season of 1815" and much of 1816 in the state, making the home of Benjamin Stout, "a well-to do saddler of Lexington," his headquarters, and traveling from association to association, soliciting funds and promoting the cause of missions. In April 1814, a year before Rice's Kentucky sojourn, "The General Convention of the Baptist Denomination in the United States for Foreign Missions," or "The Triennial Convention," had been formed in Philadelphia. Rice immediately went to work raising funds as the convention's General Agent.[72] His Kentucky work led to the formation of the Kentucky Baptist Society for the Propagation of the Gospel, usually referred to as the state's Baptist Missionary Society.

According to Spencer, Rice "visited most of the Associations in Kentucky, in 1815, and was very cordially received." Rice documented his Kentucky travels in a letter to his brother dated October 19, 1816:

> The next Sabbath, at the North District Association, Montgomery County, Kentucky, 290 miles; raining all the week, excessively bad roads, mountains, rivers, creeks, and mud—my health began to be impaired. The following Sabbath, with the Franklin Association, near Frankfort, Ky., only about 100 miles, riding for the whole week, nearly three days of which were spent in Lexington, preaching, hearing preaching, visiting, and necessary business, etc. The following Friday I was at the Union Association in Knox County, Ky., and left it the same evening, intending to be with the Caney Fork Association, in Warren County, Tennessee on the Sabbath.[73]

In Kentucky, Rice received "liberal collections," and "but for the alarm of a few preachers, who were jealous of an imaginary encroachment on church independence, or were startled at the idea of novelty," Kentucky Baptists responded favorably to Rice's pleas and began a long association with foreign mission work that would grow in the years ahead.[74] Masters asserted that, in Kentucky, "the members of Baptist churches more readily responded to mission appeals than the pastors themselves."[75] The *Christian Review* later concluded that when "the late Rev. Luther Rice first visited the churches in Kentucky and Tennessee, and brought before them the subject of Foreign Missions, the contributions were larger than in any other States."[76]

Rice's labors led to more than monetary contributions alone. As a direct result of his travels, "there was much interest and an increased zeal manifested among the churches of the state in favor of foreign missions."[77] But Rice also recognized other areas of need, areas linked crucially to missions. Masters revealed the debt that Kentucky Baptists owed to this New Englander: "He saw the importance of the relation between education and foreign missions and began to advocate a trained ministry as the greatest need of the hour. He greatly influenced Baptists to give attention to founding schools for the training of preachers. During all his life foreign missions was nearest his heart, but in later years he became absorbed in educational work only because he perceived its vital relation to the success of his first love—missions."[78]

Indeed, the history of Kentucky Baptists before the Civil War was largely defined along guidelines established by Luther Rice during his brief tenure in the state. Although Masters concluded that Rice "literally burned out his life in the cause of his Master, and died on September 25, 1836, at the age of fifty-three years," his vision continued to burn in the hearts of Baptists around the world.[79]

The glow was especially bright in Kentucky. Already, voices for missions were being raised in the Kentucky wilderness. As early as 1812, Stark Dupuy from Shelby County began publishing the *Kentucky Missionary and Theological Magazine*. Probably the first Baptist periodical in Kentucky and one of the first in the South, Dupuy's publication was soon suspended, a casualty of the financial disruption brought on by the War of 1812. It was succeeded, however, by Silas M. Noel's *Gospel Herald*, and Noel became "the primary Kentucky advocate of missionary cooperation."[80]

That is not to say that the vision of Rice and Dupuy and Noel for education and foreign missions was implemented in the state without opposition. To be sure, John Taylor, one of Kentucky's most prominent pioneer preachers, likened Rice's urgings to John Tetzel's sale of indulgences for the medieval church, a practice that led in part to the Protestant Reformation. "Though I admired the art of this well-taught Yankee," Taylor wrote, "yet I considered him a modern Tetzel, and that the Pope's old orator of that name was equally innocent with Luther Rice, and his motive about the same." Taylor was convinced that "Luther's motive was thro' sophistry and Yankee art, to get the money for the Mission, of which he himself was to have a part."[81]

Taylor was present when Rice visited the Elkhorn Association in 1815. In his deceptively titled *Thoughts on Missions*, the pioneer preacher remembered the visit with a combination of admiration and disdain:

> When Luther rose up, the assembly of thousands seemed stricken with his appearance. A tall, pale-looking, well-dressed young man, with all the solemn appearance of one who was engaged in the work of the Lord, and perhaps he thought he was. He also being a stranger, every eye and ear was open; his text was "Thy Kingdom Come." He spoke some handsome things about the Kingdom of Christ; but every stroke he gave seemed to mean money. For my own part, I was more amused with his ingenuity than edified by his discourse, and more astonished at his art in the close, than at any other time. He had the more pathos, the nearer he came getting the money, and raising his arms, as if he had some awfully pleasing vision, expressed without a hesitating doubt, that the angels were hovering over the assembly, and par-

ticipating in our heavenly exercise, and just ready to take their leave, and bear the good tidings to heaven of what we were then about, in giving our money for the instruction and the conversion of the poor heathens.[82]

By 1821, Taylor's thirty-four-page tract, written according to Masters "in the kind of style that appealed to the illiterate," and the writing of Daniel Parker, "the most persistent and effective opposer of missions who ever labored in Kentucky," were "producing a bountiful harvest of anti-mission sentiment" among the rural churches of the state.[83] Parker, who later in 1826 advocated in a pamphlet the "Two-Seeds doctrine"—described by one critic as "a very disgusting form of the Gnostic heresy"—was particularly effective in arousing sentiment against missions in Kentucky.

J. M. Peck described Parker as "one of those singular and extraordinary beings whom divine Providence permits to arise as a scourge to His church, and a stumbling-block in the way of religious effort." "Raised on the frontier in Georgia, without education, uncouth in manner, slovenly in dress, diminutive in person, unprepossessing in appearance, with shrivelled features and a small, piercing eye, few men for a series of years have exercised a wider influence on the lower and less educated class of frontier people."[84]

While rural and urban Kentucky Baptists opposed the anti-missions diatribes of Taylor and Parker, the identification of many rural church leaders with anti-missions and anti-education arguments indicated an already evident division within Baptist ranks. Although Kentucky was, of course, decidedly rural in character, the growing urban centers of Louisville and Lexington exerted an increasing influence in the state's economic and political affairs. The same could also be said of the state's religious affairs, and particularly of the affairs of Kentucky Baptists.

The anti-missions movement, and the disaffection raised by Taylor, and especially Parker, presaged still another explosive controversy that divided Baptist ranks in the 1820s and 1830s. While Taylor eventually "relaxed his opposition" to missions in the 1820s, he turned his attention to what he felt to be an even greater threat to Kentucky Baptists.[85] And unlike the anti-missions controversy, this new threat to Baptist unity influenced Kentuckians irrespective of social, economic, and educational status.

When Alexander Campbell debated the Presbyterian minister William L. McCalla on the issue of baptism at Washington in Mason County on October 23, 1823, the "Baptist denomination was probably never more prosper-

Alexander Campbell

ous."[86] News of Campbell's attack on pedobaptism was welcomed by Baptists across Kentucky. When Campbell turned his eloquence against cherished Baptist tenets, however, the results were predictably devastating. His controversial views soon "exercised a greater influence over the Baptists of Kentucky" than in any other state.[87] And it was Campbell's influence that threatened the continued growth and prosperity of the Baptist denomination in the commonwealth.

Born in Ireland, the son of a Presbyterian minister, Campbell grew up in Scotland and prepared for the Presbyterian ministry himself at the University of Glasgow. After sailing for America in 1808, he related that "I commenced my career in this country, under the conviction that nothing that was not as old as the New Testament should be made an article of faith, a rule of practice, or a term of communion amongst Christians."[88] Campbell soon gave up his Presbyterian credentials, was baptized, and joined a Baptist church in Pennsylvania. In 1820, he began a series of debates on baptism, missions, and benevolent societies, and began the publication of a religious monthly, the *Christian Baptist*.

Although Campbell at first appeared to champion Baptist beliefs, his break with mainstream Baptists came with disagreements over "conversion-initiation," over baptism "for the remission of sins," and over worship practices and denominational organization.[89] The response to Campbell's visit to Lexington's First Baptist Church, pastored by James Fishback, indicated his controversial, yet charismatic, appeal:

At the hour of meeting, the house was crowded to its utmost capacity. When Mr. Campbell rose, he appeared pale and exhausted, owing to the dyspepsia from which he had not yet fully recovered, and was unable to stand entirely erect during the delivery of his discourse. This was based on the first chapter of Hebrews, and led the speaker to dwell upon the divine glory of the Son of God—a theme upon which he was always surpassingly eloquent. It lasted two hours during which the audience sat in rapt attention.

The impression made upon the entire audience was very marked. They recognized at once in Alexander Campbell the mightiest intellect who had ever visited their city. The freshness of his thoughts, the extent and accuracy of his biblical knowledge, and his grand generalizations of the wonderful facts of redemption opened up trains of reflection wholly new, and presented the subject of Christianity in a form so simple and yet so comprehensive as to fill every one with admiration.[90]

The impact of Campbell's eloquence, coupled with the lingering influence of Barton J. Stone, whose similar views had sparked the Cane Ridge Revival, was far-reaching in Kentucky. One convert, "Raccoon" John Smith, a minister in Montgomery County, "almost single handedly carried the North District Association" of Kentucky Baptists into the "Reformation," as followers of Stone and Campbell referred to the movement. In 1828, Smith boasted to his wife Nancy that "I have baptized seven hundred sinners and capsized fifteen hundred Baptists!"[91]

Indeed, the excitement initiated by Alexander Campbell and his teachings resulted in a revival movement beginning in 1827 that swept across Kentucky, rivaling, in its impact, the earlier Great Revival. Over fifteen thousand additions were reported in the state's Baptist churches. Spencer suspected, though, that the revival's largest impact was in "those portions of the State, where Campbellism was most prevalent."[92] The Baptist historian added that while the "churches were greatly enlarged in numbers," they were "proportionately weakened in moral power" and that it was "to be feared, that a majority of those baptized during the revival, were not converted, in the Baptist definition of that term, especially in the northern and middle portions of the State."[93]

Spencer lamented the dire effects of Campbell's teachings and influence:

The effects of these teachings were felt as far as the *Christian Baptist* was circulated, and nowhere more than among the Baptists of Kentucky. The preachers who had hitherto received but a small pittance from their charges, were further reduced in their resources of living. The friends of education were discouraged in their endeavors to erect a college. The Baptist missionary societies, that started under such auspicious circumstances, were dwarfed, and ultimately perished. The ministers were brought into disrepute among those who most needed the restraints of their teaching, and practical benevolence was well nigh destroyed in the churches, at least, so far as any effort to spread a knowledge of the gospel was concerned. It required the labors of thirty years to bring the Baptist churches of Kentucky up to the standard of christian benevolence, to which they had attained, in 1816, and a considerable fraction of them continued their downward course, in this respect, thirty years longer.[94]

The schism that resulted from Campbell's teachings went beyond the Baptist benevolence movement, and the divisive impact of his influence was soon apparent. When, in 1829, the Beaver Association, "a small Baptist fraternity in Pennsylvania," withdrew fellowship from the Mahoning Association for "maintaining, or countenancing" Campbell's teachings, the fracture that eventually came to Kentucky was begun. Specifically, the charges against the Mahoning Association were:

1. They maintain that there is no promise of salvation without baptism.
2. That baptism should be administered to all who say that Jesus Christ is the son of God, without examination on any other point.
3. That there is no direct operation of the Holy Spirit, on the mind, prior to baptism.
4. That baptism produces the remission of sins and the gift of the Holy Spirit.
5. That the Scriptures are the only evidence of interest in Christ.
6. That obedience places it in God's power to elect to salvation.
7. That no creed is necessary for the church but the Scriptures as they stand.
8. That all baptized persons have a right to administer the ordinance of baptism.[95]

In Kentucky, Silas Noel, Jeremiah Vardaman, William Vaughan, George Waller, and, of course, John Taylor were the first "Baptist loyalist" pastors to take actions similar to the steps taken by Pennsylvania's Beaver Association. In Frankfort, Noel advised churches in the Franklin Association "to exclude from their membership, such of [Campbell's] adherents as could not be reclaimed."[96]

Excerpts from Noel's September 19, 1829, letter to the churches of the Franklin Association reveal the stridency of the developing schism:

> We have high authority to count those who preach another gospel accursed; to mark them who stir up strife and cause divisions. We have no authority to receive such into our houses, or bid them God speed.
>
> At this crisis, those who seek inglorious repose, by making truce with the adversaries, should have their furlough. They are unworthy of the service, unfaithful to the King. We admire charity, but let it be the uncompromising charity of the Bible. All beside is hypocrisy and spiritual venality.
>
> We viewed them [the Campbellites] as impotent, and unworthy of notice, until they have scattered discord and corruption through many churches. By our forbearance, and their partial success among the Baptists, they have become vain and impudent.[97]

By 1832, the gains of the revival begun in 1827 had been countered by exclusions of Campbell's followers in churches across the state. As Spencer noted, "The Campbellite schism began with the close of the revival, and with it, commenced a religious dirth, that continued eight years. From the apostasy of the new converts, and the Campbellite defection, the Baptist denomination lost nearly all it gained by the revival."[98] Statistics bear out such a dreary picture. In 1829, Baptists boasted 614 churches and 45,442 members. Three years later, after the initial exclusions, associational records reported 608 churches and only 35,862 members, a loss of 9,580 members. While Spencer acknowledged that Baptists were "still the most numerous sect" in the state, no longer was the Baptist expression of Christianity equal in numbers "to all others combined."[99]

The Baptist response to Alexander Campbell had far-reaching repercussions in Kentucky. And the response was a familiar refrain that had already been heard in the earliest years of the Baptist presence in Kentucky, a refrain that would be heard again and again in the years ahead. The paradoxical refrain of the 1820s and 1830s was this: Campbell's divisive influence gave way to a strong cooperative impulse, a determination by Kentucky Baptists to organize and unify behind a common mission and vision. While early cooperative ventures failed to elicit continued support, other efforts established foundations on which to build. The American Indian

Mission established in Louisville eventually languished, and the Western Baptist Theological Institute failed as well, a casualty of the growing controversy over slavery.

But if some cooperative ventures were unsuccessful, Kentucky Baptists greeted other experiments with enthusiasm. The Kentucky Baptist Missionary Society, the consolidation and growth of Baptist publications, the founding of the Kentucky Baptist Education Society and Georgetown College, and especially the birth of the General Association of Kentucky Baptists all indicated the determination of Kentucky Baptists not just to survive, but to grow and prosper.

An outgrowth of Luther Rice's work in Kentucky's associations in 1815 and 1816, Kentucky's Baptist Missionary Society, officially named the Kentucky Baptist Society for the Propagating of the Gospel, held regular meetings in Lexington. In 1819, the society opened a school for Indian children near Georgetown. The Choctaw Academy enrolled eight children in its inaugural session in the spring of 1819. Masters recorded that the academy's "students increased from year to year until it became a large flourishing school."[100]

News of the Choctaw Academy and other Baptist cooperative endeavors was disseminated through Baptist papers beginning with the *Baptist Recorder*, begun by George Waller at Bloomfield, Kentucky, in 1825. In the same year, another *Baptist Recorder* began publication in Bardstown. The early years of the Baptist press in Kentucky are clouded with a remarkable but confusing collection of papers published in various locations across the state. The name of Waller's *Baptist Recorder* changed in 1829 to the *Baptist Herald* only to be renamed later the *Baptist Chronicle*. As early as 1830, the *Baptist Chronicle and Literary Register* was published in Georgetown, and yet another Baptist paper, the *Baptist Banner*, in Shelbyville in 1834. Spencer recorded that John L. Waller "became editor of the *Baptist Banner*, a bi-weekly religious newspaper," in 1835. Later, the *Baptist Banner and Western Pioneer* was moved to Louisville from locations in Illinois and Tennessee.

A dizzying assortment of other papers followed: *The Kentucky Baptist*, published for "the diffusion of religious, literary and general intelligence" in Frankfort from 1866 to 1867; another paper, also called *The Kentucky Baptist*, published in Louisville from 1888 to 1895; *The Baptist World*; the *Baptist Argus*; and *News and Truths*, H. Boyce Taylor's paper in Murray. The list seems endless. Several of the papers merged in 1851 to become known as the *Western Recorder*. Although the *Western Recorder* did not become the official denominational weekly for Kentucky Baptists until 1919, the plethora of Baptist papers, published in locations across the state, was a unifying force among Kentucky Baptists as early as the 1820s.[101]

Discussions of doctrinal views and missions concerns, devotional materials, and church and associational news, all provided in the pages of these early Baptist newspapers, were connected both directly and indirectly to another Kentucky Baptist initiative in the 1820s. In 1829, Silas Noel, a Frankfort attorney and minister, and an erstwhile missions advocate and opponent of Alexander Campbell, persuaded twenty-four other state Baptist leaders to charter the Kentucky Baptist Education Society. These Baptist leaders surveyed the Baptist landscape of the late 1820s and decided that in light of the threat to Baptist unity posed by anti-missions advocates and by Alexander Campbell, "providing for the education and training of young ministers to preach the gospel and lead the churches was no doubt the greatest need of the hour."[102]

After considering the establishment of a Baptist college on the campus of Transylvania University in Lexington, the trustees of the education society chose instead to locate the new college on the "campus of the defunct Rittenhouse Academy," which had been established in 1798 by Elijah Craig. Located in Georgetown, with capital provided by Issachar Pawling—a wealthy patron determined "to set apart a fund for the education of Baptist ministers, and candidates for the Baptist ministry"—and others, Georgetown College was chartered in 1829 and opened its doors to stu-

Georgetown College, founded 1829

dents for the spring term in 1830 as the first Baptist college west of the Allegheny Mountains.[103]

Plagued, along with Baptists in the rest of the state, with tensions and divisions created by Alexander Campbell, Georgetown was stabilized under the presidency of Rockwood Giddings. He came to the college in 1839, bringing with him from Maine the college's first permanent faculty and initiating in the lone year of his presidency the building of an impressive main building. Established in troubled times, Georgetown brought a level of stability and vision to Baptist education that would continue to have an impact on the state in the years ahead.

Despite the positive significance of the founding of Georgetown College in 1829, the prospects for the continued growth and prosperity of Kentucky Baptists were otherwise bleak. Spencer contended that the extent of the change from the promising outlook of 1820 was substantial: "If the Baptists of Kentucky were in a most happy and prosperous condition in 1820, they had oscillated to the other extreme, at the beginning of the next decade."[104]

The founding of Georgetown College and an active, if unsteady, Baptist press provided some sense of a common cause, but anti-mission adherents and Campbell dissidents postponed any real advance toward denominational unity until 1837. Efforts at some sort of denominational organization were made as early as 1813. In that year, Silas Noel proposed the organization of a "General Meeting of Correspondence," an annual meeting for ministers and church members to provide opportunities to "consult together on mutual interests."[105] Though Kentucky Baptists failed to respond to Noel's idea, Spencer Clack and George Waller made a similar proposal in 1827.[106]

It was not until 1832 that the intensified divisions and tensions of the late 1820s resulted in the organization of a Kentucky Baptist Convention. Thirty-four delegates met in Bardstown on March 29, 1832, adopted a constitution, raised $190 for convention expenses, and named *Cross and Baptist Banner*, yet another Baptist publication, as its official organ. This Kentucky Baptist Convention met regularly from 1832 to 1836 at locations around the state: New Castle, Lexington, Russellville, Louisville, Greensburg, Frankfort, and Georgetown.[107] Still, this early organizational effort remained limited in scope.

In the 1837 meeting at Georgetown, "it was recommended that a more general body than the convention be formed."[108] Many Kentucky Baptists chafed at the convention's perceived threat to the autonomy of local churches, long a cornerstone of Baptist polity. Recognizing such fears among many local pastors and church members, the convention made attempts early on to ease their concerns. A letter sent out by the convention to local churches acknowledged that "a few of our brethren have suspected that the movers of this meeting were [led] by some other than the avowed object, and desire to usurp ecclesiastical authority over the churches." The convention official assured Kentucky Baptists that "such fears are wholly groundless." The purpose of the convention was not "to legislate for God's churches; not to form an ecclesiastical court over the Churches and Association." Rather, Kentucky Baptists were invited to "meet us in Convention, that we may know each other, and learn the condition of the different parts of the state and mutually cooperate in preaching the gospel to every creature, and aid in sustaining the actual laborers."[109]

The pleas of the letter writer failed to convince a majority of Kentucky Baptists, however. When the convention attempted "to achieve the objectives of supplying destitute places with preachers, sending out missionaries, and raising and disbursing needed funds," local churches resented perceived intrusions on local initiatives. The convention denied "any pre-eminence and affirmed that the local church is the only ecclesiastical authority" for Baptists, but local churches and associations continued to voice suspicions.[110] Coupled with the more vigorous opposition of anti-mission Baptists, the convention concept was rejected, in 1837, in favor of a "general association" plan of organization.

Familiar and comfortable with the associational concept of Baptist church organization, the idea of a more general, statewide organization proved to be amenable to the majority of Kentucky Baptists. On October 20, 1837, the General Association of Baptists in Kentucky was organized in Louisville. The old Kentucky Baptist Convention held its final meeting on October 21-23 and then transferred its remaining funds to the new General Association. In the *Encyclopedia of Southern Baptists*, Wendell H. Rone and Hugh Wamble described the organizational functions of the General Association of Baptists in Kentucky:

> Composed of representatives from Baptist churches and associations which contribute annually to the causes or co-operate through auxiliary associations, the general association has as its special aim to promote God's cause in the state. No ecclesiastical authority over churches is intended. Officers and duties, election procedure, recognition of visiting brethren, time of annual meeting, and procedure for constitutional changes are defined in the constitution. In anticipating inquiries or criticisms concerning its doctrinal viewpoint, the General Association stated that its avowed "sentiments" were those held by United Baptists (the terms of General union of 1801).[111]

Although the formation of the General Association did not ease a lingering fear of centralization that concerned many Kentucky Baptists, the new organization survived. The "Anti-missioners," responsible in a marked degree for the dissolution of the failed Kentucky Baptist Convention, now leveled repeated attacks on the new association. Arguing "that it was unscriptural to raise monies for religious purposes, that the theological education was a detriment to preachers, and that it was both unscriptural and unnecessary to preach the gospel to sinners who could not repent and believe without divine grace," these opponents harassed General Association efforts. By 1842, however, "Antimissioners" and "Missionary" Baptists "were effectively disunited." Missions-minded Baptists soon "outstripped" their anti-missions opponents in numbers and influence.[112]

Perhaps more damaging to the association than the work of anti-mission foes were the increasingly dire economic conditions in Kentucky and the rest of the nation. Founded during the panic of 1837, the General Association faced the continuing economic decline of the 1840s. Still, in "protracted meetings," held by itinerant evangelists traveling around the state, the initiatives of the General Association were promoted and large numbers were added to rolls of Kentucky Baptist churches. In 1843, for example, General Association churches reported 7,271 baptisms compared to only 476 additions in anti-missions churches.[113]

So, despite hard times economically and lingering doubts about the efficacy of centralized programs, the General Association of Baptists in Kentucky grew and prospered. The process for growth in various programs was simple and effective: "A few interested individuals formed a society through which to promote a worthy cause, and later the society turned over its work to the general association and dissolved itself."[114] Missions within the state continued to be the primary emphasis for denominational energies. At the annual meeting in 1850, the General Association stated its aim explicitly: "to secure representation from each district association in the state, to establish a Baptist church in each county seat, to sustain missionary labor in destitute areas, and to encourage the circulation of Baptist literature."[115] To implement the goals of the denomination, a general agent "was authorized to visit each district association in order to secure co-operation, to survey the needs of the state, to recommend competent men to serve as missionaries, to supervise colportage service, and to represent the general association as occasion demanded."[116]

Areas of service were further defined in 1860, and again in 1861. Specifically, the denomination was to be involved in "state, domestic, Indian, and foreign missions" and in "Bible circulation." Later, "book colportage, supervision of Sunday schools, and the hearing of reports on colleges and theological seminaries" were all included as areas of denominational concern.[117]

The Civil War had, of course, a dramatic impact on Baptists and on everything else in Kentucky and the nation. Historians of the Civil War and Reconstruction periods have argued that because Kentucky remained within the Union during the war, the state's southern identity came after the war, that Kentucky joined the Confederacy after Appomattox. For Kentucky Baptists, however, an identification with the South was established years before the firing on Fort Sumter.

In fact, the formation of the Southern Baptist Convention in May 1845 was a chief topic of discussion and action for the General Association of Baptists in Kentucky when messengers met a few months later in Georgetown. The result of a division about whether missionaries sent out by mission boards could own slaves, 310 Southern Baptist delegates met in Augusta, Georgia, on May 8, 1845, and organized the Southern Baptist Convention. Although Isaac McCoy was probably the only Kentuckian present at the meeting, the direction of Kentucky Baptists was soon clear.[118] When Kentucky Baptists met in October in Georgetown, messengers agreed on the adoption of a resolution regarding the General Association's relationship to the new region-wide convention:

> Resolved, That union among the various societies and associations of Baptists in the south, southwestern and western States and Territories, is essential to the accomplishment of the greatest amount of good. Resolved, That in order to accomplish this union, we dissolve our auxiliary connection with the American Baptist Home Mission Society, and become auxiliary to the Southern Baptist Convention. Resolved, that the terms of the auxiliaryship to the Southern Baptist Convention be the same as those by which we were connected with the American Baptist Home Mission Society.[119]

The general feeling of Kentucky Baptists concerning the growing sectional controversy was evident. Although the relationship between the General Association of Baptists in Kentucky and the Southern Baptist Convention would be long and fruitful, the widening gulf between North and South was particularly disheartening for border-state Kentuckians.

J. H. Spencer remembered that 1861 "had been another busy year with me."[120] In his autobiography, the Kentucky Baptist historian and itinerant evangelist recalled that except "while confined with typhoid fever I had enjoyed few days of rest. I had traveled by railroad 853 miles; by steamboat, 861; on horseback 1058; in buggies and wagons, 327, and on foot, 52, mak-

ing a total distance of 3151 miles. I had preached 204 sermons and witnessed 102 additions to the churches."[121] While few Kentucky Baptist ministers equalled Spencer's stamina or success, his travels indicated a continuing regard by Kentuckians for spiritual renewal after the outbreak of the
war. Although Spencer's travels were curtailed somewhat in the years of the
bloody struggle, he was never confined to one place for long; he continued
to hold "protracted meetings" throughout the war years.

According to Spencer, the "year 1861 closed with a deep gloom over all
the land." He remembered that the "great Civil War was already raging
fiercely" and that the "people in Kentucky were nearly equally divided on
the question of the hour." His memories of the war were not unlike those
of others, North and South. But Spencer's memory of the war's effect on
the religious life of the commonwealth was especially poignant:

> The people in Kentucky were nearly equally divided on the
> question of the hour. Fierce contentions prevailed in every neigh-
> borhood. Hot disputings were heard wherever two or three men
> were together. Families were divided, and many hearthstones
> where peace and happiness had hitherto prevailed were now em-
> bittered by mad passions and bitter strife. Fathers were divided
> against sons and brothers against brothers in the deadly conflict of
> opposing armies. Many preachers were carried away by the wild
> storm of excitement and some after rendering themselves obnox-
> ious to the military authorities, fled to the armies for protection.
> Others assumed the position of recruiting [sic] officers and wildly
> exhorted the young men to enlist in the armies. There was, in the
> nature of things, division of sentiment and sympathy in all the
> churches, and some of them, though much fewer than might have
> been expected, were actually split into factions, while many of
> them were left pastorless. Soldiers, "home guards" and guerrillas
> were scattered everywhere. Bad men, taking advantage of the dis-
> organized state of society, became active thieves and robbers. The
> masses of the people were in such constant fear of losing their lives
> or their property that it was difficult to get their attention to the
> gospel.[122]

Unlike many other Kentuckians who found it impossible to remain neutral, Spencer decided "early in the contest, and before actual hostilities began . . . that I could do more to advance the cause of Christ by taking no part
in the great national conflict, either in word or deed, than any other course
I could pursue."[123] Certainly, Spencer's decision to maintain neutrality was

not easy. In the years of the war, he "suffered some bitter reproaches from brethren of both parties." He bore the reproaches, in his words, "as patiently as I could, and devoted my time and energies to preaching the gospel wherever I could obtain an audience. I preached indiscriminately to federal and confederate soldiers and guerrillas, and had the happiness of seeing some Christians revived, the spirit of peace promoted and some sinners converted even during the darkest hours of the war."[124]

Still, the impact of the war was devastating for the religious life of the commonwealth. As Spencer asserted in his history of Kentucky Baptists, the Civil War "put a sudden check on all religious and other benevolent enterprises." Colleges and academies were closed, and their buildings used as makeshift hospitals for "sick and wounded soldiers." Church buildings often served the same purpose. Spencer remembered that "the people of Kentucky were nearly equally divided on the political issues out of which the War grew" and that almost "every Baptist church in the State was divided on the question of secession." Generally, Baptists in the central, southern, and western portions of the state supported the Confederacy, while Baptists in Louisville, northern Kentucky, and eastern Kentucky favored the Union, but individual churches were sometimes split as were families.[125] "The excitement was so intense," according to Spencer, "that in many communities, church members of the different parties could not worship together with any degree of comfort."[126]

Church attendance declined dramatically, and most of those who did attend "felt little or no interest in it."[127] For Baptist women, the Civil War made demands that had not been required before the war. As men marched off to war, women remained on the farms, in the homes, and in the churches. Doubtless, the foundation for the leadership roles and prominent positions in missions efforts held by women in Kentucky Baptist churches after the Civil War were laid during the lonely war years.

For Baptist ministers, the disruption was predictable. "Many faithful and valuable pastors were forced to resign their charges, because they differed in their political views from a majority, or an influential minority, of the churches they served." Spencer himself, "accused of being a rebel by unruly congregants, found himself 'threatened by a mob and a halter' during one service."[128]

Spencer's ambivalence mirrored the ambiguity felt by many during the war. The itinerant evangelist and Baptist historian "questioned the institution of slavery and frowned on secession." While "maintaining a public stance of neutrality," however, "his heart remained with white southerners as they fought what he deemed to be a war for their liberty."[129] Most churches, according to Spencer, attempted to carry on despite the conflict. Although "many of the churches had members in both Federal and Confederate armies, opposed to each other in deadly strife, in honorable warfare," upon returning to their homes and churches, "they met each other in the house of God, as brethren in full fellowship, and were recognized as such by their churches." So, when "the storm of excited passion . . . had subsided, the tempest-tossed churches righted up again . . . and sailed on seas as calm and breakerless as those traversed before the gale arose."[130]

In his 1885 history, Spencer tempered his romantic rememberings with the hard facts of the war's devastation. The receipts of the General Association declined from $14,099.82 in 1860 to $8,313.82 in 1861, to $2,154.02 in 1862; the amount increased to $3,449.37 in 1863. The cold reality of the war experience was not lost on the noted Baptist historian. He recognized that the "active piety of the churches declined in almost an equal ratio" to the association's receipts and that the "religious prospects of the country never had been so gloomy, since the close of the war with Great Britain, in 1815."[131] As much as Kentucky and Kentuckians had suffered during the war, other southern states had suffered even more. Despite the decline of revenues to Baptist causes, Kentucky Baptists were leaned on to bear the "financial burden" of the Southern Baptist Convention in the postbellum years.[132]

Spencer's conclusive paragraph on the impact of the Civil War was both telling and eloquent:

> In 1865, the War closed, and the survivors of the two great armies returned to their homes. Alas! what multitudes were left sleeping in unknown graves in the far off sunny South. Many active and valuable church members were lost in the fearful conflict that desolated our homes, our hearts and our churches. Some that survived were sadly demoralized. A few preachers, who had gone into the army, had fallen before the temptations incident to camp life. There were apostacies at home, as well as in the armies. Many were the breaches that needed to be repaired, before the armies of the Lord could be ready to march against the enemies of the Cross of Christ. But, as in the olden time, when the broken down walls of Jerusalem were to be rebuilt, "the people had a mind to work," so now, when wounds and dissensions in the churches needed to be healed, God afforded his people grace to perform the duty.[133]

Spencer likened the work facing Kentucky Baptists after the war to that of "God's ancient people on their return from Babylonian captivity. It was a time for rebuilding from ruins and repairing breaches. Not able debates nor sage counsel in conventions but earnest labor among the churches, was the need of the hour."[134]

One "breach" proved particularly difficult to repair. Before the Civil War, African American Baptists in Kentucky generally worshiped in white churches. Birdwhistell suggested that from "the earliest days of Kentucky Baptist history, slaves worshiped along with their masters in the frontier churches, often while seated in a separate balcony, or gallery."[135] Certainly, the religious expression of black Baptists was "carefully monitored" within paternalistic white Baptist churches in Kentucky as in the rest of the South.[136] Separate black congregations existed, however, in the antebellum years. In *Redeeming the South: Religious Cultures and Racial Identities Among Southern Baptists, 1865-1925*, Paul Harvey concluded that "over 150 separate black churches were formed" in the antebellum South.[137]

In Kentucky, only a few separate black Baptist churches were constituted before the war. Spencer reported 17 separate churches in 1865 with a total membership of 5,737.[138] Peter Duerett gathered the first and largest black congregation in the state at Lexington as early as 1801, and in Louisville a freedman, Henry Adams, pastored another large church. Adams was especially "active and zealous in his labors."[139] Spencer described how he "devoted himself to study, and not only improved rapidly in preaching, but also advanced in literary knowledge till he became a good English scholar and made considerable proficiency in some of the dead languages." Spencer concluded that Adams's "conduct was so uniformly exemplary, and his Christian meekness and humility so manifest, that he gained the respect and confidence of the white as well as the colored people of the city."[140]

In Paducah, the remarkable George W. Dupee in 1858 became the second pastor of the "Second Baptist Church, Colored," later renamed Washington Street Baptist Church.[141] Although Dupee had been licensed and ordained to preach while a slave, he purchased his freedom in 1856 at Georgetown and moved to western Kentucky two years later. Dupee pastored as many as fourteen churches simultaneously. In Paducah, he became the first African American pastor of the first separate black congregation in western Kentucky. When "Second Baptist, Colored" withdrew from Paducah's First Baptist Church in 1855, the separation occurred with the blessings of the white congregation. Concerned with the growing numbers of black members, white members granted blacks letters of dismissal, and the black church was established. George Brent, a white minister, served as the new church's first pastor, but was soon forced to leave Paducah "for his close association and friendship with the black church members."[142]

With Brent's forced departure, Dupee became pastor, beginning years of active service in western Kentucky. After the war, for example, Dupee was instrumental in the separation of Fairview Baptist Church from Mayfield's

First Baptist Church in 1872.[143] Separations continued in the postbellum years throughout Kentucky and the South. Harvey concluded that "the separate religious life that enslaved blacks developed before the Civil War, even while worshiping in white churches, took an institutional form after 1865, as African American believers withdrew from white congregations."[144]

In Kentucky, "congregational separation of black and white Baptists was virtually complete" by 1870.[145] On August 3, 1869, the General Association of Colored Baptists in Kentucky was organized in Lexington.[146] Comprising fifty-six churches and a membership of 12,620 at the time of its founding, the new organization elected Henry Adams as the first moderator. In 1871, Dupee was elected moderator, a position that he would hold "eleven times in succession."[147]

With the end of the Civil War came the demise of the "peculiar institution" of slavery. For Baptists in Kentucky, black and white, the war also signalled the end of the paternalistic congregational organization characteristic of Kentucky's Baptist churches before the war. After the war the separation of Baptist churches in the state exemplified the segregation evident in most areas of society in the commonwealth during the era of Jim Crow.

Ironically, it was in the divisive war's aftermath that years of strife were replaced with a renewed vision for unity within the separate spheres of black and white associations. For white Kentucky Baptists, the unity came primarily through the General Association of Baptists in Kentucky, the organization founded during the growing sectional crisis of the antebellum years. The association specifically stated its goals in 1869: "(1) to encourage closer relations between the general association and district associations; (2) to secure co-operation between churches and the general association; (3) to use experienced men as evangelists throughout the state; (4) to support the feeble churches; and (5) to establish Baptist work in neglected areas, especially in the 22 counties in the mountainous area of eastern Kentucky."[148]

Although "fewer than one third of over 1,000 churches contributed to the general association's work" as late as 1881, there was enough support to foster a remarkable array of initiatives in the years immediately after the Civil War. In 1869, for example, the Louisville Baptist Orphans' Home was founded. Educational institutions began operations around the state. In addition to Georgetown College, Georgetown Female Seminary (1845), Bethel College in Russellville (1856), and Bethel Female College in Hopkinsville (1858) were founded before the war. After the disruption of the war, the drive to establish Baptist schools by various combinations of Baptist associations continued. Lynnland Institute in Glendale (1866), Clinton

College (1874), Williamsburg Institute (1889), Oneida Baptist Institute (1899), Magoffin Baptist Institute in Salyersville (1905), and Russell Creek Academy (1906) in Campbellsville were all founded in the postwar years.[149] One scholar listed at least seventy-five Baptist schools founded in Kentucky in the years after the war.[150]

The impact of these Baptist schools and colleges on Kentucky and Kentuckians is incalculable. The institutions, of course, filled the academic void of the years before the advent of a strong public school system, but Baptist institutions met other needs as well. Amanda Hicks, a teacher at Clinton College in western Kentucky, for example, urged one student to invite his brother to a special lecture on April 10, 1893: "I am very anxious that Eugene should hear the lecture tonight. The subject is 'God's Message to the World.' It may do Eugene a great deal of good to hear it. He told me he would stay at home and that you were coming. If you can so arrange that he can come I shall be much pleased even if *you* have to stay at home. I say this because I am so much concerned about his soul."[151] Such concern for students

Bethel College, Russellville, founded in 1856 and merged with Georgetown in 1933

continued to be a hall-mark of Baptist institutions in the twentieth century.

The educational institution that exerted the largest impact on Kentucky Baptists and on the Southern Baptist Convention was not founded in Kentucky at all. Organized in 1859 in Greenville, South Carolina, the Southern Baptist Theological Seminary suspended operations during the war "and then struggled through the next two decades to develop an educational program and establish an endowment."[152] By the end of Reconstruction in 1876-77, the seminary enrolled only sixty-five students.

James P. Boyce, Southern Seminary president who moved the seminary to Louisville in 1877

Faced with dire economic prospects, the seminary moved from South Carolina to Louisville in 1877, choosing the Kentucky city over Atlanta, Chattanooga, Nashville, and Russellville in Kentucky.[153]

Under the leadership of James Petigru Boyce, the chairman of the faculty, the relocation of the institution, founded in the heart of the Old South, to Louisville, a thriving New South city, proved wise. In fact, Louisville provided an ideal base for a southern institution in need of northern capital to survive. In Louisville, rented facilities were relied on until 1888, when New York Hall—built with donations from wealthy New York donors—was built on recently purchased property on the corner of Fifth and Broadway.[154] With the move to permanent facilities, the enrollment climbed to 150.

In 1888, Boyce—only recently named by the trustees as president—died and was succeeded by John Albert Broadus, the chair of homiletics and New Testament interpretation since the institution's founding. Under Broadus, the seminary continued to make modest gains in enrollment and in the construction of facilities; Memorial Library and Norton Hall were added to the downtown campus. The seminary conferred its first Ph.D. degree in 1894. With Broadus's death in 1895, William H. Whitsitt became president, only to be succeeded by Edgar Young Mullins in 1899 following Whitsitt's brief and tumultuous tenure. During Mullins's twenty-nine-year presidency, the seminary grew in endowment and acquired a formidable reputation within the Southern Baptist Convention and outside Baptist circles as well.

Also during Mullins's tenure, educational and mission opportunities for Baptist women—already

John A. Broadus, Southern Seminary professor of New Testament and homiletics, then president, 1888-1895

well versed in Baptist church affairs from the Civil War experience—were established and nurtured. In addition to providing, in 1904, living quarters for women studying at the seminary, Mullins supported the founding of the Woman's Missionary Training School three years later.[155]

In 1840, messengers at the annual meeting of the General Association of Baptists in Kentucky in Elizabethtown issued a challenge for local churches to organize "Female Auxiliary Societies." A resolution noted that "experience has proven that in works of benevolence, the female's hand knows no miser's grip, but moves in obedience to the generous impulses of the female's heart."[156] Again, in 1857, messengers passed a resolution—this time, proposed by John Bryce, an influential pastor from Henderson—to encourage churches to form women's societies "in their respective fields of labor."[157]

The Southern Baptist Convention followed Kentucky's lead in 1876 when messengers accepted a report urging the organization of women's societies in every church. Then, in 1878, the Foreign Mission Board of the Southern Baptist Convention appointed a Central Committee for women's missionary work in Kentucky and other states.[158] Kentucky's committee included Leora B. Robinson, Lou Delph, Agnes Osborne, Emma Kruck, Susan Lucas, and Eliza S. Broadus, the daughter of Southern Seminary president John A. Broadus.[159] The committee went to work immediately. By 1880, nineteen local women's societies had been organized at the urging of the Central Committee; by 1882, forty-five had been formed.

Money collected in the local societies went directly to the Foreign Mission Board. Clearly, missions support led by Kentucky women had a substantial impact on the work of the Southern Baptist Convention as a whole. Soon, other boards and agencies—Indian Missions, the Home Mission Board, Kentucky's State Board or Executive Board—asked for and received needed funds solicited by Baptist women in Kentucky.[160] In her *Golden Remembrances of Woman's Missionary Union of Kentucky*, Ada Boone Brown wrote in 1953 that these pioneers in Kentucky Baptist women's work were "women of vision because they believed in their hearts and they wanted to share their belief with others. They saw the great possibilities in

*Southern Seminary, Old Testament class 1922-23
with Training School women*

unenlisted women and young people."[161] Another active participant described the fledgling work with a degree of sarcasm and irony: "Timidly, with doubting, hesitating steps, looking here and there for dangers seen and unseen, these organizations soon to be so great, stepped out into independent existence. Who were they that they should be willing to undertake such work as this—How dared they, with so little knowledge of finance, so unskilled in self government, so used to only whispering their advice, come boldly to the front as leaders of other women?"[162]

Women's efforts in Kentucky predated the organization of the Woman's Missionary Union, Auxiliary to the Southern Baptist Convention, in 1888. It was appropriate that when the convention organization was formed, a Kentuckian, Eliza Broadus, the chair of the state's Central Committee, was nominated to serve as a member of the Executive Committee.[163] When a similar Kentucky organization—the Kentucky Baptist Woman's Missionary Union, Auxiliary to the General Association of Baptists in Kentucky—was organized on June 16, 1903, in the First Baptist Church of Winchester, Broadus and other Kentucky women had been active in missions work for years.[164]

Within the state, missions efforts concentrated on the founding of new churches, especially in eastern Kentucky. "To establish Baptist work in neglected areas, especially in the 22 counties in the mountainous area of eastern Kentucky," was included as one of five specific goals in a report presented at the annual meeting of the General Association in 1869.[165] Churches were founded in Ashland (1882), Catlettsburg (1882), Williamsburg (1882), Pineville (1885), Harlan (1885), and Hyden (1885).[166] A. S. Petrey founded twelve churches himself and earned the title "the Prophet of Little Cane Creek." Still, by 1899, sixteen county-seat towns in eastern Kentucky remained without "missionary" Baptist churches.[167]

Despite the efforts of Petrey and others, Baptist growth in eastern Kentucky lagged behind the rest of the state. From 1830 to 1910, "the number of Baptist churches in Kentucky tripled, from 574 to 1,774, and the church membership increased fivefold, from 39,957 to 224,237."[168] Although Kentucky Baptists grew steadily in churches and membership, the growth of the Southern Baptist Convention was even more dramatic. From its founding in 1845 to 1910, the number of churches in the convention grew from 4,126 to 23,248, and membership increased from 351,951 to 2,332,464, both sixfold increases.[169]

Such remarkable growth in the Southern Baptist Convention and in Kentucky augured well for the future. Baptist leaders in Kentucky looked expectantly and confidently to years of further growth and "kingdom building" in the commonwealth. A brief period of uncertainty and anxiety brought on by World War I gave way after the war to renewed expectations of peace and economic prosperity for all Americans. For Southern Baptists, expectations of continued growth were not diminished by the war. Although the "war to make the world safe for democracy," "the war to end all wars" failed to accomplish such lofty ends, the world was changed irrevocably nonetheless. America was changed. Shell-shocked veterans—numbed by months in the trenches—now returned home to farms and towns and cities forever changed.

At the same time, evangelical Christians seemed energized by the war. At first unaware of the enormous repercussions of the conflict, southern Christians certainly found inspiration in the Great Crusade. For Baptists, this inspiration translated into renewed optimism and a determination to carry on with the work already begun.

Such fervor for the Baptist work in Kentucky was not a sudden phenomenon. The work of such far-sighted individuals as E. Y. Mullins, Eliza S. Broadus, A. S. Petrey, H. Boyce Taylor, and George E. Hays provided a solid foundation on which to build the commonwealth's Baptist work in the future. As the sesquicentennial of the Baptist presence in Kentucky—1776 to 1926—approached, it would seem that these five individuals represented the culmination of 150 years of Baptist work in Kentucky. Instead, they represented a foundation on which to build. The great years of achievement, years marked by a growing sense of cooperation—often in the midst of want and despair—were still to come.

2
chapter

Cooperation

On a summer Sunday, July 28, 1985, William W. Marshall, the executive secretary-treasurer of the Kentucky Baptist Convention, and officers and members of the Kentucky Baptist Historical Commission and Historical Society converged on the small but thriving university town of Murray in southwestern Kentucky. The small group of convention leaders drove west to take part in an important celebration, a celebration of remembrance. The convention had appointed a committee in 1979, and then voted in November 1981 "to place an appropriate marker" on the grounds of Murray's First Baptist Church "indicating Kentucky's part and the part of First Baptist Church in the beginning of the Cooperative Program."[1]

Marshall delivered the sermon during the morning worship hour, emphasizing "the Cooperative Program as a world-wide mission endeavor for all Southern Baptists." The unveiling of the historical marker, a handsome bronze marker provided by the Kentucky Historical Society, followed the morning service. Murray's pastor, Greg Earwood, Wendell H. Rone, the chairman of the Kentucky Baptist Historical Commission, Michael Duncan, the president of the Kentucky Baptist Historical Society, and H. C. Chiles, the beloved former pastor of the church, participated in the ceremony. The presence of Barry G. Allen, the treasurer of the Historical Commission and the director of the Business Division of the Executive Board of the Convention, Doris Yeiser, the secretary of both

Cooperative Program marker, Murray

the Historical Commission and the Historical Society, and other leaders from Middletown and around the state bespoke the day's significance for the convention and for Kentucky Baptists. Indeed, the observance was significant for all Southern Baptists.

The founding of the Southern Baptist Convention in 1845 preceded the founding of the Baptist church in Murray by one year. But it was the leadership of Murray's charismatic and controversial pastor, H. Boyce Taylor, that placed the western Kentucky church in the fulcrum of convention affairs. Taylor came to the church as pastor in 1897—"at a salary of $400.00 per year," as he revealed later—and served for thirty-four years in a remarkable, often tumultuous tenure that resulted in dramatic growth for the church and in dramatic changes in the cooperative work of Kentucky Baptists and eventually the Southern Baptist Convention.

On this day, in 1985, the unveiled historical marker revealed the significant highlights of Taylor's and the church's contribution to Southern Baptist work. The marker reads:

The Cooperative Program
Under leadership of H. Boyce Taylor, First Baptist Church, Murray, began in 1900 a new approach to church finance. Taylor, pastor 1897-1931, avidly promoted this unified budget plan; appointed chairman of State Baptist committee, 1913, "to consider . . . unifying our work" under one budget. During 1914-15 Taylor and layman F. D. Perkins toured state promoting unified plan.
The Gen. Assoc. of Baptists in Ky. (now Ky. Bapt. Conv.) adopted first "budget plan for the collection of funds" in 1915. Taylor served as chairman of first budget committee. This was Kentucky's part in the development of world mission budget plan adopted by Southern Baptist Convention in Memphis, 1925, known as the Cooperative Program.[2]

The story of Murray's contribution to the concept of cooperation began soon after Taylor's arrival at the church when the congregation adopted a unified budget scheme of church finance in 1900. Under Taylor's leadership, the church grew in numbers and influence. The growth and development of Murray's church illustrated the rise in membership in churches throughout Kentucky and the Southern Baptist Convention in the early years of the twentieth century. And as church membership grew, funds for new missions efforts increased as well. Although Kentucky's growth in numbers was not so dramatic as in the SBC as a whole, Kentucky took the lead in the development of a workable, cooperative system of finance, a system that would eventually have a far-reaching impact on Baptist work around the world.

In the 1913 annual meeting of the General Association, moderator J. W. Porter of Lexington appointed a "Committee of Five" to consider the question of unifying the work of the state body. Because of the success of his budget plan in Murray, H. Boyce Taylor was appointed to the committee, along with J. A. Booth, W. W. Landrum, A. F. Gordon, and O. O. Green.

In the past, of course, funding for denominational initiatives had been haphazard. In fact, weekly offerings in local churches were unusual in the nineteenth century. Before the 1880s, churches "supported local needs by an annual or periodic collections."[3] Other causes were supported by "special collections" solicited by agents sent out by the General Association or by other agencies or institutions.

When Taylor presented the report of the "Committee of Five" at the 1914 meeting in Somerset, he assured the messengers that "we have given earnest, careful and prayerful attention to the task assigned us."[4] Taylor had preached the annual sermon the year before, choosing as his topic "Kingdom Building."[5] He returned to that theme in the 1914 report: "Your committee is not unmindful of the splendid advance made by Kentucky Baptists in their missionary and benevolent contributions during the last few years. This advance, however, is not in keeping with their growth and financial strength and the growing needs of our denominational work."[6] Clearly, Taylor and the committee felt that "the building of the Kingdom" in Kentucky could best proceed through other, more innovative financial organization. The committee recommended "the unification of all departments of our work, so as to give every object, fostered by Kentucky Baptists, the support to which it is justly entitled."[7]

Upon hearing the report, messengers voted to refer the recommendations to a new "Committee of Nine." The new committee was chaired again by Taylor and instructed "to consider the whole question, give publicity to their deliberations during the year, and report" at the 1915 meeting. As chair, Taylor took seriously his instructions to "give publicity" to the plan. With layman F. D. Perkins in tow, Taylor toured the state, promoting the "unification plan" and the "unified church offering approach."[8]

Taylor's promotional work proved effective. At the 1915 annual meeting at the Baptist church at Jellico, Tennessee—at that time affiliated with Kentucky's General Association—a nine-point proposal for unification was submitted and accepted "by rising vote" of the messengers.[9] The enthusiastic acceptance of the "co-operating" budget plan preceded a similar plan for "a Co-operative Program," adopted by the Southern Baptist Convention a decade later. In fact, it could be argued that the idea for cooperation was born in Kentucky with the 1900 budget plan at Murray's Baptist church and with the plans leading up to the 1915 annual meeting of the General Association. The words "co-operate," "co-operation," and "co-operating"—rather than the more onerous "unification"—laced the 1915 report's recommendations.[10]

In 1916, another strong supporter of cooperation, O. E. Bryan, became corresponding secretary of the General Association. Serving in that capacity through 1921, Bryan implemented the budget plan of Taylor's committee. Bryan's work, coupled with his later connection with the Seventy-five Million Campaign and his cooperative work as corresponding secretary of the Tennessee Baptist Convention (1924-33), caused Tennessee Baptists to dub him "the father of the Cooperative Program." Certainly, because of the early work of Taylor, and the support of Taylor's ideas by Bryan, the concept of cooperation had found a home among Kentucky Baptists.

The resolve of Kentucky Baptists, along with the rest of the nation, was soon tested by America's involvement in World War I. Baptists in Kentucky generally supported Woodrow Wilson and the war effort. The war proved to be a turning point, however, for H. Boyce Taylor, the influential pastor of Murray Baptist Church and the architect of the newly minted cooperative budget plan. Elected as moderator of the General Association in 1917 following his high-profile role as chair of the "Committee of Nine," Taylor "was conspicuously absent from the presiding officer's chair" when messengers "overwhelmingly passed a strong resolution supporting the war" at the annual meeting.[11]

Taylor had been distressed when a resolution stating that "Jesus' teaching in the Sermon on the Mount should govern a Christian's behavior during wartime" was voted down by messengers at the 1917 meeting of the Southern Baptist Convention.[12] In Murray, Taylor's antiwar views eventually led to a public inquiry held by a committee of the Kentucky Council of Defense. Following his acquittal, Taylor resumed his leadership role in General Association affairs for a time, but a pattern of controversy prevented him from regaining the statewide influence that he had enjoyed before the war. He remained a powerful figure in western Kentucky. Even after his death in 1932, his legacy cast a long shadow over Baptist life in the Jackson Purchase.

For the vast majority of Americans, the Great War "provoked intense feelings," but feelings decidedly different from those displayed by H. Boyce Taylor. For intellectuals within the Southern Baptist Convention, "Germany had presented a philosophical challenge that had to be met." For many Baptist thinkers, the "godless ravings" of Friedrich Nietzsche symbolized "Germany's alleged combination of atheism and militarism." For A. T. Robertson,

the formidable Greek scholar and theologian at the Southern Baptist Theological Seminary, Germany presented the choice between "kaiser or Christ,
Napoleon or Jesus, Corsica or Galilee." Robertson believed that Germany, by
"exalting brute force" and scorning "Christian love, kindness, and compassion," left Christians "with no choice but to fight for their faith."[13]

Whatever the degree that individual Baptists supported the involvement
of the United States in the war, it was evident that the war had brought
change and that the end of the war was also the beginning of a "new era."
At war's end, A. T. Robertson wrote in his book, *The New Citizenship: The
Christian Facing a New World Order*, that "the old world passed away when
Belgium took her stand in front of the Kaiser's hosts. Modern history began on that date."[14]

The war's end certainly marked a "new era" in the cooperative efforts
of Kentucky Baptists. Cooperative organization already initiated before
the war developed after the war into the Southern Baptist Convention-
wide Seventy-five Million Campaign. A five-year program, lasting from
1919 to 1924, the campaign mirrored Kentucky's cooperative efforts and
was designed to increase "support for all Baptist missionary, educational,
and benevolent work."[15] One scholar suggested that "perhaps no single
innovation since the inception of the WMU would so fundamentally
strengthen the State Convention as the inauguration of the 75 Million
Campaign in 1919."[16]

While the campaign "arguably . . . stands as one of the most ambitious
denominational efforts in the history of American Protestantism," and
awakened other state conventions "to a greater, dramatic sense of the potential of cooperative action," such cooperation was not new to Kentucky
Baptists.[17] And Kentucky Baptists took leading roles in the new campaign.
In 1915, in fact, Hardy Lathan Winburn II, pastor of Walnut Street Baptist
Church, "helped set the stage for the Southern Convention's massive
stewardship campaign of 1919" with the publication of his book, *A Man
and His Money*. In the book, Winburn "mounted a formal, theologically
powerful demand for sacrificial giving to God's work."[18] Published by the
Baptist Book Concern, the book was endorsed by the convention; the
book's foreword was written by W. O. Carver of Southern Seminary,
"among the Southern Convention's most admired Bible scholars and mission advocates."[19]

The campaign surely "struck a chord in Baptist life because the nation
was just emerging victorious from the First World War." With its "resonat-
ing call to worldwide missions, to heroic, sacrificial service," the campaign
captured the imagination of the convention, building on the victorious
mood of the nation. Convention leaders even borrowed from President

Woodrow Wilson's plan for peace, offering a "Fourteen Point Plan"—a plan that outlined the goals of the campaign—to the churches.[20]

A "sense of destiny and awareness of limitless opportunity" was characteristic of Southern Baptists in the postwar period. An optimism pervaded Baptist life in Kentucky, an optimism evident in the writings of Baptist thinkers and writers like A. T. Robertson and H. L. Winburn, but also evident in the "least-educated Baptist layman." James J. Thompson, Jr., asserted in his book *Tried as by Fire: Southern Baptists and the Religious Controversies of the 1920s* that Baptists were united after the war in a common quest. Beneath social and intellectual differences, Thompson wrote, "lay a similarity too obvious to be denied. Whether illiterate laborer or seminary professor, all Southern Baptists held certain beliefs in common. They read the same Bible and went to churches that preached essentially the same message." "Equally important," Thompson continued, "they were Southerners, bound together by time and place into a distinct group that defied the pull of national conformity."[21] Baptists within the General Association of Kentucky shared the optimistic vision of other Southerners.

Kentucky was represented well as the campaign was launched. George E. Hays, the prominent layman from Walnut Street Baptist Church in Louisville, chaired the fifteen-member commission charged with laying plans for the effort. H. Boyce Taylor, despite his unpopular pacifist stance on the war, was asked to chair the committee responsible for determining Kentucky's quota. Taylor's committee then made a recommendation to the larger commission. Based on the recommendation, the commission, meeting in Atlanta in June 1918, assigned Kentucky the fourth largest quota—behind only Texas, Georgia, and Virginia—of $6.5 million for the five-year campaign effort. In a history of the First Baptist Church of Murray, Ira V. Birdwhistell wrote that "in spite of his prior opposition to the war effort and his tension with the General Association of Baptists in Kentucky, H. Boyce Taylor's heart for missions was fired by the goals of the Seventy-five Million Campaign."[22] The response of the Murray church indicated the enthusiasm for the plan around the state. In October 1919, the church voted to set a goal of forty thousand dollars as its part in the campaign. In addition, the congregation "also elected to raise three thousand dollars for ministerial education, one thousand dollars for children's homes, and one thousand dollars for a Baptist hospital, a huge sum of money in those days."[23]

When Kentucky Baptists gathered in Georgetown in November 1919 for the annual meeting, messengers not only accepted the statewide quota but pledged "our time, our talents, our means, and the loyal devotion of our hearts for the glory of the blessed Redeemer."[24] Taylor's committee divided the state's quota almost equally between Kentucky and Southern Baptist Convention causes (50.25 percent or $3,265,006 for the General Association of Baptists in Kentucky, and 49.75 percent or $3,233,765 for the Southern Baptist Convention). Specific dollar amounts were allocated for specific causes:

Foreign Missions	$1,925,098
Home Missions	1,040,000
State Missions	900,000
Children's Home	350,000
Ministerial Relief	266,000
Kentucky Baptist Hospital	250,000
Education	1,500,000
Georgetown	700,000
Cumberland	400,000
Bethel	200,000
Bethel Woman's	100,000
Russell Creek Academy	100,000
Seminaries	268,667[25]

The determination of Baptists in Kentucky to meet the quota was evident; when all the pledges were counted, Kentucky Baptists had exceeded the $6.5 million quota, pledging instead, remarkably, $7,454,000.[26]

Unfortunately, the enthusiastic response to the campaign in Kentucky was shattered and replaced by bitter disappointment by the campaign's end. The early excitement and determination to meet and exceed pledge goals were evident in the first year's pledge returns—for 1920—when Kentucky Baptists exceeded the collection goal of $1.3 million by $55,366.51. Frank Masters concluded that the collection's report "showed that Kentucky had led the South in collecting the full year's quota for the Seventy-five Million Campaign and more." Corresponding Secretary O. E. Bryan declared that the year had "been marked by unprecedented blessing in money raised for kingdom interests, in the salvation of souls and in additions to the churches. Our land has been blessed with a marvelous harvest. Temporal and spiritual blessings have been showered in abundance upon our state."[27]

Within a year, however, the expectant optimism illustrated in the 1920 report was replaced with gloomy despair. The 1921 report of the Executive Board of the General Association stated that "we are now in the midst of the most trying part of the Seventy-five Million Campaign." The collections for 1921 amounted to only $1,055,099.36, fully $175,000 short of the year's quota. The reporter lamented that "not in thirty-five years has the country faced such financial conditions."[28]

Collections in the following years were substantial, but nonetheless inadequate, in meeting the overly optimistic pledge goals at the outset of the campaign. In all, Kentucky Baptists raised $6,225,449.14 during the five-year period of the Seventy-five Million Campaign, a remarkable amount but a total falling short by over $274,500 of the initial $6.5 million quota. The total failed by $1,228,893.86 to reach the optimistic $7,454,387 goal of the pledge campaign of 1919-20. The 1924 report of the Executive Board stated bluntly that "if these unpaid pledges, made five years ago, are paid, then missions, education, and benevolent causes will be sustained; but failure to meet the payment of the pledge will mean financial disaster."[29]

That the situation was still dire was evident when the Executive Board reported the following year—in 1925—at the annual meeting at Broadway Baptist Church in Louisville. The report recalled the history of the campaign and the courage of Kentucky Baptists in the face of unprecedented challenges:

> The last General Association year was no doubt the most trying and spirit-racking in the history of that body. The first two months of that year witnessed the close of the 75 Million Campaign, the most daring adventure ever made by Southern Baptists in their co-operative work. That campaign was launched with great enthusiasm and deep spiritual purpose. The World War had trained the people to respond to large mass movements and to think in staggering terms. Prosperity abounded, and even the humblest was not lacking in financial resources. The most complete and far-reaching organization ever perfected by Southern Baptists was brought into being. That organization reached far back into the hills and made the weakest and poorest church an active participant in the great plan. There was created a varied, attractive and helpful literature, which was distributed with great prodigality. . . . For a brief period all went well, then the financial storm broke in its fury and left wreck and ruin in its track. Of course pledges were not paid—there was nothing with which to pay. Our people were hit hard by the storm. Many churches and individuals were humiliated and chagrined because of unpaid pledges. Mission boards and other institutions were alarmed and dismayed at the shrinkage of their resources. Suspicion walked abroad in the land, and the voice of recrimination

was heard. But in it all through it all Kentucky Baptists kept the faith. Every dollar was promptly remitted to the object for which it was intended by the donor, no matter how great a hardship it worked on the other interests.[30]

Despite the concern caused by what the report referred to as the "abnormal conditions which prevailed during and immediately following the great World War," conditions that "affected all civic, economic, social, educational and religious relationships," the report found cause for encouragement as well. Compared with the total receipts of the General Association during the war—$351,769.61 from November 1, 1918, to October 31, 1919—by the end of the fund-raising campaign, the receipts had increased substantially—$514,300.01 from November 1, 1924, to October 31, 1925—a gain of $162,530.40 or 56 percent in receipts.[31]

Still, the fact remained that all of the pledges were not collected. Kentucky was not, of course, the only state to fail to meet campaign obligations. Across the South, Baptists were able to collect only $58,064,365, fully $16,935,635 short of the $75 million goal. The shortfall proved especially hurtful to Southern Baptist educational institutions, many of which "had expended large sums of money on new buildings, repairs, increased current expenses, new equipment and endowment, based on the prospects of receiving the full amount allocated to Christian education at the beginning of the Campaign."[32]

While some feared the creeping modernism threatening Southern Baptist schools and colleges, the failure of the Seventy-five Million Campaign threatened the very existence of the institutions. The failure of the denomination to collect unpaid pledges hit Kentucky Baptist educational institutions especially hard. Out of the $1.5 million allotted to Georgetown, Cumberland, Bethel, Bethel Woman's, and Campbellsville Colleges, only $1,084,149.09 was actually collected, a deficit of $415,850, a substantial sum in the 1920s.[33]

The dire financial straits of Southern Baptists were of profound concern to E. Y. Mullins and the trustees of Southern Baptist Theological Seminary. In the midst of planning a move of the seminary from its downtown campus to "the Beeches," a suburban tract of tree-shaded acres on Lexington Road, the financial distress was not comforting. Mullins had outlined his "Reasons for Removal" to Southern's Board of Trustees in a 1924 report. In the report, Mullins emphasized the "antiquated facilities built of 'cheap material' as a major factor in the decision to move" from the downtown location. With windows open in warm weather, the "noise from the streets" was not conducive to scholarly pursuits, and in the winter the heating plant proved increasingly unreliable.[34] The seminary's report at the 1925 annual meeting revealed that the institution "was now in the midst of the greatest financial struggle in its history and must have in the near future the sum of $2,000,000 at least for the new buildings."[35] The $2 million estimation soon escalated to $3.5 million "because of World War I inflation."[36]

The seminary had already held groundbreaking ceremonies for Norton Hall, the centerpiece of the new campus—housing a library, chapel, classrooms, and offices—in December 1923. Determined to push ahead with the move in spite of dire economic prospects, Mullins "plunged Southern Seminary into debt, borrowing large sums from a Louisville mortgage company." The president's determination was marked by his attention to detail. For example, he worked closely with the architects, James Gamble Rogers of New York, and the landscape architectural firm, Olmstead Brothers of Brookline, Massachusetts. He insisted that protective fences be built around the beloved beech trees near the construction site for fear that unknowing workers "would injure the distinctive forested atmosphere of the property."[37]

Although Mullins's biographer referred to the president's determination to move the campus to "the Beeches" as an "obsession" and asserted that the move and the new construction "nearly brought financial ruin to the Seminary," the move to the Lexington Road site was nonetheless finished in March 1926 with "only Norton Hall, Mullins Hall (the new men's dormitory), and the heating plant completed."[38] Frank Masters concluded, more positively, that "after long and patient waiting, Dr. E. Y. Mullins . . . and faculty have now realized their inspiring dreams in being located in the new Seminary home at The Beeches." The new site "on a suburban campus of fifty-three acres, adorned with century-old beech trees, and overlooking Cherokee Park" provided just the scholarly ambience and suburban calm that Mullins desired.[39]

Considering all of the concern over the financial situation of the General Association of Baptists in Kentucky, it is ironic that advertisements for Russell H. Conwell's *Acres of Diamonds* graced the pages of the *Western Recorder* in the 1920s.[40] "The story of a $4,000,000 lecture and the wonderful man who gave it to the world," the book was written by a Baptist businessman in Philadelphia who preached that "money is power, and you ought to be reasonably ambitious to have it. . . . I say, then, you ought to have money."[41]

Victor I. Masters of the Home Mission Board warned against "dollar-lust," an evil that "threatened to subvert spiritual values that had been developed over long periods of adversity," and asserted that the South must "somehow tame its advancing affluence and show that this new prosperity could exist harmoniously with spirituality." Still, Conwell's appeal was enticing, especially since many Kentuckians were unfamiliar with the benefits of a "new prosperity."[42] Conwell assured his readers that, "If you can honestly attain unto riches in Philadelphia, it is your Christian and godly duty to do so. It is an awful mistake of these pious people to think you must be awfully poor in order to be pious."[43] Conwell's Baptist Temple in Philadelphia included a night school for working people that eventually grew into Temple University.

In Kentucky, however, Baptist schools and other Baptist causes remained vulnerable to the economy's unpredictability. While the 1920s represented economic "boom years" for many businessmen in northern cities, the increased agricultural production necessary during the war turned into agricultural overproduction after the war, overproduction that devastated southern rural economies long before the more general economic tragedy of the 1930s. For many Kentuckians, the economic prosperity of the "Roaring Twenties" was not a part of their real world experience and was instead something that they read about in newspapers or—if affordable—heard about on parlor radios.

Of course, economic decline had a disturbing impact on Kentucky's churches. And for Southern Baptists, the impact on the fund-raising campaign begun amid the optimism of the Allied victory over the Central Powers was certainly disheartening. Historian Frank Masters asserted that the "one absorbing question of Southern Baptists during this period was, what can be done about the staggering indebtedness on Southwide institutions and Boards, on the various State agencies, and on the local churches."[44]

In this atmosphere of despair, the Southern Baptist Convention decided to follow the lead of Kentucky Baptists, seeking a renewed sense of cooperation to fight the common foe of indebtedness. The precedent for a cooperative vision had been set with the Unified Budget idea of Kentucky Baptists and with the Seventy-five Million Campaign. Despite the campaign's failure to meet pledge goals, beneficial results carried over in the new cooperative venture. In *The Southern Baptist Convention, 1845-1953* (1954), W. W. Barnes discussed two beneficial results of the campaign: "The five-months' period of preparation, from July to November [1919], the subsequent whirlwind campaign for subscriptions, and the continued emphases throughout the five years [helped to enlist] church members and made them stewardship-conscious as they had never been before." Second, the campaign resulted in "the adoption of more system in raising and disbursing the finances of the Convention." Across the Southern Baptist Convention, church membership increased

40 percent between 1915 and 1929, and per-capita contributions increased 12 percent.[45]

Given the historic Baptist emphasis on the priesthood of the believer and the autonomy of the local church, the idea for financial cooperation among thousands of individual Baptists and local congregations appears perhaps as an aberration. Rather than an aberration, however, Baptist cooperation and centralization mirrored national trends toward organization. Cooperative Baptist work represented a Christian evangelical equivalent to the modern, twentieth-century "search for order" and preference for organization. Certainly, organization and uniformity was a theme of the Age of Progressivism, and Baptists took an active part—indeed, played an active role—in progressive initiatives and programs.

Baptists took part in the temperance crusade, a growing women's movement, and other progressive initiatives. And as Paul Harvey concluded in *Redeeming the South,* "the growth of commercial enterprise, the progressives understood, was essential to the rebuilding of the region and the support of denominational endeavors." According to one Southern Baptist minister, the corporation could serve as a model for the "organization and control of the total business life of the community in the service of the kingdom of God." Baptists could take "hold of the evangelization of the world as a business proposition," the minister asserted.[46] Indeed, the application of progressive principles to denominational work was crucial, according to many Baptist pastors and leaders. Yet, at the same time, such progressive sentiments clashed with long-held and cherished Baptist traditions of localism and congregationalism.

This antagonism between congregationalism and centralization continued to threaten cooperative Baptist efforts in the 1920s and beyond. Still, for many, the Cooperative Program plan represented the logical extension of the Seventy-five Million Campaign. Ironically, the recent, failed campaign, "saddling the denomination with staggering debt," also "laid the groundwork for the Cooperative Program, a system of financial collection and distribution" adopted by the Southern Baptist Convention in 1925.[47] The five-year program of the Seventy-five Million Campaign was replaced with the continuing annual plan of the Cooperative Program.

Before the Cooperative Program, the work of the convention was conducted through various agencies, each with its own financial setup and methods of raising and distributing funds. In 1924, a Commission of Future Campaigns was appointed to study the feasibility of an annual program, and the following year, a Committee on Business Efficiency initiated a study of the entire business organization of the convention. Chaired by Austin Crouch, the committee "made an exhaustive study of the entire Convention and its agencies in their several business methods" and concluded that "the constituency of this convention is becoming insistent that the work of the agencies of the convention shall be more closely correlated, and that the agencies themselves shall be brought into such relations with the convention as will guarantee in advance both efficiency of administration and the prevention of incurring any indebtedness, except for current expenses between the meetings of the convention." The committee recommended "that the Convention at this time commit itself to budget control" and "go on record as favoring a single agency to function along the lines presented in the report."[48]

Then—in the same year—the Commission of Future Campaigns recommended that upon the adoption of the commission's report at the convention's annual meeting "our co-operative work be known as the Cooperative Program of Southern Baptists."[49] The founding of the Southern Baptist Convention's Cooperative Program in 1925 inaugurated a new era of centralization and cooperation for Southern Baptists. This cooperative impulse was not new; the concept of cooperation dated back to the beginnings of the Baptist presence in America. But the commitment expressed in 1925 marked a new level of cooperation.

The Executive Committee of the convention administered the new program. In 1929, messengers at the annual convention meeting recommended "that all sums collected in the various states for Southwide objects shall be forwarded monthly by each state secretary to the Executive Committee which shall become the disbursing or distributing agent of the Convention." The program called for each state convention to set Cooperative Program goals for the next year's work and then to determine percentages dividing monies for state work and Southern Baptist Convention work. These percentage allotments differed from state to state— 50/50 in some states; 60/40 in others (60 percent for state work and 40 percent for convention causes). In states where Baptist work was just beginning, it was not unusual to divide the work on a 75/25 basis with the larger share going for state efforts.[50]

In Kentucky, the state Executive Board appointed a committee in June 1924 to recommend a plan to make the transition from the Seventy-five Million Campaign to an ongoing annual program. The committee met on July 8, 1924, at the Baptist Headquarters at 205 East Chestnut Street in Louisville. The committee's resulting report was both thorough and challenging:

> 1. That the financial objective for Kentucky Baptists for the Unified Budget for the year 1925 shall be $1,300,000, that being one-fifth of the quota of the Seventy-five Million Campaign.

2. That this amount shall be divided equally between State and Southwide interests. That is, fifty percent going to the Southwide interests and fifty percent going to State interests.

3. That the fifty percent going to Southwide interests shall be distributed on the percentage basis adopted by the Southern Baptist Convention as follows: State Missions, 23 1/2; Home Missions 10; Christian Education 10; Ministerial Relief and Annuities 5; and the New Orleans Hospital 1 1/2.

4. That the fifty percent allocated to State interests shall be divided as follows: State Missions 21; Education 17 1/2; Baptist Childrens' Homes 6 1/2; Hospital 4; and Church Building, 1.

5. That District Missions shall be included in State Missions, and be administered by the State Mission Board in co-operation with District Mission Boards.

6. That each church be asked to take as its financial objective in the New Program for 1925 at least one-fifth of its quota in the Seventy-five Million Campaign and if at all possible to go beyond that amount.

7. That, in putting on the New Program, the Campaign be so planned and executed as to place upon individual churches the burden and responsibility of putting on the program.

8. That the time for putting on the New Program for 1925 by the churches be from November 16, to December 14, and that as far as practicable the week of November 30th—December 7th, suggested by the Southern Baptist Convention, be the time for every Member Canvass and in any event that all pledges be made by December 31, 1924.

9. That while recognizing the right of every individual and church to make designations, it is earnestly recommended that all our people and churches do not make designations, but contribute to the unified budget as a whole.

10. That the Corresponding Secretary be instructed to have charge of, direct and put on the Campaign as heretofore suggested so as to get it before the District Association Boards and Churches.

11. That in carrying out the New Program the Corresponding Secretary be asked as far as possible to get the District Associations to make their objective for 1925 not less than one-fifth of their quota for the last five years.[51]

The committee's report was adopted—"after a prolonged discussion"—for 1925. This new Unified Budget would succeed the Seventy-five

Million Campaign. It is significant that this transition effort in Kentucky again preceded the effort of the Southern Baptist Convention. Kentucky made plans to support a Unified Budget in 1915, a decade before, and now a new unified plan to replace the Seventy-five Million Campaign was set fully a year before the Cooperative Program was adopted by the Southern Baptist Convention in 1925.[52]

In May 1926, the *Western Recorder* reported in an article titled "Southern Baptists in Epochal Convention," on the seventy-first session of the Southern Baptist Convention in Houston, Texas: "The Convention was in a large and unaffected way significant." The writer asserted that "messengers from every section and with remarkable unanimity expressed themselves as delighted, as feeling that we are able to face the future of our fellowship and co-operative work with optimism and hopefulness."[53] In Houston, the Cooperative Program measure passed the year before was hailed as a positive step forward in Baptist work.

Back in Kentucky, efforts to protect the integrity of the new Cooperative Program and the work of the Southern Baptist Convention generally were already underway. Early in May 1926, Seminary President Mullins—president of the SBC from 1921 to 1923, and in 1926 the president of the Baptist World Alliance—wrote an article in anticipation of the Houston meeting titled, "Safeguarding the Functions of the Southern Baptist Convention."[54] And at its annual meeting, the General Association adopted a resolution recommending that "no campaign, of any character, shall be put on by the interests participating in the Cooperative Program, namely, Foreign Missions, Home Missions, Southwide Education, Ministerial Relief, New Orleans Hospital, State Missions, Education in Kentucky, Orphanages in Kentucky, Kentucky Baptist Hospital and Church Building, as all such campaigns are unfair and hurtful to the other interests, which are not allowed to go afield."[55] Clearly the General Association of Baptists in Kentucky was determined to support the work of the Cooperative Program fully.

As with the Seventy-five Million Campaign, Kentucky Baptists received the new Cooperative Program enthusiastically. In fact, the optimism of the Executive Board's report in 1926 presented a stark contrast to the gloom and despair of the previous year. In 1925, the board asserted that the "last General Association year was no doubt the most trying and spirit-racking in the history of that body." In 1926, however—in the first year of the Cooperative Program—the board's tone changed considerably. "For more than a quarter of a century," the 1926 Executive Board writer began, "there has not been such harmony and unity as now prevails in the ranks of Kentucky Baptists." The reporter stated that "the reaction from the 75-Million

Campaign is passed, and our Baptist people are manifesting a real disposition to go forward."[56]

The optimism, in one sense, was well founded. By 1926, there were 2,049 Baptist churches, 80 Baptist associations, and a total membership of 316,467, an increase of 5,416 over 1925. Kentucky Baptist churches reported 14,357 baptisms in 1926. Because the estimated population of the commonwealth in 1926 was 2,586,000, Baptists represented one out of every eleven Kentuckians. There were 1,824 Sunday Schools, enrolling 217,316 pupils in the state, less than in 1925, but a significant number nonetheless. Fifteen Sunday Schools in the state each enrolled over 915 pupils. The largest of these—in churches scattered around the state—were Louisville, Walnut Street, 2,283; Mayfield, First, 1,917; Frankfort, First, 1,687; Newport, First, 1,547; and Owensboro, First, 1,427. Baptist Young People's Unions numbered 942, enrolling 23,995, and the 1,462 women's missionary organizations contributed $212,575.69 to missions and benevolent causes. Although this figure was again down somewhat from the previous year, Baptists in Kentucky still gave a total of $645,315.17 to denominational causes in 1926. According to historian Masters, the "one distressing fact was that 959 churches in Kentucky contributed nothing to outside causes in 1926."[57]

Still, the steady figures coupled with a renewed sense of optimism were encouraging and almost astonishing. Perhaps the most glaring irony was the fact that this new level of Kentucky Baptist cooperation, and the birth of Southern Baptist cooperation, came amid the strident controversies that wracked the convention in the 1920s. A cursory glance at *Western Recorder* articles in the April 1, 1926, issue revealed some of the pressing issues of the day. Along with an essay titled "Christ at the Door—Will Our Churches Let Him In?" other articles with titles like "The Evolution Theory," "Shall the Modernists Lay Their Hands Upon Our Children," "Louisville Baptist Ministers Endorse Anti-Race Track Gambling Campaign," and "John Barleycorn's Friends Stage a Comeback" discussed the wide range of issues confronting Baptists in Kentucky and beyond in the "Roaring Twenties."[58]

The Scopes Trial in Dayton, Tennessee, in 1925 galvanized for many the core of the controversy: the old ways versus the new ways, tradition versus modernity. The fact that John T. Scopes, the young biology teacher on whom the trial centered, was a native Kentuckian indicated that the commonwealth was not immune from the dividing controversies of the period. While many in this largely rural state remained isolated from the extremes of the Jazz Age, residents were nonetheless aware that modernity brought changes and that those changes, for better or worse, had an impact on even their rural life and work.

The changes of the post-World War I world also had an impact on the religious life of the state and nation. For Kentucky Baptists it was evident that times were indeed changing. And discussions of the raging "fundamentalist/modernist" controversy in the North crept into sermons delivered from pulpits in the South and in border states like Kentucky. The Baptist Press weighed in as well, offering advice and admonition on the dividing controversies of the period.

In Kentucky, the controversies of the day proved to be particularly perplexing for Baptists. Baptist newspapers inundated Kentucky Baptist clergy as well as lay men and women with varying perspectives on a dizzying assortment of issues. H. Boyce Taylor's *News and Truths* and *Kentucky Mission Monthly*, published by the Executive Board of the General Association and edited by the corresponding secretary, were read widely. Two other Baptist papers were published in Louisville: the *Western Recorder* (published by the Baptist Book Concern, a private group), and the *Baptist World* (published by the Baptist World Publishing Company and sponsored by Southern Seminary's faculty). William Ellis, a biographer of E. Y. Mullins, asserted that "the denominational warfare between the *World* and *Recorder* exemplified the cleavage between the moderate and fundamentalist wings of Southern Baptists."[59]

As editor of the *Western Recorder* since 1909, J. W. Porter had assumed the mantle of former editor T. T. Eaton, promising "to wage unremitting war" on what he perceived as "heretical" attacks on Landmarkism, the issue that had led to Whitsitt's resignation as president of the seminary and continued to divide Kentucky Baptists. Porter repeatedly levelled implicit and explicit attacks on Mullins and the seminary over issues ranging from Baptist origins to "alien immersion" and "unionism." In 1908, Mullins, with the aid of seminary faculty, raised the necessary money for capitalization of a new company—the Baptist World Publishing Company—responsible for publishing faculty works and the *Baptist World*, a weekly paper sympathetic to and supportive of the seminary, its president, and faculty.

A decade later—in 1919—with the challenge of the Seventy-five Million Campaign before them, Baptist leaders became convinced that a single state paper could best promote the campaign. J. B. Gambrell, president of the Southern Baptist Convention and a former corresponding secretary of the Baptist General Convention of Texas, suggested in a letter to his friend E. Y. Mullins that "Kentucky Baptists merge the two papers for the sake of denominational efficiency." O. E. Bryan, Kentucky's corresponding secretary, concluded as well that Kentucky Baptists "could only reach their financial goals through merger of the paper."[60] Bryan eventually presented a resolution at a called meeting of the state Board of Missions at Broadway

Western Recorder, *August 1919, at the time of its purchase
by what is now the Kentucky Baptist Convention*

Baptist Church in Louisville. The resolution asked the state board to "endeavor to purchase the Baptist papers of the state . . . and operate them under the direct control of the State Board of Missions."[61]

The purchase was effected in 1919 when owners of the *Western Recorder* and the *Baptist World* sold their papers—twenty thousand dollars for the *Recorder* and fifteen thousand dollars for the *World*—to the state board. The *Kentucky Mission Monthly* merged as well, but H. Boyce Taylor continued to publish *News and Truths* independently. The newly merged paper, another example of cooperation among Kentucky Baptists, retained the name *Western Recorder* and J. W. Porter as managing editor. The former editor of the *World*, E. B. Hatcher, remained as news editor of the new paper, and O. E. Bryan agreed to serve as business manager.[62]

In 1921, Victor I. Masters replaced Porter as managing editor, a position he would hold until 1942. Masters, born in South Carolina, completed an A.M. degree at Furman University in his home state as well as a Th.M. degree at Southern Seminary. Masters had long and valuable experience in Christian journalism before coming to the *Western Recorder*, having served as an associate editor for the *Baptist Courier* in South Carolina and in a similar position with the *Religious Herald* in Virginia. Then, from 1909 to 1921, Masters held the position of superintendent of the Publicity Department of the Home Mission Board in Atlanta, Georgia.[63] These varied experiences in Baptist life served Masters well during his tenure as editor of the *Western Recorder*. This is not to say that the views of the editor were always aligned with those of all Kentucky Baptists. In fact, while Mullins and seminary professors contributed to the *Western Recorder* during the tenures of editors Porter and Masters, the relationship between the state paper and the prestigious seminary remained uneasy and often tense.[64]

The publishers of the unified paper did not attempt to quell—or to steer clear of—controversy. In the 1920s, for example, with Masters as editor, considerable ink in the *Western Recorder* was devoted to searing articles on the "modernist controversy." Kentucky Baptists read an article titled "Have We Come to the Parting of the Ways?" by William James Robinson, a minister from Fort Smith, Arkansas. Robinson wrote: "Let us arise to the seriousness of the situation. No modernist has any place in the ranks of Baptists. They should be denied church membership, and denominational fellowship on the ground of vital heresy."[65]

Editor Masters assured his readers that "we are certainly not going to promise to keep quiet on Modernism, which is the evolution theory dressed up in its Sunday clothes to go to church." In the wake of the Scopes trial, the editor wrote, "It is a crying shame that American public schools should be allowed to be at the mercy of the devotees of such a system. It is a philosophy rather than a science. . . . It is a crying shame and should be corrected."[66]

The connection between evolution and education concerned Baptist leaders around the state. Messengers from the Warren Association in session in Bowling Green in September 1925, for example, passed a "Memorial" that "no funds should be given to any of the Baptist schools which shall refuse to come under the control of the General Association of Kentucky Baptists." The statement argued that the General Association should "have power to remove at any time trustees employing teachers, who teach or believe the evolutionary hypothesis as a fact, or any other doctrine subversive of the belief in the Word of God."[67]

Other Kentucky Baptists reacted differently to the controversy. W. O. Carver and A. T. Robertson at Southern Seminary, for example, thought deeply about the relationship between science and faith. Carver asserted that God had, of course, "initially created life and had sustained its development in accordance with natural law," and Robertson confessed to his friend and biographer, Everett Gill, that, "I am willing to believe in it [evolution], I rather do, but not in atheistic evolution . . . I say, write 'God' at the top, and what if he did use evolution? I can stand it if the monkeys can. . . . If he did do it that way, He still did it."[68]

As president of the Southern Baptist Theological Seminary, Mullins refused to give in to simplistic, autocratic solutions to the problem. In fact, he eventually sided with the respected president of the University of Kentucky, Frank L. McVey, against anti-evolutionary legislation in Kentucky's General Assembly. Mullins rejected the move to ban all evolutionary teaching, believing that "nothing could be more ill-advised than for Americans to attempt to employ legislative coercion in the realm of scientific opinion."[69]

In 1921, other Kentucky Baptists led by J. W. Porter persuaded the state mission board to appoint a committee to work for enactment of an anti-evolution law. William Jennings Bryan, the legendary "boy orator of the Plains," now lending his oratorical skills in the fight against evolution, spoke in Lexington early in 1922. After Bryan's address, W. L. Brock, pastor of Lexington's Immanuel Baptist Church, "introduced a resolution calling on the legislature to outlaw the teaching of evolution, higher criticism of the Bible and other forms of 'atheism and infidelity.'" When a sympathetic lawmaker introduced the proposal in Kentucky's General Assembly, Mullins induced a member of the Kentucky Senate to present a countermeasure. The Senate proposal made no reference to evolution but more moderately suggested that the state should not employ teachers "who shall directly or indirectly attack or assail or seek to undermine or weaken or destroy the religious beliefs and convictions" of their students. Ultimately, the state legislature was not amenable to either proposal. Indeed, in the mid-1920s six different bills, representing various attempts to prevent the teaching of evolution in the schools of the commonwealth, were presented to Kentucky legislators, but none survived.[70]

As president of the Southern Baptist Convention in the early 1920s, Mullins used his position to lend a calming voice. In his opening address on "Science and Religion" before the convention in Kansas City in 1923, he again refused to "advocate legislation and forestalled any such support from the Convention floor." Instead, he urged scientists and teachers to "be reasonable in their propagation of any scientific theory." Both Porter and Masters praised Mullins's Kansas City address, calling it "our Baptist gauge," and endorsed the president's forthright attempt to avoid "bitterness and faction." Mullins was satisfied that he had forestalled an open fight led by the group that he dubbed the "ultra brethren."[71] In 1927, Mullins summed up his position clearly in a letter to the famous evangelist Billy Sunday: "One of the greatest dangers facing us now," he said, "is that Christian people will be diverted from their task of saving souls into lobbying around legislatures and making out a program for the statute book rather than a program for the salvation of the world."[72]

The teaching of evolution continued to rankle Baptists in Kentucky and in other states, but that issue did not represent the only controversy in the 1920s, of course. Discussions of the Social Gospel, premillennialism, ecumenicalism, and other issues all vied for space on the pages of the Baptist press. In 1923, E. G. Sisk, a pastor in Webster County, published an article in the *Western Recorder* titled "An Argument Favoring Women Speaking in Our Churches." When H. Boyce Taylor read the article, a heated correspondence between the two fiery ministers ensued. And when Sisk insisted that "Taylor said some very hard things about some good women who spoke in our Baptist Bible Union at Memphis, Tenn.," the Murray pastor refused to publish Sisk's reply in his Murray-based paper, *News and Truths*, issuing a challenge instead: "Dear Bro.:" Taylor wrote, "Your letter is at hand. You are as rotten as the infidel women you defend. You are rotten on inspiration, God's sovereignty, the plan of salvation. . . . If you want to discuss something open your house and give me a chance at you before your own people. Put up or shut up." Taylor signed the missive, "Cordially, H. B. Taylor."[73]

Sisk accepted the challenge, and the resulting series of debates, lasting four days beginning on December 29, 1925, brought over eight hundred curious out-of-town visitors to the small western Kentucky town of Providence to witness the spectacle. The debates centered on four propositions:

1. The Scriptures teach the personal unconditional election, from before the foundation of the world, of only a part of Adam's race of salvation.
   H. B. Taylor, Affirms
   E. G. Sisk, Denies

2. The Scriptures teach that women may pray or testify in prayer meetings and protracted meetings, teach a mixed S. S. class, be a group leader in B. Y. P. U., address public mixed assemblies but not preach.
   E. G. Sisk, Affirms
   H. B. Taylor, Denies

3. The Scriptures teach that all Jews living when Christ comes again will be elect Jews and will be saved by seeing and receiving Him as their Savior and Lord.

H. B. Taylor, Affirms

E. G. Sisk, Denies

4. The Scriptures justify the use of the mourner's bench in our meetings.

E. G. Sisk, Affirms

H. B. Taylor, Denies

The fact that the Taylor/Sisk debates took place in the same year of the Scopes Trial indicates the contentious nature of the era. And Baptists in Kentucky often found themselves in the midst of the fray. The debates also indicated that theological skirmishing was not unusual within Baptist ranks.

If Baptists were not immune from divisions and debates within the Baptist family, neither did they fail to address various social concerns of the twenties. Kentuckians, despite being primarily a rural people, experienced the excitement and vicissitudes of the Jazz Age along with the rest of the nation.

After all, the 1920 census recorded—for the first time—more people living in American cities than in the rural areas of the nation. Kentucky cities grew apace, and with increased urbanization came alarming social activities associated with the excitement of urban life. Kentucky Baptists sounded the alarm. In the central Kentucky Bluegrass area, for example, the Elkhorn Association, made up of thirty-three congregations from Lexington and its environs, passed a resolution at its annual gathering in 1921, declaring that "dancing is one of the most dangerous of worldly amusements, and is making one of the greatest inroads on the churches. The dance is indecent, immoral, and immodest." The Lexington Ministerial Union objected to the opening of the Rosalind Dance Casino and specifically opposed the granting of "public dance hall licenses to any person or concern in this city." After Lexington's city commissioners granted the Rosalind Dance Casino an operating license, disregarding the ministerial union's objections, the Elkhorn Association warned local residents that "60 percent of the fallen women attribute their downfall to the dance, mostly the public dance hall."[74]

Many Baptists believed that the movie theater "was cut from the same cloth as the dance hall, the only difference being that local theaters were permitted to violate the Sabbath." The Blue Grass Baptist Young People's

Union passed a resolution declaring that moving pictures were "the out-standing evil of the day, injurious and very degrading to all that is moral, high and holy. They encourage and magnify all the things that are im-moral; they emphasize shooting, killing, gambling, divorce, elopements, unfaithfulness in the home life, free love, appealing to the sex . . . and such like."[75]

J. W. Porter, then the pastor of Lexington's First Baptist Church, criti-cized "Sunday pleasure seeking," deeming it a "deliberate disobedience to law," a practice containing the "germ of anarchy" and representing "usu-ally the first sin in the long catalogue of crime." Arthur Fox, a pastor in nearby Paris, echoed Porter's concerns. Fox asserted that "picture shows are nightly crowded" and that "whole families are becoming picture show fiends." Fox concluded that the "moving picture show is the devil's work shop." The Paris pastor publicized his views by sending letters to the edi-tors of the *Lexington Herald* and *Lexington Leader*. Inspired by Fox's bold and determined efforts, the Elkhorn Baptist Association voted unani-mously in 1921 to initiate a "united campaign against moving pictures, dancing, immodest 'undress,' mixed bathing, divorce, Sunday baseball, card playing, horse racing, gambling and violation of prohibition laws."[76] In Louisville, Bernard Spilman, recently arrived from North Carolina to attend Southern Seminary, was shocked to see the depravities of city life, especially open stores and saloons on Sunday. Spilman remembered, "All that was new to me. I saw SIN raw and rank for the first time in my life."[77]

In spite of the rancorous debates that divided Kentucky Baptists in the "Roaring Twenties," social concerns continued to provide opportunities for Baptist clergy and laity to work together. Of course, Baptists within the General Association were not reluctant to cooperate when the salvation of souls was at stake. Baptist women in Kentucky's Woman's Missionary Union organizations provided ample evidence of such cooperative efforts. Neither were Baptist women reluctant to take up the banner of social ini-tiatives such as prohibition.

In fact, prohibition, more than any other social concern, served to unite both women and men in Baptist circles during the waning years of the 1920s. This had not always been the case. In the 1800s, for example, many southern Baptists "fought bitterly against prohibition," insisting that church and state should not mingle in such prohibitive legislation. By the 1880s, however, most Baptists in the South were convinced that the "blight-ing presence" of alcohol required the "aid of the strong arm of the law."[78]

In Kentucky, few Baptists considered the Eighteenth Amendment a mistake. And when the Democratic Party settled on the anti-prohibition, New York politician Alfred Smith as its presidential nominee in 1928, many Kentuckians found themselves faced with an uncomfortable dilemma, opposing a Democratic candidate in a historically Democratic state. The fact that Kentucky's Democratic Party had already split, allowing the Republican Flem Sampson to win the gubernatorial race in 1927, did not aid the Democratic cause the next year. Smith's ties to Tammany Hall, his "wet" views, "his eastern accent, and, most of all, Catholic religion," convinced the majority of Kentucky's voters to rally behind his Republican opponent, Herbert Hoover, in 1928.[79]

E. Y. Mullins justified his vote for Hoover by declaring that the Democratic Party had "changed hands," from Thomas Jefferson's agrarian ideal—"the noble tillers of the soil"—to the "boss-ridden city masses." The *Western Recorder* reported on Mullins's address to the Anti-Saloon League in Washington, D. C., in an article titled "President Mullins Predicts Shock for Politicians Behind Smith."[80]

Mullins's stand for prohibition and against Smith healed the wounds from his various internecine battles with conservatives within the state. The great Baptist leader's death came, ironically, in November 1928, the very month of Hoover's victory over the Democratic candidate Mullins had worked so hard to defeat. When the votes were counted, it was clear that Hoover had carried the state. His 177,000-vote plurality was the largest Republican victory in Kentucky to that time.[81] Kentucky Baptists, representing the single largest religious voting bloc, certainly contributed to the Democratic defeat. Mullins's stand—in the months before his death—and the stand of thousands of Kentucky Baptists was emblematic of a general Baptist "closing of the ranks" in the latter 1920s.

During the first year of Hoover's administration, of course, the exuberance and—for some—the prosperity of the "Roaring Twenties" came literally to a crashing halt. When Wall Street "laid an egg," the economic devastation of the Great Depression had begun. One chronicler of the period noted that the depression "following upon the controversies of the previous decade, dealt the final blow to the optimism and sense of destiny that had captured Baptists' imaginations in 1919."[82]

But as the Great Depression deepened, and as the controversies that had divided Kentucky Baptists—as well as the rest of the South and indeed the rest of the nation—lingered, Baptists could still point to united victories against common foes that had marked a most remarkable decade. Perhaps the uniting causes of the 1920s served as an appropriate backdrop for Southern Baptists' most enduring advance—the decision in 1925 to begin the work of a Cooperative Program. And the enduring legacy of the Cooperative Program, a legacy that certainly overshadowed the theological wranglings and political maneuverings of the 1920s decade, had Kentucky beginnings.

H. Boyce Taylor, the controversial pastor of the Baptist church in Murray, laid the foundation for cooperation. The Cooperative Program, with the antecedent of Kentucky's Unified Budget Plan as a guide, was founded in 1925, the year of the Scopes Trial. The Scopes Trial symbolized the inauguration of a new era of modernity. The Baptist response of unity—the Cooperative Program—to the frightening changes and shifting sands of modernity gave particular poignancy to the old hymn "The Solid Rock," cherished and sung in Baptist churches across the convention: "On Christ the Solid Rock I stand; all other ground is sinking sand. All other ground is sinking sand."

3

Hard Times:
Kentucky Baptists
in the Great Depression
1929-1937

The aging professor began class at Southern Seminary in his usual way that afternoon in September 1934. A. T. Robertson, a little out of breath from his walk up the stairs to his second-floor classroom, checked the ventilation, clasped the edges of the "little box-like stand" on his desk, and stated abruptly, "Let us pray." After a short prayer, the teacher called roll, read any excuses that had been placed on his desk, made the assignment for the next session, and began the "recitation." Calling for books to be closed, he scanned the class roll as the students "waited in suspense to see who the first victim would be."

A former student recalled a typical inquisition: "Having fixed upon his man, he would say with the solemnity of a judge summoning a prisoner to his feet to be sentenced, 'Mr. Blank, will you recite?' Brother Blank stands, bracing himself for the worst. 'Brother Blank, what is the title of the lesson?' Brother Blank, clearing his throat for time, replies weakly, 'The lesson is about the healing of the man who was let down through the roof.' 'Yes, but what is the title of the lesson?' 'I don't remember.' 'Well, did you ever know? That will do.'"

At seventy, the renowned Greek scholar was held in awe by his sometimes trembling students—for his scholarship and for his rare combination of academic rigor and personal compassion. Pronouncements from his classroom lectern were widely quoted: "The greatest proof that the Bible is inspired is that it has stood so much bad preaching"; "Tell the truth even if you are a Baptist preacher"; "If God wants you to preach he will find somebody—who will stand it"; "Give a man an open Bible, an open mind, a conscience in good working order, and he will have a hard time to keep from being a Baptist"; and "God pity the poor preacher who has to *hunt* for something to preach—and the people that have to listen."[1]

As a teacher, "Dr. Bob's" classroom demeanor, as well as his lectures, were legendary. If students came to class unprepared, they were to place a note on the professor's desk at the beginning of class. "Upon a pretender," however, a student recalled, "he had no mercy." A former student remembered that "one of his determinations, that amounted to almost an obsession, was his attitude toward . . . big-headed young preachers." At the same time, Robertson's compassion for troubled, though sincere, students was just as famous: "He loved us enough to humiliate us if that seemed necessary to purge us of the pride that so often mars preachers; but he loved us enough to lift us too when we were down."[2]

In New Testament scholarship, Robertson was without peer. In his forty-five years of teaching, he produced as many books. In addition to his Greek "Big Grammar," Robertson published forty-four other books, including four grammars, fourteen commentaries and studies, six "Word Pictures of the New Testament," eleven histories, and ten character studies. His work ethic and "his capacity and penchant for hard work [were] the wonder of his scholarly friends on both sides of the Atlantic." He wrote "with a sort of fury of concentration." Robertson's

A. T. Robertson, Greek scholar and professor at Southern Seminary

biographer concluded that "so intense was this love of work that it was impossible for him to comprehend a lazy preacher."[3]

In celebration of his seventieth birthday, Robertson's friend and former student, Edwin McNeill Poteat, the pastor of Pullen Memorial Baptist Church in Raleigh, North Carolina, sent a poem of congratulations:

> There is a professor of Greek
> Unrivaled, unresting, unique,
> Who at three-score and ten
> Keeps pushing his pen
> And producing a volume a week!
>
> One would think that at seventy years
> Greek would weary the wisest of seers;
> But the older he grows
> The more grammar he knows
> And more eager for study appears.
>
> He seems to have gotten that way
> By working twelve hours a day.
> So this Louisville Hellene
> Keeps writin' and sellin'
> Not for coin but for love of Koine![4]

Characteristically, Robertson spent the morning of September 24, 1930, working in his office, walked home for lunch, and then returned to resume his writing until his 3:00 afternoon class. Leaving his books open and scattered on his desk, he left for class, or as his biographer put it, "He went to meet his class; and then to meet his Lord." Although the day was not exceptionally warm, once the class session had begun, the professor began to perspire. Feeling ill, Robertson paused, stated, "I don't know what is the matter with me, but I don't feel well. I'm going to dismiss class," and abruptly—at 3:30—left his bewildered students.

A colleague, recognizing that something was amiss since Robertson "never dismissed his classes ahead of time," accompanied the professor home. A doctor was called, but little could be done. Mrs. Robertson read to her dying husband until the physician came, but by that time the stroke had left the great Greek scholar with just a few minutes to live. News of Robertson's sudden death stunned the seminary community and all of Louisville. One student later wrote: "If a storm had blown away the buildings and left Doctor Robertson, the Seminary would have been more real than it was with him gone."[5]

Robertson's funeral service on September 27 in the sanctuary of Louisville's Fourth Avenue Baptist Church was a celebration of a remarkable life. The congregation sang one of his favorite hymns, "O Love That Wilt Not Let Me Go," and various speakers, including A. R. Christie, Robertson's pastor, John R. Sampey, the seminary president and Robertson's life-long friend, and J. R. Cunningham, the president of Presbyterian Theological Seminary, remembered Robertson as church member, seminary professor, and "neighbor." The great man was buried in Louisville's Cave Hill Cemetery beneath a granite cross bearing the inscription, "To me to live is Christ, and to die is gain."[6]

The death of A. T. Robertson in the middle of the Great Depression was one of several losses that diminished the ranks of Kentucky Baptists, the largest denomination in the commonwealth. Eliza Broadus, for more than fifty years a promoter of the work of Kentucky Baptist women and a founder of the woman's missionary movement among Southern Baptists, died in 1931. In that same year, W. M. Stallings, the much-loved superintendent of the Kentucky Baptist Children's Home in Glendale, one of the founders of the home, a past moderator of the General Association, and "a preacher of wide influence," died at the age of sixty-two.[7] Also gone—in 1932—was the inimitable H. Boyce Taylor, the pastor of the First Baptist Church, Murray, for thirty-five years and more than anyone else the initiator of the movement that resulted in the Southern Baptist Cooperative Program. Taylor's ally and friend J. W. Porter died at his home in Lexington in 1937. Porter pastored Lexington's First Baptist and Immanuel Baptist Churches, and founded the city's Ashland Avenue Baptist Church. Porter had also served as the editor of the *Western Recorder* from 1909 to 1921.[8]

The *Western Recorder* published eulogies of each of these Kentucky Baptist leaders as well as other prominent individuals whose life and work influenced state and denominational affairs. For example, in the October 16, 1930, edition, the photograph of Richard H. Edmonds adorned the cover of the state Baptist paper. Although he was not a Kentuckian, Edmonds's death on October 4 provoked considerable comment because of his promotion of the "New South" in the pages of his own *Manufacturers Record*. Born in Norfolk, Virginia, and spending most of his years in Baltimore, Edmonds was described in the *Western Recorder* as a "Patriot, Statesman (without office), Chief Prophet of the New South and unsurpassed Interpreter and Defender of the Old South." According to Victor Masters, Edmonds's "brain and heart grasped in a measure not equalled by another of his generation all that concerned the life and welfare of the South as a section and as a part of America." More important, "Mr. Edmonds was a devoted Christian," a beloved deacon of a Baptist church, and the *Manufacturers Record* through its "high moral vertebracy" was used to "build up righteousness irrespective of denominational alignments."[9]

The deaths of Robertson, Broadus, Stallings, Taylor, Porter, and Edmonds foreshadowed other traumatic events in the 1930s for Kentucky Baptists, events that could not be foreseen in the comparatively prosperous, if not peaceful, 1920s. George W. Truett, the great pastor of Dallas's First Baptist Church and the president of the Southern Baptist Convention, sent a letter to messengers at the 1928 meeting of the General Association on November 13 of that year. Truett wrote that he "would join you in profound gratitude for God's signal favor upon you and in fervent prayer that He will guide and crown all your convention enterprises with constantly enlarging usefulness. Let us all face the incomparable opportunities and responsibilities now confronting Southern Baptists."[10] Truett's optimism and the "enlarging usefulness" of Southern Baptists would be sorely tested in the following decade.

In the 1920s, however, there had been room for optimistic hope for expanding programs and missions opportunities. After all, Kentucky certainly shared in the "material display of progress and prosperity" of the twenties. According to the 1930 census, of the 2.6 million residents of the commonwealth, more than 300,000 owned automobiles as "car dealers advertised their inventory as the answer to everyone's vocational and recreational needs."[11] Although the prevalence of radio ownership "lagged behind the national average by one-half," more Kentuckians than ever tuned in to radio broadcasts, introducing themselves and their families to new programs and new consumer goods.

Throughout Kentucky in the twenties, chambers of commerce and other civic organizations "extolled growth, expansion, and profit." Material gain, rather than spiritual well-being and growth, dominated the decade, and the pronouncement by President Calvin Coolidge that "the business of America is business" only accentuated the emphasis on material prosperity. In Kentucky, Republican governor Flem Sampson supported the national trend by appointing businessmen to the new Kentucky Progress Commission, an organization designed to "advertise Kentucky to the world." The promotion of material gain in the twenties was in fact bipartisan in the commonwealth. With mixed metaphors, Keen Johnson, a Democrat, editor and copublisher of the *Richmond Daily Register*, and later governor, lauded the merits of industrial growth and economic wealth: "There is romance in the routine of industry, there is artistry in the skyscraper; there is a melody fragrant with meaning in the symphony of sound which emanates from the plants of productivity. There is poetry in progress be it expressed in asphalt or whirling dynamos."[12]

Despite the lavish optimism of Republicans and Democrats alike in the roaring twenties, by all accounts, Kentucky lagged behind the rest of the nation in the progress and prosperity of the decade. An accurate description of the decade as the roaring twenties could only be applied to the urban scene, and Kentucky remained largely rural. While the 1920 census indicated—for the first time—that the majority of Americans lived in towns and cities, in Kentucky only 25 percent were city-dwellers. Kentucky followed the trend of increased urbanization in the nation, but still by 1930 fully 70 percent of commonwealth residents remained country folk.[13]

Of course, the rural nature of the state had an impact on the emphases of the General Association of Kentucky Baptists. In 1930, W. A. Gardiner of the General Association's Bible School Department directed an admonition to the state's "country churches": "I would make an appeal to the pastors and superintendents of our country churches right now. It is that you teach your teachers. They are in desperate need of your teaching. It is so important for a number of nights for a study of doctrines, Bible history and other things of importance to your church life."[14]

Because of the state's rural identity, the strength of Kentucky Baptists continued to lie in its small-church heritage. Although Lexington took on the airs of an urban metropolis in the 1920s, Louisville, with its three hundred thousand residents in the late 1920s, was clearly "the only genuinely urban area in the state."[15] Not all of the largest Kentucky Baptist churches were located in Louisville and Lexington, however. Baptist churches—often with large memberships—located in small cities and towns, continued to thrive in the 1920s and into the 1930s. The *Western Recorder* regularly listed Baptist Sunday School attendance of churches reporting an attendance of over five hundred. In the *Recorder*'s January 16, 1930, issue, for example, Sunday Schools reporting an attendance of over five hundred for the Sunday of January 5 were: Louisville, Walnut St., 1,104; Owensboro, First, 914; Louisville, Parkland, 904; Newport, First, 900; Mayfield, First, 767; Bowling Green, First, 742; Lexington, Calvary, 651; Louisville, 9th and O, 637; Louisville, Baptist Tabernacle, 618; Middlesboro, First, 601; Frankfort, First, 592; Owensboro, Third, 589; Louisville, Carlisle Ave., 563; Hopkinsville, First, 531; Louisville, 23rd & Broadway, 518, Somerset, First, 511; and Harlan, 510.[16] Strong churches in Louisville, to be sure, but also in smaller communities like Mayfield and Hopkinsville in the west and Middlesboro and Harlan in the east, attested to the significant statewide presence of Baptists in Kentucky.

Enrollment, attendance, and offerings in Baptist churches continued to grow in the 1920s despite the serious decline of staple Kentucky industries. Even before the stock market crash, Prohibition had all but destroyed the state's distilleries and breweries, businesses that because of Baptist leadership in the temperance movement had minimal impact on Baptists' economic prosperity. The decline of another important Kentucky industry—coal mining—was more keenly felt. Because of the high price of coal, and the development of such alternative forms of energy as electricity and oil, the number of mines and coal miners in the state had declined from 600 mines and 64,000 workers in 1927 to 451 mines and 57,000 workers in 1929, the year of the crash.[17]

Even more tragic for Kentuckians and Kentucky Baptists, though, was the precipitous decline in agriculture. Throughout the 1920s, farmers produced too much. Overproduction brought crop and livestock prices intolerably low, a phenomenon that particularly affected farmers of dairy goods, corn, and livestock. Only tobacco farmers prospered during the decade; by the late twenties, Lexington had become the largest loose-leaf tobacco market in the world, and in 1929 the income of Kentucky's tobacco farmers stood at $71 million, up considerably from the previous year.[18]

Except for tobacco, Kentucky did not share in the vaunted economic prosperity of the roaring twenties. By the time stock prices plummeted in October 1929, many Kentuckians had already experienced a decade, indeed a lifetime, of hard times. The stock market crash signalled the beginning of a national economic depression, but for Kentuckians the Wall Street disaster simply exacerbated already difficult economic misfortunes. Thomas D. Clark, then newly appointed to a position in the Department of History at the University of Kentucky, recalled that "a great many U. K. professors dabbled in the stock market." Clark, a Baptist, remembered that he was worried about three things during the depression: "getting fired, having enough money to buy the essentials, and what would be the future of our country."[19]

Despite the stock speculation of certain history professors at the state university, less than 5 percent of Kentucky's total income in 1929 came from dividends on stock investments. When the crash hit, Kentuckians in both the eastern and western coal fields, and farmers throughout the state, had already struggled for years to make do. In central Kentucky—around Lexington—residents and football fans of the University of Kentucky seemed to be more concerned with the gridiron exploits of John "Shipwreck" Kelly, the Wildcats' star player. A column by humorist Will Rogers published on the front page of the *Lexington Herald* revealed the general attitude of most Kentuckians. "What does the sensational collapse of Wall Street mean?" asked Rogers. "Nothin. Why, if the cows of this country failed to come up and get milked one night it would be more of a panic. . . . An old sow and litter of pigs make more people a living than all the steel and General Motors stock combined."[20]

While Rogers and many Kentuckians dismissed news of the Wall Street crash, its impact was keenly felt. Bank and business closings and continued coal and agricultural decline brought a deeper sense of despair to the state's residents. Before the crash, Kentucky's per-capita income of $371 stood just above one-half of the national average. By 1933, per-capita income for Kentuckians had fallen to $198. Such dire economic straits had a dramatic impact on Kentucky Baptists along with everyone else in the commonwealth. And just as Baptists had played important roles in earlier reform campaigns—against "the liquor trust" and racetrack gambling—they also held significant positions in the campaign to deal with the depression.[21]

Governor Ruby Laffoon's choice for the post of Kentucky relief commissioner, for example, was R. Harper Gatton, the superintendent of public schools in Madisonville, the governor's hometown. A member of Madisonville's First Baptist Church, Gatton had been appointed to serve on the

General Association of Kentucky Baptists' Committee on Schools and Colleges in 1928. Already in financial distress, Kentucky Baptist educational institutions faced cutbacks and closings. It was the responsibility of Gatton's committee to recommend where retrenchment should be made. A well-known Democrat in western Kentucky, Gatton was later named as Kentucky's relief administrator under Franklin D. Roosevelt.

C. M. Thompson, executive secretary, Kentucky Baptists, 1921-1938

Although he reported in 1933 that

relief work in Kentucky was "progressing splendidly," and Gatton was generally praised for his administration of relief in the state, his work on the Kentucky Baptist committee—a thankless task—was to be fraught with controversy and criticism.[22]

Plummeting stock prices did not keep messengers away from the annual meeting of Kentucky Baptists in Lexington in November 1929, only a few days after the crash. In fact, the *Western Recorder* reported that "the attendance at Lexington seemed to be larger than for a number of years." Calvin M. Thompson, the corresponding secretary of the executive board since 1921, a former pastor in Paducah, Hopkinsville, and Winchester, and the former editor of the *Western Recorder*, gave the annual sermon. Significantly, the sermon addressed the issue of "Christ's Teachings on Stewardship." Thompson prophetically encouraged the messengers to consider the temporal nature of material gain. "Money isn't wealth," he said. "It is merely a means of exchange whereby real values may be secured." The preacher suggested that "this world is God's great Business College. All are enrolled in its courses. The money we have is not real money with the eternal values in it. Learn how to use that money in God's Business College so when promotion day comes you will be able to handle true riches which God will entrust to you."[23]

That money or the lack of money continued to absorb the thoughts of Kentucky Baptists was evident during 1930 in the issues of the state Baptist paper. The *Recorder* ran a series of articles in June by Frank G. Sayers, articles adapted from his address before the Northern Baptist Convention. With titles such as "Mammonism, Chief World Rival of Jesus Christ," "How Goes the Pursuit of the '1930 Gold-Rush' Worshipers?" and "Wherein Lies the Peril of Modern Mammonism," Sayers made clear the dangers of the love of money.[24] For an increasing number of Kentucky Baptists in the Great Depression, however, there was little money to love.

The executive board reported in 1930 that "drought, crop failure and financial depression have brought about a most serious situation. Thousands of people, for the first time in their lives, are without employment. Financial disaster has taken up its habitation in many homes and multitudes are feeling the terrible influence of its uncanny spell." The depression certainly had an impact on the work of the General Association. Although the *Western Recorder* had stated a goal of $550,000 in offerings for 1930, the executive board reported total receipts of only $426,058.91. The board admitted that "want with its gaunt figure is anything but a desirable companion. It would be unfortunate, however, to the last degree if the horizon of Kentucky Baptists was obscured by a huge dollar mark and their thinking limited to the temporalities of life." The State Missions Committee revealed that "in spite of the financial depression, the drought and other difficulties," 1930 had been "a very successful year," with "advancement made in most departments of our State Mission work."[25]

Despite hard times, Southern Seminary held its second annual Bible conference in March 1930. According to participants, "God smiled with gracious favor" on the conference as "a conservatively estimated aggregate attendance for all the sessions of 22,000" from 17 states and 19 "other lands" came to Louisville. For "the first time in the history of Louisville," because the large auditorium of the Crescent Hill Baptist Church and the seminary auditorium could not hold the conferees, the voices of speakers were carried by electrical transmission to adjoining rooms, "where large numbers listened to the amplified voice."[26]

The amplified voices belonged to some of the preeminent individuals in evangelical Christianity. George W. Truett as well as missions specialist Kenneth Scott Latourette gave a series of lectures, lectures that made a dramatic impact on conference participants. One listener exclaimed that "Dr. George W. Truett lifted us up and Dr. Kenneth Scott Latourette showed us the fields. Dr. Truett increased our faith and Dr. Latourette gave us work to do. Dr. Truett sounded the height and depth and breadth of the Gospel and Dr. Latourette brought us face to face with unredeemed millions in need of the Good News."[27]

Simultaneous revivals in Louisville in 1931 followed the success of the seminary's conference. Throughout October 1931, services in some forty Louisville churches resulted in 761 baptisms upon professions of faith and in a total of nearly 1,300 added to Louisville's churches. And as with all "spiritual revivals," the *Western Recorder* suggested that the revival series was "deeply significant as well because of the improved spiritual condition brought about in the life of the churches and their members."[28]

While spiritual renewal occurred, however, the lack of rain in 1930 prompted physical distress for Kentuckians across the state. Precipitation averaged below half the state's normal levels. The drought persisted throughout the summer and into the fall. In some areas of the state, it failed to rain for a month and a half. The drought was discussed in the weekly meeting of the Louisville Baptist Pastors' Conference. Pastors reported that members of their congregations "had approached them in the interest of prayers for rain." In typical Baptist fashion the pastors decided to appoint a committee "with power to act" to consider "an opinion or pronouncement on the drought and the possibility of securing rain by means of prayer." While prayer was deemed appropriate, the committee concluded somewhat ambiguously that "it was the sense of the body that we might have rain if it were God's will."[29]

The *Western Recorder* printed articles addressing the efficacy of "prayer and rain." One pastor quoted A. T. Robertson on "prayer and drought." The *Recorder*'s editor, V. I. Masters, commented that "one great blessing which has come to God's people in connection with the broadspread and long-continued drought this summer has been a certain wholesome stock-taking of the reality and extent of their faith in God." The drought coupled with the depression proved particularly distressing in eastern Kentucky and resulted in the increase in the number of needy students in mountain Baptist schools. The *Western Recorder* assured Kentucky Baptists that "twenty-five to forty dollars will pay their tuition in one of the schools. Shall we turn them away for lack of funds?"[30]

Of course, funds were lacking as the depression deepened. And Baptists found themselves flooded with requests from their local pastors not only to support church budgets, but to continue to pledge support for General Association causes as well. And various Southern Baptist Convention causes asked—indeed begged—for help. The SBC's Foreign Mission Board issued this plea in the April 3, 1930, edition of the *Western Recorder*: "We beg our Southern Baptist brethren to face the fact that they must increase at once their gifts to their Foreign Mission Board or the Board will be forced to abandon some of its fields. The situation is just as serious as this. Let us face it in the fear of God."[31]

It seemed that almost everyone was in some way affected by the trying times. Bank closings had a direct impact on some institutions. Southern Seminary had about $50,000 on deposit and over $17,000 in an "open checking account" when the Louisville Trust Company failed early in 1931. George E. Hays reported that "on account of the closing of the Louisville Trust Company, and the general depression, it has not been possible to reduce the bonded indebtedness on the Hospital during the year." The hospital's problems mounted when state newspapers carried "sensational headlines in connection with the speculations" of the hospital's bookkeeper. Hays, the hospital's chairman, accepted the resignation of Superintendent Howard E. Hodge and agreed to his own appointment as acting superintendent. Hays assured patrons that the secular press had overstated the fraud and that only "$5,000 were missing, an amount comfortably covered by bond."[32]

The recriminations in the secular press prompted the *Western Recorder* to promote the benefits of subscribing to the state Baptist paper. The deepening depression made sound literature essential for believers. The editors asserted that "big dailies and many magazines minister to the fleshly life and interests," while the "religious weekly alone ministers similarly to spiritual life and interests." The *Recorder* included a "line-up" to illustrate the differences:

Secular Press Line-up	Baptist Paper Line-up
Controlled by wets	Fights for prohibition
Opens to atheism	Confutes atheism
Trumpets materialism	Exalts spirituality
Favors moral laxity	Shames lust and impurity
Flatters human pride	Preaches Christ's cross
Discredits Bible authority	Contends for the faith
Destroys reverence	Exalts church and pastor
Breeds lawlessness	Teaches law and order.[33]

The contrast between the secular and denominational press was carried over to another area of controversy that engulfed Kentucky Baptists in the 1930s—the issue of Christian education. At the annual meeting of the General Association in 1929, R. Harper Gatton's Schools and Colleges Committee reported their recommendations concerning Kentucky Baptist educational institutions. The report was long and thorough.

After praising school administrators and teachers for rendering "unselfish, qualified service under grave difficulties," Gatton launched into a history of secondary education in the commonwealth, complete with footnotes. As school superintendent in Madisonville, Gatton was sensitive to any duplication of services between public and private institutions. In 1929, Kentucky Baptists operated four high schools, all in eastern Kentucky, four schools listed as junior colleges, and Georgetown College, the state's only senior college. Each of these schools faced financial crises: the high schools faced a debt of $41,000, the total debt of the junior colleges stood at $221,000, and Georgetown College, operating at an annual loss of $30,000, was "on the verge of bankruptcy."[34]

Gatton concluded that the fact that Georgetown remained on the list of accredited colleges was remarkable considering its subpar equipment and teacher shortages: "A high school graduate from any one of the best fifteen high schools in the State finds less equipment in the laboratories at Georgetown than they left in their home high school." This woeful lack of facilities had convinced the state's better secondary students to choose, upon their graduation, "State, Vanderbilt, Yale or Purdue." Kentucky's mountain schools faced a particular dilemma, as "the mountain appeal has been divested of its romance and no longer [stirs] the heart of the benevolent." Indeed, progress in the Appalachian hollows of eastern Kentucky made former benefactors reassess their philanthropic goals: "Perhaps those who ride the concrete mountain roads, visit her splendid, progressive cities, and talk with her prominent citizens have returned to the dirt and gravel roads, the mud and depression of Western and South Central Kentucky wiser men."[35]

Although Gatton realized that "it is not the function of this report to offer the solution of our educational problem, a responsibility of the General Association's Survey Committee," the chair concluded his dismal report with the following comments:

1. We have had confusion of names too long. Cumberland College is 41 years old and yet as late as 1917 there were but 10 pupils in the college department. Cumberland Academy would be better.

2. We should consider our denominational high schools as missionary efforts and discontinue them when the localities concerned become interested in education. This policy will be followed by stronger State high schools in these localities.

3. Any desire to educate all our children in strictly Baptist high schools is impracticable and visionary.

4. Junior colleges should discontinue high school work if a public high school is available.

5. In order for our senior college to live, at least half of our junior colleges should be discontinued. Kentucky Baptists will never render adequate support to the present educational program.

6. Discontinuation of Georgetown would help all the junior colleges.

7. The State high schools will continue to grow. We should welcome their advance and contend for Christian men for school board members.

8. Because the field of the junior college is new and prosperous a word of warning should be given against permitting too many dying Baptist academies from trying to save themselves by giving a type of work for which they may not be prepared.

9. The junior college, in depriving the senior college of its large freshmen and sophomore classes, creates a serious financial problem for the future of the senior college and hence for the future of higher Christian education.

10. Seemingly the facts indicate that we should either close all denominational high schools and half our junior colleges and support our institution of higher Christian education, or close our college and build the high schools and junior colleges. Surely the Survey Committee will urge Kentucky Baptists to rally to the urgent needs of Georgetown after her 100 years of leadership.

11. Finally, it is to be hoped that definite action will be suggested by the Survey Committee at once, and that this association will not be persuaded to prolong discussion and agitation
until our schools are lost.[36]

The Survey Committee had been appointed by a committee of five in
1927 to improve the denomination's educational program. The committee
had hired "experts"—including the director of the Bureau of School Service at the University of Kentucky, the president of Franklin College in Indiana, and representatives of Mercer University in Georgia and Christian
College in Missouri—at an approximate cost of two thousand dollars to
conduct the survey. Based on the results of the survey, the committee explained that the facts suggested that Kentucky Baptists were faced with
the prospect of "saving some or losing all." Kentucky Baptists were solely
responsible for the "maintenance and promotion" of Georgetown, Campbellsville, Cumberland, Bethel Woman's, and Bethel Colleges. Academies
at Hazard, Salyersville, and Barbourville were maintained by the Home
Mission Board of the SBC, and Oneida Institute relied "upon extra state resources." The committee recommended that Kentucky Baptists "maintain
one standard four year college, namely, Georgetown College; and two junior colleges, Cumberland College, at Williamsburg, for men and women,
and Bethel Woman's College at Hopkinsville." The controversial nature of
the proposal led to extended discussion. Eventually, Lexington's J. W.
Porter moved to refer the matter to the State Mission Board, which was to
report back to the body in 1930.[37]

Although the *Western Recorder*'s Masters believed that the "spokesmen
of the various Baptist schools have been wonderfully modest and quiet
through all of these trying months when the question of their existence
had been placed in the balances," Gatton's report and the report of the
Survey Committee met with immediate concern and criticism. O. W.
Yates, the president of Bethel College in Russellville, an institution per-
petually on shaky financial ground, wrote an article for the *Western
Recorder* titled "Fallacies of the School Survey." Yates argued that the first
fallacy concerned the measurement of "our schools and the services rendered by purely materialistic standards." Gatton's standards in his work as
a relief administrator, work that entailed a constant juggling of dollars and
a determination of an individual's fitness for relief, did not apply to the situations of Baptist education, according to Yates. When administrators of
various institutions were interviewed by Gatton's committee, the committee "marched out each school and asked it: 'Have you any debt?' The answer was, 'Yes.' The second question was, 'How much money have you?'

the answer was 'None.'" The last question "upon which hangeth 'all the Law and the Prophets,'" was "How much money can you get?"[38]

Yates believed that such questioning indicated that "if materialistic coma has not seized our people and the modernistic anestheticists [*sic*] are not undertaking to administer anesthetics to us, I am not able to discern spiritual values." Bethel's president argued that "a bow of this kind to Materialism is not easily lived down." Another fallacy of the Survey Committee's report was the implication that closing six schools would guarantee the life and prosperity of the other three. Yates queried, "Would we kill a church just because it was poor?"[39]

The concerns of Yates and others certainly had an effect on the General Association's decision in 1930 not to pronounce a death sentence on Baptist institutions. Instead, it was decided "that each school be accorded complete freedom to solicit funds for current expenses, equipment or endowment whenever they may find an open door." The resolution further recommended that "the State Board now go on record as favoring an intensive support of our Baptist Educational program and of Georgetown College in particular."[40]

The decision to allow the individual schools, in effect, to fend for themselves produced mixed results. Although Georgetown, Cumberland, Campbellsville, and Bethel Woman's College survived the depression, along with Magoffin Institute and Oneida, other schools were forced to make the hard decision to close. A. S. Petrey's Hazard Baptist Institute, Barbourville Baptist Institute, and Bethel College in Russellville eventually closed their doors. The picture of Frank M. Masters, the historian and president of Bethel, presiding—with no salary—over the liquidation of his school was especially tragic and heartrending. Bethel's few assets were merged with Georgetown in 1933. Georgetown's president, Henry E. Watters, praised Masters "for the splendid ability and leadership manifested in the manner in which he was able to close out Bethel College so as to conserve the traditions of the College, the sympathy and the interests of the alumni, and especially the friends and creditors of the college."[41]

Support for Georgetown became increasingly important in 1930. In April, the college chapel and library building had been completely destroyed by fire. Although the library, heating plant, chapel room, biology laboratory, and classrooms were destroyed, Malcom Browning Adams, Watters's predecessor as Georgetown's president, assured supporters that the state's only senior Baptist institution was "determined to fight ahead and will succeed if our people come to our help." Alumni and friends rallied to help, but the rebuilding task proved to be too much for Adams. Georgetown's president, having led the school for seventeen years, announced his decision to step down in October.[42] Following Adams's retirement, the college chose H. E. Watters to lead the school. Then, after Watters's brief tenure, Georgetown's Board of Trustees turned to Henry Noble Sherwood, an assistant professor of history at the University of Louisville.

Several months after Sherwood's appointment, it became known that the new president had once been a minister in the Christian Church, but later united with a Baptist church in Indiana "without having been baptized on the authority of that church." In 1927, after coming to Louisville, Sherwood joined Highland Baptist Church by letter from the Baptist church in Indiana. At the General Association's annual meeting in Henderson, J. W. Porter of Lexington presented a resolution in the Tuesday evening session, asking Kentucky Baptists to "withhold all funds from Georgetown College, so long as the College has a President, who has not received baptism authorized by a Baptist church." Intense discussion followed Porter's resolution motion, including the reading of a "Memorial" from the West Union Association condemning the "Unionism and Modernism in one of the leading Baptist schools of the state." Discussion continued until it was decided to review the issue at 9:15 the following morning.

On Wednesday morning the essence of the Porter resolution was adopted by the messengers, with the executive board "holding all funds in reserve allotted to Georgetown College, pending the adjustment of the relation of that institution to the General Association." The controversy was reignited in annual meeting after annual meeting until 1941, when Georgetown's Board of Trustees voted 12 to 9 to dismiss Sherwood. Sherwood eventually moved to Lexington, joined the Central Christian Church, worked for a time at the University of Kentucky, and then accepted a position as chancellor of Transylvania University.[43]

The lingering question of Georgetown's presidency in the late 1930s overshadowed other positive advancements in the work of Kentucky Baptists during the years of the Great Depression. As early as 1931, reports from the executive board pointed to specific achievements in the work. In 1931, 77 state Baptist missionaries reported 2,789 additions to the churches and an increase of 263 baptisms over the previous year. Forty-one new Sunday Schools were organized, and 66 training schools enrolled 5,181. In 1932, although the executive board reported $312,009.90 for all missions and benevolences, down by $59,513.09 from 1931, statistician E. P. Alldredge asserted that the "churches achieved in 1932 results in their local work, which, on the whole, has not been surpassed in our entire history." The 2,054 Baptist churches in Kentucky showed 17,697 baptisms and a total membership of 342,687, a remarkable net gain of 8,698 over the previous year.[44]

Baptist church growth in the state was remarkable considering the economic straits of individuals and churches. On the other hand, perhaps hard times actually served to increase the faith of individual believers, encouraging them to depend on spiritual rather than economic resources. Despite the substantial growth in numbers, executive board members appointed a committee of eleven to propose changes in the organization and institutional life of the missionary and benevolent work of the General Association in the interest of economy and efficiency. The committee's report was eventually adopted—with only minor changes—by messengers at the annual meeting in Bowling Green. The proposals included decreasing the expenses of the *Western Recorder*, combining the departments of Enlistment and Brotherhood into the Promotional and Brotherhood Department, increasing emphasis on evangelism, and promoting better coordination and cooperation between the Sunday School, B.Y.P.U., and State Missions departments. The moderator of the General Association was to take on a greater responsibility in "promoting our denominational work in the State throughout the year," and the salaries of all General Association employees would be reduced on a percentage basis.[45]

The recognition of the need to streamline the work of the General Association came none too soon. From a financial standpoint, 1933 proved to be the "most trying" year in the history of Kentucky Baptists. Cooperative Program offerings declined steadily throughout the year, and in 1933 the leaders decided to close Bethel College the following year. The funding for Baptist children's homes in Louisville and Glendale reached a crisis by 1934 as well. In that year, the General Association initiated a Thanksgiving offering to help. The depression also diminished activity at Kentucky Baptist "summer assemblies," the popular annual programs designed to provide instruction as well as inspiration for clergy and laity. Assemblies at Georgetown College from 1908 to 1931—known as the "Kentucky Baptist Assembly"—at Dawson Springs from 1910 to 1914 and Bethel College from 1915 to 1924—the "West Kentucky Baptist Assembly—no longer provided programs. By the depression years, the "Clear Creek Mountain Springs Assembly," developed from the purchase of some 450 acres of land near Pineville in southeastern Kentucky in 1924, remained as the only summer assembly in the state.[46]

By 1934, Kentucky Baptists owed in "outstanding obligation" $668,270. The debt, itemized institutionally, indicated the degree of concern for the well-being, if not the survival, of various areas of state Baptist work: the Kentucky Baptist Children's Home, $28,000; Kentucky Baptist Hospital, $302,000; Georgetown College, $143,062; Bethel Woman's College, $86,000; Campbellsville College, $13,500; Cumberland College, $30,000; and the

State Mission Board, $65,708. The executive board, concluding that "the time has arrived, when serious attention must be given to the liquidation of this debt," proposed that Kentucky Baptists adopt the Hundred Thousand Club debt-paying plan of the Southern Baptist Convention. Under this plan, raised funds would be equally divided between Kentucky Baptist and Southern Baptist causes. Of Kentucky's percentage, 50 percent would go directly to aid the Kentucky Baptist Hospital. The plan, adopted at the annual SBC convention in 1933, was designed to secure one hundred thousand subscriptions of one dollar per month to be used to pay existing debts of state and Southern Baptist Convention causes.[47]

Well-laid plans to deal with the debt and the efficient reorganization of the structure of the General Association indicated the degree that Baptists sought to deal with the hard times of the depression years. Despite economic difficulties, however, Kentucky Baptist churches continued—encouragingly—to add to enrollments and programs. By 1936, Baptists boasted of 80 associations, 2,066 churches, and 368,217 members. In 1936 alone, churches reported 14,835 baptisms, and the state's Woman's Missionary Union had increased from 2,097 organizations to 2,251. In the area of giving, as always, the WMU led the way. Kentucky Baptist women gave gifts totalling $168,273.89, fully $18,120.22 more than in 1935. WMU gifts were indeed substantial when compared to the total offerings of $375,764.98, a gain of $37,325.92 over the previous year, given by all Kentucky Baptist churches.[48]

Kentucky Baptist women continued to serve as inspirational examples of courage in the depression years. A long heritage of faith and practice was recalled at the state WMU's annual meeting in Winchester in 1936. Mrs. Joe Dills, in 1896 one of four charter members of the first missionary society in the Boone's Creek Association, recalled her experience of leading a "Sunbeam Band" at the turn-of-the-century. In one meeting a small girl offered this prayer: "God make me a missionary like you would have me to be." The girl, Helen Ford, eventually became a Sunbeam leader and still later a missionary to Brazil.[49]

Baptist men and women learned to rely on prayer in the depression years of the 1930s, but Baptist women in Kentucky institutionalized a program of prayer by joining the Intercessory League of the the SBC in 1933. An "Inner Circle" of prayer partners, determined to enlist shut-ins and elder believers in prayer groups around the state, the Intercessory League enlisted hundreds of "inactive women" in "this phase of the work." At the time of the initiation of the league, one WMU leader was convinced of the power of prayer: "Far reaching could be the results, for more things are wrought by prayer than people dream of and every individual may have a part."[50] Baptist women continued to influence the work of Kentucky and Southern Baptists through prayer and through the Annie Armstrong offering for home missions. Formerly the "Self-Denial Offering," the name was changed in 1933 to honor the early Baptist leader.

In 1936, a group of Kentucky Baptist pastors received special recognition. Eight had served at the same church for a quarter-century, "through the perilous years" of World War I, through the twenties, and the depression that followed: D. S. Smith, Annville, and T. P. Edwards, Chestnut Stand, for twenty-five years; Benjamin Connaway, Providence, First, and J. W. Campbell, Bullittsburg, for twenty-six years; Fount Brock, Mt. Ararat, for twenty-seven years; T. C. Ecton, Calvary in Lexington, and W. T. Parrish, Boiling Springs, for thirty-one years; and John T. Cunningham, Oak Grove, for forty-six years.[51] The long tenures of these pastors was remarkable when considering the trying times in which they served.

Kentucky Baptists also made an impact on Southern Baptist affairs outside the state. Following E. Y. Mullins as president of Southern Seminary, John R. Sampey served as president of the Southern Baptist Convention from 1935 to 1938. A native of Alabama, Sampey attended Howard University in Birmingham and later Southern Seminary, where he studied under Boyce, Broadus, Manly, and Whitsitt. At first, Sampey felt called to service as a foreign missionary, but President Broadus persuaded him to stay on at the seminary to teach following his graduation in 1885. Assisting the great Broadus in New Testament and homiletics, Sampey also encountered A. T. Robertson as a student in one of his Greek classes. When Robertson graduated, Sampey voluntarily—selflessly—stepped aside in New Testament and Greek to make room for the brilliant Robertson. Following four years of "intense concentration on the study of the Old Testament," Sampey then began his distinguished career as an Old Testament scholar. His versatility was astounding; he served on the International Sunday School Committee for forty-six years, helped found (along with Robertson) the Baptist World Alliance, and even served as seminary librarian from 1894 to 1928.[52]

Sampey's tenure as president of the seminary—from 1929 to 1942—spanned the years of the Great Depression. Following Mullins's death in 1928, Sampey served as acting president until the following year when he was named president. Through an aggressive building campaign, Mullins secured pledges to pay for the new construction at the Beeches. With the crash, however, thousands of dollars in pledges were not honored, and Sampey found himself strapped with a building debt of $992,000. Through Sampey's determination and perseverance, and through the sacrifices of the seminary faculty—salary cuts were endured—the seminary avoided foreclosure, and by the end of Sampey's tenure the debt was liquidated.

John R. Sampey, Old Testament professor,
Southern Seminary president, 1929-1942

The seminary actually experienced steady growth during the depression years. An attendance of 353 in 1934 grew to almost 500 by 1942. The depression years were busy ones for the president. Not only did he preside over administrative affairs on campus, but Sampey rose to the forefront of convention affairs in the United States and abroad. Following his tenure as president of the SBC from 1935 to 1938, he preached in Japan and China. In 1937, he served as the Southern Baptist representative to Oxford's Conference on Life and Work, and in 1939 to the Conference on Faith and Order in Edinburgh. At his retirement as seminary president in 1942, he had served the institution as teacher and administrator for fifty-seven years.[53] In 1931, the seminary endowed the John R. Sampey Chair of Old Testament Interpretation to honor its teacher, president, and friend.[54]

The courage of leaders like John R. Sampey inspired Kentucky Baptists—indeed Baptists around the nation and around the world—during the Great Depression. The perseverance of thousands of other Kentucky Baptist men and women prompted inspiration, too. Their quiet determination through the hard years of the depression later provided vivid memories of lives well lived in sometimes desperate circumstances. Julia Woodward, a young wife and mother in the depression years, would later serve two terms as president of the state WMU. The Lexingtonian recalled that "we brought our family up in the very middle of the depression," and "I am grateful today for the effects of the Great Depression." "We had nothing, but I think our family formed a closeness during that time. There wasn't anything to do except to depend on each other; that was a necessity."[55]

Families depended on each other, but also on the church. Mrs. Woodward recalled that "we were so church involved. Of course, offerings were down. People gave what they could, but we were so involved trying to keep ourselves together." Despite hard times, "people probably were more regular at church. They turned to the Lord because there wasn't anyone else to turn to."[56]

Kathryn Jasper Akridge, later the executive director of Kentucky's WMU, agreed that the church "was the center of our lives. Everything we did was pretty much centered around the church. It influenced every part of our lives." Mrs. Akridge remembered that she was "reared back in the days where if we had a revival, school was dismissed while the revival services went on like from 10:00 to 11:00." According to her, "it was a different concept altogether than what it is today. And that influenced my life tremendously. Everything that was going on of any consequence was at church."[57]

At times—despite the solace of family and church—the problems of the economic collapse seemed insurmountable. Such was the case in 1937. In that year, many Kentuckians felt they had weathered the worst of the depression: unemployment, terrible drought, financial disaster. Surely, the worst was over. But then the flood waters came.

Less than seven years after the months of drought in the summer and fall of 1930, record precipitation in January 1937 swelled rivers across the state. Martial law was declared in Maysville and Louisville. All businesses were closed in Carrollton. Paducah "was virtually abandoned," and half of downtown Frankfort was inundated. In the state capital, flood waters isolated the Old State House, and prisoners had to be evacuated from the nearby Kentucky State Prison. In all, damage was estimated at $250 million. Kentucky historian James C. Klotter has written that "dead animals filled the streets and rivers; homeless people sought shelter throughout the area; the economy once more was devastated."[58]

Frank Masters concluded that "all Christian work was at a standstill in all the flooded areas for weeks." Dixie Mylum, a future leader in state WMU work, attended the seminary training school for women in Louisville in the mid-1930s. She remembered that the training school, then located on Broadway, dismissed classes for two weeks during the flood. Some 250,000 of Louisville's 350,000 residents were evacuated. The *Western Recorder* reported that employees, with flood-filled homes, were housed in the paper's offices for weeks. Flood waters damaged church property, as well as homes.[59]

The flood, coupled with Georgetown College's continuing Sherwood controversy, detracted from the General Association's centennial celebration at the annual meeting in 1937. A review of Baptist achievements since the General Association's founding in 1837, special addresses, and historical papers printed in the *Western Recorder* marked the yearlong observance. At the annual meeting, the State Missions report emphasized "a century of missionary progress in Kentucky." A comparative chart revealed the changes of a hundred years:

1837	**1937**
One Baptist to twenty in population	One Baptist to seven in population
43 associations	80 associations
664 churches	2,043 churches
39,269 members	351,555 members
200 to 250 ministers	2,451 ministers
$643.03 raised for all purposes	$380,494.10 raised for all purposes.[60]

Historian and minister William D. Nowlin delivered an address titled "The Challenge of a Hundred Years of Achievements," and F. M. Powell preached a centennial message on "One Hundred Years! 1837-1937," in which he challenged Kentucky Baptists to persevere. Powell agreed that "Christianity is on trial as never before, but where Christianity is evident this debt-ridden, sin-weary, war-crazed, and dictator-ruled world is turning to it." The preacher concluded that "what Baptists are and do in these precious, pregnant, present years, will largely determine Christian history for the coming century." Both addresses were particularly poignant given the most recent challenges faced by Kentucky Baptists.[61] Despite the challenges presented by flood and controversy, and the looming spectre of a European war that threatened to spread worldwide, Kentucky Baptists pushed ahead.

4

chapter

War and Worship: Kentucky Baptists and the Impact of World War II 1938-1945

"Three sons were called by Uncle Sam and two will not return."[1] The words that accompanied the photographs of the fallen Kentucky World War II soldiers provided little more than a terse biographical account of their brief life pilgrimages. Perhaps the subtitle of the July 19, 1945, *Western Recorder* article said it all: "Somerset Parents Lose Two Heroes." The brothers, Chaplain Hubert E. Thompson, Jr.—killed when his plane, attacked by German Stuka bombers, crashed near Sbeitle, Tunisia—and Sergeant Garland Lee Thompson—wounded and killed in the Normandy invasion—were both buried in foreign graves. Their church home had been the High Street Baptist Church in Somerset, and surely their decisions for Christ provided solace for their Kentucky families back home.

Only a month before the *Western Recorder* reported the tragic news of the deaths of the Thompson brothers in 1945, the state Baptist paper published a series of articles hailing the victory of Kentucky Baptists over financial debt. "For the first time in more than a century," the writer rejoiced, "the Baptist denomination in Kentucky is free from indebtedness."[2] Not since the founding of Georgetown College in 1829 had the General Association been debt-free. The oversubscription of the Seventy-five Million Campaign, and especially the hard times of the Great Depression, had plunged Kentucky Baptists into financial despair.

Now the debilitating interest payments were no more, and Baptists in Kentucky could send money to the state treasurer assured that the offerings would go directly to state, home, and foreign mission causes and "that not one penny of it has been deducted for interest charges." A photograph showed a determined secretary-treasurer, J. W. Black, surrounded by other state Baptist leaders "diligently searching records . . . for a possible debtless year" before 1945. The examination was fruitless. History had been made.

Notes of congratulations poured in from around the state and from all over the South. Powhatan W. James, the president of Bethel Woman's College, asserted that the "achievement marks the beginning of a new era of Christian Education as fostered by Baptists in Kentucky." Ellis A. Fuller, the president of the Southern Baptist Theological Seminary, expressed a distinct sensation of "feeling good all over." And E. F. Glenn, the superintendent of the Kentucky Baptist Children's Home, was simply ecstatic: "How refreshing to breathe the pure air of a debtless atmosphere, free from the 'odors' and notes and bonds! How exhilarating! How stimulating!"[3]

The range of emotions—expressed only a month apart—between news of the deaths of the Thompson brothers and the letters of congratulations for a debt-free General Association of Baptists marked all the years of the leadership of J. W. Black, years that coincided with World War II. Indeed, the period in Kentucky Baptist life from 1938 to 1945 proved to be tumultuous as well as exhilarating. At the same time, these years paved the way for a greater advance for Kentucky Baptists in the postwar period.

In 1938, of course, it was impossible to foresee the circuitous route that Kentucky Baptists and the rest of the nation would take as the lingering financial disaster of the depression was finally left behind. Having led Kentucky Baptists through the worst of those years, Calvin M. Thompson retired on June 30, 1938, after sixteen years as the general secretary and treasurer of the General Association. So appreciative was the General Association of his work that provisions were made to pay the retiring leader one hundred dollars a month for the remainder of his life.[4]

Victor Masters, editor of the *Western Recorder*, hailed Thompson for bringing stability to the General Association. Thompson had performed his tasks, he said, "with quietness and with no confidence in anything remotely akin to sensationalism." The fact that Kentucky Baptists had contributed more than eleven million dollars to denominational work during Thompson's tenure was "testimony to their devotion and to the leadership of Dr. Thompson as General Secretary." Most significant, the editor pointed to the absence of bitterness and strife among Kentucky Baptists. A committee of the executive board, made up of Lewis C. Ray, George E. Hays, and T. C. Ecton, agreed. When Thompson became secretary in 1921, the committee remembered that "factions of long standing among our Kentucky brotherhood" with "doctrinal differences, and sharp divisions as to policies and leadership" divided the fellowship. Under Thompson, the differences seemed to diminish, and "now Kentucky Baptists are united in a measure probably unequalled in the past."[5] Along with Thompson's calm and quiet leadership, the depression and hard times actually strengthened denominational ties as well as the faith of many believers.

The years of the Great Depression were not void of rancor and differences of opinion. The 1938 Democratic senatorial primary, pitting Governor A. B. "Happy" Chandler against incumbent Alben W. Barkley and FDR's New Deal, divided Kentuckians. Despite Barkley's handy victory, seemingly a validation for the New Deal, editorials in the *Western Recorder* made clear the disenchantment of some Kentucky Baptists with the president's program. Southern Seminary faculty denounced a proposed congressional bill to strike out a clause in the original 1935 Social Security Act excluding ministers and churches from taxation. In 1940, pastors in northern Kentucky voiced similar concerns about the preservation of the historic Baptist belief in the separation of church and state by decrying Roosevelt's appointment of an American envoy to the Vatican. Writing for the pastors, Jesse M. Rogers of Fort Thomas feared that the "doctrine of the separation of Church and State for which our forefathers suffered, bled, and died, is about to be lost."[6]

One *Western Recorder* writer asserted that "our national government has been spending billions of dollars on what it calls the New Deal. It is now forty billions of dollars in debt because of it, and has only started its spending." What was needed, according to the writer, was not a New Deal, but rather an "Old Deal." This "Old Deal" was nineteen hundred years old: "Seek ye first the kingdom of God and his righteousness and all these things will be added unto you." If Christians would only "obey this Old Deal, as we promised we would, all the good things the New Deals are striving for and failing to get, would be obtained speedily—yes, in ten days!" Another Baptist pastor, C. W. Elsey of Shelbyville, took a more indirect jab at FDR when he accepted his reelection as moderator of the General Association in 1940. Upon resuming the chair, Elsey brought "gales of laughter" from the gathered messengers when he "drawled out" in his usual way, "Now remember, brethren, this was not for a third term."[7]

While New Deal politics provided topics of lively debate for all Americans, meeting sites for the annual meetings of the General Association presented a more parochial source of concern for some Kentucky Baptists. Joseph Gaines from Glasgow expressed dismay that the site chosen for the 1938 meeting was Murray in far western Kentucky. The issue of the appointment of a new general secretary and issues concerning Baptist schools and colleges remained undecided, and Gaines feared that Murray's location would keep messengers from attending. Stung by the criticism, Murray pastor Sam P. Martin replied in an "Open Letter to Kentucky Baptists" in the October 27, 1938, issue of the *Western Recorder*. Martin and former pastor J. E. Skinner had worked hard to improve the Murray church's relationship with the General Association, a relationship that had remained strained in the latter years of the pastorate of H. Boyce Taylor. Martin assured Kentucky Baptists that despite Murray's location, "we are all brethren and deeply interested in the advancement of the kingdom of our Lord." The Murray pastor invited messengers to "come to Murray, we will do our best to make you happy."[8]

Apparently, Martin fulfilled his promise. The *Western Recorder* asserted that the 1938 meeting "was considered to be one of the best for years." A reporter wrote that "it would not be too much to use superlative terms to describe how the visitors were charmed with the hospitality of Murray Baptists and their friends." The attendance was larger than in past meetings. As usual, messengers sang hymns, heard sermons, voted on resolutions, and accepted reports. Financial reports by various state agencies were encouraging. Debts for state missions and the Kentucky Baptist Hospital were significantly reduced despite the lingering depression, and churches reported 16,807 baptisms, a gain of 3,095 over the previous year. A new department of the General Association began operations in 1938, the Baptist Student Union. Designed to develop "Kentucky Baptist students for denominational leadership and to magnify Christ on every college campus," BSU work in Kentucky—a child of the Great Depression—made an immediate, dramatic imprint on the campuses of both denominational and state institutions.[9]

A Baptist Student Union report was read at the 1938 meeting for the first time. The report of the Executive Board was notably silent about the board's progress in securing a successor to C. M. Thompson.[10] It was not until the board's December 6 annual meeting two weeks after the General Association gathering that a decision was made. At that meeting, almost a year after Thompson's retirement, the board appointed the distinguished pastor John William Black, chosen earlier as the moderator-elect of the General Association.

The sixty-one-year-old pastor of the Latonia Baptist Church in Covington immediately resigned his pastorate to assume his new duties. Black's pilgrimage to the top post in Kentucky Baptist affairs was remarkable in many respects. Born in Rowan County, he taught school, then studied law, passing the bar exam in 1908. He was elected County Attorney of Rowan County six years later. Having already made a profession of faith, the young lawyer felt the call to preach two years into his tenure as County Attorney. Black pastored two small churches while serving simultaneously as County Attorney. In 1918, however, he decided to devote his full energies to the ministry. He pastored churches at Morehead, Jackson, and Dry Ridge, before his call to Latonia, where he served for almost thirteen years before being named to the association post.[11]

Despite the encouraging reports at the 1938 annual meeting, the new general secretary faced a daunting task. Ministers and their church members, devastated by the 1937 flood and discouraged from years of financial strain from the depression, presented Kentucky Baptist leaders with a formidable challenge, and Black did not shy away from the challenge. He made clear his threefold program, his priorities of ministry and leadership: "First, to bring about a spirit of unity among Kentucky Baptists;

second, to work out a well-rounded State Mission Program, and develop in the churches a State Mission conscience; and, third, to promote in Kentucky, the whole program of Southern Baptists." His leadership would be crucial as Kentucky Baptists faced a world wracked by depression and war.[12]

In a letter printed in the *Western Recorder*, the new general secretary thanked Kentucky Baptists for their "manifestation of confidence" in a letter printed in the *Western Recorder*. Black was convinced that he would "have the united support of the brethren in all parts of the State." He made plain his stance for "certain well-defined principles in Baptist life":

J. W. Black, executive secretary of Kentucky Baptists, 1939-1945

> The sovereign right of a Baptist church, however large or small, or wherever located, to manage its own affairs free from all outside interference, and that the pastor called and set in the church by the Holy Spirit is God's man and spiritual leader of His people. And further that these independent churches have the sovereign right, if they choose, to co-operate in carrying forward Christ's program for his churches as expressed by the Great Commission. This principle is wrapped up in the Co-operative Program of Southern Baptists which includes our own state.[13]

The regard for Black in his Latonia church was unquestioned. Northern Kentucky Baptists in and around Covington paid tribute to him with a "testimonial dinner" on January 23, 1939. T. C. Sleete, pastor of Covington's Immanuel Baptist Church, served as master of ceremonies, and various pastors from the North Kentucky Baptist Pastors' Conference praised the new state Baptist leader with "two-minute testimonials." A resolution prepared by the executive board of the North Bend Association described Black as "a true Christian gentleman, a man of wide experience, one who lends himself to co-operation." "He possesses the qualities of an executive, a missionary, an evangelist and an under shepherd," it declared, "and is thoroughly indoctrinated in the revealed faith that has made Baptists a great and distinctive people."[14]

These qualities would serve Black well in the trying years ahead. And the resolution also sounded the themes that he would emphasize during his tenure as the state Baptist leader: cooperation, unity, and integrity. Black immediately made clear his intention to represent all Kentucky Baptists, not just his familiar northern Kentucky constituency. In April, he traveled to eastern Kentucky, an area previously neglected in denominational initiatives. Black spoke and held "round table" discussions at five regional conferences in Pineville, Hazard, Paintsville, Ashland, and Maysville. The new leader asserted that he was "deeply interested in every man who has a problem connected with our work in Kentucky."[15]

At conferences around the state, Black emphasized the need to deal with debts lingering from the disappointing Seventy-five Million Campaign. He knew that systematic tithing by individual men and women in Baptist churches would solve the financial woes of the denomination. Members such as J. H. Anderson of Hopkinsville were already aware of the personal "spiritual blessings of tithing." By 1938, Anderson had been "fifty years a tither." As he related to students at Southern Seminary's Founders Day, when he decided to open the "Lord's Account" on his ledger, he experienced "an ever-increasing joy and satisfaction."[16]

Black encouraged other Kentucky Baptists to follow Anderson's example by participating in the "Hundred Thousand Club" of the Southern Baptist Convention. Adopted in 1933 by the SBC to secure one hundred thousand one-dollar-per-month subscriptions, the General Association of Baptists in Kentucky joined the effort in 1935 for the specific purpose of paying off state and SBC debts. Funds from the plan would be divided on a fifty-fifty basis for state and southwide causes, and, according to Black, the plan worked well. The general secretary-treasurer reported that since Kentucky's adoption of the plan in 1935, Kentucky Baptists had contributed $70,397.82. In the state, funds were distributed to apply to debts of the Kentucky Baptist Hospital, the State Board of Missions, the Kentucky Baptist Children's Home, and Bethel Woman's, Cumberland, and Campbellsville Colleges. Funds were not allocated for Georgetown College, however, because of the lingering Sherwood controversy there.[17]

With the continuing success of the plan, Black encouraged more Baptists to participate. In 1939, Lewis C. Ray, a member of the Kentucky Baptist Hundred Thousand Club Committee, outlined the "history and work" of the club in the February 16 issue of the *Western Recorder*. Testimonials poured in from all over the state. John R. Sampey, the president of Southern Seminary, wrote that the plan "pays our debts and satisfies creditors." Letters from Benton to Fort Thomas, and from each of the state agency leaders, attested to the plan's widespread popularity.[18] Pastors in city and rural churches alike were urged to promote the plan even more vigorously to their congregations. Black's emphasis on dealing with Baptist indebtedness paid dividends: debts gradually diminished in the early 1940s.

Black, Kentucky Baptists, and all Americans found themselves distracted increasingly by world events in the late 1930s and early 1940s. Significantly, Black assumed his duties as general secretary-treasurer in 1939, the year Adolf Hitler's invasion of Poland ignited World War II. Already, the pages of the *Western Recorder* were filled with references to war, totalitarianism, and world affairs. As early as April 20, 1939, Charles B. Veach from Williamsburg posed the question, "Can the World Find Peace?" in a letter to the state Baptist paper. Veach's letter offered a chilling reminder of the disaster of a world at war: "At the present time some of the world's nations are engaged in deadly combat, destroying countless lives and bringing about untold property damage, wrecking beautiful, artistic buildings with their valuable contents, murdering innocent, helpless women and children in cold blood! Could peace ever be bought in such a way?" While nations like the United States remained neutral, Veach wrote that "each nation waits in a state of nervous expectancy, wondering what the next step of the other nations will be." Veach concluded that peace would come only "by implanting the Christ in the hearts and minds of the people of every nation."[19]

Other articles with titles like "World Domination and Universal Peace" were published regularly in the *Western Recorder*. Baptists argued over the merits of pacifism versus a "just" war. Remarkably, W. C. Taylor, a foreign missionary to Brazil and the brother of H. Boyce Taylor, argued against absolute, doctrinaire pacifism in an article titled "Be Fair to Jesus, Pacifist!" H. Boyce Taylor had expressed pacifist views in Murray during World War I. W. C. Taylor himself had recently witnessed a pageant performed in a foreign mission program at Ridgecrest, the Baptist retreat in North Carolina, in which his son played a combatant who fell "before guns in the hands of soldiers." Taylor watched his son "lie motionless on the simulated field of battle" and knew "that is the way it might be, if we were drawn into war." Still, W. C. Taylor was convinced that pacifism along with "propaganda against the doctrine of Hell is doing more to undermine faith among students than any single hostility to New Testament truth in our Southern student life."[20]

Editorials written by Victor Masters in the *Western Recorder* concluded that "war has a place in the plans of God." Masters chided "our pacifist friends" who relied on the Sermon on the Mount for scriptural support of non-resistance. Christ himself, he said, will "come to this earth as a great warrior, marshalling the hosts of heaven against all the hordes of Satan and sin." The editor continued, "For in winning for us an eternal citizenship in glory our Lord is no pacifist. He is the victorious God of battle, who puts down all sin and wickedness and who has on His vesture at His Second Coming to earth, 'King of Kings and Lord of Lords.'"[21]

Lest Baptists should become overzealous warmongers, Masters in January 1941 published an article by the Baptist ethicist T. B. Maston about "Baptists and Conscientious Objectors." Maston, a professor at Southwestern Baptist Theological Seminary, warned that because of the historic Baptist belief in liberty of conscience, "Baptists cannot be consistent unless they defend and respect the rights of the conscientious objector." Masters concluded that while Christians might disagree with the pacifist's position, "anyone who is willing for the sake of religious convictions to suffer the social ostracism and ridicule that a position entails should be respected."[22]

Several *Western Recorder* writers equated European affairs with spiritual concerns among Baptists. George Ragland, the pastor of Lexington's First Baptist Church, compared Hitler's "fifth column activities" with similar diversions that threatened the church. Just as subversive Nazi "fifth columnists" weakened European countries from within, subversive forces weakened churches as well. Ragland, citing a *Lexington Leader* column that described the confusion created by Nazi agents in Holland dressed in the uniforms of Dutch soldiers, argued that "what the fifth column is now doing in national activities, a fifth column is doing in religious activities." "It is certain," the minister asserted, "that fifth column activities in a spiritual sense are going on here—certainly here in America, definitely here in Lexington." While Ragland feared "false brethren" determined to undermine the church in Lexington, other writers suggested a movement toward totalitarianism in religion. Some Kentucky Baptist leaders feared that the Federal Council of Churches represented "fifth-columnists-in-chief this hour to deceive God's people into a totalitarianism that is at bottom as spiritually warped and disobedient to God as the Papal system."[23]

At the same time, Hoyt E. Porter of Hyden was concerned about the immediate tragedy of the war for millions of dislocated victims. Porter argued that with "more than 5,000,000 people said already to have been swept from their homes by the fiery lava stream of war," Kentucky Baptists must "awaken fully to this previously undreamed-of opportunity to witness to the multitudes of helpless, and often hopeless, men, women, and children." The writer ended his plea with a bold admonition, "LET US PRAY! LET US PREPARE! LET US SEND! LET US GO!"[24]

Although Porter issued his plea in August 1940, it was another year and a half before Americans officially entered that war on the side of the Allies. Kentuckians had witnessed, along with the rest of the world, the Italian invasion of helpless Ethiopia; the German advance into Austria, Czechoslovakia, and Poland; and the Japanese conquest of parts of China. With the exception of isolationist mountain Republican John M. Robsion, Kentucky's congressmen had voted with the majority on measures concerning neutrality and defense spending.[25] When Japanese pilots bombed Pearl Harbor on December 7, 1941, a day, in President Roosevelt's words, that would "live in infamy," it was Howell Forgy, a Presbyterian minister from Murray, Kentucky, and a chaplain for the USS *New Orleans* who cried out in the middle of the attack, "Praise the Lord and pass the ammunition." Kentucky Baptists could sympathize with the Presbyterian chaplain as emotions—a mixture of anger and relief—were soon replaced by determination to win the war.

Only a short article made note of the Pearl Harbor attack in the December 11, 1941, issue of the *Western Recorder*. "America has been forced to wake up to the fact that the Republic is at war with Japan," the writer declared; and "American Christians are under the necessity, along with all other citizens, of adjusting themselves to this vast bulking fact." Although the "cost to America was bitter of the first blow struck by Japan. Yet in a certain high way we see it as a blessing of God. Within an hour's time of the flash throughout America of Knowledge of the perfidy of the Japanese attack there had been accomplished a unification of all elements within this nation and which . . . will not fail before this war is ended to bring to defeat and powerlessness the mad scheme of world rule by conquest and enslavement of free peoples." The writer could not help but associate the Japanese attack with philosophies alien to Christianity:

> To us the major significance of this treachery and perfidy by a nation still claiming to be friendly, is to be found in the worse than beastly assumptions of the new Superman Philosophy which was born in Germany, and lies at the bottom of the course it has diligently pursued since the first World War. Into this superman philosophy Italy and Japan are now drawn by like-minded leadership. Whatever may betide America and other so-called Christian nations in this great world holocaust, it is of deepest importance that it shall strike home to the hearts of all who in sincerity believe in a fear and love of God, that the way of Liberal philosophy is the way of a sliding scale on a slick surface, leaving God out and ruling mankind by super-beast tactics.[26]

It did not take long for the United States, already under a policy of preparedness, to gear up for war. Kentucky Baptist churches lent support and honored soldiers preparing for battle. Less than two weeks after the Pearl Harbor attack, the churches of Elizabethtown hosted more than 150 officers and soldiers of the Fifth Armored Division. The soldiers were transported in a truck convoy from Fort Knox to attend morning worship services at Elizabethtown's Severns Valley Baptist Church. After the service, the men were entertained in church members' homes for lunch. That evening a united service in the high school auditorium was attended by over twelve hundred, about half of whom were soldiers. The Army Band and the Fifth Armored Chorus provided a "wonderful program of inspiring and worshipful music," and Chaplain Owen W. Moran "brought a strong Gospel message."[27]

The service served as a spiritual prelude to the horrific years ahead. Before the end of the war, 306,715 Kentuckians would enter various branches of the armed forces. Kentuckians, thousands of them Baptists by denominational preference, fought and died in every theater of the war. Eight thousand Kentuckians never returned to their bluegrass homes.[28] Local papers and the *Western Recorder* reported news—good and bad—about local soldiers. The January 7, 1943, issue of the *Recorder*, for example, published a photograph of a smiling Lillard Bishop. Posed in his Navy uniform, young Bishop had escaped a troop transport ship after the vessel was torpedoed by a German submarine off the coast of Casablanca in north Africa. He had learned to swim in the Nolin River as a boy while living at the Kentucky Baptist Children's Home at Glendale and thus was "thoroughly prepared to abandon ship" when the time came.[29]

Others were not so fortunate. The war's tragic toll was most deeply felt by parents, spouses, and children left behind. The *Western Recorder* printed a growing number of photographs of fallen servicemen. Lieutenant James S. Rogers, Jr., from Covington, an officer in the Naval Reserve, was called into active duty before Pearl Harbor. Later commissioned a lieutenant in the Marine Air Corps, he lost his life when his plane crashed in the Pacific. Former pastor Lewis C. Ray remembered that, while away, Rogers still regularly sent back to his local Latonia church his tithes and offerings: "His quiet unassuming spirit made one know of his sterling character." Ray described a moving service of tribute at his local church, in which Rogers's long-time pastor and current secretary-treasurer of the General Association, J. W. Black, returned to speak. Rogers's parents and sister, Ray wrote, could be consoled in knowing that their family member was "a noble Christian, and gave his life in what he believed to be for the good of humanity."[30]

Another short article reported the death of Pfc. John W. Gregory. Only twenty-three, Gregory was killed in action on October 13, 1943, on the Volturna River while serving with the Fifth Army in Italy. "Loved by all who knew him," Gregory had accepted Christ as his Saviour and joined the Sorgho Baptist Church only two years before his death.[31] In 1944, Paul Cagle, the son of A. F. Cagle, pastor of Third Baptist Church in Owensboro, became another casualty of war. Cagle had joined the British Army as an ambulance driver after being turned down by the United States Army and Navy because of poor hearing. He was killed in action—literally while saving the lives of others—taking wounded soldiers from the front.

In tragic irony, news of young Cagle's death reached his father as the elder Cagle was en route to Omaha, Nebraska, to attend an annual reunion of his World War I regiment. A chaplain for the regiment in France, Cagle was to speak on the subject of "Death." The parting words of the dying son remained etched in the memories of his parents and others that recalled his life: "If I saved the life of only one man, my service at the battlefront will not have been in vain."[32]

The *Recorder* article on Cagle's tragic death was accompanied by a poem titled "This Son of Mine":

> I saw him go—this son of mine,
> That day, when hardly six, he started off to school
> He seemed so small—and yet
> I knew he did not seem so to himself
> Had he not said to me, "I'm a big boy now, see how tall,
> You needn't call me darling any more, just call me Paul."
>
> I let him go—I knew it had to be,
> The time had come.
> No longer could I hold him, close and sheltered, there at home.
> I asked myself, "would I, if I could?"
> The answer came, "No, it is for his good."
>
> Again, I saw him go—this son of mine;
> This time he was a youth
> I wonder why
> This boy, who once shared all with me, was now so shy—
> I seemed left out.
> Try as I might, whose confidences, once so frank and free
> Were shut up tight—and I must wait.
>
> So again, I let him go—There was naught else that I could do—
> As I waited, trembling, alone,
> I knew that God was speaking to my son—
> "It is at times like these," I said,
> "That boys grow up and men are made."
> Yesterday, once more I saw him go—this son of mine;
> A young man now—and yet
> It seems so short a while, since he first came to share our home.
> He looks like such a lad—
> But he had heard the call to service, and was gone.[33]

The deaths of Rogers, Gregory, and Cagle represented thousands of Kentuckians who paid the supreme sacrifice in World War II. Heart-wrenching poems provided little solace for those left behind. Stories about the constancy of the faith of many soldiers, faith made more real on the battlefield, provided inspirational reminders that strengthened the faith of thousands of readers back home in Kentucky.

The experience of World War II served as a watershed event for those who fought. Veterans remembered harrowing battles, the loneliness of years away from family and friends, and the forging of new and enduring friendships. If the war provided a watershed event in the lives of thousands of Kentucky soldiers, civilians on the home front remembered, too. The war changed the way people thought and lived. When Marion Palmer Hunt, the long-time Kentucky Baptist pastor and leader, died in 1944, an eloquent eulogy titled "Great Warrior Lays Down Arms" was published in the *Western Recorder*. According to the article, the Baptist minister "surrendered his commission . . . and went to be with his Commander-in-chief, after having served Him as a minister of the Gospel for 59 years."[34] The myriad activities of Hunt's life—pastor, leader of the Anti-Racetrack Gambling movement in the state, initiator of the movement that resulted in the founding of the Kentucky Baptist Hospital, and prolific writer of books and articles—were pictured as campaigns akin to the battles against the evil forces of Hitler or Mussolini or Tojo. Life and death occurrences in the commonwealth during the war years were associated inevitably with the European and Pacific campaigns. And just as M. P. Hunt made significant contributions to Baptist life at home in Kentucky, Baptists contributed to the war effort overseas.

Even before the United States entered the war, Kentucky Baptist ministers sometimes left their congregations to become chaplains in the National Defense program. Captain Clarence Q. Jones, the pastor of the Baptist church at Falmouth, served as a chaplain at Fort Sheridan in Illinois. Using Bibles furnished by the American Bible Society, Sunday School Board materials, and "a folding organ and plenty of Army and Navy hymnals," Jones conducted services for the 350 officers and men of the battalion. Pastors often took leaves of absence from their churches. Such was the case for Reverend Evans T. Mosley, the pastor of Beaver Dam Baptist Church. Mosley left Kentucky for a chaplaincy at the Reception Center at Fort Sill in Oklahoma. He explained in a letter to the *Western Recorder* that three chaplains ministered to 39 officers and 266 enlisted men at the center. Chaplains also worked with thousands of individuals just entering the armed forces; from January to May in 1941, thirteen thousand selective service men were processed at the Fort Sill center.[35]

After Pearl Harbor, chaplains' work became even more crucial. Mosley eventually became the division chaplain in the South Pacific, where his division met Japanese forces in several major engagements. H. B. Woodward, formerly a pastor in Paducah, served as a chaplain late in the war. He recalled the large numbers of wartime professions of faith: "There are always professions in the services. Last year 575 men made professions of faith in

Christ in services which I conducted, the largest number in any one service being 150."[36]

In "God in the Pacific," an article written specifically for the *Western Recorder*, Major Harry W. Hargrove, the assistant chaplain of the 81st Infantry Division, wrote about the "spiritual side" of the duties of a chaplain. Before leaving the states, Hargrove received authority from his home church, the First Baptist Church of Mayfield, to administer baptism to those who made decisions overseas. Hargrove described himself as "the circuit rider of the division"; he typically travelled over a hundred miles on Sundays to conduct numerous worship services. Often subjected to enemy fire, Hargrove stated that men came from huts, tents, and foxholes to join in worship.

Hargrove recalled his conversation with one wounded soldier, covered in bandages:

> With his one free hand he gave me a metal bound testament with a bullet hole almost entirely through the center. This book was in the breast pocket of his jacket and diverted the course of the projectile thus saving his life. No need to say that he was deeply moved to realize that God had used His own book to protect the life of one of His. I said, "It will protect your soul also if you let it," and he answered, with tears showing under his eyelids, "I've read some portion of the scripture and prayed every day." I couldn't help but quote the 91st Psalm just there, "He that dwelleth in the secret place of the most High shall abide under the shadow of the Almighty.[37]

The ministry of Kentucky Baptist chaplains like Jones, Mosley, Woodward, and Hargrove—work that has been neglected in recountings of the Kentucky Baptist influence in the twentieth century—made an imprint on countless lives during the war years.

As reminders to pray for servicemen overseas, local Baptist churches in Kentucky and across the South often posted a "service flag" in a prominent place in the sanctuary or other building. A star on these flags represented each local church member in the armed forces.[38] Church members continued to pray, and pastors often informed congregations about scraps of news from the front.

The war, of course, changed Kentuckians whether they served overseas or remained at home. Certainly, governmental intervention in the economy increased, but, then, the New Deal had already introduced the national government more prominently into the lives of individuals. Governmental rationing of sugar, coffee, butter, and meat, along with tires, fuel oil, and shoes, proved to be a burden for some. The rationing of gasoline was set at around three gallons per family per week. Again, the hard times of the Great Depression, immediately preceding the war, prepared Kentuckians for such sacrifice. Victory gardens furnished vegetables for the home, and generally good weather during the war years helped farm production. No major droughts or floods marred growing seasons or harvests as in the thirties.[39]

While stepped-up war production had a dramatic impact on the American economy, and more than anything else ended the depression, the war disrupted American society. In Kentucky, the state fair did not open in 1942 or 1943, and attendance at the Kentucky Derby was limited to local racing fans because of gasoline rationing. Although attendance at motion pictures increased significantly, college sports teams, with rosters depleted, cancelled seasons. One Kentucky historian has concluded that "Kentuckians knew matters were serious when their sport teams were affected by war."[40]

Kentucky Baptists felt the sting of war in more than one way. A weekly issue of the *Western Recorder* was not published in 1944 because of limitations placed by the War Production Board on the amount of paper stock. Since the *Recorder*'s circulation had grown to more than 30,600, the paper used more than twice as much paper stock than in 1942. Readers were forced to read a shortened version of the paper until the limitation was lifted. Editors reminded Kentucky Baptists in bold, underlined print:

> *We are at war!*
> *Rigid self-denial is the price of victory!*
> *The Western Recorder is your paper and more than ever*
> *before needs your loyal support.*[41]

While the annual meeting of the Southern Baptist Convention was postponed in 1943 and cancelled in 1945, the General Association of Baptists in Kentucky continued to meet yearly during the war years. In 1942, the first annual meeting since Pearl Harbor was held in Princeton. In a gesture of support for Kentucky's only senior Baptist institution following the years of dissension of the Sherwood controversy, Samuel S. Hill, the new president of Georgetown College, was elected moderator. At Princeton, the messengers recognized the years of service of V. I. Masters, who retired from his twenty-one-year editorship of the *Western Recorder*.[42] Masters had already given his "valedictory" in the September 24, 1942, issue of his beloved paper. Acknowledging that "we live in a time of vast and disconcerting world ferment, of the reappraisal of all values, holy revealed faith included," the retiring editor—in typical Masters' fashion—did not mince words: "We live in a crucible. The Axis-powers in World War II are frankly set to establish totalitarian world rule with God left out. Their god is Nietzschean evolutionism. Their open confession of this is a burning Baal challenge to world Christendom, itself now broadly and guiltily attracted by the kitchen odors of the Egyptian fleshpots." Masters concluded that "Baptists have an opportunity vast beyond expression in these days that try men's hearts, if we shall give ourselves to understanding and paying the price of full length return to God."[43]

The new editor, John D. Freeman, was presented at the Princeton meeting. A native of Arkansas, Freeman had served pastorates at West Broadway in Louisville and at Springfield. In 1925, Freeman became editor of the *Baptist and Reflector*, Tennessee's state paper, and then in 1933 was elected as executive secretary of the Tennessee Baptist Convention.[44] Freeman brought his vast experience in Baptist life to his new Kentucky post and continued the *Recorder*'s tradition of providing inspirational articles and practical advice for Kentucky Baptists.

Many pastors, of course, continued to struggle with local financial and spiritual concerns during the World War II years. Pastors emphasized various promotions designed to increase church attendance and to replenish pews left empty by soldiers gone off to war. The *Western Recorder* carried advertisements for bronze-aluminum Sunday School and Training Union registers available at the Baptist Book Store in Louisville. The ad encouraged churches to place one on each side of the church auditorium; the registers allowed members and visitors to track enrollment, attendance, attendance "last Sunday," offerings, offerings "last Sunday," and the number of "daily Bible readers." From the late 1930s, the registers became a popular device to encourage church growth.[45]

The health of rural churches concerned Baptist leaders in the state and across the Southern Baptist Convention in the 1940s. Leaders recognized that thriving rural churches sustained the denomination throughout state and southern conventions. J. W. Jent of Oklahoma Baptist University in Shawnee presented a resolution at the SBC annual meeting in 1940. Jent recognized that the SBC was "rural in its genius" and that "ninety percent of all our churches and seventy percent of our total membership [were located] in the open country or in villages of less than 1,000 population." Jent called for the convention to create a standing Committee on Country Churches for the purpose of developing and supporting rural churches.[46]

The editor of the *Western Recorder* supported Jent's proposal, believing that it would "stir every sympathetic and understanding Baptist heart." The editor cautioned, however, that organization alone would not help; leaders must strive to understand the specific needs of the rural church. The *Western Recorder* did its part to promote rural ministries, publishing articles on rural churches and churches in small county-seat towns. For example, a photograph of the meetinghouse of Leitchfield Baptist Church graced the cover of the *Recorder*'s December 9, 1943, issue. An accompanying article cited Leitchfield as a good example. With a small but stately edifice, the pastor of a church like Leitchfield could "do much to lead in getting rural churches to enlarge their one-room church buildings." The writer lauded Leitchfield's sound organization, an organization that provided solid Sunday School, Training Union, and missions programs.[47]

Before his retirement in 1942, Victor Masters concluded that an obstacle to church growth and prosperity in Kentucky had historically been the reluctance of congregations to pay pastors an adequate salary. Masters asserted that it was obvious in a study of "our Kentucky churches that where the churches have supported their pastors the church has grown and thrived whether in the densely populated or sparsely populated communities." In Kentucky, however, it had taken a long time for Baptists to be convinced that "They who preach the Gospel shall live by the Gospel." A study of the salaries of Baptist pastors indicated that a group of pastors of fifteen large churches had an average salary of $4,209.28 in 1942. In churches with memberships from 1,000 to 1,500, the average was $3,384.50, while churches with memberships of 500 to 1,000 paid average salaries of $2,100.23. For the large group of churches with memberships from 100 to 500, Masters was unable to obtain an accurate assessment. And for churches with fewer than 100 members, the average salary was only $127.53.[48]

Larger churches with large budgets found it easier to attract and retain capable ministers. In 1939, for example, Lexington's Calvary Baptist Church honored their pastor, T. C. Ecton, for thirty years of service. President Lee R. Scarborough, president of Southwestern Seminary and of the Southern Baptist Convention, delivered the sermon at the morning hour. During Ecton's pastorate, 4,485 individuals had been added to the congregation, 1,891 by profession of faith and baptism. Contributions totaled $645,000 during his tenure.[49]

Smaller churches continued to rely on open-air "brush arbor" meetings and revivals led by associational missionaries and pastors at sister churches to bring new members into the church. Pastors unable or unwilling to attend the annual General Association meetings often participated in local associational meetings instead. These meetings, like the larger state meetings, were sometimes inspirational and sometimes controversial. W. W. Wood of Louisville recognized the potential for associational meetings:

"The preacher of the Association Introductory Sermon has the priceless op-portunity to start the Association on a high spiritual plane by a well pre-pared Gospel message. A warm-hearted Gospel sermon, from the preacher's own experience can give spiritual tone to the whole Associational meeting and send the messengers away, resolved to see that their churches make a better showing in every way next year."[50]

Wood admonished leaders to provide prepared reports for the associa-tional meetings. He had been disheartened to attend one meeting in the late 1930s "where there was not one prepared report presented during the two days' session." According to Wood, the lack of organization was "a shame to an intelligent community and to the churches." Wood advised that "if a chairman has twelve months to prepare his report, there can be no good ex-cuse for him to come to the Association and beg some brother to help him write his report under a shade tree at noon on some hot summer day."[51]

As for revivals, the *Western Recorder* encouraged churches to conduct "open-air" preaching services. Outdoor revivals attracted individuals re-luctant to attend conventional services. One writer asserted that the "Methodist revival in England, in which George Whitefield was also a leading factor, went to the open fields. . . . The multitudes flocked to hear them in the fields, the gatherings often numbering many thousands." The writer reminded Kentucky Baptists in 1939 that "our mandate is to go, not to ask sinners to come to us. We are to ask them, when we go, to come to Christ!"[52]

In July 1943, Angel Martinez, the Texas-based preacher described as a "youthful evangelist and earnest contender for the faith," held meetings for the Valley View Baptist Church near Louisville. Martinez had been con-verted at age twelve "through the work done in a Mexican mission near the Alamo in San Antonio." In order to accommodate the expected crowds, an "old-fashioned brush arbor" was constructed for the services. Valley View, founded only in 1940, experienced "one of the most refreshing and fruitful revivals of the season." The revival added 64 members to the church's membership of 121. The number included five pairs of husbands and wives. In all, twenty-five parents were added to the congregation.[53] Revivalists like Angel Martinez, Mordecai Ham, and Gypsy Smith, Jr., had a dramatic im-pact on Kentucky's Baptist churches.

While additions to churches were reported at associational and state Baptist meetings in the late 1930s and early 1940s, Secretary-Treasurer J. W. Black continued to worry about the finances of the General Associa-tion. Particularly distressing were the financial concerns of state Baptist educational institutions. In April 1939, Campbellsville College, already fi-nancially strapped, suffered the loss by fire of the school's administration building. The building housed ten classrooms, several laboratories, and a library. The *Western Recorder* described the fire as "a major loss to the institution, to its supporters and to Baptists of Kentucky."[54] The quick response of alumni and friends of the college resulted in the completion of a new building by November. Local gifts and pledges from around the state, insurance money, and a temporary loan of twenty-two thousand dollars provided funding for the building that would house offices, classrooms, a library, auditorium, and laboratories.[55]

In Williamsburg, Cumberland College also struggled with financial concerns. Like Campbellsville a junior college, Cumberland boasted "a splendid and beautiful campus and a group of nine attractive and serviceable buildings" located in the mountains of southeastern Kentucky. Founded in 1889, the institution, like other Baptist schools, struggled to secure a sufficient endowment for its programs.[56]

At the time of America's entry into World War II, a third Kentucky Baptist junior college, Bethel Woman's College in Hopkinsville, was one of only eight Baptist junior colleges for women in the United States. Founded in 1854, Bethel was "the only college for women of its type" in the commonwealth. J. W. Gaines led the school from 1919 through all the years between the wars until he was succeeded in 1940 by Kenneth R. Patterson. At the May 1939 commencement, three cousins—Professor R. E. Gaines, a dean at the University of Richmond and president of the Foreign Mission Board of the SBC; W. W. Gaines, a Georgetown College graduate and attorney in Atlanta; and Joseph A. Gaines, pastor of the First Baptist Church in Glasgow—assisted President Gaines in the festivities. A writer explained that "during the depression there have been so many losses, that it ought to be a boon to Bethel Woman's College to have so many Gaines."[57]

As with other institutions in the state, Bethel faced serious financial decline during the Great Depression; by 1935, the college's debt stood at $106,914.76. Although the debt was reduced during the early 1940s, the institution in 1942 was forced to close its doors to students, at least temporarily. Soon after its closing, dormitories were used to house officers and enlisted men from nearby Camp Campbell. The college's administration used the income to reduce the debt further and to renovate existing buildings.[58] The hope of school officials to reopen the institution—which, after the closing of Bethel College in Russellville, was the last Baptist institution in western Kentucky—was not fulfilled until 1945, when the Board of Trustees appointed Powhatan W. James as president. James, a law school graduate of the University of Richmond and the son-in-law and biographer of the revered Dallas pastor George W. Truett, was accompanied by his wife, Jesse Jenkins Truett James, a much-loved writer for Sunday School quarterlies and magazines. The *Western Recorder* assured readers that the presence at Bethel of the daughter of "the late lamented and matchless preacher . . . will be a decided asset both to her president-husband and to the young ladies who matriculate there."[59]

The financial plight of colleges like Campbellsville, Cumberland, and Bethel paled in comparison to the theological concerns swirling around Georgetown, the state's only senior Baptist institution, in the late 1930s and into the 1940s. When the college's Board of Trustees appointed Henry Noble Sherwood president in 1934, a dispute concerning his previous pastorate at a Disciples of Christ church threatened both his presidency and the relationship of Georgetown to the General Association of Baptists in Kentucky. J. W. Porter's resolution at the annual General Association meeting at Henderson in 1934 to "withhold all funds from Georgetown College, so long as the college has a President, who had not received baptism authorized by a Baptist church," was substituted with a motion to give the college's board until January 20, 1935, to remove Sherwood. When the board refused, the General Association began in 1935 to hold all funds for the college in reserve.[60] By the late 1930s, while articles praised the work of other Baptist institutions in the state, mention of Georgetown had all but disappeared from the pages of the *Western Recorder*. The dispute continued to cloud sessions of the General Association's annual meetings until Sherwood was finally dismissed in 1941.

After almost a year, Georgetown's board appointed, in 1942, Samuel S. Hill, the pastor of Louisville's Deer Park Baptist Church, a decision cheered by alumni and friends of the college and by Kentucky Baptists generally. Hill had already established a close relationship with the General Association, having served as chair of the Executive Board and on the Board of Trustees of the Kentucky Baptist Hospital. White-haired and handsome, Hill presented the dignified image of a college president, and his educational background—including degrees from the University of Richmond, and master's and doctoral degrees from Southern Seminary— gave him the academic standing needed by a senior Baptist institution.

The *Western Recorder* heralded Hill's appointment: "The wise choice of Georgetown's Trustees should mean general restoration of confidence on the part of all groups in Kentucky Baptist fellowship." And the *Recorder* issued a plea for a restoration of confidence in the school: "We plead that the unfortunate events of the past years shall be forgotten, and as our new President takes up his difficult duties, let every Baptist assure him of our loyal support."[61] Hill's inaugural address, delivered on November 17, 1942, immediately put skeptics at ease. The new president told listeners that the "past is a fixed something we cannot change . . . but we can gather from it much that will assist us in choosing and directing our objectives for today and tomorrow." Hill assured supporters that he would lead the college financially and theologically: "We shall seek to make adequate all our facilities and to establish here through both faculty and students a school which shall be the answer to the desires and prayers of the Baptists of Kentucky." Lifting dramatically his right hand in "pledge to God" and to Kentucky Baptists, Hill promised to "launch a program for a new day at Georgetown."[62]

Hill's electrifying address brought relief to and approbation from the leaders and laity of Baptists in the state. Already, some $47,233 had been released by the General Association after Sherwood's dismissal. With the world at war, however, increases in enrollments and endowment would have to wait. Still, Hill's assurances eased the tension that had marred Georgetown's relationship with the state body.

At the heart of the controversy was the issue of control. In an article written for the *Western Recorder* by Joseph A. Gaines, the Glasgow pastor wrote that while institutional control and financial responsibility should rest entirely in the hands of the boards of trustees of each institution, those boards should be elected by the denomination.[63] Until the 1930s, the ambiguous relationship of Kentucky's Baptist schools to the General Association caused little concern. With the appointment of Sherwood by Georgetown's Board of Trustees in 1934, however, the issue of control came clearly into focus. In 1941, recommendations made by the Committee on Christian Education provided for closer cooperation between Baptist institutions and the General Association. According to the report, schools sharing in Cooperative Program funds could not change school charters or articles without the approval of the General Association. Each school was to present annually to the nominating committee of the General Association two names for each vacancy on its Board of Trustees. From the two names the nominating committee would propose one. The recommendation did not preclude other nominations in General Association sessions.[64]

Upon his appointment as president, Samuel Hill made clear his desire to cooperate fully with the committee's recommendations. When a campaign was launched to raise $1.5 million for Baptist education in the state, Georgetown was again in the good graces of the General Association. By 1943, advertisements for Georgetown, touting the "only senior Baptist College in Kentucky," again graced the pages of the *Western Recorder*.[65] Hill's appointment and leadership as president provided stability for the institution during the war and into the postwar years.

New initiatives begun in the war years had a far-reaching impact on Kentucky Baptists. In 1943, a resolution calling for the creation of the Kentucky

Baptist Foundation was presented at the association's annual meeting in Bowling Green. Later that year, the executive board drafted a charter for the foundation. The new corporation would serve benevolent, educational, and missionary undertakings of the General Association by receiving bequests or gifts "either absolutely or in trust . . . and to administer such property . . . in such manner as in the judgment of the Directors will best promote such objects."[66] When the foundation was "firmly established" the following year, all trust funds held by the General Association were transferred to the new corporation.[67]

With the addition of the Baptist Student Union as a General Association department in 1938, Baptist student work grew in the early 1940s with the appointment of J. Chester Durham as the state student union secretary. Durham was converted in the Baptist church in Berea and while attending Eastern Kentucky State Teachers College became actively involved in the fledgling BSU movement. Following his graduation from Eastern, Durham taught school for a year in Paintsville and then was named as the student secretary of the BSU at Murray State at the other end of the state. In 1943, he was appointed secretary of the state department.[68] His enthusiasm energized a work that was already off to a strong start under A. S. Gillespie.

Baptist Student Unions played an important role on the campuses of denominational and state schools alike during the war years. At Cumberland College, James M. Boswell, the director of education and professor of mathematics and physics, served as a faculty adviser on the State BSU Council. Boswell concluded that because of the BSU, Cumberland students "leave our campus [as] more mature Christians and are better equipped from the standpoint of zeal and knowledge for assuming a leading role in the denominational work." Professor C. C. Ross of the University of Kentucky's Department of Education wrote that the BSU served as the "most constructive religious force among the students on the campus." The president of the University of Kentucky praised BSU work as well. Herman L. Donovan, a staunch friend of any organization that is "keeping students close to their church," hailed the BSU as "a live, vital, dynamic Christian organization on the campus of the University of Kentucky."[69]

From the outset, the state BSU held annual student conventions. These student-led annual meetings attracted large numbers of students from campuses throughout the state. Kentucky Baptist leaders and ministers from across the Southern Baptist Convention addressed the participants and directed various "forums" dealing with important issues of the day. In 1941, the convention met in Hopkinsville. Sessions were held in the auditorium and Sunday School rooms of the First Baptist Church and on the campus of Bethel Woman's College. In the Saturday morning session, students chose to attend one of three forums: "Race Relations," "Present World Conflict," or "Love, Marriage, and the Home."[70]

Over 80 percent of the students attended the session on "Love, Marriage, and the Home" led by the University of Kentucky Professor C. C. Ross. The other sessions, featuring Clarence L. Jordan, superintendent of Long Run Associational Missions, and E. A. McDowell, professor of New Testament interpretation at Southern Seminary, included provocative discussions on world conflict and race. McDowell asked why Baptist students should bother with the race question at all? "We can preach the Gospel and attend our white churches, and go about our business, and be fairly successful as church members and preachers and church workers, without paying any attention to Negroes." McDowell assured the students, however, that Christians have a responsibility to change attitudes of prejudice and injustice because "the Negroes are discriminated against in almost every field in this country which claims to be a democracy." The professor asserted that while black Southerners made up one out of ten of the population, their wealth amounted to only "one-four hundredth" or only $215 in per-capita income compared to $3,000 for whites. McDowell did not mince words as he compared white Southerners to Hitler: "You find all sorts of Hitler's treatment of the Jews in Germany, but in the South we are fifty years ahead of Hitler in our treatment of the Negroes. Hitler has not done anything we have not done to the Negro."[71]

McDowell's effort to arouse Baptist students to see the evils of racism was coupled with only tenuous efforts by the majority of white Baptists in Kentucky. In 1938, black Baptists in the state numbered 90,000 compared to 365,000 white Baptists in churches affiliated with the General Association. The Kentucky Colored Baptist General Association held annual meetings, and the General Association sent a "fraternal messenger" to represent the white body. In 1938, Victor Masters, the *Western Recorder* editor, was commissioned by Moderator W. H. Horton as the messenger. Horton asked Masters to "express the hope that this token of fellowship would be reciprocated . . . by appointing a similar messenger to the white body." Introduced by W. H. Ballew, president of the black convention, and by W. H. Jones, pastor of the Green Street Baptist Church in Louisville, Masters gave a brief address "keyed to the thought that Baptists have a great faith, alone adequate to compose all racial or other group differences, but that most Baptists have not let that great faith in Christ have enough of them." Masters reported on the meeting in the *Western Recorder* and concluded that "there is abundant reason for good cheer in regard to race relations in the South."[72]

The *Western Recorder* regularly reprinted articles from the *National Baptist Voice*, a black Baptist paper "of broad circulation and influence" published in Nashville. Following what some black leaders referred to as the "accommodationist" appeal of Booker T. Washington, the *Voice* called for segregation in the social sphere, a policy endorsed by the editor of the *Western Recorder*. When the Baptist World Alliance met in Atlanta, Georgia, in 1939, the *Western Recorder* reprinted an article first published in the *Voice* under the heading "A Remarkable Statement in a Negro Baptist Paper." The article addressed the question of "separate entertainment of whites and blacks," and listed several reasons for the wisdom of separation: "It is better for both races that there be no amalgamation of whites and Negroes. . . . We also think it ordered of God that after the Civil War the colored people, with the encouragement and aid of their white brethren established churches of their own, separate from those of the whites. Under this arrangement both white and colored Baptists of the South have had a development that is little short of marvelous." Almost as an afterthought, the writer stated that "at the Atlanta meeting there should not be, and will not be, any racial discrimination in anything that pertains to the purposes and business of the Baptist Congress."[73]

Notices of the deaths of prominent black Baptist leaders in the state appeared frequently on the pages of the *Western Recorder*. In 1941, two prominent leaders in Louisville—father and son—died only a few days apart. The death of John H. Frank, Jr., an attorney and probate commissioner for Jefferson County, was followed three days later by the death of his father, John H. Frank, Sr., pastor emeritus of the Fifth Street Colored Baptist Church and former editor of the *National Baptist Union Review*. The elder Frank had studied theology and medicine in Leipzig, conducted research in history and Egyptology in London, and, according to the eulogist, "was at home in Latin, Greek, and German, as he was in English."[74]

In 1938, the *Western Recorder* announced the death of John H. Smiley, a well-known preacher and gospel singer in the state. Only fifty-eight years of age, Smiley "had a wide circle of friends among both White and Negro races throughout the South and the North." One of the first black chauffeurs at the beginning of the automobile age in Louisville, Smiley had impressed Theodore Ahrens, the Louisville manufacturer, with the quality of his baritone voice. Ahrens had encouraged the chauffeur to study music seriously. As a soloist, Smiley sang frequently at annual sessions of the Southern Baptist Convention, and he served as the "General Missionary among Colored Baptists in Kentucky," singing and preaching across the state.[75]

Although segregation remained the policy of choice for many white and black Baptists in the 1940s—before the civil rights movement of the 1950s and 1960s—the veneration paid to black Baptist leaders like Smiley and the Franks in the white Baptist press indicated a high level of respect for the black clergy. The *Western Recorder* praised "the Christian spirit and sound good sense of the Negro Baptist preachers and leaders in the South" and gave credit to white Baptists for creating "an intimacy scarcely equalled by that of any other group."[76] Still, as sailors and soldiers served and fought in segregated units on World War II ships and battlefields, segregation remained the norm at home in Kentucky's restaurants, hotels, schools, and churches. And just as the end of segregation in the military came after the war, progress in other areas of civil rights accelerated in the postwar years.

Halting progress in race relations in Kentucky was accompanied by more striking progress in other areas of the work of Kentucky Baptists. Missions efforts by the WMU, the Girls Auxiliary, and the Royal Ambassadors for boys increased; and new initiatives like the Jefferson Street Mission in inner-city Louisville and a renewed emphasis on mountain missions in eastern Kentucky were implemented.[77] The Kentucky Baptist Hospital continued to provide hospital services with missionary zeal.

In 1941, the hospital's superintendent, H. L. Dobbs, received a telephone call from a small-town pastor. A nine-year-old boy in the pastor's community had a ruptured appendix, and because the boy's family was poor the pastor wondered if the hospital could help. Dobbs suggested that they rush the boy to the Kentucky Baptist Hospital and that the matter of finances would be worked out. The morning after the operation, Dobbs received the following letter:

> Dear Friends in Christ: Some time ago, I ran across some of your literature and have been intending sending an offering for your Charity fund for hospital care. I think you have a splendid plan for doing the Master's work and hope what I am sending will heal someone's body and that their soul will also be healed while there. I do not wish any thanks and am trusting the Lord to see to this getting there safely and being used to His glory.
>   Sincerely, A FRIEND

Enclosed in the letter were seven ten-dollar bills. Superintendent Dobbs never knew the source of the letter or gift, but he wrote that "I cannot express the joy and privilege that was received in marking the child's Hospital bill in the amount of $65 'Paid in Full By a Christian Friend.'"[78]

News of battlefield victories in Europe and in the South Pacific were coupled with ecstatic reports of financial victories in Kentucky Baptist

churches and agencies of the General Association in the 1940s. Burned
mortgage notes at West Broadway Baptist Church in Louisville and at
Baptist churches in Hardinsburg and Falmouth were only a sampling of
joyful reports from around the state. At Falmouth, in Pendleton County,
a new edifice had been constructed in 1928 for forty-five thousand dollars. Although the congregation thought that pledges would be sufficient to pay off the debt in short order, the crash in 1929 "rendered many
of the pledges valueless." When Clarence Q. Jones came as pastor in
1939, renewed efforts were made to deal with the debt. After he was
called away to chaplain duty, the effort to reduce the debt continued under the direction of Mrs. Jones and "supply pastor" W. H. Branyon, a recent graduate of Southern Seminary. Chaplain Jones returned from his
army post "to rejoice with his people" at the note-burning ceremony on
October 30, 1941.[79]

Just as individual churches celebrated freedom from debt, the General
Association of Baptists in Kentucky rejoiced in June 1945 at a "victory
day" observance for the cancellation of the indebtedness of the state Baptist body. With his work complete, Executive-Secretary J. W. Black announced his retirement late in 1945. The seven years of his tenure had
been momentous years indeed. The new financial stability of the early
1940s followed decades of hard times for most Kentuckians. At the same
time, financial gains were coupled with the inevitable losses of war. Black's
determined leadership in these bittersweet years provided a solid foundation for the postwar years.

Certainly, the war had wrought great changes for the commonwealth
along with the rest of the world. The war's end returned many people to
the state with changed attitudes and lives. Kentucky historian James C.
Klotter wrote that the "lives of women and blacks would not be the same
again, for brief glimpses of possibilities would not be forgotten in later
years. Nor would Kentucky remain the same, for the mass migration had
taken many of the young, seldom to return. The greatest change, though,
came among those who had left to fight. Some brought back wounds, others scarred memories."[80]

Sergeant James T. Monroe, a Kentucky soldier from Mt. Eden, anticipated "when G.I.'s come home again" in a letter published in *The Spencer
Magnet* and later in the *Western Recorder*. Monroe wrote that "some day
we are coming home to stay. We are coming back, most of us, but we will
be changed." When soldiers return, they "will be ready to go to church to
thank God for their deliverance and ready to dedicate their lives to serve
Him." The writer wondered how returning soldiers would be received by
those back home: "Friends, how about you? Has the war sobered your

thinking? Have you prepared for the return of all us service men?" Monroe advised Kentuckians that returning soldiers would need assistance in adjusting to a postwar world:

> And, dear Christians, what will our fighting men think of you when they come home to stay? Will the tragedy of the last war be repeated? Will you let slip through your fingers the greatest opportunity of this generation? These men will want to hear God's word; they will have to be grounded in the faith; they will need to be encouraged; they will want real spiritual Christian fellowship. Let them not be disappointed. Be living closer to God and His Word so these returning will see His love flowing through you.[81]

"Postwar Christians" was the title of an article written in October 1945 by W. C. Boone, the fifty-three-year-old pastor of Louisville's Crescent Hill Baptist Church. Writing after Hiroshima and Nagasaki, the respected pastor was aware that the discovery and use of atomic force had "brought in an entirely new era." Boone referred to President Harry S. Truman's declaration that one result of the bomb and the victory over Japan "would be to reaffirm and re-establish the value and importance of the individual." Asserting that the responsibility of the individual soul remained a principle dear to Baptists, Boone encouraged Kentucky Baptists to rededicate themselves to "our privilege as postwar Christians." That privilege involved a renewed emphasis on missions. Boone was adamant in his belief that the only hope for a better world was the Gospel of Christ: "They are telling us that we shall have to re-educate all the people of Germany and Japan to avoid a future, more terrible war. But education alone will not do it. We need to teach them the way of life in Christ Jesus. . . . Only a world-wide missionary program, big enough and challenging enough to call for our best, for the best of all Christians, will be sufficient for this day."[82]

With his 1945 article, Boone issued a clarion call for Kentucky Baptists to make the most of the opportunities in a postwar world. His encouragement was appropriate and prophetic. The year marked the one hundredth anniversary of the founding of the Southern Baptist Convention. Kentucky joined other states in a "Centennial Crusade" to mark the anniversary. The crusade's goal was to "win one million souls for our Saviour" and "to complete, celebrate, climax and crown a century of services for Christ." Carroll Hubbard, the assistant to Executive Secretary J. W. Black, was chosen to coordinate the crusade effort in Kentucky. Under Hubbard's direction, a goal of seventy-seven thousand conversions out of the convention goal of one million was set for Kentucky.[83]

Kentucky's prominent role in the centennial observance set the stage for the boom years following World War II. And with J. W. Black's retirement, it was appropriate that W. C. Boone, the energetic and ambitious writer of "Post-war Christians" and the pastor of Crescent Hill Baptist Church, would be chosen to lead Kentucky Baptists into the postwar world.

5
chapter

Boone and the Boom Years
1946-1961

Kentucky Baptist leaders prepared for the November 1946 annual meeting of the General Association in Ashland with unusual anticipation and hope. As always, missions and Christian education took center stage. Reports from representatives from the Southern Baptist Convention's Home Mission Board and Foreign Mission Board, and a message from Louie D. Newton, president of the Southern Baptist Convention, highlighted the meeting. Newton's address proved particularly poignant. Arriving late, having spoken the night before to the Tennessee Baptist Convention, Newton found a "full house" of Kentucky Baptist messengers in the large auditorium of Pollard Baptist Church, located in the rolling hills of suburban Ashland. The waiting messengers eagerly anticipated a positive word from the Southern Baptist leader.[1]

Newton's message was anything but positive. His message was disturbing, even heart-rending. Newton dispensed with any obligatory congratulations for packed Kentucky sanctuaries and burgeoning enrollment figures. No pats on the back here. Instead, he immediately warmed to his subject of the hour: his observations of perilous conditions in the postwar world. With "the atomic bomb staring us in the face, and the very nations which fought together in war being unable to get together in peace," Newton further described a world far removed from the prospering and promising security of home.

"Never have I seen the world in such throes of travail," Newton preached. "We have come to the let-down of humanity. Oh how we need to go to God and ask Him for a word to take to the people at this hour!" Recently returned from a trip to Russia, Newton dramatically displayed a chalice—"the oldest thing that Russian Baptists had"—that had been presented to Southern Baptists in the United States by Russian Baptist preachers. The weary preacher then related that of the sixty-one Russian preachers whom he had met on his visit, every one of them had been in jail.[2] Clearly, the postwar boom for Kentucky Baptists was not shared by Baptists in other areas of the world. Indeed, the postwar world was fast becoming a cold war world. Newton's message was a clear call for Kentucky Baptists to respond to a world crying for help.

Kentucky Baptists did respond. Like the Great War a generation earlier, World War II had a dramatic impact on Baptist work in the commonwealth. "World War II marked," according to church historian George M. Marsden, "another major turning point in American cultural history."[3] Soldiers returning from the European and Pacific theaters of the second conflict had literally seen the world. The narrow, provincial attitudes of many young men and some young women—many of them never having been outside home-state borders—were abandoned.

The wars produced, however, decidedly different postwar societies. Marsden argued that while "the First World War brought to the United States a temporary, wild enthusiasm for its international mission, it soon led to disillusion and a period of cultural pessimism. The Second World War, on the other hand, led not only to America's role as a world leader, but also to a widespread revival of faith in America and America's religions."[4] To be sure, for some, World War II shattered safe, secure worlds. Far too many never returned to their homes. For returning men and women of faith, however, the war made missions opportunities more real and the need for "winning the world for Christ" more pressing.

The United States experienced an "extensive religious revival" from the 1940s to the early 1960s. Religious groups of nearly every description grew and prospered. Polls indicated the breadth, if not the depth, of the faith of Americans. One national survey conducted soon after the war showed that two out of three Americans attended religious services at least once a month, 42 percent as frequently as once a week. Nineteen out of twenty Americans said they believed in God, nine out of ten prayed, and six out of seven viewed the Bible as the "divinely inspired word of God." Three out of four Americans believed in life after death. America's poll figures were higher than in any other industrialized country in the world.[5]

From 1940 to 1960, church membership rose from 64.5 to 114.5 million, from 50 percent to 63 percent of the population. A century earlier, only 20 percent of all Americans belonged to a church. For a majority of Americans, religious affiliation became synonymous with the "American way of life."[6] A writer observed in 1956 that "One comes early to get a seat in suburban churches; they overflow, and new ones are being built every day." In 1954, Congress added the phrase "one nation under God" to the Pledge of Allegiance. The following year, the phrase "In God We Trust" was made mandatory on all American currency.[7] In 1957, British observer Denis Brogan put it succinctly in business terms: "Religion like many other things is booming in America; it is a blue chip."[8]

Other observers, like Reinhold Niebuhr, questioned the depth and genuineness of America's religious revival. Yet another postwar poll revealed that more than half of adults were unable to name any of the four Gospels.[9] Rather than experiencing a religious revival, some critics pointed to the increasing uneasiness—even despair—of the Cold War era. At the same time that Americans packed churches in unprecedented numbers, tranquilizers were the "fastest-growing new medication in the country." Apparently, "considerable anxiety" accompanied America's growing economic affluence and religious faith. One historian noted that "many people, living uneasily amid the moral and social dilemmas of the postwar period, were profoundly anxious about the meaning of life in general and their lives in particular."[10]

Of course, the obvious postwar religious revival and Cold War anxiety were connected. For many individuals in an increasingly urban nation, churches and synagogues served as suburban havens; others looked to religious institutions as "social arenas" replacing "the communal life previously supplied by kin or neighborhood."[11] Still others experienced a dynamic spiritual renewal, an assurance that only the church could offer.

Kentuckians experienced the same paradox of religious fervor mixed with emotional anxiety evident in the rest of the nation. At the same time, the war reminded Kentucky believers that there was much to do outside the boundaries of the Bluegrass. With a wide world before them—seen for the first time by many veterans—Kentucky Baptists were made aware of the scope of the challenge. In short, following the war, Baptists in Kentucky developed a wider world vision. This vision became a hallmark of the state's mission efforts in the last half of the twentieth century.

This wider world vision was inextricably linked to a renewed regard for the past. Just as the Israelites of the Old Testament were encouraged to remember what Yahweh had done for them, twentieth-century Kentucky Baptists recognized the need to document—indeed use—the inspirational record of the past in the postwar modern world. The Kentucky Baptist Historical Society, first organized in 1871, was reorganized in 1903 only to go defunct in 1919 at the end of World War I. The society was revived in 1939 during the Second World War following the organization of the Southern Baptist Historical Society.[12]

After the war, calls for a genuine regard for Kentucky Baptist history filled the pages of the *Western Recorder*. In "An Appeal for the Past of Kentucky Baptists," Bailey F. Davis concluded that "there are invaluable lessons to be learned from Kentucky Baptist history" and that "more interest should be manifested in preserving the records which narrate these lessons." Believing that "it is a sad commentary on Kentucky" that valuable collections such as the Draper, Shane, and Durrett collections were not kept in the state, and that many Baptist records had come to rest in the archives at Western Reserve and Colgate, Bailey pled with Kentucky Baptists "to not forget that as we are making history we should preserve it" as well.[13]

Leo T. Crismon, the librarian at the Southern Baptist Theological Seminary, took Bailey's plea to heart. Crismon read papers at the annual meetings of the General Association on the itinerant preacher and historian John Henderson Spencer (1947), the early Baptist minister John L. Waller (1954), and "the Lincoln Family and the Baptists" (1958). In 1955, a reinvigorated historical society began the important work of microfilming minutes of the General Association as well as minutes of the executive board. By 1958, the project also included district association minutes. In 1955 and 1956, the Kentucky Baptist Historical Society participated fully in preparing Kentucky materials for the new *Encyclopedia of Southern Baptists*.[14]

In 1946, Crismon recommended that Frank Mariro Masters be commissioned to complete a new volume of Kentucky Baptist history covering the period from 1885 to 1946. Masters's task was formidable, for he was to continue the historical project first begun by John Henderson Spencer in 1865. Spencer's massive two-volume work, *A History of Kentucky Baptists*, documented Kentucky Baptist life from 1769 to 1885. Like Spencer, Masters took to the task with astounding vigor. When the new volume was finally published in 1953 as *A History of Baptists in Kentucky*, it was clear to readers that despite hardships and setbacks, the story of Kentucky Baptists had been a story of growth and progress. It also appeared clear that with two world wars behind them, Kentucky Baptists were poised for an unprecedented period of growth and achievement. Masters ended his history with an optimistic, albeit guarded, injunction: "If Kentucky Baptists will all work together in unity, and understanding, with faith and vision, they can transform this commonwealth into a State wherein dwelleth righteousness, and where Christ shall really reign in the hearts of men."[15]

Masters's words were not his own. The historian's concluding injunction repeated words from a 1949 address delivered by the individual responsible for leading Kentucky Baptists through the postwar boom years. William Cooke Boone, the beloved pastor of Louisville's Crescent Hill Baptist Church, was the product of a long line of Kentucky pioneers. His family tree, in fact, could be traced back to Daniel and Squire Boone. In 1946, the same year that Boone took up his duties as the new general secretary of the General Association, the historical society published Crismon's "The Boone Family and Kentucky Baptists," a paper claiming that a Baptist preacher was included in every generation of Kentucky's Boone family from Squire Boone to W. C. Boone.[16]

In his quiet, thoughtful way, the twentieth-century Boone displayed the same pioneering spirit of his famous forebears. Years of service—before accepting the call to lead Kentucky Baptists—had been spent in western frontier areas in Arkansas and Oklahoma. A graduate of William Jewell College in Missouri and of Southern Seminary, Boone had already published two books, *What God Hath Joined Together* and *What We Believe*. Despite his scholarly accomplishments and his professorial demeanor, Boone proved that he was a man of action. He pastored churches in Mississippi, Arkansas, Virginia, and Tennessee in addition to two Kentucky pastorates in Owensboro and Louisville. He had served as vice president of the Southern Baptist Convention, on the Board of Trustees of Union University, and on the executive boards of the Kentucky and Tennessee conventions. For three years Boone had served as president of Oklahoma Baptist University in Shawnee. His wide range of experience in various areas of Baptist life made the leader uniquely qualified for his new leadership role.

Upon taking office, Boone—unlike his predecessor, J. W. Black—found a General Association much better positioned for organized service. Certainly the work of Black helped the associa-

W. C. Boone, executive secretary of Kentucky Baptists, 1945-1961

tion rebound from depression and war. Black was, according to one observer, a "great man" in his own right. A. B. Colvin, who would later head the General Association's Department of Evangelism and Missions, recalled that Black "did a tremendous work and took a personal interest in people." Colvin knew this from personal experience. As a young minister struggling to discern the Master's direction, Colvin paid a visit to the general secretary at his East Chestnut Street office. He later recalled that "as a kid not knowing whether I should accept a church or not I went to Black's office in downtown Louisville to ask him about it and I heard him say to his secretary, 'I can't see anyone else today; I'm too busy.' And I said, 'I'll come back,' and he heard me and he knew who I was. . . . After an hour with him on our knees I left there knowing very well that that was what I was supposed to do." Much later, long after Black's death, Colvin observed that "I really appreciated a man like that with all of his responsibilities taking time out for a kid."[17]

During Black's tenure from 1939 to 1946, steady growth was evident in all departments. In a final "Appreciation and Request," he highlighted the growth during the World War II years: "From a missionary personnel of four general workers in 1939, we now have around forty missionaries on the field in various types of direct mission work. Total receipts in 1939 amounted to $388,588.11; 1945 receipts amounted to $1,309,874.09. The 1938 *Annual* shows a membership of 369,232 in the churches reporting. The 1944 *Annual* shows 426,194. Partial reports indicate that 1945 will show the largest number of baptisms in many years." The retiring general secretary requested that his successor "receive the same loyal co-operation and support given me."[18]

When W. C. Boone took office, he found active departments and leaders already engaged in meaningful work: Sunday School, W. A. Gardiner; Training Union, Byron C. S. DeJarnette; Woman's Missionary Union, Mary P. Winbourne; Christian Education, J. G. Cothran; Student Union, J. Chester Durham; Rural Church Work, R B Hooks; and City Missions, W. K. Wood. Although *Western Recorder* editor John D. Freeman retired in 1946, the new editor, R. T. Skinner, pastor of First Baptist Church, Bowling Green, continued to provide inspirational and provocative articles. The Kentucky paper increased its circulation from eighteen thousand in 1940 to over forty-five thousand within six years. By 1946, the *Western Recorder* ranked third in circulation among all Baptist papers, following only the *Baptist Standard* of Texas and the *Baptist Record* of Mississippi.[19]

Four Baptist colleges, an institute for mountain youth, a hospital, and two children's homes provided institutional support for Baptists in the state. Twenty state-supported "missionary pastors," thirty county and asso-

ciational missionaries, and five local missionaries employed by local associational boards were striking evidence to the fact that Black and the General Association had made evangelism a top priority.[20] Boone was determined to emphasize evangelism even more.

Soon after beginning his work as general secretary, Boone wrote an article for the *Western Recorder* on "Kentucky Baptists in 1946." "Our first
emphasis should be on evangelism, winning the lost for Christ," Boone
wrote. "It is well that we had decided to major on evangelism, else the sudden end of the war and the uncertainty and confusion which followed
might have led to a lessening of our efforts and decrease in the visible results. Now, we should go forward, conserving these good results and putting our very best into the effort to do more than ever before in this greatest work of all, leading the lost to the Saviour."[21]

In "A Message to Kentucky Baptists," another *Western Recorder* article
published in 1947, Boone added "stewardship" to "evangelism" as a point of
emphasis for the new year. A series of rallies in eight different regions of
the state were planned for March 1947. State and national denominational
leaders led meetings in Somerset, Corbin, Ashland, Lexington, Louisville,
Glasgow, Owensboro, and Paducah. Boone lamented that the Southern
Baptist Convention goal of one million baptisms for 1945, the centennial of
the southern convention's founding, was not met. Indeed, churches reported only 256,699 baptisms—only a quarter of the goal—that year. In
1946, only 249,981 baptisms had been reported. Kentucky's figures mirrored the general regional trend: 18,233 in 1945, the centennial year, and
17,379 in 1946.[22]

For 1947, Boone encouraged every Kentucky Baptist pastor to preach
evangelistic sermons and every church to have at least one revival meeting
each year; he asked a million believers across the convention to "pray for a
Heaven-sent revival." Statistics indicated that almost half of Kentucky residents were unchurched. Of a total population of 2,733,090, it was estimated that 1,109,643 were without a church home. In Kentucky's cities, 62
of every 100 were unchurched; and in 32 eastern Kentucky mountain
counties (with a population of 821,594), 690,479 had no church home (approximately 81.5 of every 100). In one mountain county where over four
thousand young men were enlisted in a branch of the service during the
war, only 2 percent reported a church affiliation.[23] The need for evangelism
was evident.

The need for more faithful stewardship was also evident. The SBC set a
goal for a million tithers for 1947. Kentucky's share of the goal was seventy-five thousand. Reed Rushing of Greenville, chosen as the statewide director of stewardship revivals, also served as the state director of a "tithers'

enlistment movement." Clearly, Boone's emphasis on evangelism and stewardship was not without direction and organization. The need was evident, the opportunity clear. And Boone's determined leadership translated into immediate results. Frank Masters wrote that "no years in the history of Kentucky Baptists have been more fruitful in spiritual results, and in marked advance along all lines of endeavor than 1948-49." More baptisms—22,907—were reported in 1948 than in any previous year in the history of the convention. That record was broken the following year when 24,874 were reported.[24]

Statistics from Boone's tenure as general secretary indicated the wisdom of the leader's emphasis on evangelism and stewardship. Membership in Kentucky Baptist churches increased from 458,572 in 1946 to 617,507 in 1960, Boone's last full year. Some eighteen thousand additional members were not included in the Kentucky statistics after the founding of new conventions in Ohio in 1954 and Indiana in 1958 even though the Ohio and Indiana conventions were begun through Kentucky Baptist evangelistic initiatives. Total baptisms increased from 17,427 in 1946 to 21,274 in 1960, and total offerings from $7.6 million to $24.6 million. It was not surprising that Departments of Evangelism and Stewardship Promotion were two of the five new departments created during the Boone years. New departments of Relief and Annuity, Brotherhood, and Church Music, the development of the Kentucky Baptist Foundation and the Cedarmore Assembly, and the organization of three Baptist hospitals and three children's homes indicated that Boone promoted a well-rounded program. Perhaps his "crowning achievement in a material way," as one writer put it, was the building of a new General Association headquarters, the Kentucky Baptist Building near Middletown on Louisville's east side.[25] Accomplishments during Boone's tenure were indeed impressive.

Certainly, Baptists benefited during the Boone years from the postwar boom. The return of servicemen resulted in record gains in church membership and Sunday School and Training Union enrollments across the Southern Baptist Convention. For the first time, per-capita giving for missions exceeded the high mark of the Seventy-five Million campaign. The experience of Kentucky Baptists in this period could aptly be described as "Boone and the Boom Years."[26]

The moniker is ironic considering Boone's quiet demeanor; the "boom" did not come from him personally. Indeed, Boone always relied on close friends for advice before making decisions. A. B. Colvin remembered that Boone was especially close to Harley C. Chiles, a distinguished pastor at Barbourville and, later, Murray. When faced with an important decision, Boone would invariably say that "I've got to talk to Brother Chiles about

H. C. Chiles: pastor, teacher, and writer

this" before rendering a decision.[27] Colvin remembered hearing someone criticize the general secretary one time for not "reacting suddenly" when "a vital issue came up." The man remarked that Boone "could have so much influence if he just talked more." Hearing the remark, another individual replied that "if he got up and talked more he wouldn't have so much influence!" Upon the announcement of Boone's retirement in 1961, after taking up his own General Association responsibilities under Boone only three years before, Colvin told Boone teasingly, but with a note of remorse, that "if I happened to think that you were going to retire in a couple of years I wouldn't have come." Years later, Colvin remembered Boone simply as "a great man."[28]

Boone's quiet leadership and sound organizational skills provided encouragement for ministers, missionaries, teachers, and state and associational workers. In 1951, a new combined department of missions and evangelism was established with Eldred M. Taylor as its first director. The City Mission Program, the Rural Church Program, the Mountain Mission Program, and associational, county, and local missions were all included in the new department. In 1952, G. R. Pendergraph, a regional rural church worker, was appointed as head of the statewide Rural Church Program. A. B. Cash, connected with the SBC's Home Mission Board, helped establish the Mountain Mission Program, and Wendell Belew, a minister from Rockcastle County, became the program's first director.[29]

With the encouragement of Boone and Belew, missionary pastors like R. E. Sasser served heroically under the new structure. Sasser, a native of the mountains, pastored the Baptist church in Booneville in Owsley County. After four years, Sasser had led the church to construct a new building, and the church had grown from a membership of 80 to 224. When he arrived, the church's annual budget was $350; four years later, church members gave $5,128 to all causes in one year, including $620 for missions. Eleven church members conducted weekly mission Sunday Schools.

As a missionary pastor supported by the state Missions Board, Sasser's work was not limited to the Booneville church. He preached Saturday evenings—"when roads permitted"—in a rural church or "missions point" and two more times on Sunday afternoons. In all, Sasser preached regularly at four places in addition to his Booneville church and at a dozen other places "as times and conditions permit." At one rural church, Sasser "courageously preached tithing," and church members who had "in the main held against the doctrine of stewardship, accepted the Bible teaching and followed." Under Sasser's leadership, "with about sixty-five members widely scattered, with only dirt roads, they not only attend in splendid numbers but give from sixty-five to eighty dollars monthly, of which amount one-third is for missions."[30]

The selfless dedication of such missionary pastors as Sasser made a difference in the lives of individuals and in the growth of mountain churches. Boone's emphasis on evangelism and stewardship was not limited to work in the eastern Kentucky mountains or to remote areas in the western part of the state. Under Boone, Kentucky Baptists extended missions initiatives beyond the commonwealth. For example, Kentuckians were instrumental in the founding of the Ohio Convention of Southern Baptists in 1953 and 1954 and the Indiana convention in 1958.

In the 1930s and 1940s, large numbers of eastern Kentuckians moved to Ohio—especially to Dayton, Cincinnati, and Hamilton—to find work. Although these men and women left the commonwealth, they were not willing to leave behind their religious roots. While some Baptist transplants joined churches affiliated with the American Baptist Convention, others helped found churches aligned with the Southern Baptist Convention. Interestingly, one individual instrumental in the founding of both the Ohio and Indiana conventions hailed not from eastern Kentucky but from Murray in extreme western Kentucky. Van Boone Castleberry, a member of H. Boyce Taylor's church in Murray, and along with his wife a veteran of Taylor's missionary work in Brazil, was called as pastor of West Side Baptist Church in Hamilton, Ohio, in 1943. Since 1941, the White Water Baptist District Association in southwestern Ohio—the association that included the West Side church, other churches in Hamilton, and churches in Indiana such as Blooming Grove Baptist Church—had cooperated with Kentucky's General Association. Castleberry, who resigned the pastorate at West Side to become the district associational missionary of the White Water Association, and other ministers from the North Bend Association in the Covington area of northern Kentucky sought to expand the White Water Association into full-fledged state conventions for Ohio and Indiana.[31]

At the annual General Association meeting in Owensboro in 1953, the White Water Association presented a petition to Kentucky messengers calling for a statewide Ohio convention. Kentuckians W. C. Boone, Solomon F. Dowis, and Judge Eugene E. Siler assisted the White Water Baptists with a state constitution. Ohio Baptists expressed "their deep appreciation for encouragement and tangible assistance" of Kentucky Baptists in the new work. On January 8, 1954, the Ohio Convention of Southern Baptists came into being.[32] Significantly, Ray Roberts, former pastor of First Baptist Church, Danville, Kentucky, was elected as Ohio's first executive secretary. Ron Deering, baptized as a young man by V. B. Castleberry, was elected as the first clerk of the Ohio convention. Deering, licensed to preach by the West Side church, would later go on to a venerable life of service as the head librarian at Boyce Library at Southern Seminary and as an active leader in the Historical Commission of the Kentucky Baptist Convention.

Baptists in Indiana organized themselves into a state convention on October 3, 1958. This new Baptist convention comprised about one hundred churches that had previously been aligned with district associations in Illinois and Kentucky. In Kentucky the West Kentuckiana Association and the Long Run Association worked with Baptists in southern Indiana. Kentucky Baptists contributed $3,364.84 to the new Indiana convention.[33] Kentucky Baptist dollars, but especially the efforts of former Kentucky Baptist laymen and ministers like V. B. Castleberry, paved the way for the expansion of Southern Baptist work north of the Ohio River.

Kentucky Baptist dollars continued to assist in the work of the Southern Baptist Convention through the Cooperative Program. In 1947, Kentucky Baptist monies given through the Cooperative Program were equally divided between Kentucky and SBC causes. Of the 50 percent remaining in Kentucky, gifts were allocated in the following way:

19 percent	State missions
17.5 percent	Education
6 percent	Kentucky Baptist Children's Home
2.5 percent	Louisville Baptist Orphan's Home
4 percent	Kentucky Baptist Hospital
1 percent	New church building

The 50 percent that went outside the state was divided in the following way:

23 percent	Foreign missions
9 percent	Home missions

2.5 percent	Southern Seminary
2.5 percent	Southwestern Seminary
2.5 percent	New Orleans Seminary
.5 percent	WMU Training School
1 percent	American Baptist Seminary
7.5 percent	Relief and Annuity Board
.95 percent	Radio Committee
.5 percent	Baptist Brotherhood
.05 percent	Southern Baptist Hospital

Significantly, the largest percentage of funds from Kentucky Baptist Cooperative Program givers went to foreign missions.

In addition to Cooperative Program funds, Kentuckians were asked to share in the burden of world relief. After the war, the Committee on Relief of the Baptist World Alliance initiated a program for Baptists to donate clothing and food for war-ravaged Europe. Acting on the Baptist World Alliance initiative, the executive committee of the Southern Baptist Convention called for the SBC to play a major role. Boone encouraged Kentucky Baptists to provide clothing "for about fifty thousand people and raise fifty thousand dollars to buy food for the hungry in Europe."[34] Two world wars had made Kentucky Baptists aware of the need for a world vision for missions and service. In 1947, the motto, "All Together For All the World," emphasized the need for a world vision.[35]

V. V. Cooke
Baptist lay leader, philanthropist

As has almost always been the case with Baptists in Kentucky, however, periods of growth and expansion were not without controversy and disagreement. The first controversy weathered by Kentucky Baptists during the tenure of W. C. Boone was not related to world missions or world relief. Rather, the controversy concerned relief for homeless, orphaned children within the commonwealth. In the first year of Boone's tenure, the Children's Commission, appointed by the General Association the year before, along with the trustees of the Louisville Baptist Orphan's Home and the Kentucky Baptist Children's Home at Glendale, decided to merge the two homes under one board and build a new institution. In January, Boone wrote persuasively of the plan in the *Western Recorder*. Other *Western Recorder* articles announced confidently, "Orphanages to be Combined." R. T. Skinner, the new *Western Recorder* editor, had presided over the merger meeting as the chair of the Children's Commission.[36]

At the 1946 annual meeting of the General Association in Ashland, however, the merger plan was defeated. V. V. Cooke, a prominent layman from Louisville, presented the merger proposal and "forceably outlined the advantages that would accrue." Cooke explained that the plan would eliminate needless duplication and unite Kentucky Baptists behind the ultimate goal of caring for homeless children in the state. C. W. Elsey of Shelbyville spoke against the plan "with equal zest and vigor," arguing that the homes should remain under separate boards. Following a spirited discussion between supporters and opponents, the plan was defeated.[37]

The defeat of the merger plan did not diminish the work of providing quality child care for orphaned and troubled children in the common-

Spring Meadows Children's Home
new Middletown campus, 1950

wealth. Under capable leadership, the work grew as Kentucky Baptists carved out a niche as a leader in Christian child care. In 1946, A. M. Vollmer resigned as the superintendent of the Louisville Baptist Orphan's Home—a position he had held for two years—to take up his new responsibilities as the secretary and treasurer of the Kentucky Baptist Foundation. Virginia R. Fields, the assistant superintendent, served as acting head of the home until Sam Ed Bradley was elected to the post in 1947. Coming from pastorates in Glasgow and Fulton, Bradley presided over the move of the Louisville home to a new site. Cooke, the home's board chairman, had long dreamed of a more rural site. The home, founded in downtown Louisville in 1869 in the wake of the Civil War, purchased property near Middletown in 1948. The year before, it had been decided that the trustees of the home would be elected by the General Association, and the home's name would be changed to Spring Meadows. On January 20, 1950, Bradley, his staff, and ninety-two children moved to the new campus.

At the same time that the Louisville home was being transformed into Spring Meadows, dramatic changes came to the Kentucky Baptist Children's home at Glendale. E. F. Glenn, its superintendent since 1942, resigned in 1948, and was succeeded the following year by C. Ford Deusner, a native of western Kentucky. A graduate of Bethel College and Western Kentucky Teachers College in Bowling Green, Deusner came to his new post from the Tabernacle Baptist Church in Paducah after having served in other western Kentucky pastorates. Under his leadership, a long-needed building program was begun. Deusner led the Glendale home toward a "cottage plan" of operation, providing a more hospitable environment for the home's young residents.[38]

Although the original attempt at merger had failed in 1946, the Children's Commission had continued to function under its initial assignment, "to study the problems involved in consolidating the two homes under one board of trustees." Finally, in 1953, arguments for efficiency and quality won out as the boards of the two homes were merged with the Children's Commission to form the Kentucky Baptist Board of Child Care. The identity, location, and assets of each home were to be preserved under the new board. In 1954, the persistent efforts of V. V. Cooke were recognized as the Louisville layman was elected by acclamation as the president of the board. In 1957, a third children's home was built near Morehead, and the experienced, able Virginia R. Fields was chosen as the resident director.

In 1958, a central administration—of sorts—for the three homes was secured with the naming of Lawrence J. Dauenhauer, a Baptist layman, as director of finance. Dauenhauer, working from his base at Spring Meadows,

Kentucky Baptist Hospital, 1924

"became" the central office. In 1959 Sam Ed Bradley was promoted from his position as superintendent at Spring Meadows to the new position of general superintendent for the Kentucky Baptist Board of Child Care. J. D. Herndon, himself a member of the board, was then asked to replace Bradley at Spring Meadows. With the official name change of the Kentucky Baptist Children's Home to Glen Dale in 1956, Kentucky Baptists could boast of three distinguished institutions of child care under a central administration. And each institution boasted a picturesque name—Spring Meadows, Glen Dale, and Pine Crest—to match its wholesome, worthwhile work.[39]

Kentucky Baptist hospital work, referred to in annual General Association minutes as "the ministry of healing," expanded dramatically in the decade after the war. The Kentucky Baptist Hospital, a 150-bed facility, opened in Louisville in 1924. The hospital weathered the depression and war years, and completed major additions after the war—in 1948 (to a total capacity of 285 beds and 36 bassinets) and in 1953 (to 345 beds and 50 bassinets). By 1954, over two hundred thousand patients had been treated. Patients came not only from Louisville and Jefferson County, but also from across the state and beyond. In 1952 alone, 7,189 operations were performed and 2,803 babies delivered in the hospital. Patients representing a wide range of denominational preferences were admitted that year: Baptist, 5,696; Catholic, 2,099; Church of Christ, 366; Methodist, 1,801; Christian Scientist, 21; Jewish, 333; Presbyterian, 1,376; Evangelical, 486; others, 2,905; and 928 listing no faith affiliation. Hospital officials sought to provide a spiritual as well as a healing ministry. A full-time hospital minister, B. B. Hilburn, a former minister at Greensburg, was called "to look after the spiritual welfare of patients and employees."[40]

In the 1940s, Kentucky Baptists, recognizing the value of Louisville's hospital ministry, decided to expand the effort into western and central Kentucky. Local associations initiated the work in Paducah and Lexington. When work stalled because of lack of funds, the General Association established a Hospital Commission to find ways to finish the work. In 1950, Harold D. Tallent, the chairman of the commission, recommended that the Central Baptist Hospital in Lexington and the West Kentucky Memorial Baptist Hospital in Paducah "be brought into the Cooperative Program and share according to the percentages set up by the Budget and Appropriations Committee." The commission's report stipulated that the sharing of Cooperative Program funds "is predicated on the assumption that each of these Boards will change their charters so that the trustees hereafter will be nominated and elected by the General Association in the same way its other trustees are elected." An additional fund-raising drive was also recommended. Messengers adopted the Hospital Commission's report, and eventually the General Association pledged $144,000 per year to secure a loan of $3,150,000 to complete the hospitals. Significantly, Louisville's Kentucky Baptist Hospital gave $378,000 to the new hospitals.[41]

The Paducah hospital was formally dedicated on October 18, 1953, as Western Baptist Hospital. On that occasion, W. C. Boone served as master of ceremonies, Frank Tripp delivered an address, and a ninety-voice choir sang. Nine thousand individuals toured the facility the day of the dedication service, along with six thousand the following day. A similar ceremony was held in Lexington the following year—on May 9, 1954—to dedicate the new Central Baptist Hospital. Both facilities, along with the hospital in Louisville, continued to serve the state's various regions well in the years ahead.[42]

The benevolent work provided by three Baptist children's homes and three Baptist hospitals represented the historic Kentucky Baptist belief in service to others. In no way, however, did such benevolent work interfere with evangelism and missions. Indeed, such benevolent initiatives were viewed as an extension of evangelism. It was appropriate that C. Ford Deusner, the future superintendent at Glen Dale, presented the foreign missions report as chair of the Foreign Missions Committee at the 1946 annual meeting of the General Association. After all, both efforts—missions and child care—were linked. Kentucky Baptists were committed to evangelism at home and abroad. Like the Master, Kentucky Baptists sought to help the dispossessed and hurting, young and old alike. The expansion of Kentucky Baptist hospital work was yet another example of the humanitarian impulse of Kentucky Baptists in the postwar years.

An aspect of Kentucky Baptist work that historically held the attention of messengers at annual meetings was Christian education. Baptist institutions of learning experienced both growth and decline in the postwar years. At the 1946 annual meeting in Ashland, education received an unexpected boost from E. C. Routh of *The Commission*, a magazine of the SBC's Foreign Mission Board. The respected editor reported on foreign missions work in the convention and noted that "when Luther Rice came back to this country more than a century ago and gathered Baptists into one body and strengthened their missionary interest, the first things he did were to found a Baptist school and a Baptist newspaper." Routh then turned his attention to Adoniram Judson who, while talking with a friend, said, "I wish I had $1,000. Do you know what I would do with it?" The friend answered, "I suppose you would invest in missions." "No," the great missionary replied, "I would put it in a school." Routh went on to say that by founding a school, an individual "would be laying the foundation for a great mission work, whose influence would be felt around the world."[43]

Cumberland College, Williamsburg

Campbellsville College, 1950s chapel service

Throughout his tenure W. C. Boone echoed Routh's emphasis on Christian education. Kentucky participated each June in Christian Education Month, an effort promoted across the Southern Baptist Convention. Boone asserted in 1946 that Kentucky's six colleges and schools all needed "more buildings, more endowment, and more money for current support."[44] Although world relief remained an important stewardship priority, Boone challenged Kentuckians to "not forget our schools."

Kentucky Baptist colleges continued to struggle financially, but heroic gains were made. Georgetown, Kentucky's oldest Baptist college, flourished under the presidencies of Sam S. Hill (1942-1954) and H. Leo Eddleman (1954-1959). When Robert L. Mills became Georgetown's twentieth president in 1959, the college was debt free and poised to take its place among the commonwealth's elite private liberal arts institutions.

Two Kentucky Baptist junior colleges expanded into four-year institutions in the 1950s. After a long tenure (1925-1947) as president of Cumberland College in Williamsburg, J. L. Creech retired and was succeeded by James Malcolm Boswell. A. T. Siler, the vice president of Cumberland's Board of Trustees (and a former lay moderator of the General Association), announced Boswell's appointment at the institution's fifty-eighth commencement ceremony in 1947. With degrees from Georgetown and the University of Kentucky, Boswell taught mathematics and physical education before being named as acting president at Creech's retirement. He also served as a deacon at Williamsburg's First Baptist Church. Boswell's pastor, Herbert C. Gabhart—who would himself later serve as president of Belmont College, a Baptist school in Nashville, Tennessee—remarked that the new president "is one of the most energetic and positive Christians I have ever known." Gabhart concluded that "Kentucky Baptists have every reason to expect Cumberland College to continue to be an outstanding Christian institution, and have every cause to rejoice in the selection by the trustees of this young man as its leader."[45] Under Boswell's distinguished leadership, Cumberland grew in enrollment and facilities. In 1957, the General Association authorized the school to become a four-year institution, along with Campbellsville College in Taylor County.

Russell Creek Academy opened for classwork in 1907, and became Campbellsville College in 1924. In 1933, Campbellsville was admitted with other institutions in the state into the Kentucky Association of Colleges and Secondary Schools. Under the leadership of John M. Carter, the college was fully accredited as a junior college in 1949 by the Southern Association of Colleges and Secondary Schools. Carter, a native of Stanford, Kentucky, held degrees from the University of Kentucky and Southern Seminary. In 1940, he was awarded a Ph.D. in biblical archaeology. Following a research tour of Palestine, Egypt, and other middle eastern countries, the scholarly Carter served as pastor of churches in Louisville and Harrodsburg.[46] After his coming to lead Campbellsville in 1948, the school was fully accredited, and the transition to four-year status was completed by 1959.

General Association work went beyond Christian education. The bulk of the work of the General Association's executive committee centered on state missions. Eldred Taylor's service as the director of the Evangelism and Missions Department resulted in statewide growth. Indeed, it was during Taylor's tenure that a longtime goal of the General Association was finally realized. As early as 1841, at the fourth annual session of the General Association at Russellville, a resolution was adopted emphasizing the importance of "the establishment and fostering of Baptist churches at our county seats and other towns."[47] In 1899, there remained sixteen county-seat towns, all located in the mountains of eastern Kentucky, without Baptist churches.

By 1950, however, sixteen county-seat mountain churches had been founded. On September 3, 1950, following a revival led by F. C. Tuttle, a county missionary in Powell County, and A. B. Cash, the director of the Mountain Mission Program, a church was organized at Frenchburg, the county seat of Menifee County. The organization of the Frenchburg church fulfilled the dream of J. W. Black and a long line of general secretaries of the General Association. The present general secretary, W. C. Boone, the descendant of a family famous for the development of frontier areas, witnessed the founding of the new church and made the motion for the church's organization.[48]

Along with the founding of the last county-seat church in Frenchburg, the building of a new sanctuary in tiny Mouthcard in extreme eastern Kentucky indicated the statewide growth and stability of Kentucky Baptist churches. The new church building in Mouthcard was located just four miles from the Virginia line.[49] Baptist churches aligned with the General Association dotted the state from Mouthcard in extreme eastern Kentucky to Hickman on the Mississippi River in Fulton County in the far west.

Other groups choosing not to join the General Association represented other manifestations of the Baptist presence in the commonwealth. Primitive, "hard shell" Baptist congregations could still be found throughout the state. Various independent Baptist congregations in the Kentucky mountains, African American Baptists aligned with the National Baptist Convention and the black state convention, and a small, but thriving, General Baptist convention centered in western Kentucky indicated that vibrant groups identifying with various strains of the Baptist heritage existed outside the dominant General Association.[50]

Still, the growth of these groups paled in comparison to the growth of churches aligned with the General Association of Baptists in Kentucky. And the growth of the General Association was due to the postwar religious "boom" and to W. C. Boone's continuing emphasis on evangelism. From his post as head of the Evangelism and Missions Department, Eldred Taylor organized a statewide evangelism conference at Louisville's Walnut Street Baptist Church in 1948. The Walnut Street conference became a popular annual event for pastors and laypeople seeking inspiration and information on successful evangelistic strategies. The General Association coordinated "simultaneous revivals" throughout the state in 1951, 1952, 1955, and 1959.[51]

A. B. Colvin succeeded Taylor as secretary of the department in 1958 when Taylor was called to be pastor of the First Baptist Church of Somerset. Taylor, the Department of Evangelism and Mission's first secretary, had built the department from its inception. Colvin would continue Taylor's strong leadership. Born in Pendleton County, Colvin attended school in Grant County, graduating from Williamstown High School in 1934. He then went on to the University of Kentucky (graduating in 1939) and Southern Seminary, where he received a Th.M. degree in 1942. He pastored two part-time churches, Lawrenceville and Bethany, before serving in the Army Air Force from 1942 to 1946. The young Captain Colvin ended his wartime service to become pastor of Southside Baptist Church in Coving-

ton. He was elected president of the executive board of the General Association in 1955. Then, when Taylor was called as pastor of Somerset Baptist
Church in 1958, Colvin was selected to head the Department of Evangelism
and Missions, where he served until 1985. Colvin simultaneously served on
the SBC's Sunday School Board from 1956 to 1964 as well as in other positions in Kentucky.[52]

The General Association's emphasis on evangelism filtered down to the
associations and local churches. Various district associations sponsored
one-day evangelism clinics throughout the 1950s. Under Colvin, these one-
day clinics were eventually held annually in every association in the state.
Colvin encouraged pastors to emphasize evangelism from church pulpits
and through outreach programs in the community. In eastern Kentucky,
Colvin's close friend Frank R. Walters pastored the Manchester Baptist
Church for fifty-four years, from 1916 to 1970. In fact, during a two-week
revival at the Manchester church, Walters convinced Colvin that he should
resign his pastorate in Covington to head the Department of Evangelism
and Missions. Perhaps it was Walters's example that inspired the young
Colvin to take on his new responsibility. In addition to his church in Manchester, Walters preached at seven other smaller churches on Sunday afternoons. His records indicated that he had preached an average of once a
day for twenty-three years.[53] His impact on his community and county was
so significant that the Kiwanis Club of Manchester presented him with
"Clay County's Most Outstanding Citizen" award in 1957. The citation
characterized Walters as "an unconquerable spirit that would fight alone
for what he thought was right, and against odds that would have driven
lesser souls to surrender."[54]

The First Baptist Church of Fulton celebrated the third-year anniversary
of their young and enthusiastic pastor, John David Laida, in 1956. During
Laida's first three years as pastor, 320 new members joined the church, 175
coming by baptism. Sunday School attendance increased from an average
of 380 to 609, and Training Union from 75 to 175. The church's budget
doubled, and improvements were made to the church buildings and
grounds.[55] In Lexington, Rosemont Baptist Church under the leadership of
O. W. Yates added 500 members in three years, rising from 40 active members to 548.[56] Although few pastors and churches could match the evangelistic fervor and dramatic growth of the Manchester, Fulton, and Rosemont
churches, other congregations around the commonwealth benefitted from
the postwar boom.

Following the war, a decade-long emphasis on evangelism was capped in
1956 with a month-long Billy Graham Evangelistic Crusade beginning on
September 30 at the Kentucky State Fair Grounds in Louisville. A South-

ern Baptist, Graham held a crusade in India earlier in the year, returning to the states in the summer to preach at the Southern Baptist Convention in Kansas City. Despite the General Association's emphasis on
evangelism, the *Western Recorder* remained oddly silent on the Graham
crusade in the weeks leading up to the event. Perhaps controversy
swirling around the critical comments of famed theologian Reinhold
Niebuhr, along with the ecumenical nature of the Graham meetings,
contributed to the state paper's reluctance to push the event. In 1951,
the editor of the *Western Recorder* R. T. Skinner had written that while
"Graham is a Baptist," he "inclines, almost altogether, to give himself to
interdenominational evangelism, or, as most of us put it, union meetings." Skinner regretted that the evangelist "does not give himself entirely to revivals either in Baptist churches or for groups of Baptist
churches."[57]

Secular weeklies like *Time* and *Newsweek* highlighted the controversy
raised by Niebuhr in a May 23, 1956, *Christian Century* article titled
"Literalism, Individualism, and Billy Graham." Niebuhr specifically criticized Graham's emphasis on individualism and pietism as cures for so-
cietal ills. While Niebuhr held that society must be corrected, Graham
preached that "society can be saved only as individual men have a re-
generating experience with Jesus Christ."[58]

Graham himself refused to take part in the debate, and the controversy was covered in only a few *Western Recorder* articles. The crusade
itself was mentioned only in passing in the September issues of the state
paper. Once the Louisville crusade began, however, writers praised the
sincerity and humility of the dynamic evangelist. Over three hundred
"Kentuckiana" churches "co-operated" with the crusade, providing choir
members, ushers, and counselors to supplement the Graham team,
which included the bass-baritone soloist George Beverly Shea, choir director Cliff Barrows, and musicians Tedd Smith and Paul Mickelson.

Governor A. B. Chandler invited Graham to speak on the Capitol steps
in Frankfort and at the opening service welcomed the evangelist to the
podium. The governor stated that Graham was "the most dynamic and
the most forceful young man who has come across my path. I want to
pledge to him our confidence and our good will, and ask that he show us
the way and bring about the spirit of good will in the hearts of all our
people."[59] Well over half a million people attended the crusade, and thousands of individuals made "decisions for Christ." Crusade officials
worked closely with local pastors, and R. T. Skinner, the one-time reluctant editor, now praised Graham's methods, concluding that "in every
case those expressing a church preference have been turned over to the

pastor."[60] The impact of the Graham crusade, however incalculable, only added to a decade's emphasis on evangelism by Baptists in Kentucky.

The great evangelist was invited back to the state by seminary president Duke K. McCall to speak at Southern's mid-session 1957 commencement. Preaching in the seminary's Alumni Memorial Chapel, Graham, "an honorary alumnus" of the seminary, urged some one hundred graduates to "speak with fervency and fire." Graham advised the graduates to be authoritative in their preaching, to make their message one of simplicity, to make their message relevant, and to make their message decisive.[61] Generations of Kentucky ministers, old and young alike, were influenced by the advice and example of Billy Graham. A Billy Graham Center for Evangelism was later established at Southern Seminary to continue the evangelistic work of the greatest evangelist of the twentieth century.

The 1956 Billy Graham Crusade brought national attention to Louisville and Kentucky. The state's reputation was enhanced further when the Southern Baptist Convention met in Louisville three years later. The convention had met in Russellville in 1866, in Lexington in 1880, and in

Billy Graham Crusade, Cardinal Stadium, Louisville, 1956

Louisville in 1870, 1887, 1899, 1909, and 1927. Kentuckians had long supported the work of the convention, and many state pastors and some laymen had been appointed to key SBC posts. Kentucky Baptist pastors attended SBC annual meetings religiously. A 1961 photograph in the *Western Recorder* pictured the "Front Row Club," and noted that for ten years or more John Kruschwitz, pastor of Versailles Baptist Church, George Jones, pastor at Lawrenceburg before moving to First Baptist Church in Beaufort, South Carolina, and Eldred Taylor, pastor at Somerset, had sat together and occupied front-row seats at the Southern Baptist Convention.[62] Clearly, Kentucky Baptists continued the legacy of E. Y. Mullins and others, remaining highly visible in Southern Baptist Convention affairs.

Within the state, General Association departments other than the Evangelism and Missions Department provided important services for Kentucky Baptists during the boom years of W. C. Boone's tenure as general secretary. J. Chester Durham transformed Baptist student work from weak, fledgling, haphazard attempts to minister to Kentucky's college students to an organization that owned and operated seven student centers on college and university campuses across the state. In 1946, ground was broken for the first Baptist student center in Kentucky on land adjacent to the campus of Murray State College. The project was finally completed in 1949.

The work at Murray had been strong from the start. Durham himself had served from 1941 to 1943 as the Murray State BSU director before his appointment to the General Association post as the director of the Baptist Student Department. The support of Murray's First Baptist Church convinced the General Association to build the first center in Murray. The church gave land for the new center and contributed five thousand dollars for the building. Several church members—Wallace Key, R. H. Falwell, Sr., Thomas Hughes, Jabe Outland, and Dottie Brizendine—served on the center's building committee.

Brizendine, the campus BSU director, worked in that capacity from 1945 to 1950, and, according to Murray's pastor, H. C. Chiles, "wielded a splendid influence over the lives of hundreds of young people." Brizendine herself was transformed by her BSU work. She admitted that "when I came to Murray I was hardly interested in spiritual things. But after a few months of worshipping in your church and finding a little place of service in the BSU on the campus, I realized that God has a plan and a will for every life and I began to seek that plan for my own."

God's plan for Brizendine included her marriage to Paul Mosteller, a fellow Murray State BSU leader, as well as seminary study at Southwestern and Southern seminaries, and service as foreign missionaries to Thailand, where the Mostellers worked from 1956 to 1991.[63] Innovative student leadership at Murray continued under the direction of Joe Priest Williams from 1956 to 1961. In 1961, Williams was called as the pastor of the Baptist Tabernacle Church in downtown Louisville, where he served long and well. The work of BSU leaders like Durham, the Mostellers, and Williams led to dramatic growth in Baptist campus ministries in Kentucky. In 1957, another campus center was erected in Bowling Green. The new center served students at both Bowling Green Business University and Western State College.[64] By 1959, ten campus directors—nine full-time and one part-time— led the work on seven campuses across the commonwealth.

While Baptist student ministries nurtured believing young people through their college experience, the work also placed an emphasis on evangelism. Also closely aligned to the key Kentucky Baptist theme of the postwar years was stewardship. The executive board created a Program of Stewardship Revivals in 1946, and in 1957 a Forward Program of Church Finance was established. Thomas B. Chaney led the new program, and during the first year fifty-eight churches signed on. Over five hundred thousand dollars in budget increases were reported in the first year.

A new Music Department began in 1956 with Eugene Quinn serving as a part-time director. Lucian E. Coleman, Sr., became the first full-time Brotherhood Secretary in 1953, and in 1955 the Royal Ambassadors, a popular missions organization for Baptist boys, was transferred to the Brotherhood Department from Woman's Missionary Union. Forrest R. Sawyer became Brotherhood director in 1958, when Coleman accepted a position with the Southern Baptist Brotherhood Commission.[65]

Garnett Morton began his duties as business manager for the General Association in 1952. W. A. Gardiner led the work of the Sunday School Department—while also organizing activities for eastern Kentucky youth— from 1921 to 1952. Roy Boatwright succeeded him as state Sunday School director and promptly organized a campaign called a "Million More in Fifty-Four," an effort that increased Sunday School enrollment by 35,461 in one year. Byron C. S. DeJarnette retired as director of the Training Union Department (formerly the Baptist Young People's Union) in 1953, after nineteen years of service. The popular DeJarnette and his department had sponsored the first "M" (mobilization) Night to promote Training Union work in 1949. In that year twenty-three "M" Nights were held in associations throughout the state with a total attendance of 7,152.[66] The program continued to be a popular and well-attended annual meeting under James H. Whaley, the individual succeeding DeJarnette as Training Union director.

In 1946, in cooperation with the Relief and Annuity Board of the SBC, the executive board appointed Baynard F. Fox to direct and promote various retirement plans for pastors in the state. As director of retirement

Baptist Building, Middletown, 1957

plans, Fox served throughout the 1950s. By 1961, 805 churches—representing 63 percent of all Kentucky Baptist churches—participated in the program. Rollin S. Burhans and Grady L. Randolph served as Kentucky trustees of the SBC's Annuity Board.[67] Also in 1946, A. M. Vollmer became the first executive secretary and treasurer of the Kentucky Baptist Foundation. When $27,500 in new money was received in 1947, foundation monies totalled $211,283.12, producing an income of $7,328.86 for Baptist causes. In 1948, the assets of the Ministers Aid Society, first organized in 1887, were transferred to the foundation. The foundation remitted the new monies—some $65,515.00—to the Relief and Annuity Board to provide relief benefits for retired Kentucky ministers.[68] By 1961, the foundation, still under the direction of Vollmer, had holdings of $1,672,475.84 and produced an income of $76,226.06.[69]

Two important changes—the move of the state Baptist offices and the election of C. R. Daley as editor of the *Western Recorder*—both coming in 1957, had a dramatic effect on General Association work and on all Kentucky Baptists. On June 21, 1957, the state Baptist offices moved from 127 East Broadway in downtown Louisville to a new Baptist Building at 10701 Shelbyville Road near Middletown. Adjacent to Spring Meadows Children's Home, the new facilities provided dignified and appropriate space for the headquarters of the state's largest denomination.

The move to suburbia was in keeping with a national trend of postwar America. The home for the state offices was located for thirty-four years at 205 East Chestnut, later the site of the offices of Kentucky's Woman's Missionary Union and still later the Jewish Hospital. Then, in 1943, the headquarters were moved to 127 East Broadway in the former educational building of Broadway Baptist Church. Although many leaders thought the

East Broadway site would be adequate for at least fifty years, the growth of state Baptist work, the increase of office personnel, and downtown traffic and parking woes soon made the urban space cramped and inadequate. The much-needed new building was dedicated on July 1 with a message from W. R. Pettigrew, the General Association's moderator. In his dedicatory address, Pettigrew stated that the new building was "simply another evidence of the way God has blessed and led a group of 40,000 Baptists—the membership of the association when it was organized in 1837—to prosper into a group of 600,000."[70] The four-hundred-thousand-dollar, two-story, brick-and-stone structure provided space for an assembly room, departmental offices, and a reception room, including room for the offices of the state executive board and the Woman's Missionary Union.[71]

Also housed in the new facility were the offices and print shop of the *Western Recorder*. The *Recorder*'s editor, R. T. Skinner, had announced his retirement early in 1957. Skinner had served well, diligently documenting the growth and development of churches, associations, and General Association work in the years of the postwar boom. In 1949, Skinner included a weekly "Sunday School Lesson," written by H. C. Chiles, the pastor of the First Baptist Church at Murray. A later editor called the lessons "among the most appreciated features of the state paper."[72] Chiles continued to write the lessons until 1991. Skinner included other features in the state paper and worked hard, along with Robert L. Pogue, his business manager since 1944, to increase circulation.

When the executive board named Chauncey Rakestraw Daley as Skinner's successor in 1957, however, they appointed a new kind of editor, one who would have a far-reaching impact on the social and religious consciousness of Kentucky Baptists for a generation. Called to his new office from the pastorate of Harrodsburg Baptist Church, where he served from 1954 to 1957, Daley had taught at Georgetown College, first as a professor of Greek and Latin (1949-1950), and then as a professor of Old Testament and philosophy (1950-1954). He had also served Georgetown as dean of men from 1952 to 1954. Daley's educational background included degrees from Brewton-Parker Junior College and Mercer University in his home state of Georgia and from Southern Seminary (B.D., 1946; Th.M., 1947; and Th.D., 1955).[73] The scholarly Daley also brought to the editor's office a keen social consciousness and a courage that would translate into a distinguished career as "one of the most influential editors in the Southern Baptist Convention."[74]

Daley refused to ignore the pressing issues of the day. Through his editorial writings—his "Daley Observations"—the editor spoke out on disturbing issues that divided Baptists and the rest of the nation. For example, at the same time that many white Southerners pressed for a continuation of segregation in the South, Daley wrote about his personal stand on the issue. In 1956, W. A. Criswell, the powerful pastor of First Baptist Church, Dallas, Texas, attacked integrationists, alleging that they were "dead from the neck up." Criswell stated that "We built our lives according to deep intimacies that are dear and precious to us. We don't want to be forced by laws or statutes to cross into those intimate things where we don't want to go." Although the Dallas pastor later altered his views, in 1956 Criswell favored segregation in worship as well, insisting that it would be best for religious groups to "stick to their own kind."[75]

C. R. Daley, Western Recorder *editor, 1957-1984*

Daley countered these arguments several years later in a "Daley Observations" editorial titled "A Personal Conviction." The editor made it clear that his was "a purely personal stand," that his views were his own and "in no way an official viewpoint of Kentucky Baptists, nor any Baptist church, nor the Board of Directors of this publication." Daley assured his readers that "it is my testimony and I grant every other Baptist the same liberty of conviction without questioning his sincerity or Christian experience." Daley's "testimony" on the race question was this: "As a Christian and a believer in the New Testament concept of the dignity of man, I cannot but espouse the cause of the Negroes. Discrimination on the grounds of color of skin simply doesn't seem right to me." Daley made his point clear: "When I stand and see whites rough up and arrest blacks who seek admittance to public eating places, there is no question of whose side I espouse." Ever the visionary, Daley concluded that "the years ahead will likely make Baptists who champion segregation today appear as ridiculous as those now appear who championed slavery in the 19th century."[76]

Samuel Southard, an associate professor at Southern Seminary, agreed. In a *Western Recorder* article titled "When Negroes Attend Your Church," Southard foresaw that the question of church integration would become more significant in the future. He argued that pastors, deacons, and church members could ease integration tensions by simply asking the question, "What would Christ have me to do?"[77] The General Association took tentative steps to ease racial tensions in the 1950s. By 1957, a good working relationship had been established with the 150,000-member General Association of Colored Baptists in Kentucky and that organization's superintendent, M. H. Gant. The Executive Board of the General Association of Baptists in Kentucky contributed to the salaries of African American Baptist missionaries and pastors like J. M. Stevenson, U. O. Johnson, and J. B. Porterfield.[78]

In 1959, Daley called on Kentucky Baptists to set "an example for integration." With integrated churches already in the General Association, he wondered if Kentucky could serve as a laboratory for the rest of the Southern Baptist Convention. The editor concluded that "the chief difference between Kentucky and some of the other states of the Southern Baptist Convention in church integration seems to be that integration will take place smoothly but slowly in places where it is needed in Kentucky, but this is too much to expect anytime soon in the Deep South."[79]

Editor Daley included discussions on race, temperance, and church-state issues in his editorials and in articles by guest writers. The relationship between church and state, a signal concern of Baptists since the time of John Clarke, Roger Williams, and John Leland, continued to evoke strong responses from Baptists in Kentucky and in the rest of the nation. In 1958, a new Committee on Public Affairs, a standing committee consisting of nine members, made its first report at the annual General Association meeting held at Severns Valley Baptist Church in Elizabethtown. The committee continued to report on church-state issues—government loans, prayer and Bible reading in public schools, aid to parochial schools, and religious liberty—and on issues having an impact on society and public life—such as war, abortion, and government—in the years ahead.[80]

Daley's determination not to shy away from social issues in the pages of the state Baptist paper was evident from the start. Controversial issues relating directly to Baptist work within the state required the new editor to marshal the full range of his courage, expertise, and tact, and Daley characteristically addressed these issues with impartial grace. At the same time, the editor continued his practice of voicing his personal convictions. In his first few years as editor, he had ample opportunity to practice his considerable gift of tactful courage. In 1958, the editor consistently informed Kentucky Baptists about two controversial developments that had a decidedly unsettling effect on Kentucky Baptist life.

In that year, a serious rift developed between members of Southern Seminary's theology faculty and the president, Duke K. McCall. Southern's Board of Trustees had elected McCall as president in 1951 following the heart attack and sudden death of Ellis Fuller the previous year. The seeds of the controversy were sown with the hiring of Fuller. Historically, Southern trustees had relied on the Southern faculty for administrative decisions in addition to classroom teaching. From the beginning, faculty had exerted enormous energy to provide various administrative services; faculty also had great influence in decisions of faculty appointments. Indeed, A. T. Robertson served as a model of the scholar/teacher/administrator and was relied on heavily by scholar/teacher/presidents E. Y. Mullins and John R. Sampey.

During Sampey's tenure and especially with the hiring of Fuller, the former pastor of the First Baptist Church in Atlanta, the trustees required and expected more administrative initiative from the president. And Fuller provided that. Described as "a brilliant and powerful preacher, a popular pastor and a proven administrator," Fuller did not "claim great scholarship." Rather, Fuller proved to be "a builder and fund raiser par excellence."[81] Under his leadership, Southern Seminary grew in facilities, student numbers, endowment, and prestige. Following his untimely death, the trustees appointed McCall, yet another proven administrator.

Born in Meridian, Mississippi, in 1914, the new president studied at Furman University (A.B.) and Southern Seminary (Th.M. and Ph.D.). After a brief pastorate at Louisville's Broadway Baptist Church, McCall became president of New Orleans Baptist Theological Seminary in 1943. Then in 1946, the young administrator was elected as the new executive secretary of the Executive Committee of the Southern Baptist Convention. McCall had also served as the treasurer of the SBC and as a member of the Executive Committee of the Baptist World Alliance. His credentials as a proven Southern Baptist leader were impeccable. When McCall came to Southern Seminary, trustees changed the institution's constitution and by-laws, placing even more authority and responsibility in the hands of the president. A reorganization that provided for five deans to assist the president seemed to further diminish the prestige of the teaching faculty.[82]

Although McCall's relationships with faculty members were cordial during the first few years of his tenure, tensions increased in 1958 when a faculty report to the trustees "spoke of low morale of the faculty and pointed to the administration as the cause." Disagreements over hiring and promotion decisions heightened the tension. The controversy was decidedly not based on issues of theology. Rather, personality conflicts and differing perspectives about administrative and faculty prerogatives provided the central ingredients for the dispute. When the impasse between members of the theology faculty and the president could not be settled, thirteen faculty members were fired by the Board of Trustees.[83] The faculty members found employment at other Baptist colleges, at the newly founded Midwestern Seminary in Kansas City, and as pastors. One professor, J. J. Owens, sought and obtained reinstatement at Southern.

The American Association of Theological Schools, the seminary's accrediting agency, deferred any decision to remove accreditation for one year; the accrediting committee placed the blame for the "intolerable conditions" at the seminary on the president and trustees.[84] The seminary continued to suffer embarrassment in the secular press. In the Baptist press, C. R. Daley referred to the firings as "an unprecedented action in the 99 year history of Southern Baptist Theological Seminary." "Nothing like it has ever happened in the history of this or any other Southern Baptist institution," Daley wrote. "The recent controversy at Southern Seminary that resulted in the dismissal of thirteen professors is the Baptist story of the year and very well could be the Baptist story of the twentieth century."[85]

Another important story filled the pages of the *Western Recorder* late in 1958. In 1957, messengers at the annual General Association meeting in Harlan voted to appoint a committee of fifteen "to study the entire State Program of Kentucky Baptists." This Survey Committee, chaired by Robert E. Humphreys of Owensboro, engaged the services of Booz, Allen and Hamilton, a consulting firm from Chicago, to conduct the survey and offer recommendations. Later, the firm derisively referred to by J. D. Grey, a Kentuckian who eventually became pastor of First Baptist Church, New Orleans, as "Booz, Allen and Budweiser," presented a sixteen-page report at the annual General Association meeting in Elizabethtown in November 1958.[86]

The report recommended sweeping changes for the entire work of the General Association and especially for Baptist higher education in the state. For his part, C. R. Daley indicated his approval of the substance of the report and noted in his October 23, "Daley Observations" that "it's now or never" for Kentucky Baptists. Daley concluded that "there is little doubt that any meeting of the General Association since 1837 will be judged by history as more significant" than the 1958 meeting at Elizabethtown.[87] Other Kentucky Baptist constituents immediately voiced strong opposition to the report. Wilbur T. Chapin, president of the Kentucky Baptist Foundation, objected to the recommendation that the responsibility of the promotion of endowment giving be taken away from the foundation. W. Edwin Richardson, president of Bethel College, John M. Carter, of Campbellsville, and D. M. Aldridge, of Clear Creek, jointly composed an article for the *Western Recorder*, citing information not included in the survey report.[88]

The presidents had cause for concern. The report called for the withdrawal of General Association support for Clear Creek Baptist School and for Magoffin Baptist Institute, and that Bethel, Campbellsville, and Cumberland be invited to merge with a new Kentucky Baptist University to be located in Louisville. As for the state's oldest Baptist institution, Georgetown College was to serve as "the nucleus" for the new Louisville university. Georgetown's board of trustees would eventually "develop a plan which will over a period of years gradually transfer its principal educational program to the Louisville site."[89]

Fear and controversy over the survey report, especially the portions relating to Christian education, resulted in the General Association's decision to refer the report to the executive board without the controversial Section IX dealing with Christian education. Rollin S. Burhans, pastor of Louisville's Crescent Hill Baptist Church, and the newly elected moderator of the General Association, offered a substitute motion on Christian education that would allow the continued operation and support of the existing colleges and schools. The substitute motion also reapproved the 1956 action of the General Association to start a Baptist junior college in Louisville—rather than a four-year university—as a branch of Georgetown College. In addition, Burhans's substitute motion reaffirmed the action of messengers in 1957 to grant four-year status to Campbellsville and Cumberland.[90]

Daley referred to the much-anticipated 1958 meeting as "a do-nothing meeting." According to the editor, "the most that we can say is we started to look at ourselves, but, outside of a few glances at Christian education, we didn't even hear a word on the rest of the $25,000 examination of Kentucky Baptists." "All in all," the editor lamented, the 1958 meeting "might well be remembered as the General Association where there was more interest and less accomplishment than any in our history."[91]

Despite the editor's pessimism, positive changes did come from that 1958 General Association meeting in Elizabethtown. The abbreviated survey report was referred to the executive committee, which then appointed a new Committee of Seventeen to study the report and bring recommendations to the board. In 1959, the board presented an eleven-page report to messengers in Lexington, most of which was accepted. Then in 1960, yet another report, this time six pages in length, was submitted. The new report included the change of the name of the General Association of Baptists in Kentucky to the Kentucky Baptist Convention. The name change, in line with the practice of other states, was coupled with a change in the title of the presiding officer of the convention. Beginning in 1961, this officer would be referred to as president rather than moderator. This last report submitted by the committee chaired by Carroll Hubbard was finally accepted by messengers, and the committee was thanked and dismissed.[92]

Along with the disruption at Southern Seminary and the clamor over the survey report, one other controversy was settled during the final years of the tenure of W. C. Boone as general secretary. The involvement of women in churches and denominational affairs was always crucial for the growth—indeed, the survival—of the Baptist presence in the commonwealth. Of course, the beginnings of the Woman's Missionary Union had strong Kentucky connections. The WMU continued to make an impact on missions education and on missions endeavors in the postwar boom years. Mary Nelle Lyne served as the state executive secretary during the Great Depression and into the war years. With her resignation in 1942, Mary P. Winburne was appointed and served from 1942 to 1948. Mrs. George R. Ferguson began her long and effective tenure as executive secretary in 1949. With her leadership, participation in the state WMU increased from 51,898 women in 1949 to 72,939 in 1959. An auxiliary to the General Association, the WMU worked closely with the executive board in all phases of missions work in Kentucky.

The visibility and participation of women in General Association affairs had been all but invisible, however. As early as 1908, some 100 women were included among the 433 messengers at the annual meeting in Louisville. The following year, however, the constitution was interpreted to allow for male messengers only. Since 1909, women were not included as messengers even though the Southern Baptist Convention had allowed women messengers at SBC meetings since 1918.[93] Not until 1956 was the issue raised again in Kentucky.

During a Wednesday afternoon session at the 1956 meeting in Madisonville, "a woman visitor" sought the floor and asked whether it was customary for a woman to speak. The moderator, Murray's H. C. Chiles, replied that "it was contrary to the practice of the body." Edwin F. Perry, the pastor of Louisville's Broadway Baptist Church, then moved that if she was a messenger to the association she should be given the opportunity to speak. In the meantime, the woman made it known that she was not a messenger. When the question of seating women messengers was raised, Chiles ruled that the question would be addressed at the next period of "Miscellaneous Business." Later, when Paducah's Frank F. Norfleet moved that "all who have been elected by their churches as messengers be accorded the privilege of voting," the motion was accepted.[94] Still later, Perry moved that Nor-

fleet's motion be extended to future meetings, that "all duly elected messengers from co-operating Baptist churches be so registered in future
meetings of the General Association of Baptists in Kentucky."[95]

Although men continued to read WMU reports submitted by WMU leaders throughout the 1950s, by 1956 the process had been initiated to allow
women the same participatory rights in Kentucky that they had shared at
meetings of the Southern Baptist Convention since 1918. This change was
indicative of the many changes experienced by Kentucky Baptists during
the tenure of W. C. Boone. Great progress and growth had occurred, even
though the controversies of the late 1950s had averted the attention of
Kentucky Baptists from the general secretary's primary emphases of evangelism and stewardship.

C. R. Daley grieved in 1958 that records indicated that Kentucky Baptists
fared poorly when compared to other states. In 1956, for example, Kentucky
Baptists gave for all church causes an average of only $33.41, ranking Ken-
tuckians last in per-capita giving among the twenty-six bodies that comprised the Southern Baptist Convention. The figure would have been lower if
not for town and city churches. The per-capita gifts for "open country
churches" totaled only $19.18 compared with $48.16 for city churches. Daley lamented the fact that of the $33.41 average, $27.48 stayed with the local
church and only $5.93 went for mission causes through the Cooperative Pro-
gram. Of that amount, $4.37 stayed within the state, and a mere $1.56 went
outside the state for the rest of the world.[96] By 1959-60, distribution of gifts
showed that 66 percent remained within the state and only 34 percent was
used convention-wide.

Throughout the 1950s, monies for SBC causes were further diminished by
certain "preferred items" taken out of the convention-wide share. For example, the Cooperative Program budget goal for 1951-52 was $1.5 million, with
60 percent designated for state causes and 40 percent for SBC causes. Because the General Association made a commitment to pay $144,000 per year
on the debt owed by the state's three Baptist hospitals, plus $50,000 for Bap-
tist schools and $25,000 for Baptist children's homes in the state, the "pre-
ferred" list was extended dramatically. In all, $394,000 or 26.3 percent of Co-
operative Program money was spent before the announced 60/40 division.
Actual figures indicated that 70.5 percent of total gifts stayed in Kentucky,
leaving only 29.5 percent for other SBC causes in 1951-52.[97] Boone's vision
for Kentucky Baptists to win the world for Christ was yet to be accomplished.

Despite these disappointing statistics, it is still accurate to refer to
Boone's tenure as the "boom years" in Kentucky Baptist life. As the leader
of Kentucky Baptists, Boone played an important role in bringing positive
changes to the General Association. Thoughtful, but at the same time en-

ergetic, he seemed to be everywhere around the state. A *Western Recorder* writer described his many and varied activities:

> A Sunday afternoon may find him speaking at the dedication of a new church. On Monday he may meet with a committee of the Executive Board. Tuesday may find him in conference with the department secretaries of the Board. On Wednesday he may visit one of the thirteen institutions in the state. Thursday may see him in conference with the Business Manager, studying the receipts and expenditures for the past month. On Friday he may attend a Convention-wide conference outside the state.[98]

Boone's "aggressive, dedicated, and wise" leadership resulted in important gains for the state organization. Membership and attendance in Kentucky Baptist churches rose, baptisms increased, and total gifts through the churches jumped from $7.6 million in 1946 to $24.6 million in 1960, Boone's last full year in office. Cooperative Program gifts rose from about $775,000 to over $2,225,000. New departments, new hospitals, and new children's homes had been founded, and a new headquarters built. Kentucky Baptists had played a seminal role in the organization of two new state conventions in Ohio and Indiana.

Then, as if in recognition for the contributions of Kentucky Baptists, the Southern Baptist Convention met in Louisville in May 1959. C. R. Daley encouraged the state's Baptists to attend the Freedom Hall sessions, describing the event as a "last-in-a-lifetime chance."[99] Because Kentucky had inadequate facilities "to care for the hordes of Southern Baptists these days," the commonwealth would likely never entertain the convention again. The fact that 1959 was also the one hundredth anniversary of Southern Seminary convinced SBC officials to hold the convention in Louisville.

Daley welcomed convention messengers to Kentucky: "To many the Bluegrass State is best known for bourbon whiskey and blooded horses but to the thousands of visitors to Louisville this week, it ought to be emphasized that Kentucky is also a land of Baptists."[100] A land of Baptists indeed! From Squire Boone, the brother of Daniel Boone and probably the state's first Baptist preacher, to W. C. Boone, a descendant of Samuel Boone, another of Daniel's brothers, Baptists had made an indelible imprint on the history of the state. By the end of the 1950s, one of every five Kentuckians—over six hundred thousand—was a member of a Baptist church affiliated with the Southern Baptist Convention. In addition, as Daley put it, "there is about every other kind of Baptist in Kentucky that can be found anywhere and then some." General Baptists, Regular Baptists, Freewill

Baptists, United Baptists, and the "No-Hellers" of eastern Kentucky all represented different hues of the Baptist rainbow in Kentucky.

Daley gave credit to W. C. Boone, the "quiet, mild-mannered man of God," for bringing "peace, tranquility and progress to Baptists in Kentucky." When Boone announced that he would retire on September 30, 1961, Daley wrote that Kentucky Baptists would lose a leader of "dignity, poise, and self-restraint." Boone's retirement announcement to the ninety-two members of the executive board in May brought, according to Daley, "a profound stillness over the whole group."[101] The stillness belied the peripatetic nature of the executive secretary's work in all the years since 1946.

6
chapter

Gains and Losses
1961-1972

Called upon to present the Woman's Missionary Union report for the first time at the 1962 annual meeting of the Kentucky Baptist Convention in Owensboro, Mrs. George R. Ferguson, executive secretary of Kentucky's WMU, simply rose to move the adoption of the report. Then, after the motion was seconded, she promptly called on newly appointed state WMU president Julia Woodward to discuss the report.

From Lexington, the quiet and unassuming Woodward had been active in WMU work for years. She remembered that her mother had belonged to a local WMU circle in the early years of the twentieth century. Mrs. Woodward took Julia to Sunbeams, a mission program for young children, and during one program the young, impressionable girl "heard that there was a place called China, and people didn't know about Jesus there." Later, Woodward remembered "turning over and over in my mind, 'Why doesn't someone go to tell them?' And I guess that was my first realization that somebody needed to go."[1] Woodward did not go herself, but she became deeply involved in Kentucky's Woman's Missionary Union for the rest of her life, first as a circle chairman and president of local societies, and then in 1961 as president of the state organization.

Now, late on Tuesday afternoon, November 13, 1962, Woodward rose hesitantly to address the gathered messengers in the sanctuary of Owensboro's Third Baptist Church. The tired and hungry messengers had al-

173

ready heard numerous reports and an address by Verlin Kruschwitz, prominent pastor of Severns Valley Baptist Church who was also the convention president. The afternoon session had already lingered almost an hour past the anticipated 4:30 adjournment. And messengers were to return at 6:30 for the music service preceding the evening session.

Years later, Woodward recalled that she was "scared to death." Then, as she proceeded to the podium, men began to rush toward the back exits, beating a hasty retreat for a hurried supper before the evening program. President Kruschwitz, recognizing the significance of the slight, banged his gavel loudly on the desk and stated sternly, "Now, men, you voted for these women to make their report. Now you come back and listen!" Woodward remembered that the departing pastors and laymen promptly "turned around and came back" to hear the report. Woodward said, "We've laughed about that for a long time, but Brother Kruschwitz didn't pull any punches."[2]

In "A Message from Our New President" printed in the May 11, 1961, issue of the *Western Recorder*, Woodward stated humbly that Kentucky Baptists had "bestowed upon me the highest of honors and I am very conscious of my unworthiness." "The disturbing age in which we live is a testing time for every Christian," Woodward wrote. "As members of Woman's Missionary Union, let us prepare ourselves through study and prayer to give and go, in order to bring Christ and His message to those who have never heard." In light of her role in the continuing drama of the missionary work and participation of both men and women in Kentucky Baptist life, it was appropriate that Woodward ended her article with a quote from a John Oxenham poem as she described the ongoing pilgrimage:

> So make we—all one company,
> Love's golden cord our tether,
> And, come what may, we'll climb the hill
> Together—aye, together.[3]

Kentucky Baptists often failed to take Oxenham's verse to heart during the decade of the 1960s, but not because of Woodward and Ferguson. Woodward served well as president of the state's WMU, not once, but twice, during the decade. First elected as president in 1961, the member of Long Lick Baptist Church in Scott County returned to the office in 1968. The long tenure of Mrs. George Ferguson as executive secretary ended with her retirement in 1970. Ferguson had been named to the post in 1949 after serving as state president. A native of Hancock County in western Kentucky and a graduate of the WMU Training School (later the Carver School of Missions), Ferguson was honored at the 1970 WMU convention at Paducah's First Baptist Church.

The Paducah meeting featured Baker James Cauthen, executive secretary of the SBC's Foreign Mission Board. Characterized as "a man with the whole world in his heart," Cauthen delivered "ringing challenges" to continue the work of Southern Baptist missions, especially in Laos, a country only recently opened to SBC missionaries. With the new work in Laos, Southern Baptist missionaries worked in seventy-two countries around the world. The executive secretary's wife set the mood for each session with devotional meditations, messages emphasizing the convention's theme:

Mrs. George R. Ferguson,
executive secretary,
Kentucky WMU, 1947-1970

"Sealed with Witnessing Power." During the convention, Mrs. Ferguson was honored with a tea in the "Ladies Parlor" of nearby Immanuel Baptist Church.[4] For twenty-one years, her work had furthered missions causes in the state.

In September 1970, Mrs. Ferguson accompanied Mary Kathryn Jasper to various regional meetings around the state, introducing her as the new executive secretary. Jasper, a Somerset native, was a graduate of Eastern Kentucky University; like her predecessor, she received a Master of Religious Education degree at the WMU Training School in 1949. It was her father's pastoral work in Harlan in eastern Kentucky that first taught her the need for missions. Robert Fulton Jasper, a medical doctor and Baptist pastor, was called to Harlan, across the mountain from Hazard, where the famed A. S. Petrey ministered; both areas had few Southern Baptist churches. In Harlan, Jasper practiced medicine and organized and pastored churches, churches unable to pay regular pastors' salaries.[5]

It was in this home—in Somerset, Harlan, and also in Cumberland and Verda—that Jasper developed an intense love for the church and for missions. At the Cumberland Baptist Church, her Sunbeam leader, Mother Jacobs, had moved from Rome, Georgia. With "her beautiful southern brogue," she "made missions just absolutely live." Mother Jacobs also traveled extensively; during one trip to England, she purchased demitasse cups for each child in her Sunbeam group. The cups made an impression on the young Sunbeams, and, more importantly, Mother Jacobs's stories of missionaries were not forgotten. Years later, Jasper recalled thinking after one particularly vivid missionary story that "some day I'm going to grow up and I'm going to see one of those missionaries." She remembered Cumberland as a "very restricted" area surrounded by mountains. "I'm going to go over that mountain sometime," she told herself, "and I'm going to see these people she's talking about." Mother Jacobs "simply ministered to our imaginations," and "from that early day I became interested in missions and it just grew and grew."[6]

Jasper had already had an effective career in mission work and Baptist administration around the South before being named executive secretary of Kentucky's WMU. She served as BSU director at her alma mater in Richmond, at Mississippi State College for Women in Columbus, and then as the citywide director in Jackson, Mississippi. She had also served as youth director of First Baptist Church in Owensboro. Immediately preceding her new position in Kentucky—from 1961 to 1970—she had worked as activities director for the School of Nursing at Memorial Baptist Hospital, an affiliate of Houston Baptist College in Texas. Then, in 1970, Mrs. Chester Durham, chairman of the WMU personnel committee, and Julia Woodward flew to Houston to discuss the position with Jasper. Although flattered, Jasper was initially not interested, but later was convinced that she should accept the invitation.[7]

The inspirational work of Kentucky Baptist women like Ferguson, Woodward, Jasper, and Mother Jacobs belied the extent of women's involvement in leadership positions in Southern Baptist and Kentucky Baptist denominational affairs. C. R. Daley, editor of the *Western Recorder*, wrote in 1969 that "the question now is what place do women have in official leadership roles among Southern Baptists." Daley surveyed denominational committees and boards and found that in the states and in the SBC women were "almost completely left out so far as leadership roles are concerned." For example, only two women were among the sixty members of the SBC's executive committee; six women served on the sixty-six-member Foreign Mission Board. In Kentucky, the numbers were even lower. On Kentucky's 141-member executive board, the state WMU president in an ex-officio capacity was the lone woman representative. Only six women made up "the entire crop of women in official Kentucky Baptist Convention service."[8]

Daley underscored the discrepancy in official and actual service in Kentucky's Baptist churches: "Whatever we believe the New Testament teaches about the role of women, in actual practice we look to them for more than a subordinate place. They carry the burden of the teaching load in nearly every Baptist church. Women are also the backbone of the music program and without them missionary education in many churches would be almost nil." John C. Huffman, pastor of Mayfield's First Baptist Church, praised Daley for the timeliness of his editorial. As chair of the KBC's nominating committee, Huffman suggested to committee members that they nominate a woman for each vacancy to be filled. Huffman hoped "that the condition you correctly lament will change." Daley also raised the issue of women's ordination. Although ordination of women "is fairly common in some evangelical denominations and is practiced by American Baptists," he wrote, there was no indication that "Southern Baptists are ready to ordain women or will be ready for this any time in the foreseeable future."[9]

Less than a month after Daley's column appeared, however, the *Western Recorder*'s assistant editor, Bob Terry, reported in the February 6, 1969, edition the ordination of two women—the first women to be ordained in a church affiliated with the Kentucky Baptist Convention—as deacons of Georgetown's Faith Baptist Church. Harold Sanders, the KBC's executive secretary, recognized the ordinations as a first in Kentucky Baptist life: "I know of no other church affiliated with our convention that has women deacons. Only one or two in the entire SBC have women deacons that I am aware of."[10]

The *Recorder* reported that Mrs. Robert Snyder and Mrs. Wallace Williams were ordained along with William Vessels and Gayle Johnson in the service conducted by Robert Mills, president of Georgetown College, and Grady Randolph, superintendent of missions for Elkhorn Association. Snyder, an M.R.E. graduate of Southwestern Seminary and the holder of a Ph.D. in speech from Northwestern University, had served as a minister of youth and education in several churches in Virginia and Texas, including Ft. Worth's University Baptist Church. Williams, a native of Mayfield, had grown up under the ministry of John Huffman at Mayfield's First Baptist Church. "My background is strongly conservative," Williams stated. "I've spoken in churches near my home where it was most unusual for a woman to speak. When I worked on mountain youth teams I was expected to give my testimony for Christ but I got myself in ticklish situations more than once." Both Snyder and Williams emphasized that they would continue as deacons to minister to college girls and single women in Georgetown.[11]

Response to the ordination of women at Faith Baptist was immediate and contrasting. Reed Rushing from Russellville wrote that Faith's action was scriptural, that Romans 16:1 identified Phoebe as a "diakonon" or deaconess to "tes ekklesias" or the churches. Franklin P. Rowe from Pikeville disagreed. Rowe quoted Acts 6:3 and 1 Timothy 3:12 and lamented, "What next? Women preachers! God forbid."[12]

The question of women's ordination was only one issue that divided Southern and Kentucky Baptists in the 1960s. Indeed, as early as 1962, James Leo Garrett, a professor of Christian theology at Southern Seminary, published an article in the *Western Recorder* titled "Ought Southern Baptists to Divide?" Garrett recognized that current disagreements among Baptists were not unique to the 1960s. Historically, "from the advent of Landmarkism in the 1850's to the eschatological rumblings of the early 1950's Southern Baptists have encountered divisive issues." Even the fundamentalist/modernist controversies of the twenties did not prove to be ultimately "divisive or separative."[13] The theological controversies of the 1960s seemed to present a more imminent danger.

By the mid-1960s, Southern Baptist Convention churches boasted the largest membership—10,393,039—of any Protestant church body. Only the Methodist Church with 10,304,184 members rivaled Southern Baptists in numbers. In Kentucky, over six hundred thousand individuals—or one of every five Kentuckians—belonged to a church affiliated with the Kentucky Baptist Convention.[14] Certainly, the dominance of the Kentucky Baptist Convention and the Southern Baptist Convention among Protestant expressions of faith appeared to be threatened from within as the Cold War continued into the 1960s. In the SBC, prominent pastors like W. A. Criswell, minister at First Baptist Church, Dallas, the convention's largest church, sometimes encouraged disgruntled Baptists to find a new denominational home. In state organizations, however, leaders were not anxious to preside over the dismantling of conventions under their watch. In Kentucky, the trying—and exciting—1960s came during the tenure of an individual who had previously spent little time in the state.

Upon the retirement of W. C. Boone in September 1961, Harold G. Sanders, pastor of First Baptist Church of Tallahassee, Florida, since 1946, was elected by the executive board as the new executive secretary-treasurer. Although some Kentucky Baptists felt that a Kentuckian should fill the post and had considered Carroll Hubbard, the chair of the executive board, "a choice prospect for the job," Hubbard did not seek the nomination. The election of Sanders was conducted in executive session by secret ballot. On the first ballot he garnered 76 percent of the vote; when a motion for a second vote prevailed, he received 93 out of the 102 votes cast.[15]

Harold Sanders, executive secretary, Kentucky Baptists, 1961-1972

A native of Missouri, Sanders attended both Southwest Baptist College and William Jewell College in his home state and received both Th.M. and Th.D. degrees from Southern Seminary. While a student at Southern, Sanders pastored churches in Indiana and Kentucky, including Christiansburg Baptist Church in Shelby County and River View Baptist Church in Nelson County. As a Navy chaplain in the Pacific theatre during World War II, he baptized more than four hundred soldiers in New Guinea and the Philippines. After the war, he remained active in veterans' organizations and in 1955 served as president of the Southern Baptist Chaplains Association. He was called to the pastorate of the Tallahassee church immediately after the war. Under his leadership the church flourished: the budget increased from $28,000 in 1945 to $337,000 in 1961, and church membership grew to 4,500, making it the second-largest Baptist church in Florida.[16] Wide experience in various SBC agencies made Sanders an attractive choice to lead Kentucky Baptists into the sixties.

Franklin Owen, pastor of Calvary Baptist, the influential Lexington church, recalled that upon coming to Middletown, Sanders "hit the ground running."[17] "Energetic" and "gifted," the new executive's plans were ambitious, optimistic, and far-reaching. His dreams included adequate funding for Baptist schools and colleges, a first-rate assembly center and program at Cedarmore, harmony among the state's black and white Baptist bodies, and a reorganization of the KBC's executive board. While the new executive secretary realized some of his goals, other plans met opposition or went unfulfilled. The Sanders Era proved to be a period of gains and losses in Kentucky Baptist life.

Sanders's tenure fell in the middle of what has been called America's second reconstruction. The Civil Rights movement, pushed along by the *Brown v. Board of Education of Topeka, Kansas*, Supreme Court decision in 1954 and the Civil Rights Act a decade later, continued into the last years of the 1960s. In 1968, the racial crisis in the nation and the Southern Baptist response to it was voted the top news story of the year by the editors of thirty Baptist state papers around the nation.[18] More than a hundred years earlier, during the first Reconstruction, white Baptists in Kentucky had elected a committee on "Our Relations and Duties to the Colored population." The General Association of Baptists in Kentucky often worked jointly with the General Association of Colored Baptists to strengthen African American churches.

In 1963, white Kentucky Baptists addressed the issue of race relations as a convention for the first time. A statement adopted by the messengers was described by *Western Recorder* editor C. R. Daley as "very likely the strongest statement ever made by one of the older Southern Baptist state conventions on racial equality." The statement was by no means an attempt to "do away with Negro churches or conventions," the editor asserted. "As long as separate churches and conventions can do a better job of what New Testament churches are commissioned to do, they should remain separate," he said. "The point is that color alone should not be the deciding factor in accepting or rejecting blacks who want to join white churches or whites who want to join Negro churches."[19]

The race question came to the forefront not only in Kentucky's Baptist churches, but in the arena of the commonwealth's other major interest—regarded by many Kentuckians as a major Bluegrass religion—basketball. Although Adolph Rupp, the revered coach of the University of Kentucky Wildcats, had, along with other southern collegiate coaches, been reluctant to recruit black athletes, the recruiting battle for Butch Beard, the impressive guard at Breckinridge County High School, and his apparent signing by the University of Louisville, caused C. R. Daley to devote an entire column in the *Western Recorder* to college basketball recruiting. Although Daley did not mention race, the issue was apparent as the editor lambasted the intensity of the recruiting battle between the University of Louisville and the University of Kentucky:

> What offers have been dangled before this lad will likely never be known. What effect they will have even upon such a fine boy is yet to be seen. One can remember a few years ago when Louisville's Cassius Clay was billed as a clean, quiet youth. Now look at him! Butch Beard now shows no tendency to fall into the

errors of Clay, but he is not being helped by the recruiting tactics of college officials.[20]

Daley ended his column with a plea for sanity: "Long live basketball in Kentucky! But the sooner such recruiting tactics die, the better!"[21] As it turned out, Beard signed to play basketball at the University of Louisville, a program already desegregated in 1965; it would take several more years before the University of Kentucky's basketball team would be integrated.

In Kentucky Baptist life, however, closer cooperation between the state's black and white conventions was proposed at the 1965 meeting of the Kentucky Baptist Convention in Lexington. Presided over by Franklin Owen, the pastor of Calvary—the host church—the recommendations were made in a report presented by the convention's Christian Life Committee. Owen's church had received its first black members before 1960, but most Kentucky Baptist Convention churches remained completely white.

A two-year study conducted by the KBC's Public Affairs and Christian Life Committees showed that in 1965, more than a decade since the Brown decision, integration was slow in coming to Kentucky Baptist institutions. Out of a total of 253 faculty members in Kentucky Baptist colleges and schools, none was black. No African Americans served as college trustees. Only thirty-two black students—twenty-nine of them Americans—had enrolled in the state's four Baptist colleges. All three Kentucky Baptist hospitals admitted black patients, but only one hospital had black doctors serving on its staff; two of the three employed black nurses. The survey committee concluded that "practices in integration have not caught up with official policy."[22] Still, progress had been made, and Kentucky Baptists should be grateful, Daley asserted, that "racial turmoil among so many of our fellow Southern Baptists" was absent and that long-established segregation traditions were not so rigid in the commonwealth.

At the KBC's Lexington meeting, messengers voted to invite members of the General Association to the convention's meeting the following year in Bowling Green, and plans were made for the two state organizations to meet jointly in Louisville on November 10, 1967. Messengers at the 1966 Bowling Green meeting voted to establish a Department of Interracial Cooperation, and Herman Ihley became the department's first secretary. Before Ihley's untimely heart attack and death in 1970, the secretary had led several black churches to align dually with both conventions. One white KBC church had also dually aligned with the black General Association. Lauded as "a deeply warm-hearted Christian with the unusual ability of remembering to do for others those 'little things' which became great things that were meaningful and unforgotten by his friends," Ihley was described by W. R. Grigg, associate secretary of work with National Baptists for the SBC's Home Mission Board, as "one of the more creative men that we have had in this type of work."[23] William H. Rogers, the pastor of Louisville's Melbourne Heights Baptist Church, was chosen in May 1971 to continue Ihley's work. By 1972, the work of Ihley and Rogers had resulted in the dual alignment of twelve black churches and two white churches.

The 1967 joint meeting marked the first time the two conventions had met together officially since the organization of separate conventions in 1865. (The General Association had invited white Kentucky Baptists to attend General Association sessions at Norris Chapel Baptist Church in Henderson in 1966, and Harold Sanders had preached one of the annual sermons.) Sessions of the historic joint meeting took place in the sanctuary of Louisville's Walnut Street Baptist Church; an evening youth rally was held in Freedom Hall. Two of the "outstanding Baptist preachers in Kentucky" were featured in the afternoon session: Garland Offutt, an African American pastor and teacher at West Chestnut Street Baptist Church in Louisville, a graduate of Southern Seminary, and according to one writer "one of the ablest pulpiteers and gentlest spirits Kentucky Baptists will ever hear and know"; and Keevil Judy, the pastor of Henderson's First Baptist Church, former president of the KBC, and "dean of Kentucky Baptist preachers."[24] The Freedom Hall Youth Rally drew over twenty thousand young people and featured a five-thousand-voice youth choir directed by Genter L. Stephens of New Orleans Baptist Theological Seminary. The success of the joint meetings resulted in a series of race relations conferences the following year led by the leaders of the two Baptist conventions in the state, A. R. Lasley, moderator of the General Association, and Sanders.

In the early months of 1968, progress in race relations in Kentucky and throughout the Southern Baptist Convention was evident. The resolve of leaders received a stern test, however, when news spread of the tragic assassination of Martin Luther King, Jr., in Memphis, Tennessee, on April 4. Daley wrote that despite recent gains, "the harvest of hatred and the ravages of racism continue to heap shame on our land and make shambles of the claim of freedom, equality and justice in America." In his editorial titled "He Died to Make Men Free," the *Western Recorder* editor declared that King's murder "should haunt the consciences of all Americans." Though the civil rights leader was "felled by one demented assassin," everyone who contributed to racism and "blind prejudice" was to blame. "This includes Southern Baptists," he asserted, "who more than any other religious group have responsibility for the part of America that produced him and murdered him." Although King was a Baptist, he was rejected and criticized by most white Southern Baptists. Daley concluded that this "often has been so, the heroes of succeeding generations are rejected by their fellowmen."[25]

That Daley's words were true was evident when H. W. Wood of Harlan responded on May 9, 1968, with a letter to the editor. Wood wrote in obvious disgust with the editor's praise for the late civil rights leader: "It seems to me there are more important and interesting things to write about than Martin Luther King," he insisted. Wood charged that J. Edgar Hoover of the FBI had "classed King as a communist" and "you are lowering the opinion Baptists and others have of our denomination by such editorials."[26]

Despite the setback of the King tragedy, groups of Kentucky Baptists continued to work for racial harmony. Students led the way. Soon after King's assassination, over 325 Baptist student leaders gathered in Berea for an annual BSU leadership conference. The students pledged themselves to "personal sacrifices" in working for racial harmony and justice and stated that in light of the recent tragedy it was clear "a new intensity of dedication resulting in fresh approaches and departures from existing attitudes and actions is urgently in order." The students pledged to work to eliminate all vestiges of discrimination in Baptist Student Unions, fraternities and sororities, clubs, student housing, and employment. Ever evangelistic, they further pledged to involve themselves "in an aggressive program of witnessing to bring students of all races to a knowledge of Jesus Christ and to enlist them in the fellowship and service of our churches."[27]

Other white Kentucky Baptists caught the students' enthusiasm for constructive change. Pastors from across the state responded with sadness to the King murder. "Race Relations Sundays" were held around the state, and white and black pastors exchanged pulpits in observance of the event. A week of special services held at Louisville's Crescent Hill Baptist Church, pastored by the young and dynamic John R. Claypool, featured Charles E. Boddie, president of the American Baptist Seminary in Nashville. Wesley Shipp, recently dismissed from a church in another state because of his determination to promote racial harmony, was called to Louisville's Twenty-Third and Broadway Baptist Church in 1970. Located in a demographically changing area of west Louisville, Shipp led the predominantly white congregation to integrate and open church doors to black families in the area. Joe Priest Williams, pastor of Baptist Tabernacle, another inner-city Louisville church, was also prominent in efforts to promote interracial cooperation.[28] A joint evangelistic conference held at Southern Seminary in January 1969 prepared black and white Baptists for participation in the Crusade of the Americas planned for that year.[29]

SBC President H. Franklin Paschall, pastor of Nashville's First Baptist Church and a native of Hazel, Kentucky, suggested that a major statement on race relations would be forthcoming at the June 1968 meeting of the Southern Baptist Convention in Houston. Paschall's prediction proved true when convention messengers overwhelmingly approved "a historic statement of confession for silence and inaction on racial injustice and other social evils and pledged determined efforts to eliminate conditions that produce such evils." The day messengers adopted the statement—June 5, 1968—proved to be a day of "triumph and tragedy," however, as news spread that morning of the assassination of yet another national leader, Robert F. Kennedy, the respected brother of John F. Kennedy. Baptists in Kentucky and throughout the SBC joined the rest of the nation, in the words of editor Daley, in "searching for ways to restore American society to sanity and stability."[30]

In the same *Western Recorder* issue that announced the historic SBC vote, another article described race riots in Louisville. The riots had been precipitated by a report that the activist Stokely Carmichael's planned visit to Louisville was delayed by white Louisvillians; two rioters were shot and killed. Duke McCall, president of Southern Seminary, signed a statement along with other clergymen in the city calling for restraint on the part of policemen and for an end to the rioting and looting in the city.[31]

As the state's largest city, Louisville became a focal point in the ups and downs of progress in race relations. Later that summer—only weeks after the rioting and looting in the city had been calmed—the General Association of Baptists in Kentucky observed a centennial celebration. More than two thousand black Baptists met at Louisville's Fifth Street Baptist Church to commemorate one hundred years of struggle and progress. Significantly, Harold Sanders, Herman Ihley, and Mrs. George Ferguson were invited to speak during various sessions. The event was accorded a full-page article in the *Western Recorder*.[32]

It was appropriate that the article was written by Sanders because it was the executive secretary's energy and determination—along with progressive pastors like Crescent Hill's John Claypool—that had led to progress in tense, difficult times. In 1971, the last year of Sanders's tenure as the leader of Kentucky Baptists, KBC messengers elected Charles N. King, the African American pastor of Frankfort's Corinthian Baptist Church, as second vice president of the convention, the first black pastor to be elected to a high convention post. By 1971, other black pastors contributed devotional columns regularly in the pages of the *Western Recorder*.[33] Clearly, much progress in race relations had been made among Kentucky Baptists during the Sanders years. It was equally apparent that much work was still needed, but as with the state's model for cooperative giving in the early years of the century, Kentucky Baptists again proved to be leaders—this time in race relations—in constructive change among Southern Baptists.

In the turbulent sixties, Kentucky Baptists took an active part in the work of the Southern Baptist Convention. By 1962, SBC news and devotional meditations were broadcast on over twenty-five Kentucky radio stations on "The Baptist Hour." Four stations carried the convention's "MasterControl" programs, and five stations broadcasted the "Sunday School Lesson" issued by the convention's Radio and Television Commission in Fort Worth. Televangelism programs could be seen on Lexington's WKYT-TV and WPSD-TV in Paducah.[34]

Individual Kentucky Baptists played prominent roles in SBC affairs. As part of the Baptist Jubilee Advance, an effort to mark the sesquicentennial of the first organization of Baptists in North America (the 1814 establishment of the Triennial Convention in Philadelphia), Kentucky Baptists founded—by 1964—691 new churches and missions, only 9 short of Kentucky's goal of 700. Kentuckians James W. Cox, Leo T. Crismon, Gordon Clinard, James Leo Garrett, William Latrane Lumpkin, William Arthur Mueller, Clyde Penrose St. Amant, and G. Hugh Wamble contributed to *Baptist Advance*, a volume of essays published to commemorate the event. Kentuckians remained active on SBC boards and agencies. In 1969, Mayfield's John Huffman chaired the convention's Committee on Boards, and Harold Purdy, Madisonville, Ted Gilbert, Frankfort, and H. B. Kuhnle, Lexington, served on the Executive Committee. C. R. Daley was a representative on the Baptist Joint Committee; Lynwood Montell, Campbellsville, on the Education Commission; and D. E. Meade, Forest Hills, on the Foreign Mission Board. The names of other Kentuckians could be found on boards of trustees of SBC seminaries.[35]

Just as Kentucky Baptists participated fully in the programs of the SBC, national issues drew a full range of opinions and comments by the state's Baptist leaders and laity. Along with the Civil Rights Movement, the Vietnam War occupied the attention of Kentucky Baptists and the rest of the nation. "America's Longest War," in the words of the University of Kentucky's eminent historian George Herring, Vietnam divided the nation much like the debates over civil rights.[36] As America's troop involvement escalated from sixteen thousand in the Kennedy administration to more than five hundred thousand under President Johnson, Kentucky Baptists—along with a growing number of other Americans—questioned the legitimacy of the nation's role in the conflict. Henlee H. Barnette, professor of Christian ethics at Southern Seminary, asserted that "we should never have become involved in the land war in Asia." Barnette argued that "the U.S. is driving more Vietnamese into the communist camp than are being converted to America's side." The professor concluded that "I cannot square what we are doing there with either revelation or reason."[37]

Kentucky Baptist college and seminary students reacted to the war in differing ways. During the week of October 15, 1969, students observed the National Moratorium Day around the state. Tom Riner, a student at Southern Seminary who was later elected to the state General Assembly, led a group to the Jefferson County Courthouse, where they burned a Viet Cong flag. Later in the week, Riner reminded students at a National Moratorium Day chapel of the mass murders committed by the Viet Cong following the sacking of Hue and insisted that thousands more would be killed if American troops were withdrawn. "How can we as Christians reconcile withdrawing our forces?" Riner asked.[38]

As a protest to America's involvement, other seminary students held a public reading of the names of the American dead. When students gathered outside Louisville's Walnut Street Baptist Church, the state's largest church, pastor Wayne Dehoney invited them into the sanctuary to pray for world peace. At Southern Seminary, Walter Delamarter, Frank Stagg, and Barnette addressed an overflow chapel crowd in opposition to America's involvement. Seminary administrators found copies of "a new left magazine" slipped under their office doors.[39]

Activities at Georgetown, Cumberland, and Campbellsville were planned by students and administrators. A teach-in at Georgetown featured an antiwar lecture, and at Cumberland, President J. M. Boswell led students and faculty in what he termed "appropriate readings from the Scriptures" and prayer for world peace. Students sported various-colored armbands on campus: black armbands as a sign of protest or American flag armbands as a sign of support.[40] In November 1969, four hundred of Southern Seminary's eleven hundred students signed a petition in "support and encouragement to President Nixon's efforts to secure a just and honorable peace in Vietnam." Kentucky Baptist messengers at the 1969 annual meeting of the Kentucky Baptist Convention passed a resolution "not only to be in prayer for the President and the leaders of this country but also [to] stand firmly and patriotically united in our support of his efforts to seek an honorable solution to the war." Harold Sanders sent a telegram to President Nixon informing him of the resolution and assuring the chief executive "of our continued support, and our prayers for you and our national leaders in seeking a peaceful and early cessation of the war in Vietnam."[41]

Nixon's decision to extend bombing into Cambodia made Kentucky Baptists rethink their support of the president's policies. In May 1970, campuses across the country exploded in what Columbia University's president called "the most disastrous month of May in the history of American higher education."[42] The Kent State tragedy, in which four student bystanders were killed by Ohio National Guardsmen, was coupled in Kentucky with demonstrations on the University of Kentucky campus in Lexington. The Euclid Avenue classroom building was burned, and state police and Kentucky National Guardsmen confronted crowds of students. Joseph M. Smith, minister of UK's Baptist Student Union, was working late in his office at the BSU center on Tuesday evening, May 5, when students told him about the demonstrations just south of the BSU. With the burning of a classroom building and additional damage to a nearby dormitory, students found it difficult to study for the next day's final examinations. Smith concluded that the demonstrations at UK would continue and "among devotedly Christian students" a "heightened political awareness and more definite political decisions in regard to the war and national priorities" would occur at UK, at the state's regional colleges, and at Baptist schools as well.[43]

The trial and conviction of Lt. William Calley for the brutal murder of over two hundred civilians in My Lai village prompted *Western Recorder* editor C. R. Daley to ask, "Can Brutality Make a Hero?" in his "Daley Observations" column of April 17, 1971. Daley, troubled by the popular reaction in favor of Calley, maintained that "no other American has ever been made a hero for such conduct." When President Nixon pardoned Calley soon after his conviction, Daley hoped that the commander in chief's intervention was based on "personal convictions and not on public pressure or political expediency." The editor asked, "Do we not need to reexamine our views in light of the teachings of Jesus?"[44]

While arguments about the war raged at home, soldiers fought and were killed "In Country," as Graves County native Bobbie Ann Mason made clear in her best-selling novel of that name published in 1985. Kentucky Baptist pastors joined hundreds of others as chaplains in Vietnam. Some churches, like Oak Grove Baptist near Ft. Campbell, sent copies of the *Western Recorder* to its members in military service. Editors of the state Baptist paper urged other churches to follow Oak Grove's example. Any church in Kentucky presumably could afford the $1.50 a year for a subscription, but if this were not the case, the *Western Recorder* promised to send the paper free of charge to servicemen in Vietnam "for the duration which we trust will not be long."[45]

But the duration was long. America's longest war dragged on and on, dividing the country at home and spawning disenchantment and a spirit of rebellion among the nation's youth. Antiwar demonstrations and peace rallies at Southern Seminary and the state's Baptist colleges indicated that Kentucky Baptist students were not immune from the most divisive issue of the times. Remarkably, however, the rebellious nature of the sixties and disenchantment with Vietnam were channeled for thousands of Christian youth into the "Jesus Movement," a phenomenon that challenged the nation's youth to "turn on" to Jesus and his love. In the summer of 1971, the *Western Recorder* published the Baptist Press's five-part series on the movement. The last installment of the series asked, "How Will the Church Respond?" While some Kentucky Baptist pastors criticized the perceived superficiality of young people's response, others were convinced that the church should embrace the movement.

The editor of the Southern Baptist *Home Missions* magazine, Walker Knight, had "no doubt we are in the presence of a religious phenomenon within the youth culture." Knight praised the "youth explosion" as one of the "revitalizing movements of history," and using an analogy with which Kentuckians would be familiar, asserted that "this turning to Jesus is as fresh and new as dogwood blossoms in spring." Another pastor, alarmed by the superficiality that he perceived, was not so positive. When he asked a girl about the implications of the gospel for pollution, racial injustice, and poverty, she responded indifferently, "Oh, they're bad. But the main thing is to love Jesus."[46]

In the early 1960s, officials at the Kentucky Baptist Convention had foreseen the Jesus Movement's appeal to youth. Executive Secretary Harold Sanders observed that few young people took the time to attend the annual KBC meetings. Beginning in 1962, Sanders organized youth rallies held on the last evening of the convention. Emphasizing evangelism and music, the rallies were typically held in sports arenas in the cities where the convention was held: the Owensboro Sports Center in 1962; Lexington's Memorial Coliseum in 1963 and 1965; Louisville's Freedom Hall in 1964 and 1967; and Bowling Green's Diddle Arena in 1966. Attendance at the 1964 Louisville rally reached twenty-eight thousand, and the 1967 rally was sponsored jointly by the KBC and the black General Association of Baptists in Kentucky.[47]

In 1969, Arthur Blessitt, described as the "hippie evangelist" of Sunset Boulevard, Hollywood, California, led several youth rallies in Louisville. A Southern Baptist, Blessitt owned a Sunset Strip night club—named His Place—and had gained a national reputation for his work with Black Panthers and members of the counterculture. Walnut Street Baptist Church sponsored Blessitt's fifteen-day March crusade. Some services were scheduled, but "after that we don't know what will happen," explained Walnut

Street's associate pastor, Robert Young. Young understood that "things just begin to happen" when Blessitt led meetings. When the charismatic evangelist led crusades in major cities around the nation, youth meetings "just broke out" in schools, drive-ins, shopping malls, and night spots. Young hoped "the same thing would happen in Louisville.[48]

Young was not disappointed. After Blessitt's visit to Louisville, C. R. Daley wrote that "no preacher has made such an impact on this city in a long time." Even older Baptists, skeptical of Blessitt's methods, were convinced. "Many who might have come to scoff remained to pray," Daley wrote. Services at Walnut Street drew overflow crowds, and the televised services reached untold thousands. The evangelist ranged out to shopping centers and schools, wherever a crowd of people could be gathered, to proclaim the message of Christ. Despite recent Supreme Court rulings, Blessitt spoke in Louisville and Jefferson County high schools, lecturing on his experiences in Hollywood. Blessitt impressed members of the Southern Seminary community, students and faculty alike, as the largest chapel attendance of the year turned out to hear him speak. Seminary professors spoke of him in glowing terms: "authentic," "genuine," "valid," and "New Testament" described his preaching.[49]

An ecstatic Harold Sanders proclaimed that "no one ever so stirred youth as he under the leadership of the Holy Spirit." Sanders reported that Blessitt spoke in twenty-one high schools and preached in person to more than sixty thousand people. When Blessitt returned for a Freedom Hall youth rally sponsored by the Kentucky Baptist Convention on April 4, he preached to more than twenty thousand. At a Blessitt-led youth rally in May, six hundred Baptist young people and adults joined him in a "Walk for Jesus" down Fourth Street. Sanders and Blessitt marched in the parade, each shouldering one side of an eighty-pound cross with a banner proclaiming "A Cross to Carry and Christ to Share." More than five hundred individuals among the eight thousand in attendance made decisions for Christ at the evening Freedom Hall rally on May 9.[50]

Much like Billy Graham, Arthur Blessitt had taken the city by storm. Unlike Graham, however, Blessitt's appeal was geared to disenchanted youth affected by the war and by the alienation produced by a drastically changing world. Yet Blessitt's message was the same: the answer for a dying, alienated world was Christ alone. Kentucky Baptist youth came away from the Blessitt meetings with a new sense of purpose, with a renewed faith. Others, many on the edge of despair and hopelessness, made commitments to Christ for the first time. Older Kentucky Baptists realized the universal nature of the gospel in an age of change. For Blessitt, the Louisville rallies served as a launching pad for a remarkable life of radical

Christian ministry. Later in 1969, Blessitt embarked on a mission to carry a twelve-foot wooden cross around the world. By 1999, Blessitt and his wife Denise had carried the cross to every country in the world—277 countries, 7 continents, 32,765 miles. The walk was listed by the Guinness Book of World Records as "The World's Longest Walk."[51] Blessitt's explosive crusades in Kentucky had launched a wider world vision for the evangelist himself.

The phenomenon of the Jesus Movement made clear that while the message of the gospel remained the same, methods of disseminating the message—at least for young people—had changed dramatically. Change marked the history of the Kentucky Baptist Convention during the tenure of Harold Sanders. The expensive and extensive Booz, Allen, and Hamilton report (the document that called for a complete reorganization of the work of the convention) was not adopted at the 1958 Elizabethtown meeting. As Franklin Owen, a member of the committee that hired the Chicago firm to produce the report, put it, the convention "voted decisively to dismiss the embarrassed convention committee and scrap the report that 'eye has not seen, nor ear heard.' (1 Cor. 2:9 with apologies to the great apostle for quoting him out of context)." During the Sanders years, however, many of the ideas of the report were systematically, albeit gradually, adopted with "solid approval" from the convention.[52]

Perhaps no area of Kentucky Baptist life changed more in the 1960s than Baptist higher education. Along with racial harmony and an emphasis on youth, Sanders made Baptist education a priority during his tenure. He toured the state's Baptist institutions repeatedly, surveying the capital needs of the schools along with the BSU centers. Of course, pleading for resources for Baptist schools was an old refrain, ofttimes sounding—as C. R. Daley put it—"too much like a funeral dirge." Under Sanders, though, the refrain seemed to carry a new lilt. Daley concluded that "if we don't get headed out of the educational muddle under the leadership of this dynamic executive secretary, we might as well give up."[53]

Accompanying Sanders on his numerous visits was Doak S. Campbell, described by Daley as the "foremost educational expert among Southern Baptists." It was clear to Sanders and Campbell that one conclusion of the controversial Booz, Allen, and Hamilton report was accurate: Kentucky Baptists had too many schools. No group of Baptists seemed to be doing so much with so little. In 1961, Kentucky Baptists numbering 620,000 gave $191,795 to Georgetown College with its 1,600 students, $63,873 to Cumberland College and its 1,501 students, and $59,730 to Campbellsville College with 826 students. Little was left for Bethel College, Magoffin Baptist Institute, and Clear Creek Baptist Bible College. In comparison, Oklahoma Baptists, 461,000 in number, gave $318,000 to Oklahoma Baptist University, that state's lone Baptist college enrolling 1,649. Louisiana Baptists—401,000 in number—gave $63,612 more to a single Baptist institution, Louisiana College, to educate its 1,515 students than 620,000 Kentucky Baptists gave to three senior colleges to educate 3,927 students.[54]

Sanders concluded that Kentucky Baptists could do more—must do more—if their institutions were to survive. In 1962, a "Christian Education Capital Needs Funds Campaign" with a goal of $12 million was launched. Doak Campbell, Sanders's friend from Tallahassee, a Baptist deacon, and the retired president of Florida State University, was retained as a consultant. V. V. Cooke, the respected Louisville philanthropist, was named general chairman of the campaign. Despite the hullabaloo, the ambitious figure of $12 million was revised downward to $9,056,000 in 1963, and the campaign edged forward under the name Christian Education Advance or CEA. The campaign was deemed so important that the Friday afternoon session of the 1963 meeting of the Kentucky Baptist Convention in Lexington was designed as a rally to promote CEA. KBC personalities from around the state—Cooke, John Claypool, W. R. Pettigrew, Mrs. Duke McCall from Louisville; John Huffman, Keevil Judy, Mat Sugg, and T. L. McSwain from western Kentucky; Verlin Kruschwitz, the "pastor chairman," from Severns Valley in Elizabethtown; Harold Sanders and C. R. Daley from Middletown; Franklin Owen and Julia Woodward from Lexington; M. R. Rhoads from Newport; and C. L. Smith from Harlan and J. B. Gatliff from Williamsburg in the east either served on the CEA Executive Committee or were featured in the rally's program.[55]

By 1964, the CEA reported more than seven thousand individual donors and donor churches.[56] Still, the campaign was in trouble, for pledges and gifts failed to make a dent in the goal. Sanders and others discussed the possibility of securing a $6 million loan to meet the goal. In his weekly *Western Recorder* column, "Yours and His," Sanders pleaded with Kentucky Baptists to "put our hand to the CEA plough—again, or for the first time." Sanders included BSU centers and missionary camps in the campaign, asserting that these institutions and "our Baptist schools . . . must be given the facilities they need for this great day." Daley chimed in, writing that "the present crisis of our Baptist colleges poses one of the most serious challenges in all of Baptist history." Daley asserted that Kentucky Baptists must "come across with the funds for our cadillac school program or tailor the program to fit our pocket book."[57]

Funding continued to lag. By 1966, the situation became so pressing that convention officials decided to ask for a special session of the convention "to study the feasibility of a long term loan or bond issue of approximately $6 million for the immediate capital needs of the Christian Education Advance participants." Registered messengers (1,079 in number) met at Walnut Street Baptist Church on June 17 and 18 at the first called convention in the 129-year history of the KBC. Messengers voted 561 to 299 against permitting colleges to borrow money from the federal government, approved a plan to allocate three hundred thousand dollars from the convention for capital needs, and tabled a motion by John Claypool calling for a study of the relationship of the colleges to the convention and the feasibility of the KBC's becoming less involved in higher education.

Despite the resounding vote against government loans, within five months the convention reversed itself at the annual November meeting in Bowling Green. Following a remarkable presentation by Georgetown College president Robert Mills, messengers voted to reaffirm a 1949 policy to allow trustees of Baptist colleges to make decisions concerning school funding. In effect, the action opened the way for trustees of individual schools to borrow money from government sources. Mills's presentation, which "literally left everyone speechless," made it clear that Georgetown would seek government loans if his motion passed. His motion did pass, and the results of the historic special session in June were reversed. Editor Daley wrote that "Baptists do the strangest things, and Kentucky Baptists are more Baptistic in this respect than most any other Baptists."[58]

The issue highlighted Kentucky Baptists' strong history of support of higher education. At the same time, church-state issues became increasingly confused in the volatile sixties. As for the CEA campaign, by August 1967 only $1,162,882 in individual CEA gifts had actually been received; by 1969, when the CEA campaign closed, less than $3 million had been pledged or given. The convention essentially bailed out the campaign by pledging three hundred thousand dollars for twenty years to make up the $6 million remaining toward the goal.

As the failed CEA campaign sputtered along, it became obvious that other measures would have to be taken, that Kentucky Baptists were unable or unwilling to maintain what Daley had called a "cadillac" education program. Kentucky was not unique in closing struggling institutions. In 1968, Maryland Baptists closed the doors of Maryland Baptist College—before those doors were ever really opened—when the state missions board turned down a request for funds.[59] In Kentucky, Magoffin Baptist Institute closed in 1961. A grammar and high school in Salyersville in eastern Kentucky, the institution had been established by the SBC's Home Mission Board in 1905. The board had hoped to serve mountain children "for time and eternity"; but when the SBC board suspended its support, individuals, churches, and later the convention were forced to take up the cause. The school was moved to Mountain Valley in Breathitt County in 1940. By 1950, the school operated a farm and served as a Baptist assembly in addition to its educational function.[60]

In a sense, modernity caught up with Magoffin and similar private, church-related institutions. By 1960, school buses rambled over paved roads taking once-isolated mountain children to public schools. KBC leaders cast about for other ways to make use of the facilities, but nothing seemed feasible. In the end, on August 31, 1961, the school closed for good, and the property—buildings, equipment, and some two thousand acres of woodlands and farm land—was transferred to Oneida Baptist Institute in Clay County.[61]

Just as changes brought on by modernity led to the demise of private, secondary schools like Magoffin Baptist Institute in the east, a venerable Baptist institution of higher learning in western Kentucky also felt the strain of change. Bethel College in Hopkinsville had begun as a high school in 1854. Another Baptist institution, Bethel College of Russellville in Logan County, had ceased operations in 1933, its endowment and records transferred to Georgetown College.

Hopkinsville's Bethel, also begun as a high school before the Civil War, became Bethel Female College in 1859, and then Bethel Woman's College, a junior college, in 1916. During World War II, the school closed from July 1942 to the fall of 1945, and the campus served as officers' quarters for soldiers training at nearby Fort Campbell. The rental income temporarily paid off the institution's indebtedness. With the demise of Russellville's Bethel, the Hopkinsville campus became coeducational in 1951, changing its name to Bethel College. The future looked bright as the school seemed to prosper in the postwar boom. By 1962, the college had more students than rooms.

Despite the seeming prosperity, Bethel, like Magoffin, was already in its final years, yet another victim of changing times. When a rally was held in the Bethel College chapel on January 27, 1963, to announce a new $250,000 campaign to modernize the campus, plans for a new two-year community college to be located in Hopkinsville were already in the works. Hopkinsville Community College, eventually one of fourteen two-year institutions connected with the burgeoning University of Kentucky Community College System, made Bethel College obsolete. Bethel's inadequate endowment, antiquated equipment, and stately, but out-of-date, buildings simply could not compete with the sleek, efficient, and inexpensive education provided by the state university system. Sadly, the rally proved to be a memorial service, and messages by Harold Sanders and Doak Campbell and "Why I'm Sold on Bethel" testimonies by Hopkinsville businessmen—really eulogies for the doomed institution—proved inadequate to save the school. The $250,000 campaign never materialized, and the school officially closed following the spring semester of 1964. Library books were distributed to the surviving Baptist colleges. After all debts were paid, some ninety-seven thousand dollars was turned over to the Kentucky Baptist Foundation; income from this money would be parceled out to Campbellsville, Cumberland, and Georgetown as well.[62]

The Magoffin and Bethel closings saddened alumni and supporters of the schools. However, it was the rise and fall of another Baptist institution that dominated the story of Kentucky Baptist education in the 1960s. As

Rollin S. Burhans, president
Kentucky Southern College,
1960-1969

early as 1955, the executive committee of Long Run Association centered in Louisville promoted the idea of developing an extension of Georgetown College. In 1959, the plan was changed. The school should stand on its own. A fund-raising campaign began for the Greater Louisville College of Arts and Sciences. The name of the fledgling institution became Kentucky Southern College, and in 1962 ownership of the college was transferred from the Long Run Association to the Kentucky Baptist Convention.[63]

When the college opened for its first term in the fall of 1962, classes met at Southern Seminary. A library and faculty offices were set up on the third floor of Boyce Library, and administrative offices on the Whitsitt wing of Mullins Hall. A committee headed by Edwin Perry, pastor of Louisville's Broadway Baptist Church, selected a 238-acre site on Shelbyville Road for a new campus, and the land was donated by Baptist layman L. Leroy Highbaugh. A president's home already had been erected in 1960 for Rollin Scofield Burhans, elected as the school's first—and only—president in May of that year. A classroom and administration building, the school's signature structure, was completed at the new site by 1963.

Boarding students moved to the Shelbyville Road campus when additional dormitories were completed in 1964.

From the beginning, the founders envisioned a college of academic excellence with a decidedly Christian character. The mission of the school would be centered unabashedly on Christ. The philosophy of the institution stated unequivocally that "Jesus Christ is to education what breath is to life. He is the point of departure for all search of truth and He is the point of final return for all seekers after Truth."[64] V. V. Cooke, Sr., contributed extensively to the new college. Others gave sacrificially. President Burhans, the former pastor of Louisville's Crescent Hill Baptist Church, persuaded leading scholars from around the nation to take part in the experiment. For example, Wade Hall left a position at the University of Florida to head the Department of English. Thirty years later, Hall likened the challenge to "a wonderful example of the shining city on a hill." Other distinguished professors made a mark on Kentucky Southern and other institutions. Physics professors Perry Morton and Dave Roper went on to head departments at Samford University and Virginia Tech. Bill Parsons,

*Burhans Hall, Kentucky Southern College,
now University of Louisville, Shelby Campus*

head of the speech and theater department, retired after a notable career as the dean of the College of Fine Arts at Stephen F. Austin University in Texas. Academic dean John Killinger later taught at Vanderbilt University's divinity school. Ray Stines, the school's registrar and director of admissions, eventually became the director of student services at the University of Louisville.

Burhans did not attract this remarkable array of faculty and staff because of the prospect of lucrative contracts or academic prestige. Rather, scholars came because of a sense of calling to a unique experiment in Christian higher education. The school's new seal—of course, everything about the enterprise was new—presented images of a parchment and quill pen, the world, a dynamo, and, in the center, an open Bible and cross surrounded with a chain. The words "They Whom a Dream Hath Possessed" scrolled across the top of the seal. The dream included several innovations—"distinguishing traits"—in higher education. A trimester system, dividing the academic year into three fifteen-week terms, replaced semesters and quarters. At the time only two other schools in the nation used that format. The system promised to allow students to complete four years of college work in two years and eight months.[65]

The institution's "most unique feature" anticipated a reform later adopted by colleges and universities around the nation. An interdisciplinary requirement served as the common core of each student's academic experience. One three-hour class combined art, science, history, religion, and literature. Students were required to complete eight such courses. In addition, each student wrote a senior paper based on his or her wide-ranging interdisciplinary studies. The college's stated philosophy held that "there is a body of knowledge which every educated person, regardless of avocation or vocation, should possess and that the primary task of the liberal arts college is to identify and impart this knowledge in such a way as to demonstrate the unity of knowledge."[66]

Stines described the interdisciplinary requirement as "the heart of Kentucky Southern." The registrar asserted enthusiastically that a student "might discuss art of western civilization one day and the next day a physics professor would be talking about a lot of things that happened in science that affected religion." Former student John Carter, who later practiced law in Louisville, remembered that the institution's academic rigor attracted a small cadre of students who "went to school to learn and not to prepare to make a living." Carter concluded that "the education I received there you couldn't have received anywhere else." The college's family atmosphere invited academic exchange outside of classroom walls, according to Charles Mullins, a student and graduate who later went on to become senior attorney for the United States Nuclear Regulatory Commission in Washington, D.C. Mullins remembered walking into the college cafeteria to dine with a diverse group of students, faculty members, perhaps a dean, and two custodians.

The lively experiment in Baptist higher education, the dream of developing a premier academic institution in an urban setting, became the victim of the economic perils of the sixties. Plans for eleven additional buildings by 1967 never materialized. Inflation set in. The convention fought over the issue of government loans, and whether individual Baptist colleges could solicit funds independently of the convention. Operating funds were used for capital needs. The $9 million CEA campaign only realized one-third of its goal. Without the meager endowments that the state's three other Baptist institutions had developed, Kentucky Southern was doomed, the grand experiment shattered.

The college's last years were marked by heroic, heart-rending, but inadequate attempts to ward off the inevitable. On March 10, 1967, the KBC executive committee acted on a request from the Kentucky Southern board to be released from its relationship to the convention. President Burhans was convinced that funds outside the convention must be sought and that government loans were needed to survive. New buildings and new resources were necessary for accreditation. In releasing Kentucky Southern, the convention also agreed to give the school $885,000—a $500,000 loan and $77,010 per year for the next five years—to smooth the transition to independent-college status.[67] The transition proved to be anything but smooth.

In November 1967, after seven years as a Kentucky Baptist institution and eight months as a private, Christian school, Kentucky Southern announced its intention to merge with the University of Louisville. Only a month later, however, the merger was called off after students led a remarkable "Save Our School" fund drive that netted the school more than $1.3 million in cash and pledges in less than a month's time. Board chairman LeRoy Highbaugh, whose family had provided the land for the campus, personally gave eight hundred thousand dollars for the campaign.[68]

Although the heroic drive staved off the proposed merger for a while longer, by December 1968, the board unable to hold on, again asked the University of Louisville to assume operation of the institution. Without additional resources, the college simply could not survive with short-term debts of $1,051,000 and a long-term indebtedness of $3,245,000. The University of Louisville assumed all debts as well as assets totalling $7.1 million. The merger proved to be awkward for Kentucky Baptists because the convention had agreed to pay the school monies over a five-year period beginning in 1967. Louisville's Liberty National Bank went to court to force the KBC to honor the convention's financial pledge. The convention had faithfully honored the pledge until the merger with U of L was announced.

Certainly, this was not the way that Kentucky Baptists had envisioned the future of Kentucky Southern College when it opened for classes in 1962. The school's brief history belied the promise and excitement of the experiment. The founding of the school also left a legacy of unanswered questions. Why would Kentucky Baptists enthusiastically embark on such a bold experiment in higher education when an institute and a junior college had just been forced to close? Why would the convention pledge precious funds for such a challenge while Georgetown, Cumberland, and Campbellsville—already proven assets—went lacking? Why open a new college so close to Georgetown? The rise and fall of Kentucky Southern College served as a microcosm of the gains and losses of the sixties during the tenure of Harold Sanders.

Despite the focus on the decline and fall of Kentucky Southern, Kentucky's other Baptist colleges grew during the decade and through their endurance laid the foundation for greater days. In 1969, Campbellsville College named William Randolph Davenport to replace retiring J. K. Powell as the school's president. Davenport possessed the "rare combination of academic excellence, administrative ability and Christian commitment necessary for leadership of a Christian college."[69]

Davenport came to Campbellsville from the University of Michigan at Flint, where he served as the chair of the Department of Education. He brought to Campbellsville a dignified demeanor in addition to proven academic excellence. The new president joined Robert Mills at Georgetown and James Boswell at Cumberland as an innovative leader in Christian education for Kentucky Baptists. Despite the disappointment of the CEA campaign and the demise of Kentucky Southern, increased enrollments resulting from the coming of age of the baby-boom generation ensured a new era of growth and service for Kentucky's three remaining four-year colleges.

The growth of the schools did not come without controversy. At Georgetown a decision of the Board of Trustees to allow on-campus dancing brought the issue before messengers at the 1968 annual KBC meeting in Florence. Messengers adopted two resolutions calling on Georgetown trustees to reconsider their decision and to desist from taking action "which is contrary to stated convention position or violates the known moral conviction of a large segment of Kentucky Baptists." C. R. Daley made the motion for one of the resolutions and later referred to 1968 as "The Year of the Dance" in his "Daley Observations" column.[70] In his December 12, 1968, feature, the editor tied the Georgetown controversy to a lag in Cooperative Program giving. Cooperative Program receipts left a $250,612 deficit for the first quarter of 1968. Daley suggested that the Georgetown story "certainly didn't help matters" and that "it might have been just enough to discourage some Kentucky Baptists and even some churches who were already reluctantly contributing through the Cooperative Program."[71] Despite the convention's action and criticism offered by the *Western Recorder*'s editor, Georgetown trustees decided to let the decision stand and to allow "social dancing to be a part of the students' on-campus social program."[72]

*Barkley Moore, president,
Oneida Baptist Institute, 1972-1994*

Other institutions struggled with more crucial matters in the 1960s, matters of survival. With the closing of Magoffin, Oneida Baptist Institute took on an even more important role in the decade. Founded in 1899, Oneida continued to provide a crucial Baptist presence in an isolated area of eastern Kentucky. Located at the head waters of the south fork of the Kentucky River in the Cumberland Mountains, a poverty-stricken area where the per-capita income of $650 was one-half that of the rest of the state, Oneida served as a beacon of light for mountain youth. By the 1960s, President David Jackson and a staff of twenty-five, including twelve full-time teachers, taught classes and supervised the work programs of some two hundred students.[73]

Despite the ending of its mountain isolation brought on by modern road building in eastern Kentucky, Oneida survived public school competition by including in its mission education to disadvantaged youth, "special cases," and even to young people from foreign countries. The international flavor of the Oneida experience made the school unique. When Barkley Moore, an alumnus of the school, became president in 1972, the institution continued to make innovative changes that enhanced its unique role in the mountains. Moore graduated as valedictorian in the class of 1958, and after receiving a bachelor's degree and completing one year of law school at the University of Kentucky, returned to Oneida as assistant to President Jackson in 1963. In 1965, Moore joined the Peace Corps, spending six years in Iran, where he organized a kindergarten and thirty-two libraries among the people of Gonbad-e Kavus. When he returned to the United States, he held the distinction of having the longest term of service in the history of the Peace Corps.

Innovative changes at Oneida included the first high school Baptist Student Union in Kentucky, founded in 1949; the international initiative of the 1950s; and under Moore, a summer school program, a tutoring lab, and a middle school program. Under Moore's leadership, enrollment increased fivefold, as did the number of faculty and staff. A print shop, a band/choir room, a track and soccer field, a computer lab, a chapel, and a piano lab were all built during his presidency. Moore never lost sight of the original mission of the school, a mission adopted upon its founding in 1899. He wrote, "What is Oneida Baptist Institute? Oneida is people. It was founded to help people. It was founded to minister to sinners."[74]

Clear Creek Baptist School carved out a unique niche in Kentucky Baptist education. Providing Bible training for men and women intent on following the Master's call for service, Clear Creek trained workers for full-

Chapel service, Clear Creek Baptist Bible College

WMU Training School, Lexington Road Campus

time Christian service. A unique "in-service type program" provided hands-on experience for a wide range of Christian ministries. The school received statewide recognition in 1969 from Governor Louie Nunn. Nunn had expressed his desire to know more about the school when he passed by the campus while attending Pineville's Mountain Laurel Festival. D. M. Aldridge, Clear Creek's president, subsequently invited the governor to campus. In a brief address, Nunn commended the faculty, staff, and students and asserted that training ministers was the "hope of the world."[75]

Although not affiliated with the KBC, Southern Seminary as an institution of the SBC added new programs and grew in students and prestige in the sixties. In 1963, the beloved Carver School of Missions and Social Work, known originally as the Woman's Missionary Union Training School, merged with the seminary. The Training School had become the Carver School in 1953, and in 1956 ownership and control of the school passed from Woman's Missionary Union to the seminary. Under Southern's administration the school's social work program received full accreditation, and the mission of the school continued under the new arrangement.[76]

In 1965, Southern established the new Billy Graham Chair of Evangelism in honor of the denomination's most famous evangelist. A joint announcement by Graham and seminary president Duke McCall was made from historic Greenville, South Carolina, where the seminary had been founded more than a century earlier. The Billy Graham Evangelistic Association financed the chair for the first three years with a grant of thirty thousand dollars. A permanent endowment of five hundred thousand dollars was secured during this time. Kenneth Chafin, head of the Department of Evangelism at Southwestern Baptist Theological Seminary, was named the chair's first occupant. Praise for the chair's establishment came from throughout the Southern Baptist Convention. C. E. Autrey, director of evangelism for the SBC's Home Mission Board, called the appointment of Chafin to the chair "the greatest development in evangelism in my generation," while Wayne Dehoney, president of the SBC and soon to be pastor of Louisville's Walnut Street Baptist Church, lauded the appointment as "the most significant event to occur during my service as president of the Southern Baptist Convention."[77]

Another major change that came to Southern Seminary during the sixties was the retirement of Hugh Peterson from the seminary staff after thirty-two years of service. "Dr. Pete" was revered by the seminary community. He recalled thousands of students by name. As a member of the seminary faculty and staff, Peterson held fourteen different job titles, including faculty member, registrar, secretary of the faculty, dean of students, director of admissions, and administrative dean. Known throughout the state, he had pastored Sonora Baptist Church from 1935 to 1944, and had served over thirty churches as an interim pastor.[78]

Kentucky Baptists continued to be concerned with the denomination's educational institutions, but issues of church and state increasingly dominated the attention of Kentucky Baptists. Supreme Court decisions on prayer in public schools, ministers and Social Security taxes, federal loans and grants to church schools, and the possible appointment of an American ambassador to the Vatican kept the KBC's Committee on Public Affairs busy throughout the decade. Baptists had always been visible in Kentucky's General Assembly as well as in the governor's mansion. Bert Combs, Kentucky's governor from 1959 to 1963, had graduated from Cumberland College. In 1962, the *Western Recorder* pictured Combs, executive secretary Harold Sanders, and actor Warren Hammack at a performance of *The Book of Job* at Laurel Cove in Pine Mountain.[79]

Through the Committee on Public Affairs, Baptists like Malcolm Lunceford, pastor of Frankfort's Immanuel Baptist Church and chair of the committee, kept in close contact with legislators. In October 1963, the first Kentucky Convention on Church-State Affairs was held at Lexington's Trinity Baptist Church. The program featured sessions on four major areas of concern: public funds for parochial schools, Sunday closing laws, Bible reading and prayer in public schools, and public funds for sectarian hospitals. Kentucky's Attorney General John B. Breckinridge, *Western Recorder* editor C. R. Daley, Lexington attorney Robert Turley, and Crescent Hill pastor John Claypool read papers that were then discussed by some fifty participants chosen from religious, professional, and fraternal organizations. Early in 1970, Lunceford and one hundred other Kentucky Baptists converged on the Capitol to express opinions about House Bill 198 and Senate Bill 128, legislation that would enable the state to pay 70 percent of the salary of teachers of non-religious subjects in parochial schools. These church-state issues concerned Kentucky Baptists because of the denomination's rich heritage of religious liberty and strong stand for separation of church and state.[80]

The Kentucky Baptist hospital ministry grew and expanded during the decade. Western Baptist Hospital in Paducah experienced a minor controversy in 1969 when James V. Dorsett, the hospital's executive vice president, was dismissed and then quickly reinstated. H. L. Dobbs, president of Kentucky Baptist Hospitals, Inc., had fired Dorsett over a matter of administrative policy, specifically "where, when, what and how to build" expansions to Kentucky Baptist hospitals. Dobbs explained that the hospital program required a team effort by hospital administrators.

Upon Dorsett's firing, administrators on the Western Baptist Hospital board, the medical staff, and Baptist ministers in the Paducah area wrote strongly worded resolutions of protest against the dismissal. For his part, Dorsett sent a letter of apology to Dobbs, promising to work more closely with the president. The letter and resolutions resulted in the reinstatement of the popular Dorsett. Dobbs explained that "Jim Dorsett has been big. It takes a big man to do this," and asserted that the reconciliation was an answer to prayer. Using a hospital analogy, C. R. Daley likened the crisis to "labor pains" that "always accompany a new birth." In this case, the crisis stemmed from expansion plans in all three hospital cities— Louisville, Lexington, and Paducah. A new hospital facility was planned for the St. Matthews area of Louisville, and by 1971 expansions of the existing facilities were underway in Lexington and Paducah. Lexington's Central Baptist Hospital added seventy beds and new x-ray and laboratory departments, expanded electrocardiographic and electroencephalographic units, and opened a new physical medicine department. At Paducah, seventy-two beds were added, and surgery, X-ray, physical therapy, out-patient, and laboratory facilities were expanded.[81]

Constructive change came to the children's home ministry of Kentucky Baptists in the 1960s and early 1970s as well. In 1963, the Kentucky Baptist Board of Child Care accepted the resignation of Sam Ed Bradley, the general superintendent since 1959, and selected C. Ford Deusner as his successor. Bradley had served as superintendent of all three children's homes in Kentucky—Glen Dale, Spring Meadows, and Pine Crest—before taking over as general superintendent. From Henderson, Deusner had pastored churches in Kentucky and Missouri. He had been called from Paducah's Tabernacle Baptist Church to be superintendent of Glen Dale, where he served for fifteen years before coming to replace Bradley at Middletown.[82]

Under Deusner, Kentucky's Baptist children's home ministry continued to serve the state well. Deusner declared 1968 a "year of firsts" for the ministry. Preparations were underway to celebrate the first centennial of Spring Meadows, founded as the Louisville Baptist Orphans' Home in 1869. In 1968, Spring Meadows accepted black children for the first time in its century of service. References to race were removed from the charters and by-laws of the three Kentucky institutions. A black couple received the child care board's adoption services for the first time in 1968. Finally, the children's homes Thanksgiving offering surpassed three hundred thousand dollars for the first time. The final tally of $315,000 set the stage for a goal of $330,000 for the offering in 1968. Sadly, 1968 marked the first death among its children in twenty-four years when an eleven-year-old girl succumbed to a rare blood disease.[83]

While 1968 was indeed a year of firsts for the Kentucky Baptist Board of Child Care, the following years proved to be the last for Pine Crest Children's Home, the smallest facility in the system. In December 1969, the child care board suggested that Pine Crest could be used as a "home for the aged." John Claypool, first vice president and soon to be president of the convention, conceded that Pine Crest "had been a financial burden" to the convention for some time. Deusner offered the Morehead facility for use to the convention as a home for the elderly, but the executive board rejected that proposal in 1970. Pine Crest's services were suspended at the end of the school year in 1971, and the home's twenty children transferred to Spring Meadows and Glen Dale. In August 1971, in what was described by *Western Recorder* associate editor Bob Terry as "a historic moment for Kentucky Baptists," the convention leased Pine Crest to the Commonwealth of Kentucky. The cooperation between the KBC and the state was historic indeed. Governor Nunn signed the document that leased the property for twenty thousand dollars annually and explained that plans were being made to provide a place for mentally and emotionally disturbed girls. The action was hailed as "an excellent example of how a church group and the state can cooperate to meet human needs without compromising the important principle of separation of church and state."[84]

The initiative that bore the mark of Executive Secretary Harold Sanders more than any other was Cedarmore Baptist Assembly. Although some critics good-naturedly referred to the assembly as "Chiggermore," the development of the Shelby County site made available much-improved facilities for summer assemblies, retreats, and RA and GA camps. Boone Lodge, named after Sanders's predecessor, was completed in August 1964. This hotel-type facility provided forty-eight bedrooms built at a cost of $470,000, with an additional $106,000 set aside for equipment and furnishings. Improved facilities—permanent cabins and dining halls—for Camp Rabro, the summer RA camp, and summer camp for GAs were built in the 1960s, as was the Ferguson-Jaegle Conference Center. The new center was completed in August 1968 at a cost of $140,000.[85]

The new structures elicited praise for design and beauty. In fact, Boone Lodge—in 1964—and the Ferguson-Jaegle Conference Center—in 1968—received the Kentucky Architects' award for the most beautiful wood building constructed in the state. The new facilities concerned some members of the executive board, however. They recalled that with each board meeting—and many of the meetings then were held at Cedarmore

Boone Lodge, Cedarmore Baptist Assembly

rather than at the Baptist Building in Middletown—more money seemed to be required for improvements at the assembly. A growing number of Kentucky Baptists considered Sanders's emphasis on the assembly an extravagant and unnecessary drain on scarce convention funds.

Initially, Cedarmore had been owned by the Long Run Association, but with the coming of Marvin M. Byrdwell as the assembly's manager in 1949, ownership was transferred to the convention the following year. Byrdwell came to Cedarmore from Clear Creek Baptist Bible School, where he had served as business manager as well as manager of the Baptist assemblies and camps. Under his direction at Cedarmore, the assembly grounds grew from 415 to 1,376 acres, and an initial convention investment of $50,000 grew to a worth of more than $1.5 million. Under Sanders and Byrdwell, the lodge and conference center, eight cottages, two dormitories, a tabernacle, dining halls, a boys' camp with three cottages and fourteen "covered wagons," a girls' camp with five cottages, and modern water and sewage facilities were all added to the grounds. Byrdwell, known as "Mr. B." by his friends, justified the expense and expansion by citing over fifty-six hundred decisions for Christ during his years of service as camp manager. In 1971, Byrdwell left Cedarmore to become superintendent of missions for the Christian County Association. For twenty-one years Byrdwell and his wife had been synonymous with the Kentucky Baptist Assembly: "Cedarmore has been the Byrdwells and the Byrdwells have been Cedarmore." Arlis C. Hinson, Jr., succeeded Byrdwell as manager in 1971.[86]

In 1966, convention messengers voted to reorganize the executive board, clarifying its responsibilities and organization. The executive board was to serve as the voice of the convention between annual sessions. Within the board, responsibilities were to be carried out by the Nominating Committee, the Operating Committee, the Finance Committee, the Program Committee, the Denominational Cooperation Committee, the Christian Life Committee, the Assemblies and Camps Committee, the Christian Education Committee, and the Administrative Committee. Guidelines were drawn up to determine the personnel and responsibilities of each committee.[87]

Other agencies connected with the KBC continued to function, providing valuable service to Kentucky Baptists. In 1964, Albert M. Vollmer retired as executive secretary-treasurer of the Kentucky Baptist Foundation. Vollmer was replaced by James C. Austin of the SBC's Stewardship Commission, but Austin left after only three years to head the foundation at Southern Seminary. After months of searching, foundation directors in 1969 named Grady L. Randolph as the new executive. Randolph had served as the superintendent of missions for the Elkhorn Association.[88]

Under Randolph, the work of the foundation flourished. The foundation had been organized in 1945 to encourage Christian will-making as well as the creation of "living memorials" to be administered on behalf of the donor for Baptist causes in the state. Under Vollmer, Austin, and Randolph, foundation gifts were used to endow Glen Dale, Spring Meadows, and Pine Crest children's homes, the state's Baptist colleges, and the SBC's foreign and home mission boards. By 1969, the income of the foundation had grown to over $200,000 from an initial income of $6,911 in 1946. Total assets had increased from $184,488.50 to $4,427,449.00 by August 31, 1969. By 1972, assets approached $5 million.[89]

A committee composed of several members of the executive board reported on the work of the Kentucky Baptist Historical Society to the convention from 1961 to 1967. In November 1966, the convention approved the formation of the Kentucky Baptist Historical Commission, and the former committee was abolished. The commission consisted of eleven members elected by the convention to handle funds given by Kentucky Baptists for the important work of preserving the commonwealth's rich Kentucky Baptist history. The Kentucky Baptist Historical Society, made up of dues-paying members, continued to function along with the commission.[90]

In 1965, Thomas Hicks Shelton, pastor of the historic Latonia Baptist Church in Covington since 1950, was chosen to head the newly created Department of Evangelism. Evangelism work for years had been connected with the Department of Missions, and A. B. Colvin had performed the herculean task of overseeing both areas. Shelton was Colvin's choice for the new position because "he was doing the best job in a local church of evangelism." Colvin remained as head of the work in state missions.[91] Years later, Colvin explained that "our mission program in those days involved basically the associational directors of missions and district missionaries that served two or more associations. Then we had county missionaries, men who pastored county seat town churches and did mission work within the county. And then we had local missionaries that served as pastors of churches, and we helped assist them."

During Sanders's tenure, an anonymous donor, a Washington, D.C., attorney, asked Sanders if the convention could think of some new kind of mission program that needed funding. In 1966, Colvin responded with the idea of "a communities missions program" that involved a layman— a member of a county seat town church—who would work in county missions. Eventually, seven lay missionaries in this program received support from the anonymous donor as well as the SBC's Home Mission Board.[92]

Colvin initiated and led a wide range of other programs and activities from one end of the state to the other. In 1961, for example, the largest Mountain Missions Conference on record was held at Oneida Baptist Institute. Pastors, missionaries, and lay men and women gathered for worship and training on literacy programs, rural church development, survey techniques, and music. C. R. Daley, Ray Summers, professor of New Testament interpretation at Southern Seminary, and Mrs. George Ferguson, the WMU executive secretary, led participants in an examination of the conference theme, "Found Faithful."[93]

The challenge of the mountains became the focus of the Southern Appalachian Studies in Religion Program financed by the Ford Foundation from 1958 to 1960. The study of 190 mountain counties of Alabama, Georgia, North Carolina, Tennessee, West Virginia, Virginia, and Kentucky attempted to gather up-to-date survey information for the southern mountain region to replace statistics last provided by the United States Department of Agriculture in the 1930s. Of the region's total population of 5,765,000, only 45 percent professed to be church members compared to 53 percent in the nation as a whole. Of the 2,621,000 church members, 996,000 were Baptists, twice the number of any other denomination. Many mountain Baptists were not affiliated with the Southern Baptist Convention; and according to the report, "many are small ultra-independent groups characterized by untrained leadership and emotional type worship." The *Western Recorder* admonished Kentucky Baptists that the preponderance of Baptists in the mountains did not mean that "we have done our part in vigorous missionary and evangelistic activity." Indeed, the writer asserted that "we have made no intense effort to win the mountains."[94]

The lack of effort was certainly not evident at Clear Creek Baptist Bible School or at Oneida Baptist Institute. And it was evident that mountain preachers like D. E. Meade of Pike County did their part. In 1965, Meade received the annual "Mountain Preacher of the Year" award given at Clear Creek. Meade had helped in the organization of the First Baptist Church of Forest Hills in 1941 and remained as their pastor nearly twenty-five years later. He was selected for his "mission zeal, radio ministry, personal study, visitation and denominational work." In accepting the award, named for the first time for A. S. Petrey, the revered mountain preacher and church organizer, Meade exhorted other ministers to "always prepare" for their ministry and to preach the "whole message" of the Bible.[95]

In 1969, James E. Casey, Jr., a Kentucky Baptist mountain missionary in Morgan County, outlined the progress of Kentucky Baptist work in eastern Kentucky. Casey maintained that the goal of establishing a Baptist church in every county-seat town had been accomplished. Local churches were encouraged to establish missions in isolated mountain regions. The KBC helped by supplementing the salaries of mountain ministers in churches unable to support a full-time pastor. Each summer, scores of college students descended on the mountains to conduct Vacation Bible Schools, revivals, and religious surveys. The state WMU and mission board provided funds to build churches. Despite all the effort, Casey concluded that much more needed to be done: "We need men and women to serve as missionaries in our mountains in the fields of music, education, and recreation."[96]

At the other end of the state, Kentucky Baptists were involved in meaningful ministry in the Tennessee Valley Authority's Land-Between-the-Lakes (LBL) area. The federal New Deal project had displaced thousands of individuals and scores of churches and communities. Now, the area served as a major resort for millions of people each year, individuals seeking a few days' escape from hectic work schedules and the hubbub of suburban life in modern America. Baptists in nearby Blood River, Little River, Ohio River, and Caldwell associations wondered how they could minister to summer vacationers. In 1968, Kentucky Baptists teamed up with eight other denominations in forming a General Coordinating Council to oversee religious work in the LBL region. Earl Wofford, superintendent of missions for the Blood River Association, represented Baptists on the council. Baptist pastors took part in leading worship services at various LBL campsites. In a fifteen-week period in 1968, from Memorial Day to Labor Day, Baptist ministers conducted twenty-one worship services for more than fifteen hundred vacationers within the TVA compound.

Cooperative Program funds also provided for an LBL chaplain who moved from site to site in a trailer owned by the KBC. Although the ministry was initially funded by the Blood River Association, eventually other local associations, the KBC, and the SBC's Home Mission Board contributed to the expanding ministry. In 1969, A. B. Colvin presented keys to a new "Chevrolet suburban carryall" to Freeda Harris, the director of the Marrowbone Baptist Center, Diana Greene, a US-2 worker, and Kale Conner, pastor of the Marrowbone Baptist Church. The van was used to transport children to Sunbeam meetings and Vacation Bible Schools in the area.[97]

The KBC targeted rural areas of the state through the Rural Church Program, begun in 1944. Under the leadership of Garland R. Pendergraph, the work was referred to as "Church Survey and Enlargement" in 1960. Pendergraph's title was changed to director, Church Development Ministry, in 1964, and to Church Development consultant three years later. Under whatever title, he served faithfully until his death in 1972.

The ministry's goal was to strengthen struggling rural churches. Few of the state's rural Baptist churches could boast of the record and endurance of Pleasant Hill Baptist Church near Campbellsville. In 1965, the church celebrated its 125th anniversary. The *Western Recorder* asserted that the church was "one of the leading rural churches in Kentucky and in the Southern Baptist Convention for that matter. The buildings and grounds are a showplace and the church program is model." The church budget of forty thousand dollars allotted 40 percent to missions. D. L. Druien, pastor of the church for thirty-six years, was "the leading spirit in the life of the congregation," a congregation that had endured no serious controversy in its 125-year existence. From its very beginning, black members had been accepted into the fellowship. The *Recorder* concluded that "when all is considered, there could be no more pleasant a hill on the earth."[98]

The KBC was able to function effectively throughout the 1960s because of churches like Pleasant Hill. In fact, KBC finances flourished in the decade. In 1962, C. R. Daley declared that "the tide has turned for Kentucky Baptists, at least finance-wise." For the first time in four years, Cooperative Program giving exceeded the goal. December 1961 saw the largest Cooperative Program income for one month in Kentucky Baptist history. Over five hundred Kentucky Baptist churches gave through the Cooperative Program in that year. The KBC's executive board approved a record $2,620,000 budget for 1963. Of that amount, 64.5 percent or $1,689,900 stayed for KBC programs within the state, while Southern Baptist causes received the remaining 35.5 percent or $930,100.[99]

The KBC budget was bolstered by gifts from large churches, some of which seemed to lead in giving year after year. In 1968, the top ten givers were (in order): Severns Valley, Elizabethtown; Walnut Street, Louisville; First Baptist, Madisonville; First Baptist, Somerset; First Baptist, Owensboro; Crescent Hill, Louisville; Third Baptist, Owensboro; Calvary, Lexington; Immanuel, Lexington; and First Baptist, Bowling Green.[100] It was the hundreds of smaller churches like Pleasant Hill, though, that insured the success of the work of the Cooperative Program in the commonwealth.

Kentucky Baptists came to the aid of fellow Kentuckians suffering from natural disasters in the late 1960s. In 1969, for example, extensive flooding in eastern Kentucky damaged churches and homes. Again, it was A. B. Colvin—who seemed to be everywhere in the sixties—who surveyed the losses, reporting back to KBC offices in Middletown. Harold Sanders sent emergency funds to Harlan and other eastern Kentucky communities to help feed and care for displaced families. Damaged churches applied for financial aid through the KBC's Church Building Assistance Fund.[101] In northern Kentucky, a tornado ripped through an area near

Falmouth in April 1968. By 1969, new buildings funded in part from a state mission offering replaced three destroyed church structures.[102]

Through the Direct Missions Department of the KBC, cooperating churches extended Kentucky Baptist work beyond state borders. In 1964, Kentucky Baptists aided West Virginia Baptists in mountain work there. With no state Baptist convention, the state benefitted from Kentucky Baptist efforts in Charleston and Welch. Kentucky Baptists teamed up with Baptists in Ohio and the SBC Sunday School Board to send Francis R. Tallent to West Virginia as director of religious education. Through these efforts the West Virginia Convention joined the SBC in 1970.

Kentucky Baptists contributed to Baptists in other states as well. The Alaska Baptist Convention received one thousand dollars from the executive board of the KBC following an earthquake in 1963; Kansas Baptists were given a "special emergency mission gift" of ten thousand dollars to alleviate debt in 1970, and gifts continued to be given until the debt was paid. Mississippi Baptists received over twenty-eight thousand dollars for relief and rebuilding efforts following the devastation of Hurricane Camille in 1969, and Texas Baptists were sent over twelve thousand dollars following Hurricane Celia the same year.[103]

As early as 1962, Kentucky Baptists extended emergency aid for Cuban refugees flooding into Miami following the Bay of Pigs fiasco and during the developing Cuban missile crisis. A request for help from the SBC's Home Mission Board resulted in the formation of a committee headed by

Baptist Building, Middletown

Duke McCall, V. V. Cooke, and the ubiquitous A. B. Colvin. The committee attempted to provide food, housing, and jobs for refugee families and foster homes for homeless Cuban children.[104]

Clearly, Kentucky Baptists responded to the spiritual and physical needs of individuals at home, around the United States, and throughout the world in the 1960s. The devastating tornados and other natural disturbances serve as a useful metaphor for the sixties for Kentucky Baptists. Certainly, winds of change were evident. And as with the cultural and social climate of the decade, Kentucky Baptists and the Kentucky Baptist Convention experienced change, too. Many developments were positive as Kentucky Baptists attempted to minister to displaced, hurting, and searching individuals. Other changes especially in Baptist higher education were disturbing to leaders and laypeople alike.

It was appropriate that the state Baptist paper, the *Western Recorder*, a paper that gained a reputation under editor C. R. Daley for integrity and excellence, was sometimes dubbed the "Western Disturber." Indeed, in the sixties the moniker might be more accurately the "Daley Disturber." Executive Secretary Harold Sanders remembered the "Western Disturber" from his student days at Southern Seminary in the late 1930s and early 1940s. The term took on a new significance in the cold war sixties, a decade of disturbances in Kentucky, in the nation, and around the world. Sanders contended the paper "makes us think, makes us take stock of our old ways of thinking of things about which we really gave no serious thought." Sanders concluded that "I like the way the *Western Recorder* disturbs me—calls on me to think about the live issues of life, the issues of death, the issues of the life-giving gospel in all human relations."[105]

Daley wrestled with these life and death issues in each issue of the *Recorder*. And by the end of the decade, the struggle had taken its toll. In August 1970, the revered editor checked into the Kentucky Baptist Hospital in Louisville with a case of severe depression. A month later, he explained to his readers the reason for his absence. Daley returned to the hospital the following year when he "felt himself slipping into depression similar to that which caused his first hospitalization."[106] His struggles, however personal, indicated the tremendous stress and strain so evident in the sixties.

Harold Sanders endured his own difficulties. Less than two years after being named executive secretary in 1961, he underwent back surgery to remove a ruptured disc.[107] He soon recovered, and with renewed vigor pushed forward his plans for Kentucky Southern, Cedarmore, and other projects. He celebrated his seventh-year anniversary with the convention with a column noting changes that had come to the convention during his tenure. The name of the organization had changed from the General Association of Baptists in Kentucky to the Kentucky Baptist Convention. Verlin Kruschwitz, pastor of the historic Severns Valley Baptist Church, served as the last "moderator" of the General Association and the first "president" of the Kentucky Baptist Convention from 1959 to 1961. Sanders noted the individuals who had served in his tenure under the new title of president: E. Keevil Judy, Henderson (1962-63); J. Chester Badgett, Campbellsville (1963-64); Franklin P. Owen, Lexington (1964-65); David A. Nelson, Owensboro (1965-66); John C. Huffman, Mayfield (1966-67); and Eldred M. Taylor, Somerset (1967-68). Sanders expressed his appreciation to each president, noting that each had "served with you and me in a unique way, each was an able leader." Sanders also praised the 148-member executive board, individuals in the state's 82 associations from small and large churches, and finally the state's 680,000 Baptists.[108]

J. T. Miller, pastor of Chestnut Grove Baptist Church in the Blackford Association, assumed the presidency of the convention in 1968, and Sidney Maddox, Hopkinsville, in 1969. Sanders's own pastor at Louisville's Crescent Hill Baptist Church, John R. Claypool, became convention president in 1970. Young and dynamic, Claypool had served as Crescent Hill's pastor since 1960. C. R. Daley placed Claypool in "the new generation of Southern Baptist preachers who unhesitatingly speaks out on contemporary moral and social issues." According to Daley, Claypool was among the first of Kentucky Baptist pastors, and "by now the best known," to take a strong stand on issues such as desegregation, open housing, and the withdrawal of troops from Vietnam. Claypool's future as a leader of Kentucky Baptists seemed secure. To the surprise and consternation of many, however, Claypool resigned in September 1971 as Crescent Hill's pastor to take the pastorate of Broadway Baptist Church in Fort Worth, Texas. Although at first Claypool wished to fulfill his responsibilities in his last year as convention president, it soon became clear that this would not be possible. On October 1, 1971, he resigned as president of the KBC as well.[109] The pastor had lost his ten-year-old daughter Laura Lue to acute lymphatic leukemia. The pain of the loss was overwhelming, but Claypool labored on, centering many of his Crescent Hill sermons on grief and faith. The sermons were later published by Word Publishers in *Tracks of a Fellow Struggler: Living and Growing Through Grief*, a book that ministered to thousands suffering from loss and failure.[110]

Claypool's resignations proved unsettling for his Crescent Hill congregation and for the Kentucky Baptist Convention, but the pastor's action presaged other imminent changes in the offing for Kentucky Baptists. In the May 1969 executive board meeting, members voted to accept the recommendation of the Administrative Committee to modify the retirement policy to permit voluntary retirement at age sixty and to require mandatory retirement at age sixty-five for KBC employees.[111]

Because Sanders was near the mandatory age of retirement, Sidney Maddox, the president of the convention, appointed a special committee in November 1970 to write a job description and to seek a new executive secretary. David Nelson, pastor of First Baptist Church, Owensboro, and a former KBC president, was asked to chair the committee. Nelson and other committee members used the Booz, Allen, and Hamilton study, a 1963 description for the job of executive secretary adopted by the convention, and materials from twelve other Baptist conventions to write a new job description for the new leader. A recommendation was made to elect a new executive secretary at the November 1971 annual convention meeting and to allow the new leader to assume the role of executive secretary-elect on January 1, 1972. The new leader would then assume full responsibilities on April 1, 1972, with Sanders remaining as a consultant until his retirement at the end of August. When Sanders objected to this arrangement, the board instead agreed that the new leader would not assume "full responsibilities and title" until Sanders's August 1972 retirement.[112]

Under this cloud of debate, Harold Sanders ended more than a decade of service to Kentucky Baptists. Under his leadership Cooperative Program receipts climbed from $2,357,180 to $4,315,375. Total Cooperative Program receipts during his eleven-year tenure totalled $37,057,641. Membership in Kentucky Baptist churches rose from 620,414 in 1961 to 683,436 in 1972.[113] Growth was evident, but so was controversy. Indeed, controversy seemed to define the 1960s. Because of his years in Florida, Sanders was considered an outsider from the outset. Then, it was under his watch that several beloved institutions were closed: Bethel College, Magoffin Baptist Institute, and Pine Crest Children's Home. Of course, the closings seemed right and necessary for the convention. Was it not ludicrous to think that a small state like Kentucky could support four senior colleges while other states like Oklahoma and Louisiana supported only one? The duplication of institutions had proven to be a drain on the convention for years. Still, the closings hurt, especially for alumni and staunch friends and supporters.

The failed CEA campaign and Sanders's support for Kentucky Southern College, and its hasty demise, certainly baffled and dismayed Kentucky Baptists across the state. Sanders's dogged determination to carry through an idea did not serve him well in the end. A. B. Colvin remembered that "he took an idea and ran with it, and if you didn't like it, he'd spend most of his time with you until he had convinced you that it was the thing to do." Sometimes Sanders was less than convincing. He never had the full confidence of Kentucky Baptists. Colvin concluded that Sanders "came determined to change Kentucky Baptists and you don't do that in a lifetime, you know."[114]

Still, change did come to the Kentucky Baptist Convention during the Sanders years. Courageous men and women continued to labor faithfully throughout the 1960s and early 1970s. In western Kentucky, for example, H. C. Chiles retired quietly from his pastorate of twenty-two years at First Baptist Church, Murray in 1970. Long considered a model for Baptist pastors, Chiles was known for his "thorough and diligent preparation," performing each of his varied tasks "with dispatch and distinction." During the week, Chiles could invariably be found at his desk in his study laboring in "one of the largest and most complete libraries of any Baptist pastor in Kentucky." Even after his retirement from the pastorate, the studious Chiles continued to write his popular Sunday School lessons for the *Western Recorder*.[115]

Then, in eastern Kentucky, the ministry of Elizabeth Miller Zieger, "the little woman of Chestnut Ridge," served as a model of faithful service. Standing less than five feet tall, and weighing no more than eighty pounds, Zieger served as a missionary to Kentucky's mountain people for more than forty years. A *Western Recorder* tribute claimed that "her story is a saga of determination and selfless service rarely matched in Baptist missionary annals." Overcoming crippling illnesses, Zieger served as missionary for Mt. Vernon Baptist Church, then for the Kentucky Baptist Convention and the SBC Home Mission Board. Walking hundreds of miles in the early years of her ministry, she was later provided with a horse and saddle by a Texas radio evangelist; still later, she was presented a jeep by a WMU circle. Her selfless life of ministry served as a living testimony to a hymn that her mother had taught her while only a baby, "Where He Leads Me, I Will Follow."[116]

The various pilgrimages of faithful Kentucky Baptists like Chiles and Zieger seemed to pale in comparison to the journey of American astronauts as they landed on the moon in 1969. C. R. Daley in another poignant column wrote that the "amazing trip to the moon calls to mind another historic trip which was even more amazing and unbelievable. This was not man's journey from earth to the heavens but God's journey from heaven to earth." Without downplaying the historic moon landing, Daley wrote that "man's trip to the moon was measured in miles; God's journey to earth could be measured only in love and suffering."[117] The quiet, selfless journeys of love and suffering of Kentucky Baptists like

Chiles and Zieger mirrored the pilgrimage of the Master, but the collective pilgrimage of Kentucky Baptists in the 1960s had been trying and rocky at times. New paths threatened to divide the convention fellowship. It would take a firm, but gentle leader to steer the convention in the years ahead.

7
chapter

Making History
1972-1982

The tall, gangly, ex-basketball player from Missouri proved to be the perfect tonic for the ills that beset a Kentucky Baptist Convention reeling from the confusion and controversy of the 1960s. As the pastor of Lexington's Calvary Baptist Church, Franklin Owen was already renowned as a master pulpiteer. Colorful stories laced his sermons, illustrating biblical truths in a rustic, yet elegant, way, easily understood by plowman and professor alike. Indeed, his Calvary congregation was a cross section of Lexington's bluegrass, blue-blood elite and the city's middle-class suburbs. Yet, the pastor had a unique ability to make everyone feel right at home. Little wonder that the special committee entrusted with the task of finding a new executive secretary-treasurer for the Kentucky Baptist Convention following the mandatory retirement of Harold Sanders came knocking at his door.

The Harold Sanders years had been exciting, but the retiring executive secretary was not fully appreciated for what he had accomplished in difficult times. Described as a "dreamer and idealist," Sanders firmly believed that his initiatives rested within the will of the Almighty, once remarking that "I never recommend anything until I have prayed it through and I am convinced it is the will of God. Then I commit myself completely to it and believe nothing can prevent its coming to pass." Despite his energy and persistent optimism, Sanders often faced opposition. C. R. Daley wrote that "his type of leadership is bound to evoke some resistance and opposition, especially in a state where Baptists have a long history of independence and conservatism in methods as well as doctrine." "Some of us weren't as ready for a 'full speed ahead' pace as we thought," Daley concluded.[1]

The Christian Education Advance campaign, one of Sanders's first major initiatives, fell woefully short of the goal despite his obvious genius for organization and promotion. Despite Sanders's love for Christian education, he presided over the closing of three cherished institutions. An attempt to increase Cooperative Program giving was more successful; receipts increased more than 80 percent from 1961 to 1972. Advances in race relations were also commendable. And Sanders's work to improve Cedarmore Baptist Assembly was spectacular; he boasted that the assembly had become one of the most outstanding religious encampments in the United States.[2]

Perhaps it was the emphasis on Cedarmore in the midst of the institutional struggles of the Baptist colleges that brought the greatest criticism. Sanders's dogged determination to make the assembly into a first-rate facility was never understood by other leaders, especially presidents and boards of trustees of the colleges and schools. The executive board's enforcement of a new retirement policy made it clear that some Kentucky Baptists felt a change in leadership was needed.

C. R. Daley described 1972 as "an eventful year for Kentucky Baptists." The editor reviewed the fifty issues of the *Western Recorder* for the year and listed significant events that would no doubt have a far-reaching impact on Kentucky Baptists. At the top of the list, he placed the election of Franklin Owen on February 25. Owen took office on September 1 upon the retirement of Harold Sanders. Other personnel changes included the retirement of A. W. Walker as Annuity Department secretary and the election of Byrd Ison to fill the post; the sudden death on June 16 of G. R. Pendergraph, an executive board staff member since 1946; the resignation of David Jackson as president of Oneida Baptist Institute and the election of Barkley Moore as interim president; the resignation of George Price, Jr., as business and circulation manager of the *Western Recorder* and the election of Paul Whitler, Jr., to the vacant position; the election of William E. Amos, Jr., as executive director of the Kentucky Baptist Child Care Board to replace the retiring C. Ford Deusner; the election of Chester Durham, the director of the student department since 1942, as assistant to the executive secretary-treasurer; and the election of T. L. McSwain, pastor of First Baptist Church, Richmond, as president of the convention.

Initiatives cited by Daley included the approval of a six-year, five-hundred-thousand-dollar major expansion program at Cedarmore Baptist Assembly, the establishment of a Kentucky Baptist College Scholarship Program, a one-hundred-thousand-dollar emergency appropriation for Campbellsville College, and the dedication of a $6 million addition to Lexington's Central Baptist Hospital. The fact that Kentucky Baptists exceeded the Cooperative Program goal of $4.2 million by more than $113,000, an all-time record, indicated that the convention had emerged from the turbulent sixties with renewed commitment and determination.[3]

From the beginning, pastors and leaders from around the state hailed the decision to elect Owen as the new executive secretary-treasurer. An evaluation of the new leader's qualifications for the challenging job revealed a minister with a "shepherd's heart," "unusual insight and discernment," and "transparent honesty, integrity and openness." A "leader and not a driver," Owen had "a profound respect for his fellowman and can be disagreed with without fear of reprisal or rupture of fellowship." Owen left a church that he loved—he had pastored Calvary Baptist for eighteen years—only after agonizing for over three months with his decision to accept the invitation from the executive board. Clearly, Owen possessed the traits that many Kentucky Baptists sought in a leader, traits that some Kentucky Baptists saw lacking in Harold Sanders. But the job would not be easy, as Sanders knew all so well. After years of observation, Daley concluded that an individual would "either have to be a fool or be under divine compulsion to take on this ministry." Daley quickly added that "Frank Owen is surely not a fool, except for Christ's sake, but is, I am persuaded, under divine compulsion."[4]

The executive board voted 73-14 in favor of the recommendation from the special committee to offer the position to Owen. A discussion of Owen's views on baptism had delayed the vote momentarily when a board member suggested that Calvary practiced "alien immersion." John Huffman, the chair of the special committee, assured board members that Owen's views were fully in line with the statement on baptism in the Baptist Faith and Message. A personal friend of Owen and a fellow native of Missouri, Harold Sanders endorsed the new leader enthusiastically.

And why not? Owen had all of the experience and diplomatic skills to endear himself immediately to his Baptist constituency in the state. His experience included service on the executive board (including the position of chair in 1964-65 and the administrative committee in 1960-62 and again in 1964-65), the KBC presidency in 1964, the board of directors of the *Western Recorder*, and board service for Bethel College, Georgetown College, and Southern Seminary. His education resulted in a bachelor's degree from Southeast Missouri State College, where he lettered in basketball, football, and baseball, and a master of divinity degree from Southern. He was awarded an honorary doctor of divinity degree from Georgetown College in 1956. Owen pastored churches in La Center and Highland Park in Kentucky, and the First Baptist Church in Gainesville, Georgia, before coming to Calvary in 1954. He was prominent in the life of the Southern Baptist Convention, having served on the SBC's committee on committees, the committee on boards, and the committee on order of business.

Along with his wide-ranging experience, perhaps it was Owen's tactful way with people that served him best in his new position. One board member commented that "no matter how intense an issue might be, Frank can tell one of his famous stories and have everybody practically eating out of his hand." Like his predecessor, Owen knew how to get things done, but unlike his predecessor, the new leader proved to be much more skillful in making everyone comfortable with progress and change.

After only a year in office, Kentucky Baptists seemed to settle down into a period of quiet growth and accomplishment. C. R. Daley described the 1974 convention as "one to remember." Meeting in Paducah, messengers elected John Wood, pastor of Paducah's First Baptist Church, as convention president. The "sweetness and tranquility" of the meeting was not a result of sweeping controversial issues aside. Still, disagreements were minimal and emotional reactions absent. Perhaps the calm was due to the recent distribution of $456,139 in "overage funds," money received by the convention that had gone over the yearly budget. The monies were distributed among the KBC's ten institutions and agencies, and to SBC causes. The recent settlement of the Kentucky Southern lawsuit also brought closure to a lingering reminder of a failed 1960s venture. The Liberty Bank of Louisville had claimed that Kentucky Baptists owed $288,000 to the bank as payment of Kentucky Southern debts. When the executive board agreed to pay $125,000 as an out-of-court settlement, the issue was finally laid to rest.[5]

The increased receipts during 1974 continued a trend begun in 1972. In that year, total receipts had exceeded the budgeted goal by $115,300. In 1973, receipts exceeded the budget by more than $134,600. Messengers at the November 1974 annual meeting recommended a goal of $7 million for the following year, part of the $150 million goal for the Southern Baptist Convention.[6] In addition to the optimism brought on by record giving totals, Owen learned quickly to heal old wounds with skill and grace.

Owen also displayed a keen eye for talent as he filled staff positions at the Baptist Building. Longtime business manager Garnett Morton made plans to retire in 1975. Morton had led the all-important business office for twenty-three years. C. R. Daley noted that the business manager did his work "mostly in the background and so he hasn't had the statewide exposure some of us have." Still, Morton "has put in more hours than most anyone in the Baptist Building and he has done his work as perfectly as anyone." His responsibilities included personnel, central purchasing, payroll, accounting, building and grounds management, property, the mail room, and general services and supervision of computer programs. Daley praised Morton for his service to Kentucky Baptists: "He made every penny and every day count."[7]

Morton did not retire until June 30, 1975, but on January 1, 1975, a young, energetic native of Mississippi became the business manager-elect. The new administrator would then take over full responsibilities upon Morton's retirement on July 1. Barry Allen had come to the Baptist Building when

Franklin Owen, executive secretary, Kentucky Baptists, 1972-1983

Harold Sanders hired him as a part-time assistant in the business office in February 1971. A native of Grenada, Mississippi, Allen received a business administration degree from the University of Mississippi as well as a master of divinity degree from Southern Seminary. This combination of faith and business acuity made Allen realize a calling into this unique area of Christian service. And it was Sanders and then Owen who saw something in the young Allen that made him the perfect choice to succeed Morton. As Morton's assistant from 1971 until his retirement, Allen received the full range of the retiring administrator's expertise. Allen noted his debt to Morton: "I greatly appreciated the opportunity of working with Mr. Morton. He gave freely of his knowledge in order to assure a smooth transition for the benefit of the Kentucky Baptist Convention. Nothing in the way of information was held back from me. He is an important part of my story."[8]

Owen's confidence in Allen was obvious. He depended on the young administrator for advice and guidance. Owen surrounded himself with other able and experienced advisers. Soon after taking office, the executive board named long-time student director J. Chester Durham as assistant to the executive secretary. Newly elected KBC President T. L. McSwain explained that Durham's election had been unanimous. Durham had served as the BSU director at Murray State University for two years before moving to Louisville to direct the state's whole program of student work in 1942. An innovative leader, Durham initiated the BSU summer mission program in the state in 1947, and later an international student conference. In 1955, the Kentucky and Tennessee conventions sponsored the first international student conference in the Southern Baptist Convention. The budget for student work had grown from $4,300 in 1942 to $239,318 thirty years later. Seven Baptist student centers had been built on college campuses under Durham's direction.

In his new position, Durham would represent the executive secretary at functions which Owen was unable to attend, act as a liaison between the executive secretary and the staff, and develop promotional activities for the convention. Speaking to the board, Durham described his responsibilities more bluntly. His main job, he explained, would be "to keep this man [pointing to Owen] from killing himself." "No man," he continued, "can travel the state as he does and then do a full day's work handling the paper that goes with the executive secretary's job."[9]

Durham's appointment became the first step in Owen's plan to move toward a divisional organization of convention offices. By the 1970s, divisional organization had become common throughout the Southern Baptist Convention, and a recent two-year study of state convention organization recommended a divisional framework. Owen was convinced that a new alignment for professional staff would be beneficial for the convention, but he faced skeptics reluctant to upset the status quo. Ever the diplomat, Owen convinced his critics to try a divisional organization for a year. Division heads would be called chairmen rather than directors, and Owen assured the executive board that "we are not burning our bridges behind us just yet. If we get into this and find some problems that we do not anticipate, we might want to back out of this structure." This was Owen's way, and his way—in contrast to the more direct determination of Harold Sanders—proved to be more endearing to his Kentucky Baptist constituents.

As chairmen/directors or as assistants to the executive secretary, the executive board named James Whaley and A. B. Colvin in November 1974. Chester Durham had functioned as an assistant to the executive since 1972. Each individual would coordinate the work of specific departments. Durham directed the work of the various finance-related departments, including annuity, stewardship, promotion, the business office, Cedarmore Baptist Assembly, and the Kentucky Baptist Foundation. Colvin, the long-time head of the convention's Direct Missions Department, would be in charge of missions-related departments including direct missions, evangelism, brotherhood, and cooperative ministries. Whaley was charged with direction of various church services such as the departments of Sunday School, church training, church music, and student work.

Each individual brought a level of expertise and experience that served him well in a new, expanded role. Durham's training in business administration and Colvin's years of service in missions made them proven leaders. Whaley joined the KBC staff in 1953 to head the Church Training Department, having already served in a similar associate position in Church Training for the Alabama Convention. A frequent speaker at Ridgecrest and Glorieta, the conference centers for the SBC, Whaley had risen to a position of respect across the Southern Baptist Convention.[10] By May 1975, the restructuring plan was in place and functioning smoothly under the new coordinators. According to Owen, the new format improved communication between various departments and with the executive secretary.

The new division appointments required shufflings and hirings in other departments. In 1973, Barry Allen had already been appointed to succeed Garnett Morton in the business office, and with Durham's elevation to the position of assistant to the executive secretary, Don Blaylock was named to take his place as the director of student work. A native of Bristol, Virginia, and a graduate of Carson-Newman College, a Baptist school in Jefferson City, Tennessee, Blaylock had served in the position of music and youth at Buechel Park Baptist Church in Louisville and in three churches in Tennessee. He had also served as the associate pastor of the First Baptist Church of Cullman, Alabama.

Blaylock studied at Southern Seminary, completing a master of divinity degree there in 1969, and later served as campus minister at Morehead State and then at six campuses in the western area of the state. He had considered becoming a Christian entertainer, and his comedy routines and pantomime skits became legendary. His appointment to succeed Durham—himself a legend in Kentucky Baptist student work—allowed Blaylock to continue to use his skills as an entertainer in churches and on campuses around the state. On April 10, 1973, for example, he served as master of ceremonies for a Freedom Hall youth rally that drew over twelve thousand young people from around the state. More than 135 youths made decisions for Christ at the gathering.[11]

Blaylock's position also required skill in administration. Upon taking office, he coordinated and supervised the work of sixteen full-time campus ministers serving on thirty Kentucky college campuses.[12] As Durham's replacement in student work, Blaylock faced a formidable task. After all, Durham had literally built the Kentucky Baptist student program from scratch. Durham's competitive nature stemmed from his days as a "Little All-American" football player for Eastern Kentucky University. In 1939, he scored fourteen touchdowns as Eastern's quarterback and once threw a football seventy-three yards in the air for a touchdown. It was as a junior at Eastern that Durham, in his words, realized that "I had not been living a Christian life and I then totally committed my life to Christ and to student work." Although his new commitment helped him to lose most of the "vocabulary" of his former life, he never lost the "sense of fierce competitiveness" that he had nurtured through his involvement in athletics.

After graduation, Durham turned down an offer to play football professionally and took a job as a bookkeeper in Lexington. When J. W. Black called him with an offer to head the state Baptist youth activities office, Durham quickly accepted despite a cut in salary from the eighteen thousand dollars he was making as a bookkeeper to his starting salary of twenty-four hundred dollars with the Kentucky Baptist Convention. Durham explained that the salary cut "didn't bother me because I couldn't get away from my commitment to Christ I had made in my junior year in college."

When he began his new position, he found Baptist student work in the state virtually non-existent, or as he put it: "It consisted of wiener roasts, singing Do-Lord and mainly just entertaining students." Durham also faced a wall of resistance from Kentucky Baptist pastors, many of whom felt Durham's position to be unnecessary. Durham recalled that "it was five years before the first pastor took me out for a cup of coffee." Instead of being discouraged, Durham's fierce competitive nature took hold. He convinced the KBC to establish a campus ministry on every Kentucky college and university campus and eventually to build a BSU center at every major state campus. His work had an impact on the whole Southern Baptist Convention. In fact, nine of the last twelve new phases of Baptist Student work in the SBC were developed by Durham in Kentucky.

In July 1975, having been rewarded for his thirty-three years of service with the KBC with an appointment by the executive board as an assistant to Franklin Owen and as a division head, Durham was nearing retirement when he could spend more time with his wife Vera and more time reading the books in his seven-thousand-volume library in his Louisville home.[13] Before a restful and rewarding retirement began, however, Durham died on September 8, 1975. Despite declining health, he had insisted on working and spending at least part of each day in his Middletown office. Several times he went from his office to the hospital taking his work with him and making his hospital room into a temporary workplace.

Durham had served as the state director of student work from 1942 to 1972 when he was chosen to assist Owen. With his death, a popular, energetic Kentucky Baptist leader was gone. Already in the last few years, A. M. Vollmer, Herman Ihley, Robert Pogue, and G. R. Pendergraph had died, leaving a void in the leadership ranks of the convention. Durham's death was especially difficult for Kentucky Baptists. Doctors, lawyers, and individuals from all walks of life visited the funeral home to pay respects, many saying that "they would not be where they are except for Chester Durham." Durham had written much, and his articles had appeared in numerous professional and denominational publications. Perhaps his most poignant writing came in the form of short verses that were read at his funeral. Among them the following summed up his life and work:

> When I my rest have won
> I hope someone will say;
> "His life was never easy
> But he never ran away."
> But if none can sincerely
> Declare this by my grave.
> Then say, "He loved life so dearly
> That he died unafraid."[14]

Progress with the work among students in Kentucky continued unabated under Don Blaylock. In October 1977, swarms of students from across the commonwealth came to Louisville for the fiftieth anniversary celebration of student conventions in Kentucky. The first student convention had been held in 1927 at Louisville's Crescent Hill Baptist Church. Now, students returned to Crescent Hill to attend workshops and worship services. Among the guests was A. L. "Pete" Gillespie, Kentucky's first director of student work—and Durham's predecessor—from 1938 to 1942. After leaving the KBC work, Gillespie and his wife had gone as missionaries to Japan where they served for thirty years. Gillespie reminded the students that many former Kentucky BSUers had become leaders in Southern Baptist life. He cited Lucy Hoskins, the associate editor of *Church Efficiency*, Bob Denny, the former head of the Baptist World Alliance, and Bill Estep, a professor of church history at Southwestern Seminary, as examples. Vera Durham recalled the accomplishments of her late husband's thirty-year tenure as director of student work, and Ted Sisk, the president of the KBC delivered a sermon that brought "swells of laughter one minute

Wilderness Revival marker dedication, Harrodsburg,
April 19, 1976

and tearful emotion the next." The convention, filled with emotion and in-spiration, was an appropriate way to cap off fifty years of KBC ministry among students in the state.[15]

As it happened, the 1970s represented a decade of anniversaries and cel-ebrations. In 1975, the Kentucky Baptist Foundation observed its thirtieth anniversary. Grady Randolph, the foundation's executive secretary, re-ported that the assets and earnings had grown from $184,488 and $6,911 in 1946—according to the first annual report—to $6,052,908 and $279,570 in 1974. From 1946 through 1974, the foundation had earned a total of $2,683,986 for Christian causes. A. M. Vollmer (1946-64), James Austin (1964-67), and Randolph (since 1969) had served as the foundation's exec-utive secretary.[16]

The largest and most important anniversary celebration of the decade coincided with an even more famous national observance. In 1776, the year of the signing of the Declaration of Independence, preachers delivered the first Baptist sermons on Kentucky soil. In that year Thomas Tinsley, as-sisted by William Hickman, conducted a series of services in Harrodsburg. It was from that series of meetings, sixteen years before statehood, that Baptists marked the beginning of their history in Kentucky.

The Kentucky Baptists of 1976 were determined to mark the bicenten-nial appropriately. The Kentucky Historical Society placed a Commonwealth of Kentucky historical marker at the site of the first services. With the heading "Wilderness Revival," the marker explained the historical significance of the spot:

> Scene of the first of a series of religious revivals conducted in Kentucky during April and May of 1776. The Rev. Thomas Tinsley, a Baptist minister, was assisted by William Hickman in meetings held here under a spreading elm tree. The tree was only a short distance from "Big Spring," where Capt. James Harrod and men started Kentucky's first settlement.

A series of "Bicentennial Glimpses," written by the Kentucky Baptist historian Ira "Jack" Birdwhistell, was published throughout the bicentennial year in the *Western Recorder*. The Kentucky Baptist Convention published *Baptists in Kentucky, 1776-1976: A Bicentennial Volume*, edited by Leo Taylor Crismon, to commemorate various aspects of two hundred years of Kentucky Baptist life and work in the commonwealth. A Bicentennial Committee, chaired by Georgetown College president Robert Mills, had been named as early as 1969 to oversee the celebration. An editorial committee, chaired by *Western Recorder* editor C. R. Daley, worked with Crismon to produce the commemorative volume.[17] In November 1975, the celebration began in earnest when the annual meeting was held at historic Severns Valley Baptist Church in Elizabethtown, the oldest church in the convention.

The bicentennial celebration was capped off on April 19 with day-long activities at Harrodsburg Baptist Church near the site of the first Baptist preaching service in the state. Speakers for the event included Wayne Ward, professor of Christian theology at Southern Seminary; A. Russell Awkard, pastor of Louisville's New Zion Baptist Church; Verlin Kruschwitz, pastor of Severns Valley Baptist Church; Manuel Scott, pastor of Calvary Baptist Church in Los Angeles; and Franklin Owen. Black Baptists from the General Association of Baptists in Kentucky played a prominent role in the celebration just as they had played a prominent role throughout the history of the Baptist presence in the state. The Main Street Baptist Church choir performed "a traditional Black interpretation of Christian hymnody," and the Kentucky Baptist chorale closed out the program with the "Battle Hymn of the Republic." A. R. Lasley from the General Association and Hicks Shelton from the offices of the KBC presided over the day's proceedings.[18]

In the morning, "Baptists took over the town, at least for a little while, as they marched four abreast down Main Street, then turned up Lexington for a half-mile trek to the place where it all began, the traditional site of preaching by Tinsley and Hickman." At the site, speakers recalled "under broiling heat" events of Baptist history. The marchers walked to the nearby grounds of Harrodsburg High School for a noon dinner of that quintessential Baptist dish, fried chicken. Following the meal, which was topped off with vanilla ice cream covered with hot fudge, a black preacher remarked that he had enjoyed an "integrated dessert." The interracial aspect of the meeting made "the greatest and longest lasting impression of the day." C. R. Daley believed that the black response and participation was "a tribute to their leaders and to the cordial relationship black and white Baptists [share] in Kentucky." It was also a result of a history of racial harmony among Kentucky Baptists in the twentieth century.

It was appropriate that Charles King, pastor of Corinthian Baptist Church in Frankfort, was elected as the first black officer in the history of the Southern Baptist Convention; he was elected in 1974 as the second vice president of the SBC. He had been elected as second vice president of the Kentucky Baptist Convention several years earlier. When elected to the SBC post, he stated candidly, "Yes, I feel I'm a token, a symbol. I wasn't elected because I am so hot but I think Baptists wanted to show the world that they are making progress in racial advancement and understanding. The Lord won this election for me."[19] King's election indicated that Kentucky Baptists continued to provide leadership for the denomination in the area of race relations.

Daley asserted that "no gathering could have been more typically 'Baptist'" than the April 19, 1976, Harrodsburg gathering. "It was one of those 'Amazing Grace' and 'On Jordan's Stormy Banks I Stand' kind of meetings." Daley noted that Baptists came from the far corners of the state, overflowing the Harrodsburg sanctuary, and concluded that "there was something deeply moving about the experience. We rejoiced in recalling a noble heritage, exulted in the wonder of being redeemed and sincerely longed to perpetuate our noble heritage of gospel preaching." Franklin Owen exulted that the celebration "was the greatest day I have ever seen Kentucky Baptists have." Owen thanked God "for Kentucky Baptists, black and white, and for a great day of celebration that quickened much of the best things in the hearts of those who attended."[20]

The spirit of celebration gained momentum after the April meeting in Harrodsburg. The celebration continued during the annual meeting of the Lexington convention in November. Ted Sisk, pastor of Lexington's Immanuel Baptist Church and former president in 1968-69 of the West Virginia Baptist Convention, succeeded Louisville layman Henry Huff as convention president. Although the convention's business sessions were "delightfully dull," the spirit that pervaded the meeting had historic import.

"Long Live the Spirit of '76," proclaimed C. R. Daley. Daley stated that it was "difficult to describe Kentucky Baptists in these days. It's more of a feeling than anything else. The best that can be said is we have a spirit—a spirit of love, a spirit of unity, a spirit of mutual confidence and trust and a spirit of commitment to God's plan for us."[21]

Perhaps the euphoric feeling of many Kentucky Baptists mirrored the excitement of Baptists around the United States. The excitement and anticipation grew when Jimmy Carter, a Baptist layman from Plains, Georgia, was elected president in November of the bicentennial year. Many Kentucky Baptists rejoiced that a fellow Baptist and a fellow Southerner had climbed to the highest office in the nation. Many Baptists were delighted when Carter unabashedly called himself a "born-again Christian." Messengers at the 1976 KBC session, meeting only a week after the national presidential election, offered encouragement to the new president. The excitement over Carter's election was almost immediately coupled with concern surrounding the president's home church, however. Carter and his pastor, Bruce Edwards, had opposed the 1965 action of the majority of the Plains membership against the admittance to worship services of blacks and civil rights demonstrators. Plains church officials had locked the doors of the church on two Sundays when out-of-town black visitors tried to enter the church.

Kentucky Baptists voted to send a message to Carter and Edwards commending them for their "stand for welcoming to the Baptist worship services all persons regardless of race, color or ethnic origin." Kentucky Baptist messengers pledged to the president and his pastor "our love and prayers." Despite the opposition of some messengers that the Baptist belief in the autonomy of the local church would be violated, a third telegram was sent to the members of the Plains Baptist Church. Church members were assured of "our prayers and deep and genuine concern during these difficult days of decision for you." The message recognized the right of every church to make policies "even when we disagree," and stated that Kentucky Baptists would pray that "God guide you in making all decisions in the spirit and teachings of Jesus Christ in your total mission and ministry to all men everywhere for his glory."[22] The intent of the message was clear. Kentucky Baptists, fresh from another experience of interracial harmony at the Harrodsburg bicentennial gathering, subtly implored a church in the deep South to go and do likewise.

The presidency of Jimmy Carter proved to be both a blessing and a curse for Baptists in Kentucky and around the nation. Even more than another Baptist president—Harry S. Truman—Carter drew attention to his Baptist heritage in a way that brought national publicity to the denomination.

Some Baptists chafed under the spotlight. The stand of Carter's home church on the issue of race surely embarrassed the president and other more progressive white Baptists. Eventually, Carter left the Plains congregation to join First Baptist Church, Washington, D.C., and later helped found another Baptist congregation—Maranatha Baptist Church—in Plains. The divorce and remarriage of Charles Trentham, Carter's Washington, D.C., pastor, and the antics of family members, especially Billy, the president's beer-drinking, good-old-boy brother, further embarrassed the president and the Baptist cause. Perhaps Carter's interview with *Playboy* magazine more than anything else indicated the ambivalence that many Baptists felt in having a national figure among their own denominational ranks. Surely, there was something to admire in Carter's humanity and in his down-to-earth honesty, but the microscopic gaze of the national media made Baptists uncomfortable nonetheless.

Despite Carter's problems, other Baptists in Kentucky became increasingly active in state and national affairs during the 1970s. In 1979, John Huffman, pastor of Mayfield's First Baptist Church and a former president of the Kentucky Baptist Convention, shocked his congregation when he resigned his pastorate to work on Carroll Hubbard's campaign for governor. A United States representative, Hubbard was the son of Carroll Hubbard, Sr., a Kentucky Baptist pastor and member of the state executive board. When he decided to make a bid for governor, Hubbard chose longtime friend Huffman to serve as the state co-chairman for the campaign. Huffman had pastored the Mayfield church for twenty-four years and in addition to his KBC presidency had served as chair of the SBC's committee on committees.[23]

It was not at all unusual for Baptists to play important roles in state politics. In 1979, Martha Layne Collins was elected as lieutenant governor in a landslide. A native of Bagdad in Shelby County, she was reared in the shadow of the Cedarmore Baptist Assembly, and her parents were faithful members of Bagdad Baptist Church. Collins often attended all-day WMU meetings with her mother. As a child, she sometimes attended four different Baptist Vacation Bible Schools the same summer. She carried her Baptist heritage from her post in the state's second highest office to the governor's mansion, where she served from 1983 to 1987 as the state's first woman governor.[24]

At the same time that Carter's presidency focused the nation's attention on Baptists, the success of Martha Layne Collins did the same on the state level. And while Collins's career injected state politics with a Baptist presence, Baptist agencies and institutions in Kentucky continued to provide valuable services in other areas. When C. Ford Deusner retired in 1973 as general superintendent of the Board of Child Care after twenty-five years in Kentucky's Baptist child-care program, William E. Amos, a member of Crescent Hill Baptist Church and a pastor/director of that church's Portland Mission, was named as his successor. Amos had previously been employed by the SBC's Home Mission Board as assistant secretary of the Department of Christian Social Ministries in 1968-69. Under him, a new organizational plan for the board was adopted in 1973. Following Franklin Owen's wish for a divisional structure for the KBC, Amos led in a divisional structure for the child-care board. Two divisions, administrative services and program services, were led by heads answering directly to him. The administrative services division under the direction of Larry Dauenhauer included accounting and clerical services, public relations, personnel and development. The program services division included the two childrens' homes at Glen Dale and Spring Meadows, the foster home program, the family counseling program, and intake services.[25]

The child-care board adopted an $884,200 budget for 1973-74 and set a goal of $399,000 for the annual Thanksgiving offering. Under Amos, the board agreed to sell four acres of land to the KBC's executive board for twelve thousand dollars in 1974. The land which adjoined the site on which the Kentucky Baptist Building was located would provide for future expansion of the building. The child-care board also sold the Pine Crest facility near Morehead to a real estate firm for $620,000. The facility had been leased since 1970 to the Kentucky Department of Child Welfare.[26]

When Amos left to assume the pastorate of First Baptist Church, Plantation, Florida, the child-care board was in the middle of a major building program and, according to Eldred M. Taylor, the chair of the agency's board of directors, "in a very healthy state, moving forward in a very positive way." The election of Taylor to succeed Amos did not surprise supporters and friends of the agency. Taylor had served for twenty-three years as the pastor of Somerset's First Baptist Church. Having been a member of the agency's board for four years and chair for three years, Taylor was called by one observer "a natural" for the post. Certainly, he loved the work and was intimately knowledgeable about the role that the board played in the convention.

The announcement of Taylor's election came on July 10, 1981, at the same time of the formal dedication of twelve new cottages built at Glen Dale and Spring Meadows. The $2 million building project provided a welcome addition to the campuses replacing the older houses that were "too large, too costly to heat and cool, out-of-step with the family-oriented concept they were trying to pursue and in severe need of repair."[27] During Taylor's first full year in office, the board voted to sell the old cottages and thirty-eight acres of land to Brookside Inc. for $1 million. Brookside, a non-profit organization, planned a $20 million retirement community on the property. The board also voted to change the name of the agency from Kentucky Baptist Board of Child Care to Kentucky Baptist Homes for Children Inc. The new name more accurately identified the multifaceted work of the agency which included, in addition to the two homes for children, several temporary shelters located around the state, a Louisville home for unwed mothers, and foster and adoption services. The work of the agency flourished under Taylor's leadership. Kentucky Baptists exceeded the 1981 Thanksgiving offering goal of $550,000, an indication of the denomination's support for the work.[28]

The ministries of the Kentucky Baptist assemblies program continued to expand in the 1970s. Frank A. Heberlein replaced the resigning Arlis Hinson as manager of Cedarmore in 1977. After only a brief tenure, Heberlein retired in 1979 and was succeeded by Marshall Phillips. A native of Shelby County—the location of the assembly—Phillips graduated from Southern Seminary, pastored churches in Tennessee and Kentucky, and served as a foreign missionary in Kenya and Tanzania.[29]

Youth Week at Cedarmore meant a week of fun and spiritual growth and renewal for Kentucky Baptist young people. Young people assembled for an hour of worship and reflection each morning, followed by workshops on creative writing, puppetry, and Bible study. Recreational activities took up the afternoon, and the evenings were given over to creative services of worship and praise. Cedarcrest, the camp for G.A.s and Acteens, and Camp Rabro for Royal Ambassadors provided similar activities for girls and boys in Kentucky Baptist missions organizations. The KBC's Brotherhood Department also sponsored twice-a-year father-and-son weekends. Fathers and sons camped in restored covered wagons equipped with cots for sleeping.

In the western part of the state, eleven Baptist associations operated the Jonathan Creek Assembly located on a 120-acre tract in Marshall County. When George Gray became director of Jonathan Creek in 1972, changes came to the assembly immediately. Mary L. Gholsow, the WMU director of West Union Association, stated that "Brother Gray has literally torn that place apart and cleaned it up. He's done a wonderful job and has made Jonathan Creek an area we are very proud of." Gray had served as assistant director at Spring Meadows children's home. The tall, lanky manager emphasized that Jonathan Creek was "not just a youth camp but a place for people of all ages." Gray purchased bunk beds and mattresses from Murray State University, painted rooms, and poured new sidewalks. Because of the new manager's leadership, the assembly began to mirror Cedarmore with an array of summer camps and mission training sessions. Jonathan Creek, along

with Campbellsville College, also served as the site for "fellowship conferences," an extension of pastor-deacon retreats designed for the whole family.
In 1973, hundreds of participants heard Vance Havner, the venerable speaker
and minister, speak at a fellowship conference at Jonathan Creek.[30] Ownership of Jonathan Creek was transferred to the Kentucky Baptist Convention
in 1983.

Like the child-care and assembly ministries, the Kentucky Baptist hospital system continued to grow. In 1974, H. L. "Bert" Dobbs retired after thirty-
nine years of service to the hospital ministry. He came to Kentucky in 1935
to succeed George Hays as superintendent of the Kentucky Baptist Hospital
in Louisville. Dobbs and Helen Vincent, the hospital's director of nursing,
guided the institution through the latter years of the Great Depression and
through the troublesome World War II years when sixty-eight staff physi-
cians had been drafted into the military. After the war, administrators, having just weathered one crisis, faced another when the postwar demand for
medical care far exceeded the capacity of the hospital's facilities.[31] By 1948,
two additional patient wings were added to the facility, bringing the hospital's capacity to 285 beds. The hospital continued to grow in the 1950s when

Jonathan Creek Assembly, transferred to Kentucky Baptists in 1983

sixty beds were added in 1953, and a school of nursing building and a memorial chapel named after longtime supporter and Baptist pastor and activist M. P. Hunt were built in 1959. In the 1960s, building continued with the addition of another one hundred beds, a modern lobby, administrative offices, coffee shop, pharmacy, gift shop, and new elevators.

With the addition of Central Baptist Hospital in Lexington and Western Baptist Hospital in Paducah in the early 1950s, and with the creation of Baptist Hospitals Inc. in 1968, the convention looked to Dobbs to head the system. Dobbs became the first president. Three executive vice presidents were also named: Homer D. Coggins, the former administrator of Central Baptist Hospital and the successor to Dobbs at Kentucky Baptist Hospital; Ben R. Brewer, an administrator at Western Baptist Hospital who moved to Lexington with the appointment of Coggins to Louisville; and James V. Dorsett, the new administrator at Paducah. A twenty-four-member board of directors—eight designated to each hospital—was elected by the Kentucky Baptist Convention.

Under this arrangement, the hospital system continued to expand. In Louisville, the J. Graham Brown farm in Saint Matthews had been purchased in 1966 as a site for a new Baptist hospital to lessen the strain on the ever-expanding Kentucky Baptist Hospital. A convention fund-raising campaign, the "Second Mile Campaign," was initiated in 1970. Ground was broken for Baptist Hospital East in 1972, and the facility received its first patients in 1975. The six-story facility cost $16.5 million and was built to house 253 patients, with seven operating rooms, an eleven-bed intensive care unit, an eight-bed coronary care unit, an emergency department, and an obstetrics unit. Administratively, the hospital would be run by the staff of the Kentucky Baptist Hospital as part of the newly designed Louisville Baptist Hospitals (LBH). LBH would also operate the Mallory-Taylor Hospital, a thirty-one-bed institution in La Grange. The La Grange facility, financially troubled for years, had been taken over by Baptist Hospitals Inc. in 1974.[32]

The impressive growth of Kentucky's Baptist hospital system took a toll on its chief executive officer. Dobbs suffered from two heart attacks in 1964 and 1971. He took a leave of absence in 1973, and then after thirty-nine years of service, retired in 1974. Leadership of the corporate office with its statewide network of hospitals went to Homer Coggins. A gala celebration and recognition for Dobbs was held at the Galt House in Louisville on March 1, 1974. Duke K. McCall, president of Southern Seminary, served as toastmaster for the evening. Two hundred guests heard a long line of local and national medical and hospital leaders praise the work of the retiring administrator. The board of directors of Kentucky Baptist Hospitals Inc. presented Dobbs with an automobile in appreciation for his years of service.[33]

The state's Baptist hospitals did more than provide superb medical care for ailing patients. They provided spiritual comfort for patients, family members, and visitors as well through a well organized and effective chaplaincy program. B. B. Hilburn served as chaplain at Kentucky Baptist Hospital from 1952 until 1964. Upon his retirement, Hilburn was succeeded by Walter C. Jackson. At Central Baptist Hospital, volunteering pastors served until 1966 when Henry Buchanan was called as the hospital's first chaplain. Buchanan was succeeded by Bill B. Bailey in 1969. In Paducah, volunteers did the work until 1958 when George Miller was called as that hospital's first chaplain. Harley C. Dixon took the position in 1963. Chaplains broadcasted worship services through radio speakers in patient rooms. Closed-circuit television systems were added later.[34]

Chaplains certainly softened sterile and stark hospital environments. In 1976, Reita Moody joined Dixon at Paducah's Western Baptist Hospital, becoming the first female chaplain in the Kentucky Baptist Hospital system. She was part of a family of ministers. Husband George T. Moody served as minister of education at Murray's First Baptist Church and son Dwight pastored churches in Pittsburgh, Pennsylvania, and Owensboro before being named dean of the chapel at Georgetown College. Moody brought a special grace to her position. Dixon admitted that because of the sometimes rigid conservatism of the region, he had "some apprehensions" about hiring her. His decision proved the right one, however. Some area pastors questioned Moody's position on ordination, but the new chaplain explained that "for my situation it would be inconsequential to me." Moody was immediately accepted by the hospital community and became a caring minister to patients, visitors, and hospital personnel. Through her work, she gained "a better understanding of the church's role in crisis intervention." She explained that "when I see a patient surrounded with a community of love and support it's a special blessing."[35]

The issue of women in positions of ministry in Kentucky Baptist churches increased in intensity in the latter 1970s. At Louisville's Twenty-third and Broadway Baptist Church, John Sylvester and Joy Johnson, a husband and wife ministerial team, were called as co-pastors in 1977. The husband/wife co-pastor arrangement was believed to be a first in the Southern Baptist Convention. Both graduates of Southern Baptist Seminary, Sylvester and Johnson were called to lead the inner-city congregation of 150 members, both black and white. The church was large and prospering in the 1940s, but when white members fled the inner-city for the suburbs and joined other churches in the 1950s, its enrollment and attendance plummeted. The church was affiliated with both the Kentucky Baptist Convention and the General Association of Baptists in Kentucky. Cora Washburn, a deacon in the church, served as the chair of the pastor selection committee that called the husband and wife team. One of Sylvester's first duties as co-pastor was to lead in the ordination of Johnson to the gospel ministry.

Johnson, who made a commitment to the ministry during a W. A. Criswell revival, contributed fully to the ministry. Sylvester explained that, "we do everything together. We visit together. We make it a point to conduct funerals and weddings together. We rotate preaching duties." Johnson stated that the couple complemented each other in their ministerial roles: "I like for John to handle the business sessions and he feels more comfortable with me doing children's church," she explained. "But we both do each because we feel it is important for our ministry."[36] The pastor team built a home near the church in Louisville's west end and continued to serve the church into the 1980s.

While some pastors in Long Run Association, the couple's local association in Louisville, sometimes ignored Joy Johnson in associational meetings, the association eventually passed a resolution placing the authority for ordination in the hands of the local church. This was not the experience for Suzanne Coyle, who was ordained by the Beech Fork Baptist Church in Gravel Switch on February 6, 1977. The twenty-four-year-old Coyle hailed from the Gravel Switch area near Lebanon, attended Centre College in Danville, and then Princeton Theological Seminary in New Jersey. At Princeton, she worked part-time at Center City Baptist Chapel in Philadelphia. After graduation in 1976, she worked full-time in the area of church extension for the SBC's Home Mission Board and as a chaplain at the Center City chapel.[37]

When Beech Fork's association, the South District Association, met in October 1977, associational messengers voted to oust Beech Fork for ordaining Coyle. C. R. Daley described the meeting "as in the best Baptist tradition with opponents being careful in trying to avoid offending each other personally." Daley admitted that the Beech Fork church "was probably the first Southern Baptist congregation excluded from a local association for this reason." When a Louisville reporter contacted Coyle in Philadelphia, she expressed hurt and sadness for her home church: "I grew up there, played the piano at the church for years and I love those people." Coyle concluded that "the association is doing something it strongly believes is right and which I believe is wrong."[38]

When the Kentucky Baptist Convention met for the 140th annual session in Florence in November 1977, convention messengers reaffirmed the historic Baptist position on the authority of the local church, presenting a resolution to that effect. Bob Winstead, a messenger from Prospect, introduced a second resolution opposing the ordination of women. The first resolution eventually passed, however, making clear the messengers' desire to empha-size the prerogative of the local church in matters of ordination. At the Flo-rence meeting, messengers also elected Betty McSwain, wife of T. L. Mc-Swain—pastor of Hurstbourne Baptist Church—as the second vice presi-dent of the convention. McSwain became the first woman ever elected to a KBC office.[39]

The debate over women's ordination obscured the years of service that women had rendered for Kentucky Baptists. Women like Carolyn Ellis served faithfully through the state's Woman's Missionary Union. Elected president in 1972, the Shelbyville resident wondered, "What am I going to do now?" when her two-year term had ended. The answer was not long in coming as the nominating committee of the Southern Baptist Convention's WMU called to ask if she would serve as recording secretary. With her election, Ellis be-came one of only two elected officers representing some one and a quarter million Baptist women throughout the world.

The election was certainly fulfilling for Ellis, a lifelong advocate of mis-sions. "WMU has been a part of my life since my days in YWA's [Young Women's Auxiliary]," she explained. "As long as I can remember I have had a love for missions and a zeal to work in that area." Ellis served as WMU di-rector at First Baptist Church, Shelbyville, her home church, associational WMU director, on the executive board for state WMU for sixteen years, as regional WMU president, as state WMU assistant recording secretary, and as state president. Although elected to a national office, Ellis argued that WMU work on "the grass roots level, [in] the local church, is a full time Christian calling." "In WMU," she stated, "you realize each of us has a call to missions wherever we are." In 1981, Ellis completed six years as record-ing secretary for the national organization.[40]

Ellis continued a long tradition of Kentucky women's involvement in WMU. In 1976, the state missions offering was renamed the Eliza Broadus Offering in honor of Eliza Sommerville Broadus, daughter of John A. Broadus, president of Southern Seminary from 1889 to 1895. After coming to Kentucky from Greenville, South Carolina—with the move of the semi-nary—Broadus immediately became involved in missions work in Louisville's Walnut Street Baptist Church. She served on the state's central committee from its founding in 1878 for fifty years, serving as committee chairman for thirty-two years. By 1982, Kentucky's Woman's Missionary Union realized an activities budget of almost one hundred thousand dollars from the Eliza Broadus Offering.

In that year, the Kentucky roots of another woman, long revered for her work in missions, was remembered with the placement of a historical marker by the Kentucky Historical Society. Lottie Moon lived in Danville,

Kentucky, from 1866 to 1871, teaching at Caldwell Female Institute, a school operated by Danville's First Baptist Church and Centre College. Over eleven hundred Kentucky Baptist women witnessed the unveiling of the monument and heard Moon's biographer Catherine Allen, author of *The New Lottie Moon Story,* pay homage to the Baptist saint. Allen stated: "Lottie Moon was the angel Danville entertained unaware."[41]

A decade earlier in 1973, Gladys Hopewell, a native of Hopkins County and a Southern Baptist missionary to Taiwan for nineteen years, was found slain in her apartment. She was the fourth Southern Baptist missionary to die by violence in twenty months. A pioneer in Baptist student work in Taiwan, Hopewell had served in Tsingtao and Shanghai, China, and in Bangkok, Thailand, before being transferred to Taiwan in 1954.[42] Missionaries abroad like Gladys Hopewell and at home like Carolyn Ellis continued the grand and heroic Kentucky Baptist tradition established by Lottie Moon and Eliza Broadus years before.

Other Kentucky Baptist leaders found places of service in Southern Baptist Convention affairs and even beyond the SBC. In 1980, Ted Sisk, the pastor of Lexington's Immanuel Baptist Church and a former president of the KBC, was elected chair of the SBC's Sunday School Board trustees. In all, seventeen presidents (out of a total of thirty-nine through 1976) of the Southern Baptist Convention had Kentucky ties. Only two—E. Y. Mullins (1920-23) and John R. Sampey (1935-38), both presidents of Southern Seminary, served as SBC president while living in Kentucky. Three native sons— W. W. Hamilton from Christian County (1940-42), J. D. Grey, born in Princeton in Caldwell County (1951-53), and H. Franklin Paschall from Hazel (1966-68)—were elected as SBC president. Twelve others lived in Kentucky at one time or another during their ministerial careers.[43]

On the international level, Duke K. McCall, president of Southern Seminary, was named president of the Baptist World Alliance in 1980, the same year that Somerset native Robert S. Denny retired as the BWA's executive secretary. The involvement of two Kentuckians in the high ranks of an organization consisting of 119 Baptist bodies in 85 nations indicated the extent of the influence of Kentucky Baptists around the world.[44]

In the United States, the landscape of Southern Baptist life changed in the last year of the 1970s. Convinced of a liberal drift in the convention, conservative Baptist strategists orchestrated a plan to insure the election of an SBC president committed to the concept of "biblical inerrancy." The plan was spearheaded by Houston judge Paul Pressler and Criswell Bible College president Paige Patterson. The strategy involved a drive in some fifteen states to organize messengers to vote for an "inerrantist" candidate. Women's ordination and perceived liberalism in Southern Baptist seminaries were other con-

cerns of conservative leaders, but the inerrancy issue dominated the movement. In 1979, outgoing SBC president Jimmy Allen grieved that the movement would shift attention from the SBC's "Bold Mission Thrust" plan to
proclaim the gospel in every nation of the world by the year 2000. "There are
those who would like to change the agenda of the convention from missions
to orthodoxy," Allen concluded. C. R. Daley condemned the injection of political maneuvering in the election of the SBC president, behavior "more becoming in the back room scheming of political parties than in Southern Baptist life."[45]

But Southern Baptist allegiances became more akin to political parties after 1979. At the Southern Baptist Convention in Houston, Adrian Rogers,
pastor of Bellevue Baptist Church in Memphis, a prominent advocate of in-
errantism, was elected president. As president, he had the power to appoint
the committee which recommended scores of individuals to agency and institutional boards. In his first news conference as president, Rogers pledged
"100 percent support" for continuing the emphasis on the SBC's Bold Mission Thrust and assured Baptists he would not support a "witch hunt" in an
investigation of liberalism in the seminaries.[46]

Kentucky messengers to the Houston convention reacted to the meeting
in different ways. Eldred Taylor, at that time pastor of First Baptist Church,
Somerset, responded laconically that the convention was "pretty good." Taylor had attended thirty Southern Baptist Conventions, including twenty-
eight in a row. He did not see a shift in the work of the convention, but instead believed that "basically the Southern Baptist Convention will be the
same as before." Former KBC president Ted Sisk shared Taylor's optimism:
"I haven't seen a lot more politics here than I've seen in the past. It's just people speaking out for someone they support."

Mrs. Ray Mullendore, a member of First Baptist Church, Bowling Green,
and first vice president of the Foreign Mission Board, saw the injection of politics as a disturbing trend. "Politics has made this convention different from
any other I've attended." Mullendore wished that "we could get away from
politics." John Dunaway, pastor of Corbin's First Baptist Church, agreed.
"This has been the most political convention I've been to," he stated. He de-
cried the emphasis placed on doctrine, and believed that "if there is an attempt to force Baptists' thinking into one mode of theological belief, then it
will later lead us away from our effort at bold mission."[47]

At the center of the controversy was Wayne Dehoney, the former SBC
president and pastor of Louisville's Walnut Street Baptist Church. When a
messenger made a motion that the convention "disavow overt political activity and organization as a method of selection of its officers," Dehoney
spoke to the motion. Without mentioning Paul Pressler by name, he leveled

charges of overt political use of skyboxes at the Summit, the arena that served as the site of the convention, and referred to Pressler—again not by name—as being an illegal messenger at the convention. Other messengers rose to accuse Dehoney of "overt political activity" during his presidency of the convention from 1965 to 1967. After the short but rancorous debate, convention president Jimmy Allen expressed sadness over "the spirit that is now moving in this room." After messengers approved the resolution against political activity, Pressler, asking for a personal privilege, made "an impassioned and tearful" speech defending himself. He stated that he came to the convention as an accredited messenger because of his "honorary" membership in the First Baptist Church of Bellaire, Texas, a Houston suburb.[48]

The conservative swing of the Southern Baptist Convention mirrored a growing political conservatism in the nation. Both religious and political conservatism had an impact in Kentucky, although the Kentucky Baptist Convention steered clear of any extreme reaction one way or the other. Ronald Reagan, the Republican candidate for president, easily defeated Jimmy Carter in his bid for reelection in 1980. In the same year, the organization in Kentucky of Moral Majority, a right-wing group advocating educational and political action, indicated the presence of the conservative movement in a largely Democratic state. Frank Simon, a Louisville physician, and Robert Parker, pastor of Kosmosdale Baptist Church near Louisville, led Moral Majority's organizational efforts. Organizational meetings were held in Mayfield at Mid-Continent Baptist Bible College and in Bowling Green.[49]

As messengers prepared to gather at Louisville's Walnut Street Baptist Church for the 142nd meeting of the Kentucky Baptist Convention in 1979, James H. Cox, the *Western Recorder*'s associate editor, noted the new dynamic that the controversy had injected into the election of president for the Kentucky Baptist Convention. In his headline article of September 12, 1979, titled "Our Next President: A Pastor, Mid-stater & Ultra-conservative?" Cox noted previous trends in presidential elections. Now a "totally new factor" related to the victory at the Southern Baptist Convention for those Cox described as advocates of "biblical inerrantists, the so-called ultra-conservatives."

Cox stated that "rumors around the state now lead some to believe a similar campaign to capture the presidency of the Kentucky Baptist Convention may be in the making." Cox surmised that the Heart of America Bible Conference on the campus of Southern Seminary, held just five days before the meeting of the KBC in Louisville and featuring well-known conservative pastor W. A. Criswell and Texas evangelist James Robison, might serve as a staging ground for conservative organization and influence.[50]

When messengers voted in Louisville, however, Cox's conclusions appeared less than accurate when John Dunaway, pastor of First Baptist Church, Corbin, and a critic of the political activity at the Houston SBC meeting, was elected over four other candidates. J. Altus Newell, pastor of Louisville's St. Matthews Baptist Church, and Bill Whittaker, pastor of the First Baptist Church of Murray, were elected as vice presidents by acclamation. Rather than politics, the issue of world hunger dominated the Kentucky convention. The executive board meeting in Middletown a week before the convention was described as "the most tranquil in years."[51]

In a later December meeting, president Dunaway challenged the executive board to emphasize the obligation of Kentucky Baptists to share the gospel with "two million Kentuckians without Christ." According to the new president Kentucky must do its part in Bold Mission Thrust, the primary emphasis of the Southern Baptist Convention. Dunaway asserted that there were 735,000 Kentucky Baptists and about the same number in other Christian denominations. "This means more than half the population— youth and adult—are lost," the president concluded. Dunaway cited Pike County where 85 percent of the population did not profess Christianity.[52] He made it clear that the recent theological and political maneuvering at the SBC would not divert Kentucky Baptists from the main task of missions.

Adrian Rogers, the SBC president, surprised many Baptists when he refused to accept a nomination for a second term. Wishing to spend more time with his Bellevue congregation, Rogers made it clear that he would not be involved in the selection of his successor. With the election in 1980 of Bailey Smith as president, and with the elections of a succession of conservative candidates throughout the 1980s, the victory for conservatism in the SBC was clear. In Kentucky, however, Baptists continued to steer a neutral course, and the state was spared major upheavals that wracked other state conventions.

In Kentucky, the fact that the Southern Baptist Theological Seminary was an SBC institution made the swirling controversy prescient for Southern students and especially faculty and administrators. Away from the Southern campus, however, the laity among Kentucky Baptists continued to emphasize missions—both at home and abroad—more than theological and political controversy. Pastors of thriving churches also steered clear of the political fray, choosing to lead their congregations in evangelism, discipleship, and stewardship instead. From 1967 to 1979, the historic Severns Valley Baptist Church with pastor Verlin Kruschwitz led the state in total giving to the Cooperative Program. Indeed, even after 1979, the church continued to lead the state year after year despite expensive building debts.

After the church paid off a building debt in the mid-1960s, a church member asked Kruschwitz, "Now that we're out of debt, what shall we do with all that money?" The pastor suggested, "Let's try giving it to missions." The following year, Severns Valley jumped to first place in Cooperative Program giving in the state. The church remained perennially at the top spot despite a $1 million addition to the church in the 1970s.

Under the leadership of Eldred Taylor, First Baptist Church of Somerset often challenged Severns Valley for the top spot in giving. These large churches were not the only churches in the state committed to the support of missions through the Cooperative Program. The *Western Recorder* also reported on leading churches in "per-capita giving." Based on an average of giving per member, these churches were often medium or smaller churches in membership, but their members were no less committed to giving sacrificially. In 1979, for example, Countryside Baptist Church in the Ohio Valley Association and pastored by J. Wesley Bolin, led the state in per-capita giving. The church's forty-two members sent $82.58 per member to the Cooperative Program.[53]

Bolin represented a significant segment of the state's Baptist pastorate. In addition to the pastorate, Bolin owned a drugstore in a small, county-seat town. In fact, Bolin was a pharmacist before he was called to preach. When called to the gospel ministry at age forty, he sold his drugstore and soon left with his family for Fort Worth, Texas, where he attended Southwestern Baptist Theological Seminary. He worked a forty-hour week as a pharmacist at a large chain drugstore, pastored his first church (a small country church near a ranching community in east Texas), and took classes in theology and church history. After five years with degree in hand, he left the seminary and eventually returned to Kentucky to fulfill his call.

Out of the state's 2,201 Kentucky Baptist Convention churches in 1977, 715 pastors worked another job. Across the Southern Baptist Convention, over 9,000 bi-vocational pastors ministered in the denomination's 35,073 churches. These pastors held other jobs because their small congregations were unable to provide for a full-time pastor. In Kentucky, farmers, coal miners, and businessmen also pastored churches. Bi-vocational pastors found themselves in a unique position to minister to their congregations on Sundays and Wednesdays and to witness and serve in their communities during the rest of the week. Franklin Owen, executive secretary of the KBC, recalled his first pastorates in the Ozark hills of Missouri: "I worked in the filling stations and painted buildings. I officiated athletic events and sundry other vocational ways of earning a livelihood." On weekends, Owen preached and "shepherded some little flocks at a price they could pay." Owen described bi-vocational pastors as dedicated ministers who provided a valuable service for Kentucky Baptists. "They are witnesses and the darkness does not overcome the lighthouse windows of their modest churches to which they and their people are faithful."[54]

The role of the laity was also highlighted in the 1970s when Henry B. Huff, in 1975, became the first layman to be elected president of the Kentucky Baptist Convention in twenty-two years. A descendant of ministers and Baptist college presidents, he served as a Sunday School teacher, deacon chair, and Sunday School director at Louisville's Crescent Hill Baptist Church. He served on various boards and as a trustee of several agencies of the KBC before his election as president. An accomplished attorney, Huff brought a wealth of experiences—both denominational and secular—to his new position. James Cox, associate editor of the *Western Recorder,* hoped that Huff's election would cause other laymen to become involved in the business of the Kentucky Baptist Convention.[55]

Involvement of the laity in ministry had a long history at First Baptist Church, Arlington, in Carlisle County. Since 1949, members of the church represented their association, state, and region in more "Bible sword drills" and speakers' tournaments than any church in Kentucky. The church sponsored a first-place winner in the state Bible drill an average of once every four years. Most of the intense training for the competitions was led by Robert Hocker, an Arlington businessman, and his wife, Mary Helen. In 1973, the church held a reunion for former contestants from the congregation.[56] The church continued to emphasize this valuable ministry during the seventeen-year pastorate of Alvin York.

Kentucky Baptists from around the state gave sacrificially to the World Hunger offering year after year. In 1975, the KBC business office received close to $13,500 each month for the offering. When tornadoes ripped through the state the year before, individuals gave money that was distributed by the Kentucky Baptist Convention to aid victims of the disaster. Churches in Brandenburg, Monticello, and Bowling Green were especially hard hit. Nearly forty thousand dollars was distributed through the convention to aid damaged churches.[57]

In Louisville, the Kentucky Baptist Convention teamed up in 1979 with the St. Matthews Baptist Church to minister to the city's Spanish-speaking population. Headed by Robert Jones of the convention's Direct Missions Department, the effort marked the first major convention effort to reach a non-English language group. A 1970 census indicated that over six thousand Spanish-speaking people lived in the greater Louisville area. A 1978 *Time* magazine article estimated that over nine thousand Spanish-speaking individuals lived in Kentucky. J. Altus Newell, pastor of St. Matthews, approached Claude Mariottini, a doctoral student at Southern Seminary, with the idea of the unique ministry. Mariottini, fluent in Spanish as well as English and Portuguese, immediately accepted the challenge and began conducting home prayer meetings and Bible studies. Two professions of faith were made at the first meeting. Mariottini was supported with funds from both the convention and the St. Matthews congregation.[58]

The work of the Jefferson Street Chapel in Louisville's inner city continued to minister in the urban center throughout the 1970s and into the 1980s. Bill Fulkerson served as pastor-director of the chapel, one of the oldest mission centers in the United States. Founded by Steven P. Holcombe and the Walnut Street Methodist Church as the Holcombe Chapel in 1881, the chapel was taken over by the Long Run Association in 1941 and renamed the Jefferson Street Baptist Chapel in 1964. The chapel was one of three urban missions sponsored by the association. Fulkerson left the association's Portland Bridge Mission in 1977 to become the director of the Jefferson Street center.[59]

Kentucky Baptists responded to ministerial opportunities outside of the commonwealth in unique ways. In 1981, Bill Whittaker, president of the Kentucky Baptist Convention, led his congregation at Murray's First Baptist Church to give five thousand dollars to a summer mission project in Brazil. The gift represented only a minor part of the church's longtime commitment to Brazilian missions. The church had been involved in Brazilian missions since the early years of the twentieth century. Former pastor Richard Walker, Whittaker's predecessor, went to Brazil as a missionary after his Murray pastorate. In 1981, a nineteen-member team went with Whittaker to build dormitories at a Baptist assembly in Manaus, Brazil.[60] The church continued the Brazilian connection into the 1990s.

Kentucky Baptists continued the legacy of Lottie Moon, Gladys Hopewell, and others in ministering on foreign fields. In 1957 and 1958, for example, William W. Marshall, a native of Frankfort, Kentucky, taught English, history, and biology at the Baptist school in Nazareth, Israel. After graduating from Southern Seminary in 1961, he pastored churches and became associate secretary for the Department of Missionary Personnel of the Foreign Mission Board in Richmond, Virginia. Marshall and his wife Alice were appointed career missionaries in 1969, becoming field representatives for the Middle East.[61]

In 1973, Don and Suzanne Mantooth were among twenty-seven missionaries appointed by the Foreign Mission Board. The Mantooths were assigned to Israel, a country not unfamiliar to Don. A graduate of Cumberland College and Southern Seminary, he served as president of Cumberland's BSU during his senior year. The summer after graduation, he served as a summer missionary in Israel, an experience that changed his life. Since that summer, Mantooth "felt a definite leading to return there to serve."[62] He later returned to Kentucky for a long and fruitful pastorate at Morehead's First Baptist Church. The Marshalls and Mantooths represented scores of other Kentucky Baptists who were called from Kentucky to posts with the SBC's Foreign Mission Board.

The fact that Marshall and Mantooth were both products of Kentucky Baptist colleges indicated the importance of Baptist schools in preparing individuals for missions as well as the secular world. Because of the importance of Baptist institutions in the state, the struggle to fund them adequately posed a constant challenge for the convention. In 1977, C. R. Daley wrote that "no part of Baptist denominational life in Kentucky has made as much news and received as much attention in the last 20 years as Baptist colleges and schools. They have been in the forefront of discussion and debate almost constantly and they still pose the greatest challenge to an enthusiastic and united mission thrust for Kentucky Baptists." In 1957, seven colleges and schools were supported by the convention; in 1977, there were five. Magoffin Institute, a boarding high school in eastern Kentucky, had closed, along with Bethel College, a two-year school in Hopkinsville. Kentucky Southern College opened in 1962 and facing dire financial straits merged with the University of Louisville only seven years later. In 1977, Campbellsville, Cumberland, and Georgetown remained as four-year colleges, Clear Creek as a Bible college, and Oneida Baptist Institute as a boarding high school.

The recommendations of the consulting firm in 1958 that Kentucky Baptists drop three schools and combine four colleges into a Kentucky Baptist University located in Louisville was soundly defeated when presented to convention messengers in Elizabethtown. The most ambitious financial effort in the history of the convention—a $12 million goal for capital needs later dropped to $9 million—was approved in 1962. Although professional fund-raisers worked to raise money, the results were disappointing. Only $3 million was raised, and part of that total went to the fund-raisers. In desperation, the convention finally underwrote a $6 million loan to make up the difference. In 1977, the loan was still in the process of being paid with an annual Cooperative Program allocation of $268,650. The 1976-77 allocation for operating funds amounted to $856,950, making a total appropriation for colleges and schools of $1,125,500.

In 1976, a special committee reported to the executive board after a two-year study, listing eleven goals for Baptist educational institutions in Kentucky. C. R. Daley noted the ambitious nature of the goals and concluded that "if these goals are achieved, our schools will have recognition and financial support from the convention they have never enjoyed before."[63] Bill Whittaker chaired the committee; other members included A. B. Harmon and Joe Priest Williams of Louisville, Jim Highland of Shelbyville, and Henry Johns of Versailles. The eleven-point plan was far-reaching and visionary.

Kentucky Baptist colleges and schools were to have:

1. developed and implemented a comprehensive strategy by Sept. 1, 1978, to interpret the importance of these colleges and schools to Kentucky Baptists.

2. translated their purpose . . . of Christian values into visible, effective programs by Sept. 1, 1981.

3. encouraged Kentucky Baptists to maintain their annual investment in Christian education . . . at a minimum of 30% of the Kentucky Baptist Convention portion of the Cooperative Program by July 31, 1982.

4. designed and implemented joint programs of cooperation by Sept. 1, 1979.

5. completed a coordinated capital campaign for needed buildings and endowment by July 31, 1982.

6. encouraged the Kentucky Baptist Convention to establish and staff a full-time professional office for the promotion of Christian education and provide adequate operating funds . . . by Sept. 1, 1978.

7. a comprehensive long-range plan for the fiscal stability of each institution by July 31, 1979, to serve as a primary guideline for the fiscal operation for the period 1979-84.

8. established [by the Kentucky Baptist Convention] an effective, equitable formula for the distribution of Cooperative Program funds to Baptist colleges and schools in Kentucky by the beginning of the fiscal year 1977.

9. established a comprehensive student recruiting plan on each campus to enable each institution to achieve its optimum enrollment by July 31, 1984.

10. in cooperation with the Kentucky Baptist Convention . . . a continuing program to increase the level and quality of trustees' performance of their duties by July 31, 1980.

11. the executive board reorganize the Christian education committee by July 31, 1977, to provide leadership for the implementation of recommendations.

When the goals were presented to the executive board in November 1976, several board members questioned the merits of goal 6. T. A. Prickett of Owensboro, Chester Badgett of Campbellsville, and Bill Jaggers of Prestonsburg believed that money allocated for a staff position for educational promotion could best be spent on the schools themselves. When an amendment to strike the goal was defeated, the board went on to approve the report without opposition. At the annual meeting, the report "sailed through the convention without a comment."[64]

Daley believed that the first goal was the key to success. In a March 3, 1977, "Daley Observations" column, the editor asked, "How Vital Are Kentucky Baptist Colleges and Schools?" He noted that "some Kentucky Baptists believe we must have strong schools but not all agree. Christian education doesn't appeal to nor excite most Kentucky Baptists like state, home and foreign missions and child care." The editor stated bluntly that "until recent years we had only one senior Baptist college and its history is punctuated with controversy and poor relationship with many Kentucky Baptists."

Because of the lack of support, many Baptist families sent sons and daughters to state-supported schools. Parents were convinced that strong Baptist Student Union programs at the larger colleges and universities would provide a Baptist young person with support and encouragement at less expensive state institutions. For the rank and file, education had historically been a low priority in the bluegrass state. The ambivalence to Baptist education—and education in general—in Kentucky made higher education challenging work indeed. Daley went to the core of the problem: "Not enough Kentucky Baptists are sold on our schools," he wrote.[65]

The apathy of Kentucky Baptists for higher education was especially challenging for Campbellsville College. In 1975, it appeared that the very existence of the Taylor County school was in jeopardy. An enrollment of around seven hundred simply did not generate sufficient funds to keep the institution afloat. The school operated at a financial deficit, and the Kentucky Baptist Convention had already made a one-hundred-thousand-dollar emergency grant from mission reserve funds. A fifty-thousand-dollar advance from the convention was designed to help Campbellsville through the summer, and would be withheld from the 1975-76 monthly convention appropriations to the school. If not for a sense of calling to the school, Campbellsville faculty members could resign and take positions in public high schools for higher salaries.[66]

Campbellsville's beleaguered president, Randy Davenport, continued to persevere, leading the school courageously through the hard times. In an interview for the *Western Recorder*, he was asked frankly, "How do you justify spending what we do on Christian education?" The president answered, "It is justified by what life would be like if we did not have that influence." Davenport argued that "the history of our nation had been so positively affected by the small private and particularly Christian institutions. God forbid that we should ever let these schools go." In Kentucky, Davenport noted that in 1979, 87 percent of Kentucky students enrolled in state colleges and universities compared to the national average of 80 percent. In 1968, Campbellsville's enrollment reached an all-time high of 1,069, but with the building of a comprehensive junior college system connected to the University of Kentucky, the school's enrollment had plummeted to only 652 students in a decade's time. Twelve percent of the school's $2.7 million budget came from Kentucky Baptists through the Cooperative Program. With the dramatic drop in enrollment, additional funds from tuition were woefully lacking. The school was able to hang on, but it would be another decade before another leader was able to turn the corner and bring prosperity to the struggling institution.[67]

At the state's other Baptist institutions, a changing of the guard came in the late 1970s. In 1978, it was announced that James H. Taylor would succeed J. M. Boswell upon his retirement as president of Cumberland College. An educational legend in the Appalachian Mountains of eastern Kentucky, the seventy-two-year-old Boswell would step down. Trustees elected Taylor, the school's thirty-year-old vice president for development. Taylor was a Cumberland alumnus, having received a bachelor of science degree from the school, as well as additional degrees in higher education and administration from other institutions.

Boswell had served as the institution's president for thirty-three years, one of the longest tenures of any college president in Kentucky history. He was proud of the school's impact in the mountain area. He stated that "the school has grown in influence and service, and I believe it is being recognized by its constituency now more than ever." He was pleased that the school had a history of accepting students "who had no money but who had strong educational backgrounds and a determination to go to college." Boswell was recognized across the Southern Baptist Convention for his long years of leadership of the school. Now, the younger Taylor would lead. Words of praise from the college's board chairman David Hugg of Corbin presaged future years of growth and progress for the mountain school: Taylor "has demonstrated he is energetic, intelligent, perceptive and imaginative. He strongly supports the fundamental purposes of Cumberland College."[68]

At Georgetown, the state's oldest Baptist college, Ben M. Elrod replaced the retiring Robert Mills in 1978. Mills had led the institution for over eighteen years. He continued on in a fund-raising capacity as chancellor after his retirement. Approaching the college's sesquicentennial anniversary, Mills believed that it was "time for new leadership that would stimulate the college." With an enrollment of 990 students, the school had suffered with other private colleges. When Mills arrived as president in 1958, the enrollment had been 1,086. After eight years at the helm, an enrollment of 1,488, an all-time high, had been recorded; but along with Campbellsville, Georgetown's enrollment suffered with the advancement of the state's community college network.

Under Mills, significant changes had come to the school's campus. Major renovations of Giddings Hall, Anderson Hall, Hill Chapel, and Alumni Gymnasium were completed, and a new student center, science center, law library, and music laboratory built. C. R. Daley wrote that above all of his accomplishments, Mills was "a Christian gentleman." Deeply involved in Kentucky Baptist life, he had chaired the bicentennial committee for the state convention. Daley concluded that at Georgetown, his successor would "have big shoes to fill literally, professionally and spiritually."[69]

When trustees elected Ben Elrod as the school's twenty-first president, they chose an individual with valuable experience in Baptist higher education. Elrod came to Georgetown from Ouachita Baptist University where he served as senior vice president and director of development. Like Jim Taylor at Cumberland, Elrod represented a new breed of Baptist college president. Instead of climbing through the ranks of academic affairs, presidents came increasingly from careers in development, an indication of the significance of fund-raising for private institutions. Elrod graduated from Ouachita and then completed degrees from Southwestern Seminary, as well as a doctorate in education from Indiana University. He was elected as vice president for development at Ouachita in 1963, and then in 1968 as president of Oakland City College, a General Baptist school in Indiana. He returned to his old position at Ouachita after two years.[70]

Elrod brought a fresh sense of commitment and dynamism to the Georgetown campus. Despite finding a nine-hundred-thousand-dollar budget deficit upon his arrival at Georgetown in 1978, the institution was in the middle of a 15 percent, two-year rise in enrollment. The enrollment climbed to 1,092 in the fall of 1978, and remarkably increased to 1,110—100 more than the previous spring—in the spring semester when enrollments usually dropped.

Georgetown was also involved in a major capital campaign. Between $3.5 million and $5.5 million was solicited from individuals.[71] Backed by his years of leadership in the area of development, Elrod proved to be the perfect choice to lead the school in the exciting, but difficult, years ahead.

The enrollment issue had always been crucial for Baptist colleges in Kentucky, especially after a state-wide community college system was in place by the 1970s. The Kentucky Baptist Convention adopted a program in 1972 to assist students who preferred to continue their education in a Kentucky Baptist school rather than a state institution. The Kentucky Baptist Scholarship

Fund provided a one-hundred-dollar scholarship per semester on a matching basis, with the student's local church giving an additional one hundred dollars. The colleges later agreed to give an additional one hundred dollars. The program, designed for all first-time, full-time students, provided six hundred dollars for the first year at Campbellsville, Cumberland, or Georgetown. The program provided this assistance for sixty-three students in its first year, 1973-74, and for sixty-eight students in 1974-75.[72]

In 1976, Clear Creek Baptist Bible College observed its fiftieth anniversary as a training school for preachers. Founded in 1926 by L. C. Kelly, pastor of Pineville's First Baptist Church, the school became a full-fledged Bible college in 1944, operating eight months a year. Kelly served as the school's president until 1954 when he was succeeded by D. M. Aldridge. Aldridge came to Clear Creek from Magoffin Institute where he had served as president. He had graduated from Southern Seminary and taught missions and church history as a member of the Clear Creek faculty before going to Magoffin.

The growth of the school under Aldridge's leadership was phenomenal. The annual budget grew from $86,000 to $550,000 in 1976, and the total assets of the school rose from $612,000 to $1.5 million. The endowment increased from a paltry $771 to $525,000. Aldridge admitted that "fund raising is all we do around here—for at least 17 hours a day." The leader's tireless efforts paid off for the school and for Kentucky Baptists.

Clear Creek provided a unique educational experience for men called to preach in their middle-to-late adult years. The average Clear Creek student was male, age thirty-four, and married with children. "When a man gives up his job and home to go to school, he means business," Aldridge concluded. These men usually ministered at smaller churches, and according to the school's leader, "Clear Creek is exactly the kind of school we need to train men for the smaller churches. . . . We are filling a void." Aldridge pointed out that of 34,849 Southern Baptist churches, 25,293 had memberships under 400. In Kentucky in 1979, 1,635 Baptist churches out of a total of 2,138 had memberships under 400. Clear Creek did indeed fill a void, providing a needed educational ministry in eastern Kentucky.[73]

When Aldridge resigned in 1982, Leon Simpson, the forty-three-year-old assistant pastor of First Baptist Church, Dallas, Texas, was elected to be his successor. A native Oklahoman, Simpson held degrees from Texas Tech University and Moody Bible Institute, and a doctorate from Southwestern Seminary. The new president knew eastern Kentucky well, having served for twelve years as the director of ministerial training at Cumberland College. Simpson promised to continue the mission and ministry of his predecessor: "Clear Creek shall continue to offer the finest Biblical and practical training possible for those who have answered God's call after reaching mature years.

It shall continue to relate primarily to the Appalachian region and various areas of Kentucky."[74]

At the other end of the state, Mid-Continent Baptist Bible College had trained preachers from its founding in 1949. Supported by area churches and associations (especially West Kentucky Baptist Association) rather than the state convention, Mid-Continent has had a strong influence in small, rural churches in western Kentucky. First called West Kentucky Baptist Bible Institute, the school's classes initially met at Clinton's First Baptist Church in Hickman County. L. W. Carlin, one of the school's founders and a former student at H. Boyce Taylor's Bible school in Murray, taught the institution's first class in the basement of the church on January 10, 1949. And it was Carlin who suggested that the institution change its name to Mid-Continent Baptist Bible College in 1967.[75] The location of the school in Clinton was a recognition of the town's long heritage in Baptist education. Clinton Seminary began there in 1830, and from 1874 until 1914 Clinton Baptist College provided educational opportunities for western Kentucky students.

Mid-Continent continued in Clinton from 1949 to 1957, when the school moved to Mayfield, occupying a former church building. By 1957, the institution was supported by thirteen Baptist associations in three states. When the college outgrew its facilities in 1976, Mid-Continent moved from its downtown location to an eighteen-acre campus in Hickory, five miles north of town.[76]

In 1957, Oscar C. Markham became Mid-Continent's president. Another of the school's founders, Markham presided over the move of the campus from Clinton to Mayfield. The president's remarkable wife Ann Parrish Markham became the school's head librarian, leaving her position in the Department of English at Murray State University. For twenty years, she presided over the library, building the collection from a paltry two thousand books to over twenty-five thousand volumes. A world traveler, Markham visited Guatemala, Scandanavia, Canada, Japan, and various African countries. Two libraries were named in her honor: The Ann Parrish Markham Library at Mid-Continent and the Ann Parrish Markham Library at the Christian Academy in Guatemala City.[77]

Remarkable individuals like Ann Markham influenced countless students in a school like Mid-Continent funded by local associations and in institutions supported by the Kentucky Baptist Convention. Oneida Baptist Institute, Clear Creek Baptist Bible College, Georgetown College, Cumberland College, and Campbellsville College all struggled heroically to make a mark in the lives of students as Kentucky Baptist Convention institutions.

Franklin Owen made his mark on Kentucky Baptists, too. With a steady hand, he had guided the convention carefully and faithfully in the years of his tenure. As he approached the mandatory retirement age in 1978—lowered to sixty-five at the end of the tenure of Harold Sanders—KBC president Ted Sisk appointed a fifteen-member panel chaired by Verlin Kruschwitz to recommend a successor.[78] When the executive board met in May 1978, however, sweeping changes were made to the convention's staff retirement plan. The increase in the mandatory retirement age from sixty-five to seventy proved to be an appropriate way to recognize the quality of Franklin Owen's tenure as executive secretary. The plan would allow Owen to continue as the leader of the convention, a development that Owen himself appreciated. "I don't feel that this old horse is plum done. I don't honestly feel that this is the time for me to lay it down. I do not foresee any desire to work until age 70. But for now, we go on."[79]

C. R. Daley concluded that the invitation for Owen to continue was "a tribute to the personal popularity of Dr. Owen and to his outstanding leadership."[80] Kentucky Baptists agreed. Owen did not continue until his seventieth birthday. Instead, late in 1981 a sixty-eight-year-old Owen surprised the 170 members of the KBC executive board with the announcement of his impending retirement on December 31, 1982. In a "Daley Observations" column, the editor of the *Western Recorder* revealed that "stunned members of the Kentucky Baptist Convention executive board sat silently before responding with a standing ovation at the conclusion of the announcement." Not a "courtesy gesture," Daley concluded that the ovation resulted from the "profound appreciation" of board members.[81]

Successful in every respect, Owen's tenure was marked by an increase in Cooperative Program income from $6,693,000 in 1972 to $16,124,000 in 1981. From a $1 million indebtedness in 1972, Owen's management skills had resulted in a $4 million surplus by 1981. Baptist student centers, improvements at Cedarmore, and an impressive addition to the Baptist Building left a physical legacy of the Owen years. Yet, his most enduring legacy according to Daley would not be marked with statistics or buildings, but "in such intangibles as spirit, morale, confidence, dependability, trust, and integrity." Owen's successor in the executive office would call him "a genuine statesman."[82] High praise indeed, but largely because of the work of Franklin Owen, the Kentucky Baptist story continued as a story of cooperation into the last years of the twentieth century.

On Mission Together
1983-2000

When the retired executive secretary of the Kentucky Baptist Convention rose to address the audience gathered for the historical symposium at the Baptist Building on August 28, 1998, he acknowledged that he was not the first choice for the engagement. Joe Priest Williams, the chair of the KBC's Historical Commission, had first asked A. B. Colvin to speak on "the Baptist response" to the period of "wealth and disconnectedness" in American life from 1980 to 1998. When Colvin was unable to attend, however, Williams turned to William Walter Marshall to speak. The purpose of the meeting was to examine the history of the Kentucky Baptist Convention from 1900 to 2000. Marshall, the ex-football player turned foreign missionary turned executive secretary-treasurer of the KBC, proved to be a happy choice to provide perspective on the last decades of the century, a period that mirrored his years as the leader of Kentucky Baptists.

The dignified Marshall outlined the highlights of Kentucky Baptist achievements in carefully crafted sentences delivered in measured terms, dividing his talk into three sections: Who were Kentucky Baptists during this period? What has been the impact of "the Controversy" on Kentucky Baptists and what were responses to it? And what has been the progress of Kentucky Baptists during this period?[1] Marshall's insights were perceptive and revealing. It was clear that the speaker knew intimately of which he spoke, had experienced it, and then had thought deeply about it.

Marshall had succeeded Franklin Owen as executive secretary in 1983. His previous experience had prepared him for a tenure of leadership dedicated to missions. His weekly column penned for the *Western Recorder* was appropriately titled "On Mission Together." Born in Frankfort in 1932, Marshall grew up near the famous "Singing Bridge" on the Kentucky River. His parents, Earnest and Elizabeth, were longtime members of Frankfort's First Baptist Church, as were his Marshall grandparents. Marshall was especially close to his grandfather, Walter Marshall, his namesake who took him fishing and hunting and called on young Walt to help in his grocery store. Marshall remembered that his early years represented "among the most ideal childhoods that one could have."[2]

Marshall was baptized in the church of his parents and grandparents when he was ten, but it was not until his college years that he had a spiritual experience that changed his life. After high school, he was recruited to play football at Eastern Kentucky University as a tackle, but after an academically rocky year, the immature freshman transferred to Georgetown College. At Georgetown, he continued to play football for three years until the football program was discontinued in 1953. He then decided to go to California, where he worked and played semi-pro football until he was drafted into the Marine Corps. While stationed in Chesapeake, Virginia, Richard Moore, the pastor of a small church there, turned to Marshall and asked, "Walt, have you ever thought that part of your running away from God is that He wants you to do something special for Him?" Pastor Moore had planted the seed that would grow into a life calling in Marshall's heart.[3]

Back in Kentucky after his stint in the military, Marshall attended a revival service at Georgetown Baptist Church led by Jess Moody. Marshall made a decision for Christ, asked for re-baptism, and soon felt called to the ministry. The church's pastor, Dan Moore, asked him to teach a Sunday School class, but Marshall declined. Moore countered with a proposal for Marshall to start a church in the Highlands subdivision between Georgetown and Lexington. Marshall, along with several other Georgetown students, went door to door, and he preached on a carport before the mission moved to a rented storefront in the subdivision. While pastoring the church, Marshall completed his degree at Georgetown in May 1957, married Alice—also a Georgetown graduate and honored as Miss Georgetonian—on August 10, and left for Nazareth, Israel, two days later.[4]

Leo Eddleman, Georgetown's president, had served as a missionary in Palestine, and he provided opportunities for Georgetown students to teach and minister there. The Marshalls taught school in Nazareth and lived for a summer on a Jewish kibbootz (kibbutz) in Mizrah, on the plain of Esdraelon just south of Nazareth. They returned to Kentucky just in time to enroll for the fall 1958 semester at Southern Seminary. Another seed—a seed for missions—had been sown.

After graduation from the seminary in 1961, Marshall pastored Rosalind Hills Baptist Church in Roanoke, Virginia (1961-63), before going to the Foreign Mission Board (FMB) in Richmond as associate secretary in the Department for Missionary Personnel (1964-69). Again, an individual was used by the Lord to nudge Marshall in the direction of his calling. Marshall's predecessor at Rosalind Hills had asked Jesse Fletcher, the new personnel director of the Foreign Mission Board, to lead a revival. With Marshall as the new pastor, Fletcher kept the engagement. At the time, Fletcher was completing his first book, *Bill Wallace of China*. Fletcher's influence brought Marshall to the Foreign Mission Board. Yet again, a seed was planted.[5]

After several years in Richmond, the Marshall family, now with three children, were appointed as career missionaries in 1969. The appointment—field representatives to the Middle East—landed them in Nicosia, Cyprus, Beirut, Lebanon, and eventually Munich, West Germany. During a one-year furlough in 1973-74, Marshall completed a Doctor of Ministry degree from Southern. The Marshalls returned to the states for good in 1976 when he became the director of furlough ministries for the FMB. He was promoted to vice president for the Office of Human Resources in 1980, the position from which he was called as KBC executive secretary-treasurer in 1983.[6]

When Marshall came to serve Kentucky Baptists in 1983, his experience in the ministry, and especially in missions, had provided fertile soil for the harvest of work that would come during

William W. Marshall,
executive secretary,
Kentucky Baptists, 1983-1997

his tenure. Individuals like Dan Moore, Leo Eddleman, and Jesse Fletcher had influenced Marshall in unique ways. The years of education and experience and influence served the leader well as he approached his new field of ministry and calling.

At the historical symposium in 1998, two years after his retirement as executive secretary, Marshall could speak with confidence about the Kentucky Baptist story in the last two decades of the twentieth century. By the end of the century, the Kentucky Baptist story had been woven into the rich fabric of the commonwealth. For many years, Kentucky Baptists had long been the largest religious group in the state, and by the late twentieth century one out of every five Kentuckians was a Baptist. During the period discussed by Marshall, the number of churches affiliated with the Kentucky Baptist Convention hovered somewhere between the twenty-three hundred and twenty-five hundred mark. A large majority of those churches numbered fewer than one hundred in attendance on any given Sunday.[7]

In many ways, Kentuckians remained a diverse, even a divided people; at the least, Kentuckians were determined to maintain a strong regional consciousness. In the east, as Marshall put it, "the mountains . . . had not moved nor had Baptists of that area shown inclinations to desert their inherited mountain pride or their usually kind suspicion of outsiders." The influence of mountain institutions—Oneida Baptist Institute, Clear Creek Baptist Bible College, and Cumberland College—on eastern Kentucky churches remained strong. Clear Creek's influence carried across the state. Statistics indicated that one of every seven Baptist churches in Kentucky was pastored by a Clear Creek graduate. Most of these pastors ministered in the east, but it was not unusual to find a Clear Creek trained minister in a western Kentucky church. More than half of the state's over six hundred bi-vocational Baptist pastors, many of them Clear Creek graduates, ministered in the eastern area of the state.

When Bill Whittaker became president of Clear Creek in 1988, succeeding Leon Simpson (president in 1982-88), the institution entered a new era of service and growth. Whittaker was converted in Calvary Baptist Church in Bowling Green during his high school years. Influenced by the Baptist Student Union, he was called to preach while an undergraduate at Western Kentucky University. During and following the completion of two degrees at Southern Seminary, he pastored at Jackson Grove Baptist Church in Bowling Green (at one time pastored by W. A. Criswell), First Baptist Church, Sturgis, and First Baptist Church, Murray. During his Murray pastorate, the young minister was elected president of the Kentucky Baptist Convention in 1980. He served the convention well, consistently making the long trip to Middletown to conduct convention business. Years later, he recalled that he used to joke that "Murray was centrally located, about four hours from everything."[8] Whittaker followed other Murray pastors, H. Boyce Taylor and H. C. Chiles, as president of the KBC.

Whittaker had been approached about the Clear Creek presidency in 1982 following the retirement of D. M. Aldridge. He had visited the campus each year since 1971, preaching in chapel services and organizing various projects for the school. The time was not yet right, however. Whittaker had a strong, clear conviction that he should become more involved in missions. While a student at Western Kentucky University, he had served as a BSU summer missionary in the Philippines. In December 1982, convinced that he should return to his former mission field, he resigned the Murray pastorate and went with his family to the Philippines for service with the Foreign Mission Board.[9]

After service in the Philippines, and a brief Florida pastorate, Whittaker was approached again about the Clear Creek presidency, and feeling that the time was now right, took the leadership position in 1988. He found a languishing school, over nine hundred thousand dollars in debt from the building of a family life center. Enrollment continued to decline in the early 1990s, reaching a low point of 130 students. Then things began to happen. Simpson had started the process for the school to become fully accredited by the American Association of Bible Colleges (AABC). Under Whittaker, accreditation was achieved and later renewed for ten years. In June 1999, the institution also received accreditation with the Southern Association of Colleges and Schools (SACS), the culmination of six years of preparation and hard work.[10]

Whittaker worked to renovate existing housing, built new townhouses for students, along with a new medical health center, a new child development center, and a new classroom building. Two remodeling projects were devoted to the library. A capital campaign to raise $3.5 million produced $3.8 million. Work teams from across the state often made valuable contributions to the school's building projects. Year after year, for example, Tim and Karen Langford with children Andrea, Mary Evelyn, and Amy made the long trek across the state from Hickman in far western Kentucky to work on various Clear Creek projects. A commonwealth attorney and active farmer, Tim also served as a deacon in his church and as a member of Clear Creek's Board of Trustees. The service of the Langfords indicated that Clear Creek's mission had statewide appeal.

Clear Creek made long strides to achieve its mission under Whittaker's leadership. And that mission continued to emphasize a practical, Bible college education. Whittaker explained that "we are committed to being a Bible college; we don't want to be a liberal arts college." "We intend to be a Bible college," Whittaker explained, "and we intend to be a good one; we are a good one."[11] New programs like the center of church planting and a center for evangelism provide practical means for the school to fulfill the mission to which it continues to be committed. Kentucky Baptists can be proud of Clear Creek Baptist Bible College as it continues to fill a unique niche for Christian education in the commonwealth.

Oneida Baptist Institute served the state—indeed, the nation and the world—in a different way. A century of service provided a Christian boarding school for grades six through twelve.[12] Hundreds of Kentucky Baptist volunteers came to eastern Kentucky, many of them for the first time, drawn there by Barkley Moore, Oneida's charismatic president from 1972 to 1994. Ray and Geneva Brownfield, a retired couple from Murray, came, for example, for a year's stay in the mid-1980s to volunteer. Geneva, a former guidance counselor in Tennessee and Kentucky public schools, worked to evaluate transcripts and also provided guidance expertise for Oneida students. Ray, a retired banker, wished to work out-of-doors, so he helped organize student crews in Oneida's work-study program. The volunteering efforts of the Brownfields mirrored the work of hundreds of other volunteers impressed with the unique mission of Oneida. These volunteers played an important role in Oneida's work, and they continued to make the pilgrimage to the school year after year.

The contributions of Clear Creek and Oneida, along with the continuing influence of Cumberland College, were impressive indeed for the eastern region of the state. It was the commonwealth's western region that seemed most resistant to change. After he became executive secretary of the convention, Marshall had been told by a west Kentucky pastor that when he came to visit his church, Marshall would feel that he was back in the 1950s. Only after Marshall had spoken there did he realize that the pastor had meant his comment as a compliment to the area.[13] Certainly, old Kentucky Baptist traditions remained strong in the west. Many of those traditions related to the lingering influence of Landmarkism. Views on the observance of the Lord's Supper and women in ministry, for example, remained tied in many churches to Landmark tradition.

Just as Clear Creek made an impact in the east, Mid-Continent Baptist Bible College influenced the western area. Not affiliated with the convention, the Mayfield institution trained ministers for area churches. One of the institution's presidents claimed that one in twelve Kentucky Baptist churches was pastored by a Mid-Continent graduate. Marshall asserted that Mid-Continent, along with Union University and Mid-America Seminary in Tennessee, and Southwestern Seminary in Texas, probably ex-

On Mission Together   259

erted more influence in the Baptist churches of western Kentucky than Kentucky's three Baptist colleges and Southern Seminary.[14]

When the state convention assumed control of Jonathan Creek Baptist Assembly in 1981, "a bridge to a stronger relationship"—in Marshall's words—was built between the convention and the western region. Like the east, the west had experienced a sense of isolation, of a fashion, from the rest of the commonwealth. Numerous alumni and friends of Bethel College held lingering resentment toward the convention, feeling that their old alma mater in Hopkinsville had been left "to die on the vine."[15] Still, as a whole, the churches in western Kentucky remained loyal to the spirit of cooperation. The vision of cooperation had been conceived in Murray, after all, and churches in the west continued to be the most generous in their giving to missions through the Cooperative Program.

In Kentucky, basketball has historically been a unifying factor. With the emergence of the University of Kentucky Wildcats under Adolph Rupp as a premier big-time college program in the 1930s, basketball fans from Pikeville to Paducah rallied around the state university team. Perhaps it was the pride in the university's basketball program that unified Kentuckians more than anything else in the twentieth century. It was a combination of basketball and Christian love that transcended the state's regionalism in a unique way in 1983. In that year, the high school basketball team from Carlisle County, a small rural county in extreme western Kentucky, advanced to the Sweet Sixteen and eventually met Lexington's Henry Clay High School in the championship game of the tournament.[16]

The Comets lost the title game to the large urban school, but still completed the season with a sterling 40-4 record. Two leaders on the team were Keith York of Arlington and Philip Hall of Bardwell, both Baptists. A writer for the *Western Recorder* stated that "two young Baptist athletes received a great deal of publicity last March, not because their basketball team won, but because it lost."[17] An Associated Press photograph, made just after the Comets' season-ending loss to Henry Clay, pictured York with his arms wrapped around a crying Hall. Longtime teammates and best friends, York tried to comfort Hall after the loss, while also congratulating his friend for winning the prestigious Ted Sanford Award for sportsmanship.

The fact that York was white and Hall black was not lost on a state that had struggled—along with other southern states—to overcome racial barriers. The *Western Recorder* writer concluded that "York and Hall typify the progress that has been made in both the field of athletics and in the area of racial prejudice." When the six-foot, two-inch, two-hundred-pound senior was asked to speak before a group of writers attending a workshop at Mid-Continent, York expressed his faith in Christ and shared how teamwork, unity, and sportsmanship were instilled in the team by Coach Craynor Slone. Facing a group of Baptists was not unusual for York. The athlete's father, Alvin York, served as pastor of Arlington's First Baptist Church for seventeen years.[18] Perhaps the lessons the young York learned from his coach and from his father—lessons of faith and cooperation and unity— symbolized the goal of Kentucky Baptists to overcome regional differences to advance the cause of Christ.

If the eastern and western regions of the state felt slighted at times, the "golden triangle" represented the region having the greatest diversity and the least resistance to change. Ironically, this central area of the common- wealth which included Kentucky's three largest cities—Louisville, Lexing- ton, and Covington—boasted at once the richest institutional tradition as well as the greatest bent toward progressive belief and practice. Marshall believed that Campbellsville University, Georgetown College, and Southern Seminary provided the greatest influence on "golden triangle" churches.

Less conservative than churches in the east and west, churches in the central and northern regions of the state have been more tolerant of dif- fering practices of sister churches. For example, the practices of "open" communion, "alien" immersion, and the ordination of women as deacons were less divisive in "golden triangle" associations. These churches, espe- cially in urban areas where concentrated populations and ethnic diversity presented challenges unique to the state, continued to be more involved in social ministries.

Marshall believed that the striking regional differences of the state, and the even more striking diversity in the urban centers of the "golden trian- gle," made even "more remarkable the togetherness of our mission."[19] That togetherness of mission had been severely tested since 1979. In that year conservative leaders orchestrated an initiative to elect Adrian Rogers, the conservative pastor of Bellevue Baptist Church in Memphis, Tennessee, as president of the Southern Baptist Convention. In each succeeding conven- tion, a conservative leader stating his belief in the inerrancy of Scripture was elected president. With the presidency came the power to appoint lead- ers to boards and committees. In short order, convention conservatives controlled the agencies of the SBC as well as the boards of the convention's six seminaries.

In Kentucky, the election in 1993 of R. Albert Mohler, Jr., as president of Southern Seminary, following the productive but stormy tenure of Roy Lee Honeycutt, Jr., indicated that the commonwealth would not be immune from the controversy. Under Mohler more than half of the seminary faculty departed, either under pressure or willfully. The young president was in- tent on molding the seminary into the institution that he believed seminary founders had envisioned. His critics, however, lamented that Mohler had simply fallen in line with the neo-conservative power brokers of the SBC. According to the president's detractors, Mohler's emphasis on Calvinist doctrine proved, ironically, to be at odds with the seminary's signature program, the Billy Graham School of Missions, Evangelism, and Church Growth. Mohler's style had a way of mobilizing individuals on opposing sides of the controversy.

As executive secretary, Bill Marshall felt the full brunt of the controversy as he attempted to keep Kentucky Baptists focused on missions. Looking back on his tenure in later years, the retired executive secretary referred to the debate as "The Controversy," so significant was its impact on Kentucky Baptist life. His *Western Recorder* articles titled "On Mission Together" emphasized the convention's grand history of cooperative missions. Sadly, however, the togetherness of the mission was in danger of being lost. Characteristically, the Kentucky Baptist reaction to the controversy represented a full range of diversity. Remarkably, the controversy did not lead to a major division in the commonwealth as in other states. In Texas and Virginia, for example, rival conventions were founded to represent either conservative or moderate factions.

In Kentucky, individuals and some churches chose to give offerings through the Cooperative Baptist Fellowship (CBF), the organization founded by Baptist moderates in the wake of the conservative advance. A Kentucky Baptist Fellowship aligned with the national organization had been founded, and some churches provided ways for individuals to designate tithes and offerings for either the Cooperative Program or the CBF. While there was no major cleavage in Baptist ranks, it was clear that actions of Kentucky Baptists in the 1980s and 1990s were often determined by the controversy. The controversy loomed in the background, threatening at any time to disrupt fellowship ties that had held since 1837.

The controversy hovered over the sesquicentennial celebration in 1987. Messengers met in the splendid, paneled sanctuary of Walnut Street Baptist Church in Louisville; and Howard Cobble, pastor of the historic Severns Valley Baptist Church, was elected convention president. In the spirit of the celebration, it was agreed in 1987 not to accept resolutions for that year. A motion to eliminate resolutions for all future conventions failed, but another motion to amend convention by-law nine to require a two-thirds vote rather than a simple majority to pass resolutions carried. The two-thirds requirement represented one attempt to stave off the introduction of controversial resolutions that might threaten to disrupt harmony.

Many wondered if the election of the KBC president would become a focal point of the controversy as it had in the SBC. Unlike the SBC, Kentucky

Baptists generally elected presidents who refused to be leaders for either side of the debate. The 1994 presidential election at the annual meeting in Frankfort indicated the determination of the majority of Kentucky Baptists to steer a neutral course. In that election popular candidates from both sides of the controversy lost to a centrist candidate. Bob DeFoor, pastor of First Baptist Church, Harrodsburg, and an outspoken moderate, and Bill Hancock, pastor of Louisville's Highview Baptist Church and an architect of the conservative resurgence in the state, were both defeated by Billy Compton, pastor of Mt. Washington Baptist Church and a minister recognized to be more concerned with evangelism and discipling than with denominational politics. After a stint of service on the Kentucky Baptist Convention staff, Compton later followed Howard Cobble as pastor of Severns Valley Baptist Church.

If the annual meeting of the convention continued unscathed from the worst effects of the controversy, the yearly Pastors' Conference came to mirror the conservative advance. In the 1970s and early 1980s, the conference "included a relatively good mix of Kentucky Baptist pastors." In the late 1980s, however, conference preachers were chosen increasingly from those representing the conservative side of the debate. As attendance declined—more moderate pastors chose not to go—it was suggested that another conference be held simultaneously at a nearby location to represent moderate pastors in the state. Moderates eventually withdrew this proposal, feeling that the organization of a rival conference would deepen the controversy.[20]

The controversy filtered down from the SBC and the KBC to the associations. When selecting nominees to the executive board, a process taking place on the associational level, where one stood in the controversy sometimes became a major factor. More often than not, however, associational messengers nominated persons who were not known to be active in the controversy, much in the same way that KBC presidents were elected.

Marshall believed that the single most significant KBC action taken in response to the controversy was the adoption of "Covenants" between the KBC and each affiliated institution and agency. Concern over the parameters of trustee authority for the board of Kentucky Baptist Hospitals Inc. led to the executive board's decision to draw up specific agreements clarifying the board's relationship to the convention. At the same time, the controversy within the SBC, particularly the issue of trustee control of Baptist institutions, broadened the issue to the three Baptist liberal arts colleges in Kentucky. During an intensive two-year process from 1984 to 1986, a special committee appointed by the executive board worked to clarify the relationships of all boards and agencies to the KBC. Approved in November

1986, the covenants provided a more specific process for the selection of trustees, "greatly relieving the tensions that had been growing as a result of the controversy." With some modest amendments to the covenants, the new agreements fostered a "continuing, positive relationship" between Kentucky Baptist institutions and agencies and the convention.[21]

Marshall concluded that the Kentucky Baptist response to the controversy that had wracked the Southern Baptist Convention since 1979 indicated that Baptists in the commonwealth "as a whole, were not easily provoked or moved by religious politics" during this period. Rather, Kentucky Baptists responded "faithfully and energetically to a movement more powerful and persuasive than the Controversy." Marshall was convinced that the movement that he labeled "volunteerism" would be recognized by historians as "the most visible sign of God's own spirit during these years." The executive secretary believed that volunteerism might better be described "in Christian terminology, as a spiritual hunger to use one's resources to participate personally and actively in the mission of God in the world."[22]

Marshall witnessed the twentieth century beginnings of the movement among Southern Baptists in the 1960s when he served as a staff member of the SBC's Foreign Mission Board. In 1999, he remembered that "this energy virtually exploded through laypersons who determined they had something to share in global missions." After "considerable resistance" from the Foreign Mission Board (the board was skeptical about sponsoring mission efforts that were not led by ordained ministers), volunteer efforts gained credibility after the success of laymen-led evangelistic efforts overseas.[23] Just as impressive as the results on foreign fields was the dramatic impact these lay efforts had on the local church at home. Personal lay missions involvement abroad proved to revitalize the home churches from which the lay missionaries were sent.

By 1980, the volunteer movement had influenced the programs of the SBC's Home Mission Board. The Mission Service Corps was born out of the movement. The corps sent thousands of Baptists, many of them from Kentucky, to a multitude of volunteer mission sites in the United States, some for extended stays and others for short-term appointments. Partnerships between large and smaller state conventions developed in the 1980s. And associations within the states developed new missions projects overseas and closer to home. At home, associations noted a need for ministries for a growing Hispanic, migrant population. Significantly, this new emphasis on mission involvement at the associational level was lay-led.

A desire for "more personal, hands-on experience" gave state conventions and associations the opportunity to enlist and channel more volunteers than the missions agencies of the SBC were able to accommodate. The volunteer movement led the larger and more progressive churches to design mission opportunities of their own. The trend reflected "the emergence of what would become a growing independence and initiative of the local church as the primary missions base."[24] In short, the impact of the volunteer movement was funneled down from the SBC to the state conventions to regions within states (such as the history of volunteerism at Oneida Baptist Institute in eastern Kentucky) to state associations to the local churches and ultimately, of course, to thousands of Baptist lay men and women.

With Bill Marshall's support and under his able direction, Kentucky became a leader in the volunteer missions movement. Specific partnerships were developed between Kentucky Baptists and Kenya, Brazil, Russia, Ohio, Utah-Idaho, and later with Poland, Tanzania, and New England. The Kentucky Baptist Convention provided the first on-the-field coordinator for a state convention partnership, a development pioneered by Marshall, and a model soon followed by other state conventions.

The volunteer movement led eventually to the creation of disaster relief teams. Again, Kentucky Baptists, this time under the auspices of the state Brotherhood organization, took the lead for the conventions east of the Mississippi River. Kentucky Baptist disaster relief teams gained national praise for the quick response and food relief efforts following natural disasters. Among others, the national Red Cross noted and affirmed the efforts of Kentucky Baptists in this effort.

The volunteer movement transcended the controversy that had divided Southern Baptists. In a Kentucky partnership project in Brazil, volunteer missionaries from two churches noted to be on opposite ends of the controversy worked together to spread the gospel. Clearly, the common ground on which all Kentucky Baptist churches and individuals could agree continued to be missions. The saving grace of the Master and the call for all Christians to make others aware of the opportunity to believe had inspired and motivated Baptists like Squire Boone and Thomas Tinsley and William Hickman in the very beginnings of the work in 1776. The need to tell played a role in the founding of the General Association of Baptists in Kentucky in 1837. An effective means to spread the Word motivated the General Association to adopt a Unified Budget Plan in 1915. And the same desire caused Kentucky Baptists to participate fully in the Cooperative Program of the Southern Baptist Convention beginning in 1925. The volunteer movement and the various Kentucky partnerships that grew out of it indicated the enduring desire of Baptists to tell others about God's grace.

On April 7, 1987, the appointment service for the SBC's Foreign Mission Board brought the largest gathering of Baptists in the history of the Kentucky Baptist Convention to Lexington's Rupp Arena. Attended by 16,137 persons, the commissioning service featured inspirational music and a stirring flag display representing countries around the world. As newly appointed missionaries were commissioned for their work, the service provided a dramatic visual image of the reality of the Baptist witness around the world. It was appropriate that the service was held in 1987 under the watch of Bill Marshall as executive secretary-treasurer of the KBC. Himself a foreign missionary and former staff member of the Foreign Mission Board, he devoted his tenure as leader of the convention to a renewed emphasis on missions.

Marshall referred to the experience of KBC agencies and institutions during his tenure as a period of "innovation and expansion." The historically "modest to fragile economic status of the three liberal arts colleges and Clear Creek" improved dramatically during the 1980s and 1990s.[25] By the end of the century, Georgetown, Cumberland, and Campbellsville had each carved out a unique niche in private higher education. The schools came to acquire solid reputations in the state and beyond as programs were added and endowments increased. Clear Creek made great strides as well, carving out a niche of its own in adult Bible training. All in all, after years of struggle Baptist higher education approached the new millennium with a bright future. The confidence in Baptist schools stemmed from sterling performances by each of the institutions' presidents.

At Georgetown College, William Crouch succeeded W. Morgan Patterson in 1991. Patterson, a prominent church historian, had continued to build upon the school's reputation for scholarship and teaching. Crouch described his predecessor as an academician, a "very outstanding researcher and historian." Reared in New Orleans just blocks from the Baptist seminary campus, Patterson returned to his home city after completing an undergraduate degree at Florida's Stetson University. At New Orleans Seminary, he completed B.D. and Th.D. degrees in church history. Patterson taught and served as director of graduate studies at Southern Seminary for seventeen years before moving west to Golden Gate Seminary where he became the dean of academic affairs. He returned to Kentucky in 1984 where he served as Georgetown's president until 1991.

During Patterson's tenure, Georgetown's endowment doubled (from $8 million to $16 million), the school acquired various properties adjoining the campus as well as a 50-acre farm near the town, and various buildings were renovated and enlarged. When Patterson retired in 1991, the institution's enrollment had reached an all-time high of nearly 1,600. When Crouch arrived, he found Georgetown to be "a very stable institution" thanks largely to the work of Patterson. In Crouch, Georgetown's Board of

Trustees found a leader who could "create a new excitement and energy to prepare the college for the next century."[26]

Crouch recalled that upon his arrival Georgetown had "good students, good faculty, and good facilities."[27] At the same time, the school had not constructed a new building in twenty-five years, faculty salaries remained embarrassingly low, and student dorms were sub-par. Clearly, a leader with experience and expertise in fundraising was needed to lead the school to a greater level of prominence. Crouch filled the bill well.

Born in Louisville while his father studied for the ministry at Southern Seminary, Crouch moved to Taylorsville with his family when the elder Crouch was called to the pastorate of Taylorsville Baptist Church. From Taylorsville, the Crouch family moved south to another Baptist church in Jackson, Mississippi, and then to Ardmore Baptist Church in Winston-Salem, North Carolina. Crouch remained in North Carolina to attend Wake Forest University and then completed master's and doctor's degrees at Southeastern Baptist Theological Seminary. Following the completion of his formal education, he took a position at Gardner-Webb College to teach and serve on the institution's development staff. From Gardner-Webb, the rising young administrator became director of development for the Baptist Children's Homes of North Carolina, and then vice president for development at Carson-Newman College in Jefferson City, Tennessee. Crouch came from that post to become president of Georgetown in 1991.[28]

William H. Crouch, Jr.,
president, Georgetown College, 1991-

The new Georgetown president represented a new breed of college administrator. A generation before, the road to the presidency of a small, private institution like Georgetown generally followed a route through academic affairs; dean to vice president for academic affairs to president was not an unusual progression for academicians of ability and vision. By the 1980s and 1990s, however, more presidents—like Crouch—came from backgrounds in development. In 1991, one educational consultant predicted that by the year 2010, 50 percent of all private, denominational colleges in the country would be out of business. "Therefore," Crouch explained, "colleges have had to turn to the fund-raising side and the marketing side as an important role for the president." Crouch guessed that he spent "almost ninety percent of my time as president of Georgetown College involved in fundraising and strategic alliance type of work."[29]

The president's emphasis on fund-raising paid off for his institution. Trustees had voted to build a new library in 1972, but lack of funds had held back the project. Under Crouch, a new learning resource center was completed in 1998, a facility that attracted 225,000 visitors that year. A new athletic complex, resulting, in part, from a partnership with the National Football League's Cincinnati Bengals, was voted in 1998 the number-one new athletic complex in America, an award won the year before by the University of Nevada at Las Vegas. The new facility fit in well with the grand tradition of excellence in athletics at Georgetown. At the end of the 1990s, athletic teams—especially basketball and football—ranked at the top of National Athletic Intercollegiate Association (NAIA) polls.

In all, Georgetown added eleven new buildings after 1993. Existing buildings were also refurbished in the 1990s, and a technology infrastructure system provided computer access in every dorm room. By 1999, Georgetown's enrollment had climbed to 1,300 residential undergraduate students and 350 master's degree students in education. The academic quality of Georgetown's freshman classes rose dramatically in the 1990s. In 1991, the average ACT score of the college's freshman class was 21; in 1999, the average score had risen to 25.3. A new program aligned with Regents Park College, a Baptist college of Oxford University, attracted high-caliber students from around the nation. Students in the program could study with any of Oxford's forty-three colleges. Crouch believed that "as far as we know we are the only undergraduate college in the country that has that kind of relationship with Oxford University."[30] The Marshall Center, founded by Georgetown alumni Bill and Alice Marshall, provided for a sabbatical leave program at Regents Park for ministers. The mission of the center involved the goal of helping ministers to "stretch their minds," but also to remind students of their role as Christian missionaries.

Crouch was named in 1999 as a Fellow at Regents Park College, the equivalent of an honorary doctorate from Oxford. The president's hard work in the establishment of the Georgetown/Oxford partnership and the fact that Georgetown gave an endowment of $2.5 million to Regents Park, the largest single gift that the Oxford college had ever received, justified the honor bestowed on the Georgetown leader.

The college's public radio station, WRVG, featured "The Meetinghouse: Conversations on Religion in American Life," the first public affairs program on Georgetown's World Radio Network. The program included interviews with religious and public figures, book and movie reviews, music, and the commentary of Dwight Moody, dean of the chapel at the college. Moody believed that the program "is unique in the country," explaining that "there has been a vacuum in mainstream media in the coverage of religion in American life that we are trying to address." "The Meetinghouse" featured interviews with Jay Fannin, minister of youth at Wedgwood Baptist Church in Fort Worth, Texas, where seven people were gunned down in September 1999; former Southern Seminary professor Bill Leonard, later dean of the divinity school at Wake Forest University; Rabbi James Rudin of the American Jewish Committee in New York and Rabbi Jon Adlin of Temple Adath Israel in Israel; and former Kentucky governors Martha Layne Collins and Brereton Jones.[31]

Crouch asserted that "since 1787 Georgetown College has been involved in Baptist education." "We were founded," the president continued, "for the purpose of preparing ministers and teachers for the new frontier." Crouch stated that "today we are still preparing students for the new frontier—the new frontier today means technology, science, all of these things that are out there. So it is remarkable that from 1787 to 1999 we are still preparing students for the new frontier." Crouch's vision for the new frontier of the new millennium included "superior academics," teaching students to think. The vision also included "giving students incredible leadership opportunities." According to the president, Georgetown was the only college to have a vice president for leadership and ethics, Judy Rogers. To bring focus to the first two parts of the school's mission, the third part of Crouch's vision involved the inculcation for Georgetown students of the Christian value system. Perhaps Georgetown College—under Crouch's leadership—is the only college in the country to strategically place all three goals—academic excellence, unique leadership opportunities, and Christian values—together as a part of an institution's mission.[32]

To the east, Cumberland College in Williamsburg carved out a unique niche of its own in private, denominational education. In 1981, James H. Taylor succeeded the legendary J. M. Boswell as Cumberland's president. Born during World War II while his father was stationed at an air base in San Antonio, Texas, Taylor and his family moved north to Michigan after the war. In Michigan Taylor's father worked at Pontiac Motors. During his junior year, young Taylor contacted Boswell about coming to Cumberland after his graduation from high school the following year. Boswell told him that if he could get together seven hundred dollars, he would get Taylor through four years of college. After graduation, having scraped up the necessary amount, Taylor boarded a bus and headed for Williamsburg.[33]

Taylor worked his way through Cumberland, recalling years later that "if the president told me to sweep up something, I tried to sweep it up better than anyone else." From Cumberland, Taylor went to Vanderbilt University where he completed a doctorate, staying on to serve as a vice president at

James H. Taylor, president, Cumberland College, 1981-

Scarritt College. Taylor left Nashville to become vice president for development at Cumberland, his alma mater. Long before Crouch at Georgetown, Taylor came from a position in development to become president of a Kentucky Baptist school. Taylor stated, "I suppose as far as pure institutional development, I was one of the first, but now almost all including the president of Harvard University come out of that area."[34]

When asked to describe the school that he came to in 1980, Taylor referred to the achievement of Boswell and asserted that "we all stand on the shoulders of others and no one does much of anything alone, but we've been very well blessed." Still, Taylor did his part to make Cumberland an exemplary institution. Virtually all of the buildings on Cumberland's campus have been either built or restored since 1980. The endowment of the school increased from $800,000 to $42 million—a truly remarkable statistic—under Taylor's leadership. By 1999, Cumberland—with an enrollment of 1,662—had become the largest private college for undergraduates in the commonwealth, catering to students 18 to 21 in age. Cumberland became a true undergraduate, residential college.[35]

Cumberland built its reputation around the tried-and-true values of work and community service. Students built eighty-eight homes for the economically disadvantaged; the institution owned a warehouse and operated its own bulldozer, in addition to a fine academic program. The school boasted a second transcript that recorded practical experience and community service.

Founded by the coal barons of Appalachia, Cumberland's mission from the beginning involved providing indigenous leadership in a Christian context for the mountain region. Taylor asserted, "that's still our mission primarily, but not exclusively." "We get students from virtually every state in the nation and every continent on the face of the earth," Taylor stated. "We say that the sun never sets on Cumberland College." To bring his point home, Taylor revealed that Cumberland had produced "five military generals, an admiral of the navy, two governors—Bert T. Combs, a Democrat, and Edwin P. Morrow, who was a Republican."[36]

Clearly, Cumberland College had fulfilled its role as a leader in private education for the state, the Appalachian region, and the nation. Another aspect of Cumberland's mission became evident in November 1999 when a campus-wide revival resulted in 107 students making decisions for Christ. Campus minister Dean Whittaker explained that the school had experienced "an unreal kind of movement of the Holy Spirit among our students." Ken Freeman, an evangelist from San Antonio, Texas, led the revival, speaking at campus services, a meeting of the Fellowship of Christian Athletes, and off campus at nearby Main Street Baptist Church. Freeman also spoke at a promotional event in which area church youth groups came to Cumberland's campus as part of the Celebrate Jesus 2000 youth rallies held across Kentucky. Whittaker believed that the fact that seventy-two Cumberland students served as summer missionaries in 1999 paved the way for a revival at home.[37]

Perhaps the greatest higher education success story for Kentucky Baptists in the 1980s and 1990s was the dramatic resurgence of Campbellsville University. Cambellsville's turnaround was related directly to the coming of Kenneth W. Winters as president in 1988. Born in Crittenden County in western Kentucky, he graduated from the county high school and from Murray State University, working throughout his college years in his family's construction business and in a building-supply business on weekends, holidays, and summers. Winters's father had been a deacon and song leader at Sulphur Springs Baptist Church for over fifty years, and had sung in the

Southernaires quartet.[38] Young Winters grew up in the church. His father was one of twelve children, and his grandparents had "hundreds" of grandchildren, but Winters was the first to go off to college. It was these two great influences—education and the church—that had a lasting influence on his life.

At Murray State, Winters studied technology education, specializing in the area of construction-related studies. He went immediately into the military after graduation with an ROTC commission. Winters later taught school in Henderson but returned to the military for another tour of duty during the Berlin crisis. After teaching two more years at Henderson, he completed a master's degree at Indiana University. He eventually returned to Murray State as an assistant professor, completed a doctorate, and moved up through the ranks to a dean's position where he served for eleven years.

When a representative of Campbellsville's Board of Trustees contacted Winters about the institution's presidency, he was reluctant at first, but after a time, he felt a firm, sure call to accept. Winters simply felt that "I was supposed to go." At Campbellsville, financial problems, deferred maintenance on unimpressive buildings, and low enrollments had plagued the institution for years. Campbellsville was a struggling school with an enrollment of 660 when Winters arrived. Still, the new president saw a great underlying strength in the school, the community, and especially the students. His emphasis on students proved to be the hallmark of his tenure. He concluded that "the one thing that I truly believe in is that we have no reason for being there other than for the student."[39]

Kenneth W. Winters, president,
Campbellsville University,
1988-1999

Winters's student-centered approach paid off immediately. After making arrangements to cover the budget deficit from the previous year, he led the school to begin what he referred to as "a first impression upgrade." With help from a work team from Winters's former church—First Baptist Church, Murray—buildings were gutted and renovated and the grounds improved. Winters also recognized that "a major overhaul of the town-gown relationship" was imperative. The administration and faculty worked with the Chamber of Commerce and other local organizations, emphasizing the need to do extensive business with the community. Before long, local residents began to speak of "our college" when referring to a school that had at one time been regarded with suspicion.[40]

Winters instituted a marching band to go along with the school's new football team, men's and women's swimming teams to take advantage of the school's Olympic-size swimming pool, men's and women's soccer, and women's volleyball. These teams competed nationally, with swimmers faring especially well. To show Winters's priorities, he balked when trustees suggested the building of a new home for the president. Only when Winters made it clear that the house must be paid for with gifts from the trustees and not from other funds coming into the school (and after Winters himself pledged ten thousand dollars, the same amount given by each of the thirty-six trustees) did the project go forward.[41]

Winters's education and experience in construction served him well. The president found the school's old gymnasium, boarded up for years and considered by the board a prime candidate for demolition, to be in "atrocious" condition, yet still "solid as a rock" structurally. Built in 1923, the gymnasium was the only original building still standing. For around $1 million, the gym was converted to a student activities center with offices and an auditorium for convocations. The project was completed in 1990, changing the "whole image of the campus."[42] Other buildings were renovated, current housing was upgraded, and new dormitories—men's and women's—built. Carter Hall, a former men's dormitory, was renovated and converted to a new classroom and laboratory building.

Winters had only one regret from his tenure as president of Campbellsville University. "We work hard at telling our story to the churches," he asserted. "My greatest disappointment, I guess, is that many of the churches do not spend the time necessary to let the congregations know that this valuable resource is available." Winters argued that in 1906 the Baptists of what is now Taylor County made a commitment to fund a Christian institution of higher education. "Think about the difference between 1906 and today," he concluded. "If there was a need for such a school in 1906, how many hundred fold more important it is today!"[43]

Winters's argument is persuasive. And he had done his part to make Campbellsville University a point of pride for Kentucky Baptists. When Winters retired in 1999, the school's enrollment had increased from 660 to 1,660. His successor, Michael V. Carter, formerly the provost at Tennessee's Carson-Newman College, continues the heritage of strong leadership established by his predecessor. The transformation of Campbellsville University was nothing short of astounding. In fact, the resurgence of all three Kentucky Baptist institutions of higher learning at the end of the twentieth century made the future appear bright indeed for the new millennium.

Other areas of Kentucky Baptist life and work promised a bright future as well. Since the formation of the Woman's Missionary Association of Kentucky in 1903, the Kentucky WMU led ministry and missions efforts in the commonwealth. Under executive director-treasurers Kathryn Akridge, Dee Gilliland, Kay Trisler, and Joy Bolton, the WMU continues to pray for missionaries, lead organizations for children and youth, and raise funds for missions involvement locally and globally. Under the new dynamic director of college ministries Keith Inman, Kentucky Baptist student work continues to make an impact on the state and the world. For twelve years the campus minister at Murray State University, Inman came to lead the state work in 1999. The *Western Recorder* still sets the standard for objective reporting of news relating to the religious life of the state and nation. Following the retirement of C. R. Daley, other *Western Recorder* editors Jack D. Sanford (1984-89), Marv Knox (1990-95), Mark Wingfield (1996-98), and Trennis G. Henderson (1999-) continued to follow the standard of excellence brought to the paper by Daley. A proven editor, Henderson came to Kentucky from the editorship of the *Arkansas Baptist* in July 1999.

In 1996, Bill Marshall retired as executive secretary of the Kentucky Baptist Convention. His legacy, especially in the area of missions, left an enduring mark on Kentucky Baptists. Clearly, the phrase "on mission together" marked his tenure accurately. Missions and cooperation had been hallmarks of the Kentucky Baptist Convention from the beginning. Marshall's tenure continued the grand Kentucky Baptist tradition of cooperative missions. Significantly, Marshall—like President Jimmy Carter on a national level—redefined his post-leadership years. Not content to sit on the sidelines, the retired executive secretary founded—along with Alice, his wife—the Marshall Center at the couple's alma mater, Georgetown College. The center linked Georgetown with Regents Park College, Oxford University's Baptist college, providing sabbatical leaves for Kentucky Baptist pastors and opportunities for Georgetown students to gain an "Oxford experience." Through the auspices of the Marshall Center, workshops held on Georgetown's campus and featuring America's greatest preachers and theologians provided unique intellectual and spiritual experiences for pastors in the commonwealth.

It was not until 1998 that Marshall's successor was found. In the meantime, Kentucky Baptists relied on a faithful friend. Jim Hawkins was called on to serve as the leader of Kentucky Baptists during the interim period. Hawkins had come to work for the Kentucky Baptist Convention in 1985 as executive associate, the assistant to Marshall. Hawkins grew up in Bowling Green and in that town's First Baptist Church. His pastors included R. T. Skinner, Franklin Paschall, Joseph Estes, and Harold Purdy. After graduation from high school in 1958, Hawkins attended Georgetown College. He then went into educational administration, working on the registrar's staff of the new Kentucky Southern College in the 1960s. Just before Kentucky Southern merged with the University of Louisville, Hawkins helped open up the new Jefferson Community College, where he served for seventeen years first as registrar and then as academic dean.[44] Along the way, Hawkins completed a doctorate in higher education from Indiana University. After leaving JCC, he worked briefly with a consulting firm before coming to work for the KBC in 1985. Then upon Marshall's retirement in 1996, he was asked to serve as interim executive secretary-treasurer during the transition period. Because of his years of service for the convention and for the commonwealth, Hawkins was uniquely qualified to comment on Kentucky Baptist life and work at the end of the century.

During his tenure, Hawkins witnessed significant changes in the state and in the denomination. He believed that "there has been a tremendous renewed interest in missions" in Kentucky. "When some state conventions were having difficulties over some of the Southern Baptist Convention controversies, in Kentucky people who even disagreed on some of those issues were able to do partnership missions together and be strong friends in Christ and continued to support the work of the state convention."[45]

Hawkins particularly lauded Marshall's leadership in establishing various partnership missions projects for the state. The partnerships "showed people they could become involved in missions hands-on as well as give their dollars to it." Hawkins argued that one of the greatest benefits of partnership missions was "what it did for our fellowship. It kept people in touch with each other, and those that might think that they are opposed to each other learned that they shared much in common as they went out on the missions projects together."[46]

Hawkins believed that churches must find ways to disciple individuals more deeply in the Christian faith "so that they understand how important the body of Christ is in the local church, but they understand also how important it is that we do things as a larger fellowship together." "We still need cooperation to get done what needs to be done," Hawkins asserted. "Individual church members must realize that their vocation, whether it is teacher, carpenter, doctor, lawyer, or plumber, is their place of ministry in the world. John 17 says, 'I send you into the world.' If we are going to have an impact on our society and our communities, then Christians have to have a stronger sense of their citizenship."[47] Hawkins practiced what he preached. Like Marshall, Hawkins continued to live out his faith and citizenship after his retirement.

Bill F. Mackey, executive secretary, Kentucky Baptists, 1998-

When Bill Mackey was introduced as the new executive director of the Kentucky Baptist Convention in 1998, Kentucky Baptists welcomed back a former pastor and friend. Born in Lancaster County, South Carolina, Mackey became a Christian at the age of ten and was raised in a local, rural church where his father served as deacon and director of the Sunday School. He surrendered to the ministry at sixteen while attending a summer Royal Ambassador camp. In 1999, Mackey stated that he was "a product of Baptist life in every sense of the word."[48]

He attended North Greenville Junior College and Furman University in South Carolina where he graduated with a degree in history. He then came to Kentucky to earn a bachelor of divinity degree from Southern Seminary in 1967 and eventually a doctor of ministry degree in 1979. Mackey had served with the Home Mission Board in Pittsburgh, Pennsylvania, and as an associate pastor with Truett Miller at First Baptist Church, Middlesboro, in eastern Kentucky. Then, from 1969 to 1979, he ministered as the pastor of First Baptist Church, Whitesburg. In addition to his pastorate, Mackey took an active part in convention affairs, serving on the KBC executive board and administrative committee.[49]

Because of the quality of his service in various capacities with the convention, Mackey had been asked by James Whaley to come to work for the convention. The diligent pastor was approached again in 1977, this time by executive secretary Franklin Owen, about serving as director of the KBC's Evangelism Department. In both instances, the time was not yet right. In 1979, Mackey was called back to his home state, where he became state evangelism director for the South Carolina Baptist Convention. Eventually, the areas of evangelism and leadership development were combined and Mackey became the director of the Evangelism Growth and Leadership Development Department. When he came to Kentucky in February 1998, Mackey's background as a beloved pastor and as an experienced, diplomatic administrator proved to be the perfect combination to lead Kentucky Baptists into the new century and new millennium.

The 1999 annual meeting of the Kentucky Baptist Convention in Covington provided the usual combination of business and reports, worship and inspiration. Jim Henry, pastor of First Baptist Church, Orlando, Florida, former president of the Southern Baptist Convention, and a Georgetown College graduate, delivered a stirring convention sermon. Messenger William E. Shoulta, pastor of Louisville's Melbourne Heights Baptist Church, introduced a proposal to affirm the SBC's 1963 "Baptist Faith and Message" statement. SBC messengers had altered the document the year before, including an amendment on the family which stated that "a wife is to submit herself graciously to the servant leadership of her husband even as the church willingly submits to the headship of Christ." When SBC president Paige Patterson appointed a fifteen-member study committee to consider other changes to the 1963 statement, some Southern Baptists feared that the document would be rewritten to mirror the particular beliefs of the convention's conservative leadership.[50]

Shoulta argued that the 1963 statement "undergirds our strong heritage of religious freedom, church autonomy, and priesthood of the believer." "By reaching back to 1963, we can emphasize the numerous beliefs which have held us together rather than a few issues which tend to divide us," he concluded.[51] Messengers voted down the proposal by a narrow margin. The 408-374 vote indicated that certain issues continued to divide Kentucky Baptists at the end of the twentieth century.

In other business, messengers elected centrist candidate Terry Wilder, since 1992 the pastor of Burlington Baptist Church, as convention president. Echoing a theme that had characterized the Kentucky Baptist Convention from the beginning, Wilder asserted that "our unity must be found in what we do together to reach Kentucky for Jesus Christ." Wilder assured Kentucky Baptists that "I genuinely want to lead all Kentucky Baptists. I want to see us pull together, pray together, grow together and make the year 2000 a Great Commission year in Kentucky Baptist life."[52]

Former KBC president John Wood, in 1975 the pastor of Paducah's First Baptist Church, had asserted that "Kentucky Baptists are a special people" and that "Kentucky Baptists have a special purpose."[53] His assertions held true twenty-five years later as Kentucky's largest denomination faced a new millennium. If Kentucky Baptists are to fulfill the special purpose to which they are called as a special people, the most obvious theme of the twentieth century must continue into the twenty-first century. Former executive secretary Bill Marshall concluded his historical symposium remarks with a wise admonition: "The divisions among us are cushioned by a larger body of Kentucky Baptists who have, it seems to me, proven . . . that they prefer to listen long, speak softly, move slowly, and try as best they can to follow their conscience and the spirit of God."[54] Such has been the case with Kentucky Baptists in the twentieth century. The Kentucky Baptist story from 1925 to 2000 has been a story of cooperation.

Epilogue

Driving in from Arkansas to visit the grandparents and parents in Kentucky proved to be a precious, but exhausting, experience for the family of four: father, mother, son, and daughter. Arriving on a Friday in time for supper, the young family was treated to a royal Kentucky feast: ham, chicken, sliced tomatoes, creamed potatoes, squash, fresh hot rolls, and pies of several flavors, fare you would associate with the wife of a Kentucky Baptist bi-vocational pastor. Gorged and sleepy, the family would visit into the night, reluctant to cut the visit short with mere sleep. The children finally fell asleep, the older children droned on a little longer, and then reluctantly withdrew to bed.

Several years later, the ritual was repeated, not often enough, but the pastor father and grandfather was already gone, the victim of a heart attack. His memory remained. The family came again on a Friday, and the ritual was repeated, but the experience would never be the same. The son arose as usual before the rest of his immediate family, his mother (the grandmother) already up, of course, cooking breakfast. The son went out on his morning run. He walked down the steep driveway and broke into a jog at the street, turning right at the next drive, which led to the city lake, which he circled before climbing the slanting road to the water tower. At the tower he turned left down the familiar lane that led to the cemetery where his father was now buried.

The cemetery was, to be sure, the perfect picture of a cemetery. Nestled in the hills, it reminded one of an English graveyard. A black wrought-iron fence lined the front entrances of the place, and the son had always taken the second entrance. He followed it around in a counter-clockwise direction past his father's grave, circled the cemetery twice, and then retraced his steps back home. But this morning the son decided on a whim to take the first entrance and wind around the graveyard in a clockwise direction. The son passed his father's grave as always, but from the opposite direction. The run was revolutionary for the son. He saw for the first time the flowering bush in full bloom behind the grave. And he saw other graves with gravestones etched with the familiar names of neighbors and family friends, names that he had never noticed before. The run changed the son.

Many of the gravestone names the son saw for the first time had been members of the father's church, the town's First Baptist Church; many of the names had been customers at the father's drug store, the store that stood directly across the street from the 1938 WPA-built courthouse, the landmark of the county-seat town. The son remembered the mark that the father, a bi-vocational Kentucky Baptist minister, had made on the town, his church congregation, and his customers at the store.

The son decided that the run had been revolutionary because he had approached the cemetery from a different angle, from a different point of view. The path had been the same, but the perspective had changed. And that had made all the difference. We have before us the eloquent, sometimes encyclopedic, telling of the Kentucky Baptist story of Spencer, Masters, and Birdwhistell. It is hoped that this rendition of the Kentucky Baptist story will allow faithful readers to regard the story from a different light, from a different angle, from a different perspective. The son now considered his father's ministry in a different light. The sermons boldly delivered, the Wednesday night Bible studies faithfully prepared, the word of witness carefully crafted across the prescription counter. The father had indeed made a difference in the lives of his parishioners and customers in that small county-seat town, a difference that only eternity would register.

In the rich history of Kentucky Baptists, the stories of unnamed ministers and lay men and women have made a difference, perhaps more than the well-known names and faces that have dominated the epic of the Baptist story in the state, the names that have dotted the pages of this history. The Kentucky Baptist story is their story, too. And the story must continue to be told, and considered from the new perspective of each generation.

Perhaps no Baptist church in Kentucky has adjusted to change as well as Severns Valley Baptist Church in Elizabethtown. Founded in 1781, this historic church is not only the oldest Baptist church in the commonwealth, but also the oldest Baptist church west of the Allegheny Mountains. The church experienced a full range of tragedy and triumph. The first pastor, John Gerrard, lost his scalp and his life to Indians, and the church met outdoors in summer and around log cabin fires in winter without benefit of a sheltering sanctuary for the first twenty years of its existence. Around 1800, the congregation built "a huge log concern on the hill northeast of the courthouse." The crude structure was the first of several log buildings that served as the church's sanctuary, at least during the summer months. In 1834, a brick structure was completed at a cost of twelve hundred dollars on West Poplar near the center of the town.

The church with-
drew from Salem
Association because
of members' coura-
geous—indeed, for
the time, radical—
stand on the slavery
issue. Several early
pastors   refused
membership to slave
owners; and at times
during the church's
antebellum   years,
slave members out-
numbered   white
members. Only after
the war, in 1866, did
African   American
members   of   the
church constitute a
church of their own.
By 1897, the Severns
Valley congregation
sold the West Poplar
sanctuary   to   the
black Baptist congre-
gation, and moved to
a larger brick build-
ing in the downtown
business district.

*Severns Valley Baptist Church,
Elizabethtown, organized June 15, 1781,
as the first Baptist church in Kentucky*

In the latter half of the twentieth century, the focus of this book, the
congregation gave more money—year after year—to the Cooperative Program than any other congregation in the Kentucky Baptist Convention.
Perhaps no other church in the convention epitomized the cooperative
years of Kentucky Baptists more than Severns Valley. After Verlin Kruschwitz
was called as pastor in 1952, the church moved in 1955 from the downtown
business district to an outlying residential location on the corner of West
Poplar and Morningside Drive.[1]

A visitor ushered into the empty sanctuary on a quiet Saturday morning
in 1999 is immediately aware of the calm beauty of the place. The distinctive curve of the sanctuary ceiling, the rows of elegant pews, and the lou-

vered windows, all add touches of dignified elegance and grace. The visitor is perhaps aware of the leadership of pastors Verlin Kruschwitz, Howard Cobble, and Billy Compton, each providing a unique brand of ministry and direction. What impresses the visitor immediately, however, is the arrangement in the pulpit area of the room. No pulpit is to be found. The church secretary explains that the arrangement has been made to accommodate the early "contemporary" service, one of three Sunday morning services provided for the diverse congregation. The "contemporary" service, which includes drums, saxophone, and large doses of drama, is followed by a "blended" service, which combines contemporary and traditional elements of worship, which is, in turn, followed by a "traditional" service. Although Pastor Compton preaches the same sermon at each of the three services, praise and worship take decidedly different turns as various age groups express their faith in different ways.

As I write these words, I can look out my study window past the wood fencing of our backyard toward the lighted steeple of the Grace Baptist Church, founded as a mission of my own church over thirty years ago. The lighted steeple reminds me of the enduring, continuing grace and legacy of the Kentucky Baptist story. May the story continue—as we Baptists believe and like to say, "until the Lord returns"—and may the story continue to be told.

Afterword:
Continued Cooperation

As this book makes clear, the story of Kentucky Baptists has been a story of learning how to cooperate. Barriers of geography, culture, theology and race have had to be overcome in order to cooperate in carrying out the Great Commission. Because they place a high value on cooperation, Kentucky Baptists generally have been willing to put aside personal agendas and preferences for the higher cause of missions.

In forty-four focus group interviews I conducted across Kentucky in March 1998, Kentucky Baptists expressed gratitude that they had been spared the divisiveness of the Southern Baptist Convention controversy. Because Kentucky Baptists have always had to work at overcoming barriers to fellowship and cooperation, the latest controversy was just one more challenge to overcome. In the focus group interviews, I heard Kentucky Baptists state repeatedly that they want to keep the focus on Jesus Christ, maintain strong mission involvement, strengthen churches and work together.

Expressions of cooperation during my first two years have been increased participation in Kentucky Baptist Convention conferences and the growth in Cooperative Program gifts for Kentucky and SBC mission causes. One of the specific requests from the focus group interviews was to put a face on missions. I think one of the best ways to do this is through volunteer involvement in partnership missions. There are so many opportunities in Kentucky: collegiate summer missions, disaster relief, Campers on Mission, Baptist Builders, WMU Job Corps, ministry to international students, state missions, and mission trips, as well as many local mission opportunities. I believe the spirit of involvement in missions will continue for years to come.

God has given me four guiding principles as a part of my ministry with the Kentucky Baptist Convention, which I plan to follow for the years ahead. I believe these are key for us to be successful in reaching our state for Christ.

First, Christian ministry must be based on spiritual foundations. It is my desire to see a growth in church prayer ministries and to see Kentucky Baptist Convention staff and church staff persons walking more closely with Jesus Christ than ever before.

Second, a clear focus on God's vision is essential to effectiveness. The Kentucky Baptist Convention staff has been involved in a planning process to clarify values and write a vision statement. The core values we identified as a staff are represented by the words "integrity," "servant," "teamwork," "effectiveness," "communications," "healthy relationships," and "positive attitude." These values led us to develop the following vision statement, which focuses on serving: "As a servant team, empowered by Jesus Christ, we work with Kentucky Baptists in fulfilling their God-given mission."

Our staff has also established five focus areas, or "big objectives," which will guide our work for the next few years. The areas in which we are focusing are: authentic spirituality, leadership development, intergenerational issues, reaching and keeping young adults, and transitions/change. The entire staff is involved in research, learning, and networking in order to help churches be as effective as possible in reaching their communities for Christ. This will certainly mean helping churches assimilate and involve youth and young adults, beginning new work targeted at unreached persons, strengthening our partnerships with associations, and assisting bi-vocational pastors and smaller membership churches.

Third, relationships are essential to cooperation. We cannot stop challenges from coming but we can build a strong fabric of relationships that will enable us to work together through and beyond challenges. It is Jesus in me that identifies with Jesus in another person and enables us to overcome barriers. Only God can change and mold a person's heart. I have challenged Kentucky Baptists to take the initiative to build relationships with people outside their normal contacts and perspectives.

Fourth, we exist to serve the churches. We serve the churches in order to assist them in being more effective in reaching their communities and the world for Christ. The Kentucky Baptist Convention institutions and agencies, as well as executive board ministries, have been created to extend and strengthen the ministries and mission of the local churches. Every effort should be made to strengthen the ministries of the Kentucky Baptist Convention institutions and agencies so they can serve the churches more effectively.

Based on data from the North American Mission Board, growth in Kentucky Baptist Convention churches is more plateaued than in any of the thirteen old-line state conventions. With increased interest in spirituality, however, Kentucky Baptist Convention churches have a wonderful opportunity for exciting growth—both from within existing churches and by starting new congregations. It will require the best that Kentucky Baptists can provide in innovative and creative approaches empowered by the Holy Spirit.

The coming years look to be an exciting time for Kentucky Baptists. The challenges are certainly great but the opportunities are incredible as well. It is going to be wonderful to see what the Lord has in store as through faith in God and trust in one another, Kentucky Baptists cooperate in fulfilling their God-given mission! The Kentucky Baptist story of the twenty-first century like the story of the twentieth can be a story of cooperation.

Bill Mackey
Executive Director
Kentucky Baptist Convention

Notes

Prologue

1. *Proceedings of the General Association of Baptists in Kentucky* (1926), 8, Archives, Kentucky Baptist Convention, Middletown, Ky.; henceforth cited as *Proceedings*; *Western Recorder*, 18 November 1926.
2. *Western Recorder*, 14 January 1926.
3. Ibid., 18 November 1926.
4. Frank Masters, *A History of Baptists in Kentucky* (Louisville, Ky.: Kentucky Baptist Historical Society, 1953), 576-77; Ira (Jack) Bird-whistell, *Kentucky Baptists: 150 Years on Mission Together* (Middletown, Ky.: Kentucky Baptist Convention, 1987), 110.
5. *Western Recorder*, 11 November 1926.
6. William E. Ellis, "Edgar Young Mullins," *The Kentucky Encyclopedia* (Lexington: University Press of Kentucky, 1992), 661.
7. Ibid.
8. Ibid.
9. For Mullins, see William E. Ellis, *"A Man of Books and a Man of the People": E. Y. Mullins and the Crisis of Moderate Southern Baptist Leadership* (Macon, Ga.: Mercer University Press, 1985); William E. Ellis, "Edgar Young Mullins," *Kentucky Encyclopedia*, 661; Gaines S. Dobbins, "Edgar Young Mullins," *Encyclopedia of Southern Baptists* (Nashville, Tenn.: Broadman Press, 1958), II: 930.
10. Carrie U. Littlejohn, *History of Carver School of Missions and Social Work* (Nashville, Tenn.: Broadman Press, 1958), 104; "Eliza Broadus," *Encyclopedia of Southern Baptists*, I: 236.
11. Ellis, *"A Man of Books and a Man of the People,"* 18; Dobbins, "Edgar Young Mullins," *Encyclopedia of Southern Baptists*, II: 930.
12. Ellis, "Edgar Young Mullins," *Kentucky Encyclopedia*, 661.
13. Ellis, *"A Man of Books and a Man of the People,"* 67.
14. Ibid., 192.
15. Wendell Holmes Rone, "Harvey Boyce Taylor, Sr.," *Encyclopedia of Southern Baptists*, II: 1346-47; Edward Freeman, *H. Boyce Taylor: The Man* (Murray, Ky., 1939), 4-6.
16. William N. McElrath, "News and Truths," *Encyclopedia of Southern Baptists*, II: 977.

17. For a study of the various issues discussed in *News and Truths*, see Lynn Allan Sandusky, "A Historical Analysis of the News and Truths: Pioneer Religious Weekly Published by H. Boyce Taylor in Murray, Kentucky from 1906 until 1932" (M.A. Thesis, Murray State University, Murray, Ky., 1973).

18. Ibid., 113, 114; See also Ira V. Birdwhistell, *A Heart for Missions: A History of First Baptist Church, Murray, Kentucky, 1846-1996* (Franklin, Tenn.: Providence House Publishers, 1996), 73-77. Birdwhistell argued that Taylor was not a pacifist "in the strictest sense." When war was declared, he "advised the young men of the church to register for the draft. But he also supported the conscientious objector who refused to serve in the war because of his religious views." See Birdwhistell, *A Heart for Missions*, 74.

19. Sandusky, "A Historical Analysis of the News and Truths," 116, 117.

20. Rone, "Harvey Boyce Taylor, Sr.," *Encyclopedia of Southern Baptists*, II: 1346.

21. Birdwhistell, *Kentucky Baptists*, 119.

22. *Proceedings* (1926), 120.

23. Birdwhistell, *Kentucky Baptists*, 84.

24. Quoted in Littlejohn, *History of Carver School of Missions and Social Work*, 115.

25. *E. B. Magazine* (September 1995), 19.

26. Harold E. Dye, *The Prophet of Little Cane Creek* (Atlanta: Home Mission Board, Southern Baptist Convention, 1949), 24.

27. Ibid., 26.

28. Ibid., 38.

29. Ibid., 24, 15.

30. Ibid., 75.

31. "Hazard Baptist Institute," *Kentucky Encyclopedia*, 420.

32. Kenneth Moore Startup, *March We Onward: A Centennial History of the First Baptist Church of Walnut Ridge, Arkansas, 1889-1989* (Walnut Ridge, Ark.: First Baptist Church, 1989), vi, vii.

Chapter One

1. *Proceedings of the General Association of Baptists in Kentucky held November 9-12, 1926, Lebanon, Kentucky*, 8.

2. See J. H. Spencer, *A History of Kentucky Baptists from 1769 to 1885*, two volumes (Cincinnati, Ohio: J. R. Baumes, 1885); William Dudley Nowlin, *Kentucky Baptist History, 1770-1922* (Louisville, Ky.: Baptist Book Concern, 1922); Frank M. Masters, *A History of Baptists in Kentucky* (Louisville, Ky.: Kentucky Baptist Historical Society,

1953); Leo Taylor Crismon, editor, *Baptists in Kentucky, 1776-1976: A Bicentennial Volume* (Middletown, Ky.: Kentucky Baptist Convention, 1775); Ira (Jack) Birdwhistell, *Kentucky Baptists: 150 Years On Mission Together* (Middletown, Ky.: Kentucky Baptist Convention, 1987); see also Birdwhistell's entry on Baptists in John E. Kleber, editor, *The Kentucky Encyclopedia* (Lexington, Ky.: University Press of Kentucky, 1992), and Wendell Rone's entry in *The Encyclopedia of Southern Baptists* (Nashville, Tenn.: Broadman Press, 1958), I.

3. Lowell H. Harrison and James C. Klotter, *A New History of Kentucky* (Lexington: University Press of Kentucky, 1997), 153, 154.
4. Masters, *A History of Baptists in Kentucky*, 11, 12.
5. Quoted in ibid., 11.
6. After 1788, Hickman pastored all of his years, except for two, at the Forks of Elkhorn church. See Masters, *A History of Baptists in Kentucky*, 13.
7. John Filson, *Kentucky and the Adventures of Daniel Boone*, 51, quoted in Masters, *A History of Baptists in Kentucky*, 13.
8. Masters, *A History of Baptists in Kentucky*, 10; Harrison and Klotter, *A New History of Kentucky*, 154; George Street Boone, "Squire Boone," *Kentucky Encyclopedia*, 99.
9. Masters, *A History of Baptists in Kentucky*, 57, 60, 77; Birdwhistell, *Kentucky Baptists*, 11.
10. Masters, *A History of Baptists in Kentucky*, 24.
11. Ibid., 24, 25.
12. Ibid., 26.
13. Thomas D. Clark, "Traveling Church," *Kentucky Encyclopedia*, 897.
14. Ibid., 897.
15. Birdwhistell, *Kentucky Baptists*, 9. Thomas D. Clark also stated that Traveling Church members later founded the Providence Church in Madison County and the Minerva Church in Mason County. See Clark, "Traveling Church," *Kentucky Encyclopedia*, 897.
16. Clark, "Traveling Church," *Kentucky Encyclopedia*, 897.
17. Quoted in Crismon, *Baptists in Kentucky, 1776-1976*, 3.
18. Masters, *A History of Baptists in Kentucky*, 81.
19. Birdwhistell, *Kentucky Baptists*, 48.
20. Rone, "General Association of Baptists in Kentucky," "I. Baptist Beginnings," *Encyclopedia of Southern Baptists*, I:724.
21. Ibid.
22. Paul Harvey, *Redeeming the South: Religious Cultures and Racial Identities Among Southern Baptists, 1865-1925* (Chapel Hill: University of North Carolina Press, 1997), 7.

23. Ibid., 5.
24. Rone, *Encyclopedia of Southern Baptists*, I: 724, 725.
25. Birdwhistell, *Kentucky Baptists*, 15.
26. Ibid., 725.
27. Ibid., 15; Rone, *Encyclopedia of Southern Baptists*, I: 725.
28. Rone, *Encyclopedia of Southern Baptists*, I: 725.
29. Ibid.
30. Masters, *A History of Baptists in Kentucky*, 47.
31. Ibid., 47, 17.
32. Ibid., 47.
33. Ibid.
34. Ibid., 47, 48.
35. Ibid., 158. For the results of the Great Revival in Kentucky and the South, see John B. Boles, *The Great Revival, 1787-1805: The Origins of the Southern Evangelical Mind* (Lexington, Ky.: University Press of Kentucky, 1972) and Dickson D. Bruce, Jr., *And They All Sang Hallelujah: Plain-folk Camp-meeting Religion, 1800-1845* (Knoxville, Tenn.: University of Tennessee Press, 1974).
36. Masters, *A History of Baptists in Kentucky*, 158.
37. Ibid., 158.
38. Spencer, *A History of Kentucky Baptists from 1769 to 1885*, I: 545.
39. Ibid., 545-46.
40. The "Terms of Union Between the Elkhorn and South Kentucky, or Separate Associations" are recorded in Spencer, *A History of Kentucky Baptists from 1769 to 1885*, I: 546; Masters, *A History of Baptists in Kentucky*, 159; and Birdwhistell, *Kentucky Baptists*, 22.
41. Spencer, *A History of Kentucky Baptists from 1769 to 1885*, I: 546, 547.
42. Ibid., 505.
43. Quoted in Jerry Breazeale, "Some Contributions of the Second Great Awakening to Baptist Higher Education in Kentucky and Tennessee, 1800-1860" (Th.M. Thesis, New Orleans Baptist Theological Seminary, 1959), 10.
44. Rev. George Baxter to Rev. Alexander, *Christian Index*, January 5, 1883, quoted in Breazeale, "Some Contributions of the Second Great Awakening," 11.
45. Spencer, *A History of Kentucky Baptists from 1769 to 1885*, I: 514-21.
46. Ibid., 522-34,
47. Ibid., 521, 535.
48. John B. Boles, "Great Revival," *Kentucky Encyclopedia*, 387.
49. Birdwhistell, *Kentucky Baptists*, 19.

50. Ibid.
51. Ibid., 20.
52. Ibid., 20, 21.
53. Spencer, *A History of Kentucky Baptists from 1769 to 1885*, I: 541.
54. Masters, *A History of Baptists in Kentucky*, 159.
55. See Birdwhistell, *Kentucky Baptists*, 146.
56. Masters, *A History of Baptists in Kentucky*, 158.
57. Birdwhistell, *Kentucky Baptists*, 23, 24.
58. Spencer, *A History of Kentucky Baptists from 1769 to 1885*, I: 543.
59. Ibid., 544.
60. Harrison and Klotter, *A New History of Kentucky*, 156.
61. Spencer, *A History of Kentucky Baptists from 1769 to 1885*, I: 567.
62. R. L. Street, "New Madrid Earthquakes," in *Kentucky Encyclopedia*, 679.
63. Ibid.
64. Harrison and Klotter, *A New History of Kentucky*, 156.
65. Spencer, *A History of Kentucky Baptists from 1769 to 1885*, I: 567.
66. Ibid., 568.
67. Masters, *A History of Baptists in Kentucky*, 185.
68. Birdwhistell, *Kentucky Baptists*, 31.
69. Ibid.
70. Spencer, *A History of Kentucky Baptists from 1769 to 1885*, I: 568.
71. Ibid., 569.
72. Birdwhistell, *Kentucky Baptists*, 32.
73. Quoted in Masters, *A History of Baptists in Kentucky*, 191.
74. Spencer, *A History of Kentucky Baptists from 1769 to 1885*, I: 569, 570.
75. Masters, *A History of Baptists in Kentucky*, 191.
76. *Christian Review*, 17: 490, 491, quoted in Spencer, *A History of Kentucky Baptists from 1769 to 1885*, I: 571.
77. Masters, *A History of Baptists in Kentucky*, 191.
78. Ibid.
79. Ibid.
80. Birdwhistell, *Kentucky Baptists*, 32.
81. Quoted in Masters, *A History of Baptists in Kentucky*, 193.
82. Ibid.
83. Ibid., 194.
84. Ibid., 195, 196.
85. See Harry Trent Hutcheson, "John Taylor: Frontier Baptist Preacher of Kentucky" (M.A. Thesis, Emory University, 1969).
86. Spencer, *A History of Kentucky Baptists from 1769 to 1885*, I: 581.
87. Ibid., 587.

88. Ibid., 583.
89. Birdwhistell, *Kentucky Baptists*, 36.
90. Ibid., 37, 38.
91. Quoted in Ibid., 39.
92. Spencer, *A History of Kentucky Baptists from 1769 to 1885*, I: 598.
93. Ibid., 599.
94. Ibid., 593, 594.
95. Ibid., 610.
96. Ibid., 611.
97. Ibid., 611, 612.
98. Ibid., 642.
99. Ibid., 643.
100. Masters, *A History of Baptists in Kentucky*, 197.
101. See *Western Recorder*, 24 December 1925; *Kentucky Encyclopedia*, 944; *Encyclopedia of Southern Baptists*, 747.
102. Masters, *A History of Baptists in Kentucky*, 227; Robert Snyder, "Georgetown College," *Kentucky Encyclopedia*, 371-72.
103. Ibid.
104. Spencer, *A History of Kentucky Baptists from 1769 to 1885*, I: 644.
105. *Encyclopedia of Southern Baptists*, 727.
106. Ibid.
107. Birdwhistell, *Kentucky Baptists*, 46.
108. *Encyclopedia of Southern Baptists*, 728.
109. Quoted in Birdwhistell, *Kentucky Baptists*, 45.
110. *Encyclopedia of Southern Baptists*, 728.
111. Ibid.
112. Ibid., 729.
113. Ibid.
114. Ibid.
115. Ibid.
116. Ibid.
117. Ibid.
118. See William Wright Barnes, *The Southern Baptist Convention, 1845-1953* (Nashville: Broadman Press, 1954), 305; and Birdwhistell, *Kentucky Baptists*, 58.
119. Masters, *A History of Baptists in Kentucky*, 289.
120. "Autobiography of John Henderson Spencer from His Birth September 9, 1826 Until August, 1876 (Incomplete)," unpublished manuscript, Archives, Kentucky Baptist Convention, Middletown, Kentucky, 145. Hereafter cited as "Autobiography of John Henderson Spencer."

121. Ibid.
122. Ibid., 145, 146.
123. Ibid., 146.
124. Ibid.
125. Birdwhistell, "Baptists," *Kentucky Encyclopedia*, 48.
126. Spencer, *A History of Kentucky Baptists from 1769 to 1885*, I: 741.
127. Ibid.
128. Harvey, *Redeeming the South*, 19-20.
129. Ibid., 20.
130. Ibid., 742.
131. Ibid.
132. Birdwhistell, "Baptists," *Kentucky Encyclopedia*, 48.
133. Ibid., 743.
134. Quoted in Harvey, *Redeeming the South*, 20.
135. Birdwhistell, "Baptists," *Kentucky Encyclopedia*, 49.
136. Harvey, *Redeeming the South*, 9.
137. Ibid.
138. Spencer, *A History of Kentucky Baptists from 1769 to 1885*, II:653. See also Chris Beckham, "Race Relations and Southern Baptists in Western Kentucky, 1865-1925" (M.A. Thesis, Murray State University, 1997), 32.
139. Spencer, *A History of Kentucky Baptists from 1769 to 1885*, II: 657.
140. Ibid., 657, 658.
141. See Beckham, "Race Relations and Southern Baptists in Western Kentucky," 30-33.
142. Ibid.
143. Ibid., 36.
144. Harvey, *Redeeming the South*, 12.
145. Birdwhistell, "Baptists," *Kentucky Encyclopedia*, 49.
146. Spencer, *A History of Kentucky Baptists from 1769 to 1885*, II: 746.
147. Masters, *A History of Baptists in Kentucky*, 349.
148. *Encyclopedia of Southern Baptists*, 729.
149. Birdwhistell, "Baptists," *Kentucky Encyclopedia*, 48.
150. Georgetown College professor Carl Fields recorded at least seventy-five schools founded by Kentucky Baptists in the years after the war. See Birdwhistell, *Kentucky Baptists*, 87.
151. Amanda M. Hicks to Wesley Bolin, April 10, 1893, in the position of the author.
152. William E. Ellis, "Southern Baptist Theological Seminary," *Kentucky Encyclopedia*, 834.
153. Birdwhistell, *Kentucky Baptists*, 79.

154. Ellis, "Southern Baptist Theological Seminary," *Kentucky Encyclopedia*, 834.
155. Birdwhistell, *Kentucky Baptists*, 83.
156. Ibid.
157. Ibid.
158. *Western Recorder*, 25 December 1925.
159. Birdwhistell, *Kentucky Baptists*, 83.
160. *Western Recorder*, 25 December 1925.
161. Ada Boone Brown, *Golden Remembrances of Woman's Missionary Union of Kentucky: A History of the Baptist Woman's Missionary Union of Kentucky* (Louisville: Woman's Missionary Union, 1953), 37.
162. Ibid., 37, 38.
163. Birdwhistell, *Kentucky Baptists*, 84.
164. Birdwhistell, "Baptists," *Kentucky Encyclopedia*, 49.
165. Ibid., 48.
166. Birdwhistell, *Kentucky Baptists*, 77.
167. Ibid., 78.
168. Birdwhistell, "Baptists," *Kentucky Encyclopedia*, 49.
169. See Barnes, *The Southern Baptist Convention, 1845-1953*, Appendix B.

Chapter Two

1. "Cooperative Program Day at First Baptist Church, Murray," *Kentucky Baptist Heritage* (July 1985), 18.
2. The marker stands in front of First Baptist Church, Murray, Kentucky.
3. Birdwhistell, *Kentucky Baptists*, 95.
4. *Proceedings* (1914), 46.
5. Birdwhistell, *A Heart for Missions*, 71.
6. *Proceedings* (1914), 46.
7. Ibid.
8. Birdwhistell, *A Heart for Missions*, 71.
9. *Proceedings* (1915), 40.
10. Ibid., 40, 41.
11. Birdwhistell, *A Heart for Missions*, 73.
12. Ibid.
13. James J. Thompson Jr., *Tried as by Fire: Southern Baptists and the Religious Controversies of the 1920s* (Macon, Ga.: Mercer University Press, 1982), 4.
14. A. T. Robertson, *The New Citizenship: The Christian Facing a New World Order* (New York: Fleming H. Revell, 1919), 8, quoted in Thompson, *Tried as by Fire*, 6.

15. Frank E. Burkhalter, "Seventy-Five Million Campaign," *Encyclopedia of Southern Baptists*, II: 1196.

16. C. Fred Williams, S. Ray Granade, and Kenneth M. Startup, *A System & Plan: Arkansas Baptist State Convention, 1848-1998* (Franklin, Tenn.: Providence House Publishers, 1998), 189.

17. Ibid.

18. Ibid.

19. Ibid.

20. Ibid., 190, 191.

21. Thompson, *Tried as by Fire*, 14.

22. Birdwhistell, *A Heart for Missions*, 82, 83.

23. Ibid., 83.

24. Quoted in Birdwhistell, *Kentucky Baptists*, 104.

25. Ibid., 104, 105.

26. Ibid., 105.

27. Masters, *A History of Baptists in Kentucky*, 478.

28. Ibid., 480.

29. Ibid., 483.

30. *Proceedings* (1925), 17.

31. Ibid., 18.

32. Masters, *A History of Baptists in Kentucky*, 486, 483.

33. Ibid., 483.

34. Ellis, *"A Man of Books and a Man of the People,"* 180.

35. Masters, *A History of Baptists in Kentucky*, 486.

36. Ellis, *"A Man of Books and a Man of the People,"* 180.

37. Ibid., 181.

38. Ibid.

39. Masters, *A History of Baptists in Kentucky*, 506, 507.

40. For example, see *Western Recorder*, 15 April 1926, 28.

41. Leon Fink, editor, *Major Problems in the Gilded Age and the Progressive Era* (Lexington, Mass.: D.C. Heath and Company, 1993), 11.

42. Thompson, *Tried as by Fire*, 9.

43. Quoted in Fink, *Major Problems in the Gilded Age and the Progressive Era*, 11.

44. Masters, *A History of Baptists in Kentucky*, 505.

45. Barnes, *The Southern Baptist Convention, 1845-1953*, 224.

46. See Harvey, *Redeeming the South*, 200.

47. Birdwhistell, *Kentucky Baptists*, 107.

48. Barnes, *The Southern Baptist Convention, 1845-1953*, 225, 226.

49. Austin Crouch, "Cooperative Program," *Encyclopedia of Southern Baptists*, I: 323.

50. *Encyclopedia of Southern Baptists*, 323.
51. Masters, *A History of Baptists in Kentucky*, 484.
52. Ibid.
53. *Western Recorder*, 20 May 1926.
54. See *Western Recorder*, 6 May 1926.
55. Masters, *A History of Baptists in Kentucky*, 505.
56. See *Proceedings* (1925), 17, and (1926), 15.
57. Masters, *A History of Baptists in Kentucky*, 507.
58. See *Western Recorder*, 1 April 1926.
59. Ellis, *"A Man of Books and a Man of the People,"* 148.
60. Ibid., 149.
61. Masters, *A History of Baptists in Kentucky*, 476.
62. Birdwhistell, *Kentucky Baptists*, 105; Masters, *A History of Baptists in Kentucky*, 477.
63. Masters, *A History of Baptists in Kentucky*, 479.
64. Birdwhistell, *Kentucky Baptists*, 106.
65. *Western Recorder*, 14 January 1926.
66. Ibid.
67. Masters, *A History of Baptists in Kentucky*, 505, 506.
68. Thompson, *Tried as by Fire*, 117, 118.
69. Ibid., 125.
70. Ibid., 130-31.
71. Ellis, *"A Man of Books and a Man of the People,"* 166.
72. Ibid., 136.
73. Quoted in James Duane Bolin, *An Abiding Faith: A Sesquicentennial History of Providence, Kentucky, 1840-1990* (Providence, Ky.: Chamber of Commerce, 1990), 47.
74. Both quotations in this paragraph are quoted in Gregory A. Waller, *Main Street Amusements: Movies and Commercial Entertainment in a Southern City, 1896-1930* (Washington, D.C.: Smithsonian Institution Press, 1995), 230.
75. Ibid., 230, 231.
76. Quoted in Ibid., 231.
77. Harvey, *Redeeming the South*, 217.
78. Ibid., 216.
79. Harrison and Klotter, *A New History of Kentucky*, 356.
80. Thompson, *Tried as by Fire*, 190; *Western Recorder*, 15 December 1927.
81. Harrison and Klotter, *A New History of Kentucky*, 356.
82. Thompson, *Tried as by Fire*, 195.

Chapter Three

1. Everett Gill, *A. T. Robertson: A Biography* (New York: Macmillan Company, 1943), 133, 134, 178, 181, 179.

2. Ibid., 110, 112.

3. See William W. Adams, "Archibald Thomas Robertson," *Encyclopedia of Southern Baptists*, II: 1168, 1169; Gill, *A. T. Robertson*, 108, 109.

4. E. McNeill Poteat, Jr., to A. T. Robertson, 1 November 1933, A. T. Robertson Papers, quoted in Gill, *A.T. Robertson*, 201.

5. An account of Robertson's death can be found in Gill, *A. T. Robertson*, 238-39.

6. Ibid., 239, 240.

7. Masters, *A History of Baptists in Kentucky*, 516.

8. Ibid., 529.

9. *Western Recorder*, 16 October 1930.

10. *Proceedings* (1928), 35.

11. George T. Blakey, *Hard Times and New Deal in Kentucky, 1929-1939* (Lexington: University Press of Kentucky, 1986), 5.

12. Ibid.

13. Ibid., 6.

14. *Western Recorder*, 16 January 1930.

15. Blakey, *Hard Times and New Deal in Kentucky*, 6.

16. *Western Recorder*, 16 January 1930.

17. Blakey, *Hard Times and New Deal in Kentucky*, 7.

18. Ibid., 8.

19. James Duane Bolin, "The Human Side: Politics, the Great Depression, and the New Deal in Lexington, Kentucky, 1929-35," *The Register* 90 (Summer, 1992): 257.

20. Quoted in Blakey, *Hard Times and New Deal in Kentucky*, 9.

21. Ibid., 14.

22. Ibid., 47, 22.

23. *Western Recorder*, 21 November 1929; 5 December 1929.

24. Ibid., 12 June 1930; 19 June 1930; 26 June 1930.

25. *Proceedings* (1930), 25, 26, 44.

26. *Western Recorder*, 3 April 1930.

27. Ibid.

28. Ibid., 19 November 1931.

29. Ibid., 14 August 1930.

30. Ibid., 4 September 1930.

31. Ibid., 3 April 1930.

32. Masters, *A History of Baptists in Kentucky*, 514; *Western Recorder*, 16 October 1930.
33. *Western Recorder*, 16 October 1930.
34. *Proceedings* (1929), 23, 24.
35. Ibid., 24.
36. Ibid., 25.
37. Ibid., 27, 28, 29.
38. *Western Recorder*, 6 February 1930.
39. Ibid.
40. *Proceedings* (1930), 24.
41. Birdwhistell, *Kentucky Baptists*, 110; Masters, *A History of Baptists in Kentucky*, 519, 520.
42. *Western Recorder*, 1 May 1930; 30 October 1930.
43. Masters, *A History of Baptists in Kentucky*, 523, 524.
44. Ibid., 515, 518.
45. Ibid., 516, 517.
46. Ibid., 519; Birdwhistell, *Kentucky Baptists*, 111-12. Clear Creek served as the state's Baptist Assembly until 1951, when it became Clear Creek Mountain Preachers' School.
47. Masters, *A History of Baptists in Kentucky*, 521, 522.
48. Ibid., 527.
49. Brown, *Golden Remembrances*, 122.
50. Ibid.
51. Masters, *A History of Baptists in Kentucky*, 527.
52. Gaines S. Dobbins, "John Richard Sampey," *Encyclopedia of Southern Baptists*, II: 1182.
53. Ibid., 1182, 1183.
54. Clyde T. Francisco, "John R. Sampey Chair of Old Testament Interpretation," *Encyclopedia of Southern Baptists*, II: 1183.
55. Author interview with Julia Woodward, Lexington, Kentucky, 10 July 1998.
56. Ibid.
57. Author interview with Kathryn Jasper Akridge, Louisville, Kentucky, 9 July 1998.
58. "Flood of 1937," *Kentucky Encyclopedia*, 327, 328; Harrison and Klotter, *A New History of Kentucky*, 361.
59. Masters, *A History of Baptists in Kentucky*, 528; Author telephone interview with Dixie Mylum Lusher, 1 July 1998.
60. *Proceedings* (1937), 40.
61. Ibid., 72-83.

Chapter Four

1. *Western Recorder*, 19 July 1945.
2. Ibid., 14 June 1945.
3. Ibid.
4. Masters, *A History of Baptists in Kentucky*, 529.
5. *Western Recorder*, 14 July 1998.
6. Ibid., 23 February 1939; 25 April 1940; 11 April 1940.
7. Ibid., 20 April 1939; 21 November 1940.
8. For the interchange of "Open Letters" about the site of the 1938 annual meeting, see ibid., 22 September 1938; 27 October 1938; 3 November 1938.
9. Ibid., 24 November 1938; 21 July 1938; Masters, *A History of Baptists in Kentucky*, 530, 531.
10. *Proceedings* (1938), 36, 29.
11. Masters, *A History of Baptists in Kentucky*, 529, 530.
12. Ibid., 530.
13. *Western Recorder*, 12 January 1939.
14. Ibid., 2 February 1939.
15. Ibid., 23 February 1939.
16. Ibid., 3 February 1938.
17. Masters, *A History of Baptists in Kentucky*, 521, 522; *Western Recorder*, 16 February 1939.
18. *Western Recorder*, 16 February 1939.
19. Ibid., 20 April 1939.
20. Ibid., 4 January 1940; 5 January 1939; 26 January 1939.
21. Ibid., 27 June 1940; 4 July 1940.
22. Ibid., 2 January 1941.
23. Ibid., 20 June 1940; 24 October 1940.
24. Ibid., 8 August 1940.
25. Harrison and Klotter, *A New History of Kentucky*, 370.
26. *Western Recorder*, 11 December 1941.
27. Ibid., 18 December 1941.
28. Harrison and Klotter, *A New History of Kentucky*, 372.
29. *Western Recorder*, 7 January 1943.
30. Ibid., 6 May 1943.
31. Ibid., 4 May 1944.
32. Ibid., 5 October 1944.
33. Ibid.
34. Ibid., 17 August 1944.
35. Ibid., 1 May 1941.

36. Ibid., 4 November 1943; 15 February 1945.
37. Ibid., 12 July 1945.
38. Birdwhistell, *A Heart for Missions*, 139.
39. Harrison and Klotter, *A New History of Kentucky*, 370.
40. James C. Klotter, *Kentucky: Portrait in Paradox, 1900-1950* (Frankfort, Ky.: Kentucky Historical Society, 1996), 262.
41. *Western Recorder*, 27 January 1944.
42. See *Proceedings* (1942), and *Western Recorder*, 19 November 1942.
43. *Western Recorder*, 24 September 1942.
44. Masters, *A History of Baptists in Kentucky*, 536.
45. For a typical advertisement for church attendance registers, see *Western Recorder*, 2 February 1939.
46. Ibid., 14 March 1940.
47. Ibid., 9 December 1943.
48. Ibid., 29 January 1942.
49. Ibid., 2 March 1939.
50. Ibid., 28 July 1938.
51. Ibid.
52. Ibid., 5 January 1939.
53. Ibid., 5 August 1943.
54. Ibid., 20 April 1939.
55. Ibid., 16 November 1939.
56. Ibid., 10 June 1943.
57. Ibid., 9 January 1941; 25 May 1939.
58. Ibid., 20 May 1943.
59. Ibid., 11 January 1945; 8 February 1945.
60. Birdwhistell, *Kentucky Baptists*, 111.
61. *Western Recorder*, 18 December 1941; 15 October 1942.
62. Ibid., 17 December 1942.
63. Ibid., 15 February 1940.
64. *Proceedings* (1941), 46.
65. See *Western Recorder*, 7 January 1943, 23.
66. *Proceedings* (1943), 28, 29.
67. Masters, *A History of Baptists in Kentucky*, 546.
68. *Western Recorder*, 1 January 1942.
69. Ibid., 12 August 1943; 1 January 1942.
70. Ibid., 23 October 1941.
71. Ibid.
72. Ibid., 25 August 1938.
73. Ibid., 20 October 1938.
74. Ibid., 3 April 1941.

75. Ibid., 6 January 1938.
76. Ibid., 22 September 1938.
77. For articles on the Jefferson Street Mission operated in the 1940s by the Long Run Association, see ibid., 14 October 1943; for the need for mountain missions, see ibid., 26 August 1943.
78. Ibid., 1 May 1941.
79. Ibid., 28 October 1943; 2 September 1943; 11 December 1941.
80. Harrison and Klotter, *A New History of Kentucky*, 372.
81. *Western Recorder*, 3 May 1945.
82. Ibid., 11 October 1945.
83. Ibid., 2 November 1944; 11 January 1945.

Chapter Five

1. *Western Recorder*, 5 December 1946.
2. Ibid.
3. George M. Marsden, *Religion and American Culture* (San Diego: Harcourt Brace Jovanovich, 1990), 208.
4. Ibid.
5. Ibid., 213.
6. Elaine Tyler May, *Homeward Bound: American Families in the Cold War Era* (New York: Basic Books, 1988), 25-26.
7. George Brown Tindall and David E. Shi, *America: A Narrative History*, 5th edition (New York: W. W. Norton, 1999), II: 1443-44.
8. William E. Leuchtenburg, *A Troubled Feast: American Society Since 1945* (Boston: Little, Brown and Company, 1973), 71.
9. Marsden, *Religion and American Culture*, 213.
10. Tindall and Shi, *America: A Narrative History*, II: 1445.
11. May, *Homeward Bound*, 26.
12. Crismon, *Baptists in Kentucky, 1776-1976*, 26, 27; *Western Recorder*, 14 March 1946.
13. *Western Recorder*, 28 March 1946.
14. Crismon, *Baptists in Kentucky, 1776-1976*, 26.
15. Masters, *A History of Baptists in Kentucky*, 578.
16. *Western Recorder*, 3 January 1946.
17. Author telephone interview with A. B. Colvin, 21 October 1998.
18. *Western Recorder*, 17 January 1946.
19. Ibid., 20 June 1946. Because the letters constituted his name and not merely initials, R B Hooks used no periods in his name.
20. Ibid., 7 March 1946.
21. Ibid., 31 January 1946.
22. Ibid., 16 January 1947.

23. Ibid.
24. Masters, *A History of Baptists in Kentucky*, 552, 563.
25. Crismon, *Baptists in Kentucky, 1776-1976*, 41.
26. *Western Recorder*, 24 April 1947.
27. Author telephone interview with A. B. Colvin, 21 October 1998.
28. Ibid.
29. Eldred Taylor address, Historical Symposium, Kentucky Baptist Historical Commission, Middletown, Kentucky, 28 August 1998.
30. Ibid.
31. Author telephone interview with Ronald F. Deering, 22 December 1998.
32. *Proceedings* (1953), 34; Crismon, *Baptists in Kentucky, 1776-1976*, 36.
33. Crismon, *Baptists in Kentucky, 1776-1976*, 38.
34. *Western Recorder,* 13 November 1947.
35. Ibid., 16 January 1947.
36. Ibid., 31 January 1946; 28 February 1946.
37. Ibid., 5 December 1946.
38. Masters, *A History of Baptists in Kentucky*, 554, 555; Eldred Taylor address.
39. Birdwhistell, *Kentucky Baptists*, 116; Eldred Taylor address.
40. *Proceedings* (1953), 101, 102.
41. *Proceedings* (1950), 27; Eldred Taylor address; Birdwhistell, *Kentucky Baptists*, 116.
42. *Proceedings* (1953), 102; *Proceedings* (1954), 102.
43. *Western Recorder*, 5 December 1946.
44. Ibid., 20 June 1946.
45. Ibid., 19 June 1947.
46. Masters, *A History of Baptists in Kentucky*, 556.
47. Crismon, *Baptists in Kentucky, 1776-1976*, 32.
48. *Proceedings* (1950), 57.
49. Crismon, *Baptists in Kentucky, 1776-1976*, 33.
50. See Howard Dorgan, *Giving God the Glory in Appalachia: Worship Practices of Six Baptist Subdenominations* (Knoxville, Tenn.: University of Tennessee Press, 1987).
51. Eldred Taylor address.
52. Author telephone interview with A. B. Colvin, 21 October 1998.
53. Ibid.
54. *Western Recorder*, 1 May 1958.
55. Ibid., 22 March 1956.
56. Ibid., 26 January 1956.
57. Ibid., 19 July 1951.
58. Ibid., 29 November 1956.

59. Ibid., 18 October 1956.
60. Ibid., 1 November 1956.
61. Ibid., 28 February 1957.
62. Ibid., 18 May 1961.
63. Birdwhistell, *A Heart for Missions*, 154-55.
64. *Western Recorder*, 22 August 1957.
65. Crismon, *Baptists in Kentucky, 1776-1976*, 38.
66. Ibid., 29.
67. *Proceedings* (1961), 140.
68. Crismon, *Baptists in Kentucky, 1776-1976*, 25.
69. *Proceedings* (1961), 170.
70. *Western Recorder*, 18 July 1957.
71. Ibid., 20 June 1957.
72. Birdwhistell, *A Heart for Missions*, 186.
73. Ibid., 13 June 1957.
74. Birdwhistell, *Kentucky Baptists*, 131, 132.
75. *Western Recorder*, 8 March 1956.
76. Ibid., 4 May 1961.
77. Ibid., 9 February 1961.
78. Ibid., 29 August 1957.
79. Ibid., 23 July 1959.
80. Crismon, *Baptists in Kentucky*, 38.
81. *Western Recorder*, 5 June 1958.
82. Ibid.
83. Ibid., 19 June 1958.
84. Ibid., 18 December 1958.
85. Ibid., 25 June 1958; 24 July 1958.
86. For the text of the report and for the debate over the report, see *Proceedings* (1958), 99-125.
87. *Western Recorder*, 23 October 1958.
88. Ibid., 13 November 1958.
89. *Proceedings* (1958), 113.
90. *Western Recorder*, 27 November 1958; *Proceedings* (1958), 99-125.
91. *Western Recorder*, 4 December 1958.
92. Crismon, *Baptists in Kentucky, 1776-1976*, 37, 41.
93. Birdwhistell, *Kentucky Baptists*, 119.
94. *Proceedings* (1956), 90.
95. Ibid., 113.
96. *Western Recorder*, 20 February 1958.
97. Eldred Taylor address.
98. *Western Recorder*, 15 June 1961.

99. Ibid., 26 March 1959.
100. Ibid., 21 May 1959.
101. Ibid., 18 May 1961.

Chapter Six

1. Author interview with Julia Woodward, Lexington, Kentucky, 10 July 1998.
2. Ibid.
3. *Western Recorder*, 11 May 1961.
4. Ibid., 24 January 1970; 11 April 1970.
5. Author interview with Kathryn Jasper Akridge, Louisville, Kentucky, 9 July 1998.
6. Ibid.
7. Ibid.
8. *Western Recorder*, 23 January 1969.
9. Ibid.
10. Ibid., 6 February 1969.
11. Ibid.
12. Ibid., 20 February 1969; 27 February 1969.
13. Ibid., 24 May 1962.
14. Birdwhistell, *Kentucky Baptists*, 146-47; *Western Recorder*, 5 February 1965.
15. *Western Recorder*, 21 September 1961.
16. Ibid.
17. Franklin Owen address, Historical Symposium, Kentucky Baptist Historical Commission, Middletown, Kentucky, 28 August 1998.
18. *Western Recorder*, 9 January 1969.
19. Ibid., 28 November 1963.
20. Ibid., 24 June 1965.
21. Ibid.
22. Ibid., 9 December 1965.
23. Crismon, *Baptists in Kentucky, 1776-1976*, 51, 52; *Western Recorder*, 18 April 1970.
24. *Western Recorder*, 21 September 1967.
25. Ibid., 18 April 1968.
26. Ibid., 9 May 1968.
27. Ibid.
28. Ibid., 16 January 1971; 26 June 1971.
29. See a historical analysis of "Kentucky Baptist Progress in Race Relations" in ibid., 23 May 1968.

30. Ibid., 30 May 1968; 13 June 1968.
31. Ibid., 13 June 1968.
32. Ibid., 29 August 1968.
33. Ibid., 20 November 1971; see the devotional of H. Joseph Franklin, pastor of Washington Street Baptist Church in Paducah, as an example in ibid., 27 November 1971.
34. Ibid., 1 February 1962.
35. Crismon, *Baptists in Kentucky, 1776-1976*, 52; *Western Recorder*, 26 June 1969.
36. For the best account of the long struggle see George Herring, *America's Longest War: The United States and Vietnam, 1950-1975* (Philadelphia, Pa.: Temple University Press, 1986).
37. *Western Recorder*, 15 August 1968.
38. Ibid., 25 October 1969.
39. Ibid.
40. Ibid.
41. Ibid., 29 November 1969; 22 November 1969.
42. Tindall and Shi, *America: A Narrative History,* II: 1573.
43. Carl B. Cone, *The University of Kentucky: A Pictorial History* (Lexington, Ky.: University Press of Kentucky, 1989), 166; *Western Recorder*, 15 August 1970.
44. *Western Recorder*, 17 April 1971.
45. Ibid., 12 September 1968.
46. Ibid., 7 August 1971.
47. Crismon, *Baptists in Kentucky, 1776-1976*, 48, 49.
48. *Western Recorder*, 27 February 1969.
49. Ibid., 27 March 1969.
50. Ibid., 16 May 1969.
51. Arthur Blessitt website, http://www.blessitt.com.
52. Franklin Owen address.
53. *Western Recorder*, 22 March 1962.
54. Ibid.
55. Ibid., 7 November 1963.
56. Crismon, *Baptists in Kentucky, 1776-1976*, 49.
57. *Western Recorder*, 4 February 1965; 1 July 1965.
58. Ibid., 24 November 1966; 1 December 1966.
59. Ibid., 25 April 1968.
60. Crismon, *Baptists in Kentucky, 1776-1976*, 45.
61. *Western Recorder*, 27 April 1961; 19 October 1961; Crismon, *Baptists in Kentucky, 1776-1976*, 45.
62. Crismon, *Baptists in Kentucky, 1776-1976*, 45, 46; *Western Recorder*, 24 January 1963.

63. For more on the Kentucky Southern story, see *They Whom a Dream Hath Possessed: A History of Kentucky Southern College, 1962-1969* (published by the Kentucky Southern College Alumni Board).

64. *Kentucky Southern College News* (December 1961), 2.

65. *Western Recorder*, 9 August 1962.

66. *Kentucky Southern College News* (December 1961), 2.

67. *Western Recorder*, 16 March 1967.

68. Ibid., 9 November 1967; 7 December 1967.

69. Ibid., 29 May 1969.

70. Ibid., 21 November 1968.

71. Ibid., 12 December 1968.

72. Ibid., 27 March 1969.

73. Ibid., 9 August 1969.

74. Ibid., 8 June 1999.

75. Ibid., 23 January 1969; 3 July 1969.

76. Ibid., 8 March 1962.

77. Ibid., 8 April 1965; 29 April 1965.

78. Ibid., 2 August 1969.

79. See the photograph on the cover of the *Western Recorder*, 9 August 1962.

80. Ibid., 26 September 1963; 14 February 1970.

81. Ibid., 11 October 1969; 2 January 1971.

82. Ibid., 31 January 1963.

83. Ibid., 31 October 1968.

84. Ibid., 10 October 1970; 21 November 1970; 30 January 1971; 7 August 1971; Crismon, *Baptists in Kentucky, 1776-1976*, 47.

85. Crismon, *Baptists in Kentucky, 1776-1976*, 43.

86. Ibid., 44; *Western Recorder*, 7 July 1966; 6 March 1971; 13 March 1971.

87. Crismon, *Baptists in Kentucky, 1776-1976*, 44.

88. Ibid., 43; *Western Recorder*, 28 March 1970.

89. *Western Recorder*, 28 March 1970.

90. Crismon, *Baptists in Kentucky, 1776-1976*, 44.

91. Author telephone interview with A. B. Colvin; *Western Recorder*, 15 July 1965.

92. Author telephone interview with A. B. Colvin.

93. *Western Recorder*, 27 July 1961.

94. Ibid., 10 August 1961.

95. Ibid., 25 March 1965.

96. Ibid., 23 January 1969.

97. Ibid., 3 April 1969.

98. Crismon, *Baptists in Kentucky, 1776-1976*, 43; *Western Recorder*, 24 June 1965.
99. *Western Recorder*, 17 May 1962.
100. Ibid., 31 October 1968.
101. Ibid., 10 January 1970.
102. Ibid., 3 January 1970.
103. Crismon, *Baptists in Kentucky, 1776-1976*, 53, 54.
104. *Western Recorder*, 25 January 1962.
105. Ibid., 10 October 1963.
106. Ibid., 26 September 1970; 29 May 1971. For a collection of Daley's editorials, see A. B. Colvin and Mark Wingfield, editors, *Daley Observations: The Best of C. R. Daley's Western Recorder Editorials* (Franklin, Tenn.: Providence House Publishers, 1998).
107. *Western Recorder,* 7 March 1963.
108. Ibid., 10 October 1968.
109. Ibid., 26 August 1971; 4 September 1971; 25 September 1971.
110. John R. Claypool, *Tracks of a Fellow Struggler: Living and Growing Through Grief* (New Orleans, La.: Insight Press, 1995. The book was published originally by Word Publishers in 1974).
111. *Western Recorder*, 22 May 1969.
112. Ibid., 21 November 1970; 15 May 1971.
113. Crismon, *Baptists in Kentucky, 1776-1976*, 57.
114. Author telephone interview with A. B. Colvin.
115. *Western Recorder*, 12 December 1970.
116. Ibid., 21 March 1968.
117. Ibid., 2 August 1969.

Chapter Seven

1. *Western Recorder*, 26 August 1972.
2. Ibid., 2 September 1972.
3. Ibid., 30 December 1972.
4. Ibid., 4 March 1972.
5. Ibid., 23 November 1999.
6. Crismon, *Baptists in Kentucky, 1776-1976*, 61.
7. *Western Recorder*, 28 June 1975.
8. Ibid., 21 December 1974; 8 November 1975.
9. Ibid., 9 December 1972.
10. Ibid., 23 November 1974.
11. Crismon, *Baptists in Kentucky, 1776-1976*, 59.
12. *Western Recorder*, 19 May 1973; 6 December 1975.
13. Ibid., 26 July 1975.

14. Ibid., 20 September 1975.
15. Ibid., 26 October 1977.
16. Ibid., 10 May 1975.
17. See Crismon, *Baptists in Kentucky, 1776-1976.*
18. *Western Recorder*, 8 April 1976; 29 April 1976.
19. Ibid., 22 June 1974.
20. Ibid., 6 May 1976.
21. Ibid., 18 November 1976.
22. *Proceedings* (1976); *Western Recorder*, 18 November 1976.
23. *Western Recorder*, 17 January 1979.
24. Ibid., 8 October 1980.
25. Ibid., 28 July 1973.
26. Crismon, *Baptists in Kentucky, 1776-1976*, 60.
27. *Western Recorder*, 15 October 1980; 15 July 1981.
28. Ibid., 17 March 1982.
29. Ibid., 31 August 1977; 21 February 1979.
30. Crismon, *Baptists in Kentucky, 1776-1976*, 61; *Western Recorder*, 11 August 1973; 28 July 1973.
31. Crismon, *Baptists in Kentucky, 1776-1976*, 269.
32. *Western Recorder*, 29 March 1975; Crismon, *Baptists in Kentucky, 1776-1976*, 60, 273, 274.
33. *Western Recorder*, 16 March 1974.
34. Crismon, *Baptists in Kentucky, 1776-1976*, 272-73.
35. *Western Recorder*, 20 May 1976.
36. Ibid., 1 August 1979.
37. Ibid., 17 February 1977.
38. Ibid., 26 October 1977.
39. Ibid., 23 November 1977.
40. Ibid., 21 April 1973; 3 August 1977; 18 February 1981.
41. Ibid., 5 May 1982.
42. Ibid., 17 March 1973.
43. Ibid., 11 November 1976.
44. Ibid., 13 August 1980; 6 August 1980; 16 July 1980.
45. Ibid., 23 May 1979.
46. Ibid., 20 June 1979.
47. Ibid.
48. Ibid.
49. Ibid., 6 August 1980.
50. See Ibid., 12 September 1979.
51. Ibid., 21 November 1979.
52. Ibid., 19 December 1979.
53. Ibid., 10 October 1979.
54. Ibid., 24 March 1977.
55. Ibid., 22 November 1975.
56. Ibid., 18 August 1973.

57. Ibid., 29 March 1975; Crismon, *Baptists in Kentucky, 1776-1976,* 61.
58. *Western Recorder,* 14 February 1979.
59. Ibid., 21 March 1979.
60. Ibid., 23 September 1981.
61. Ibid., 8 December 1982.
62. Ibid., 28 April 1973.
63. Ibid., 24 February 1977.
64. *Proceedings* (1976); *Western Recorder,* 18 November 1976; 24 February 1977.
65. *Western Recorder,* 3 March 1977.
66. Ibid., 19 July 1975.
67. For the interview with Davenport, see ibid., 30 May 1979.
68. Ibid., 15 November 1978; 30 July 1980.
69. Ibid., 2 November 1977.
70. Ibid., 5 July 1978.
71. Ibid., 13 June 1979.
72. Crismon, *Baptists in Kentucky, 1776-1976,* 60.
73. *Western Recorder,* 16 May 1979.
74. Ibid., 22 April 1981.
75. *Baptist Herald,* 6 May 1977; for a collection of Carlin's sermons, see L. W. Carlin, *Earthly Preparation for our Heavenly Home: Eleven Needed Sermons from the Word of God* (author's copy given by James Courtney).
76. Ibid., 23 September 1981.
77. Ibid., 16 December 1981.
78. Ibid., 23 November 1977.
79. Ibid., 17 May 1978.
80. Ibid.
81. Ibid., 9 December 1981.
82. Ibid.; Author interview with William W. Marshall, Middletown, Kentucky, 27 August 1999.

Chapter Eight

1. William W. Marshall address, Historical Symposium, Kentucky Baptist Historical Commission, Middletown, Kentucky, 28 August 1998.
2. Author interview with William W. Marshall, Middletown, Kentucky, 27 August 1999.
3. Ibid.
4. Ibid; *Western Recorder,* 8 December 1982.
5. Author interview with William W. Marshall.
6. *Western Recorder,* 8 December 1982.
7. William W. Marshall address.

8. Author interview with Bill Whittaker, Covington, Kentucky, 16 November 1999.
9. Ibid.
10. Ibid.
11. Ibid.
12. *Western Recorder*, 8 June 1999.
13. William W. Marshall address.
14. Ibid.
15. Ibid.
16. *Western Recorder*, 15 June 1983.
17. Ibid.
18. Ibid.
19. William W. Marshall address.
20. Ibid.
21. Ibid.
22. Ibid.
23. Ibid.
24. Ibid.
25. Ibid.
26. Author interview with William Crouch, Covington, Kentucky, 17 November 1999.
27. Ibid.
28. Ibid.
29. Ibid.
30. Ibid.
31. *Western Recorder*, 2 November 1999.
32. Author interview with William Crouch.
33. Author interview with James H. Taylor, Covington, Kentucky, 16 November 1999.
34. Ibid.
35. Ibid.
36. Ibid.
37. *Western Recorder*, 7 December 1999.
38. Author interview with Kenneth W. Winters, Murray, Kentucky, 4 October 1999.
39. Ibid.
40. Ibid.
41. Ibid.
42. Ibid.
43. Ibid.
44. Author interview with Jim Hawkins, Covington, Kentucky, 17 November 1999.

45. Ibid.
46. Ibid.
47. Ibid.
48. Author interview with Bill Mackey, Murray, Kentucky, 12 December 1999.
49. Ibid.
50. *Western Recorder*, 23 November 1999.
51. Ibid.
52. Ibid.
53. Ibid., 22 November 1975.
54. William W. Marshall address.

Epilogue

1. For the history of Severns Valley Baptist Church, see Ella Cofer et al., *History of Severns Valley Baptist Church, 1781-1956* (Elizabethtown, Ky.: Bean Publishing Co., 1956), and Jack Birdwhistell, *A City Built on a Hill: A History of Severns Valley Baptist Church, 1781-1981* (Elizabethtown, Ky.: Severns Valley Baptist Church, 1980). The author relied on these works and an unpublished two-page history provided by the church office for descriptions of the church.

Index

About the Author

After graduating from Webster County High School in western Kentucky, James Duane Bolin played basketball and majored in history at Belmont University in Nashville, Tennessee, graduating with a B.A. degree in 1978.

Following a year of graduate school in the Church-State Studies Program at Baylor University where he researched the early American Baptist leader John Clarke, Bolin returned to his home state to finish his graduate studies, completing M.A. (1982) and Ph.D. (1988) degrees in history at the University of Kentucky. After teaching stints in the public schools of his home county and at Madisonville Community College in Kentucky and Williams Baptist College in Walnut Ridge, Arkansas, Bolin joined the faculty at Murray State University in 1996, where he now serves as an associate professor of history.

Author photograph by Chuck Perry

Duane Bolin

Bolin has published numerous articles on topics ranging from the Civil War to the Great Depression. His book *Bossism and Reform in a Southern City: Lexington, Kentucky, 1880-1940* was published in 2000 by the University Press of Kentucky. A Sunday School teacher and deacon, Bolin resides in Murray, Kentucky, with his wife Evelyn and children Wesley and Cammie Jo.

317